■
■
■ **Film on the Left**
■
■
■
■

D0083823

WILLIAM
ALEXANDER

Film on the Left

AMERICAN
DOCUMENTARY FILM
FROM 1931 TO 1942

Princeton University Press
Princeton, New Jersey

Copyright © 1981 by Princeton University Press
Published by Princeton University Press, Princeton, New Jersey
In the United Kingdom: Princeton University Press, Guildford, Surrey

All Rights Reserved

Library of Congress Cataloging in Publication Data will be
found on the last printed page of this book

Publication of this book has been
aided by the Whitney Darrow Publication
Reserve Fund of Princeton University Press

This book has been composed in VIP Caledonia

Clothbound editions of Princeton University Press books
are printed on acid-free paper, and binding materials are
chosen for strength and durability

Printed in the United States of America by Princeton
University Press, Princeton, New Jersey

Designed by Laury A. Egan

to Tom Brandon, Sam Brody, Leo Hurwitz, Joris Ivens, Lewis Jacobs, Herbert Kline, Ben Maddow, David Platt, Leo Seltzer, Ralph Steiner, and Willard Van Dyke

to the memory of Lester Balog, Lionel Berman, Sheldon Dick, Irving Lerner, Sidney Meyers, Arnold Perl, Harry Alan Potamkin, Henwar Rodakiewicz, Paul Strand

and to the other artists, technicians, and organizers who were film workers with the New York Workers Film and Photo League, Nykino, and Frontier Films

Contents

Preface

Inevitably in writing about the progressive films of the 1930s, I have written about the people who made them and of how their personalities, their lives, their politics, their aesthetics, and their relations to one another have been relevant to the art they were creating. Every writer who knows the value of personal interviews is aware that his or her resulting portraits cannot be entirely true. In this book it was the particular perspectives of people in their sixties, seventies, and eighties that shaded and sometimes distorted events. I came upon poor recall, sharp but conflicting memories, people eager either to over- or underplay their roles, intense friendships and bitter enmities developed either during the thirties or as a result of subsequent events.

My relations with the interviewees varied, of course, but I admire them as they were in the past, and in most cases I admire them as they are now. Although not everything they produced was, to my way of looking, commendable, and although I have distinctions to make about their art, in many ways I mean this book as a tribute to all of them as they were in the thirties—as a tribute to the use they were making of their talents. Thus, where I have, however slightly, misconstrued their lives, motivations, and decisions, I want to apologize to them. They realize, I know, through their own journeys back with me into that time, how difficult it is to locate the truth.

It is from these interviews and from watching the films and absorbing past and present discussions about them that I have put together my own particular version of the who and why of it all. In composing this version, my primary purposes were to write about social and political documentary film and to bring to light a significant and neglected group of filmmakers. At the same time that I wanted to focus on the films and filmmakers of the far left, I also wanted to put them into the context of the left-liberal filmmakers with whom they came in contact and to compare them to their colleague Joris Ivens who influenced them and who during these years filmed the same subjects as they.

As I worked, I found that I had had other goals, of which I only gradually became aware. I found that I was attempting to experience a certain aspect of the thirties in order to work out something that had been incomplete for me in the sixties. I needed to *realize* more fully than I had my personal commitment against such shames as the war in Vietnam and the corruption, the indifference, and the lethargy in American life that allowed it to happen. By engaging myself fully with a group of dedicated political filmmakers of the thirties, I hoped to further develop my own true roots in the sixties—roots I could then nourish and be nourished by in the years to come.

In this I succeeded, a little. By thinking about what I learned, I gained reaffirmation and direction. But I was also frustrated, for I could not live out in the thirties what I had failed to live out fully in the sixties. I could not deepen my actual experience, could not live in another time.

One afternoon in early October of 1974, I sat with a man my father's age in his mountainside house in Los Angeles, my tape recorder on a low table between us, the two of us, an immense distance from the thirties, trying to talk about the WPA, attempting to recreate his brief experience on the *Imperial Valley* crew, hoping to talk our way into something not present. We both sought handles for it, but neither of us could apprehend what it had been like to live in the thirties, even though one of us had done so. Warming to me, he and his wife invited me to stay on for dinner. We each had a couple of sizable martinis, and then, over a potluck dinner accompanied by red wine, he and I, our minds suddenly tuned, began to argue—about what I suppose should be called metaphysics. The dispute was both trivial and crucial. There is no present or future, he maintained, only the past: his words were past as soon as he spoke them. I argued that he would experience a blow from my fist in the present, my example, like similar ones we both chose, indicating that beliefs essential to us were under attack. I suggested that he predicated his behavior on a belief in the future. Although he was in excellent health, at seventy he faced the relative closeness of the end of his life—what his wife said he referred to as the "new adventure." Accordingly, he was fighting for a flexible, uncertain, mysterious future and for dimensions of time and space latent with untapped possibility. At thirty-five, uncertain of my career, needing self-definition, searching for paths to recognition, responsibility, and power, I battled for a practical grip on things, for the idea of an anticipated future as an active force in my present life. We were engaged in discovering who we were that October evening, and our talk had a vitality and meaning that had been lacking most of the afternoon.

What I discovered here and elsewhere was that my encounter with these filmmakers of the thirties in the present was highly important to me, important in a way that is representative of many younger people of my and other generations. At a late stage in my research, an insightful friend suggested I was seeking fathers in these older men. Until that moment, I had never had any conscious notion of such a goal, but my friend was right. My own father is a political conservative to whom I feel very close in everything except politics. In these men of the left, I was searching for political fathers, people whom in my imagination I might have drawn upon throughout life, especially during the crisis of the sixties, and whom I might draw upon now. Some meetings managed to develop into a degree of vital communication— like the one just described, like those with Sam Brody, Ben Maddow, Ralph Steiner, and, especially, like the ones with Leo Hurwitz. I found myself reaching out across the gap between thirty-five and sixty-five, or seventy-two. I was trying to find, as I do in my own father, sensitivity, vitality, curiosity, firmness, flexibility, and some wisdom, qualities I could inherit for my own sixties and seventies and for the years between. And I was seeking models, people who had continued to act upon progressive social and political beliefs throughout their lives.

I also began to find some of these filmmakers helpful to me in my own career. As a junior faculty member at a status- and success-oriented American university, narrow and for the most part dogmatic in its requirements for faculty performance, it had been inspiring for me to discover in my profession courageous people like Martin Duberman, Paulo Freire, Jonathan Kozol, and Richard Ohmann. In the same way, it was important to me to learn that in 1932, after *Philips-Radio*, Joris Ivens decided never again to make advertising films. And it is important to me to remember that in 1935 several filmmakers broke away from a filmmaking organization that seemed to them to have become dogmatic about what every individual artist in it should do. This was not a matter of Communist Party ideology or aesthetics but of defying the tired strictures by which people in power interpreted the question of political art when bound by a narrow budget. Failing to achieve change from within, these filmmakers left this organization, continuing to pursue their beliefs and insisting on exercising their vital talents. They and others in the pages that follow have provided me with an example and a resource, and their careers in the thirties raise questions for us all.

Acknowledgments

Charles Silver of the Museum of Modern Art Film Study Center often heads acknowledgment lists, and I know why. Like countless others, I could not have screened films and found resources so easily without his great generosity and his concern for my work. His colleague, Mary Corliss of the Film Stills Archive, went out of her way for me and has my gratitude for her kind, efficient assistance. I also want to thank William Murphy of the Audiovisual Archives Division at the National Archives for his assistance during my three days of screening there. And I am grateful to Tom Brandon and Leo Hurwitz for allowing me to view early films in their possession.

Several funding sources made this book possible. A seed grant in the summer of 1972 from the American Council of Learned Societies for a more general but related project enabled me to locate my subject. The following summer, a grant from the Horace H. Rackham School of Graduate Studies, University of Michigan, supported me and took me back to New York for intensive viewing. A travel grant from the same source during the academic year 1974-1975 permitted me to carry on further viewings as well as interviews in Los Angeles, New York, and elsewhere. Thanks to a Younger Humanist Grant from the National Endowment for the Humanities, I did most of my research and the early stages of the writing during the same year. Financial assistance for preparation of the manuscript came from my father, William Alexander, from the University of Michigan English Department and, again, from the Rackham School of Graduate Studies.

I am highly indebted to the filmmakers and nonfilmmakers who granted me interviews, answered letters, and were so generous with their time, memories, and ideas: the late Lester Balog, the late Louise Berman, Tom Brandon, Sam Brody, Vera Caspary, Inez Garson, June Gitlin, Leo Hurwitz, Lewis Jacobs, Herbert Kline, the late Irving Lerner, Pare Lorentz, Ben Maddow, Edna Meyers, David Platt, David Prensky, the late Henwar Rodakiewicz, Leo Seltzer, George Sklar, Hortense Socholitsky, Ralph Steiner, the late Paul Strand, Willard Van Dyke, Gunther von Fritsch, and Fred Zinnemann. I regret that Jay Leyda was unable to give me an interview. I also owe much to other writers about documentary film, especially to Erik Barnouw,

Richard Barsam, Lewis Jacobs, and Richard Dyer MacCann for the firm grounding in history, theory, and resources they have given me. Richard MacCann, who encouraged me all along the way, and John Raeburn, who worked over an early version of the first chapter with much sensitivity, invited me to speak to their seminar on thirties film at the University of Iowa in the spring of 1975. The response that came from them and their students was enormously stimulating and gave me much incentive. In February of 1974, Murray Schwartz of SUNY at Buffalo listened to me talk and sent me to Martin Duberman's *Black Mountain*, a book that has strongly influenced my notions on both teaching and writing.

Many students and young colleagues at Harvard University and the University of Michigan whom I have grown with and learned from over the years also stand behind this book. The kind of people they are and what they have said and done in difficult times have been reference points and resources as I have written. I fail to list them here only because I do not want to risk leaving anyone out. At a late stage, Sara Blackburn read and edited the manuscript with a toughness and wonderful sensitivity to my purposes, and she taught me some vital lessons about writing; she has my lasting gratitude. Also at this stage, Bill and Sally Ruddick loaned me their house on Long Island for three months of painful rewriting; the ambience they had created there and their generous friendship made this a happy time and lightened my task considerably. Cathy Dammeyer and Larry Goldstein helped me think out one final knotty structural problem, and I thank them for the wonderfully empathetic readings they gave my text. Finally, I have more than ample reason to thank Gina Alexander, the late Marvin Felheim, Joanna Hitchcock, Alan Howes, Jay Robinson, and the students and friends who formed with me the Ann Arbor Committee for Human Rights in Latin America for their many-faceted support.

I wish to acknowledge permission from the following people and organizations: Leo Hurwitz, Michael Klein, and *Cinéaste*, to quote from "*Native Land*: An Interview with Leo Hurwitz," conducted by Michael and Jill Klein for *Cinéaste* 6, no. 3 (1974); Leo Hurwitz and *Cinema Journal*, to quote from Hurwitz's "One Man's Voyage: Ideas and Films in the 1930's," *Cinema Journal* (Fall 1975); Willard Van Dyke and the Film Society of Lincoln Center, to quote from Van Dyke's "Letters from 'The River'," *Film Comment* (March-April 1965) (Copyright © 1965 by Film Comment Publishing Corporation, all rights reserved); Ben Maddow and the Modern Poetry Association, to quote from "On Signing Up," *Poetry*, May 1936; Ben Maddow and

Partisan Review, to quote from Maddow's "Images of Poverty," *Partisan Review* 2, no. 9 (October-November 1935), pp. 9-10; Jack Salzman, to use my article, "Frontier Films: Trying the Impossible," *Prospects 4*; *American Quarterly*, to use my article *"The March of Time* and *The World Today,"* *American Quarterly* (Summer 1977) (Copyright 1977 Trustees of the University of Pennsylvania); *Cinema Journal*, to use my "Frontier Films, 1936-1941: The Aesthetics of Impact," *Cinema Journal* (Fall 1975) (Copyright 1975, Society for Cinema Studies); Joris Ivens, to quote from his book, *The Camera and I*; Gerald O'Grady, to quote from the tapes from the Oral History of the Independent American Cinema Collection at Media Study/Buffalo containing the Rodakiewicz, Steiner, and Van Dyke Buffalo interviews; Olga Rodakiewicz, to quote from the interview of Henwar Rodakiewicz by Willard Van Dyke at the State University of New York at Buffalo, 8 August 1974, and to quote from Henwar Rodakiewicz's scenario for *The City*; Ralph Steiner, to quote from the interview of him by James Blue at the State University of New York at Buffalo, 12 July 1972, and to quote from his July 1975 letter to Howard Gillette; Willard Van Dyke, to quote from the interview of him by James Blue at the State University of New York at Buffalo, 2 August 1973, and to quote from his words during his own interview of Henwar Rodakiewicz in the interview just cited; Leo Hurwitz, to quote from *Native Land*; Willard Van Dyke, to quote from *The City* and *Valley Town*; Vera Caspary, to quote from her 22 June 1975 letter to me; June Gitlin, to quote from her 6 June 1975 letter to me; Ben Maddow, to quote from his 13 October 1974, 24 December 1974, 2 June 1975, and 18 August 1976 letters to me, and to quote from his poetry; Georgia O'Keeffe, Hazel Strand, and the Alfred Stieglitz Archive in the Collection of American Literature, the Beinecke Rare Book and Manuscript Library, Yale University, to quote, on a one-time only basis, from a 9 October 1935 letter from Paul Strand to Alfred Stieglitz; David Platt, to quote from his 30 July 1975 letter to me; George Sklar, to quote from his 4 July 1975 letter to me; Hortense Socholitzky, to quote from her 18 August 1976 letter to me; Gunther von Fritsch, to quote from his 18 August 1976 letter to me; and Fred Zinnemann, to quote from his 18 April and 4 June 1975 letters to me.

List of Abbreviations

Periodicals

DW	*Daily Worker*
EC	*Experimental Cinema*
FF	*Film Front*
NBR	*National Board of Review Magazine*
NM	*New Masses*
NR	*New Republic*
NT	*New Theatre*
WT	*Workers Theatre*

Interviews (by the author unless otherwise noted)

Balog and Brody interview	Lester Balog and Sam Brody—3 October 1974
Brandon interview	Tom Brandon—14 October 1973
Garson interview	Inez Garson—30 April 1975
Hurwitz interview 1	Leo Hurwitz—7 June 1973
Hurwitz interview 2	—22 August 1973
Hurwitz interview 3	—21 November 1974
Jacobs interview	Lewis Jacobs—20 August 1973
Kline interview	Herbert Kline—7 May 1975
Lerner interview	Irving Lerner—1 October 1974
Maddow interview	Ben Maddow—1 October 1974
Meyers interview	Edna Meyers—11 May 1975
Rodakiewicz interview	Henwar Rodakiewicz—15 May 1975
Rodakiewicz Buffalo interview	—8 August 1974 interviewed by Willard Van Dyke at SUNY, Buffalo
Seltzer interview	Leo Seltzer—13 May 1975
Steiner interview	Ralph Steiner—17 August 1973
Steiner Buffalo interview	—12 July 1973 interviewed by James Blue at SUNY, Buffalo
Strand interview	Paul Strand—18 February 1975

van Dongen Buffalo interview	Helen van Dongen Durant—1 August 1974 interviewed by Willard Van Dyke at SUNY, Buffalo
Van Dyke interview 1	Willard Van Dyke—22 August 1973
Van Dyke interview 2	—12 May 1975
Van Dyke Buffalo interview	—2 August 1973 interviewed by James Blue at SUNY, Buffalo

Film on the Left

I The Workers Film and Photo League, 1930-1935

Beginnings

"A WORKING-CLASS CINEMA FOR AMERICA?" So blazed the title of Seymour Stern's own lead article in the cinema section he edited for the short-lived *The Left*. It was the spring of 1931, and the new magazine's cinema section was graced with a definitive epigraph from Lenin, the renowned statement that "among the instruments of art and education, the cinema can and must have the greatest significance. It is a powerful weapon of scientific knowledge and propaganda." Stern, the most exuberant and one of the most knowledgeable of the writers in the early left, or revolutionary, film movement in America, began:

> A working-class cinema for America? A cinema completely freed from the influence of (1) capitalist, racketeer, politician, State official, (2) Socialist, reformer, censor, parlor 'pink,' woman's club, liberal, (3) the Hollywood-minded film-practitioner schooled in the tradition and 'technique' of the Hollywood entertainment-movie? A cinema reflecting the struggles and growth of the revolutionary proletariat of the United States? A cinema relentless, merciless, in its analysis of the American bourgeoisie? A cinema passionate, ultimate, in its indictment of the capitalist slave-system of America? In its exposé of the fundamental *lie* underlying American society? A cinema, in a word, that offers the exploited class of America precisely the opposite, in spirit, technique and ideology, to the Hollywood Movie,—the advertisement for American Money? . . .

What a possibility! What a vision! What a drum-beat to Revolution! Films in the name of the American Revolutionary Proletariat! Films in the name of Centralia, of Sacco and Vanzetti, of Mooney and Billings, the Imperial Valley prisoners, the swinging bodies of negroes, of Gastonia and Ella May! Think of a motion picture as blazing as the blood of the 322 convicts who burned to death like animals in a caged trap, in the Ohio State Penitentiary Fire of last year! Think of a cinema as terrific as the sweep of a nation-wide demonstration—for food, for work, for the triumph of the working-class!

"The vision of such a possibility," Stern proclaimed, "reduces the feeling of impotence and transforms it into a demand for practical action."[1]

And practical action there was. In addition to the still photographers who carried their prints and negatives to the *Labor Defender*, the organ of the International Labor Defense (a radical version of the present American Civil Liberties Union), and in addition to a small newsreel group in the hire of the ILD, there also existed in early 1931, a "scattered, but ideologically united, *left-wing* kino-group," composed of Stern in Hollywood, Barnet G. Braver-Mann in Detroit, Lewis Jacobs in Philadelphia, and Samuel Brody and David Platt in New York. These and other men, Stern announced, had recently formed both the Workers Film and Photo League of America, which was committed principally to newsreels, and his own unit, the American Prolet-Kino,[a] which was rooted in Eisenstein's experimental achievements in montage and dedicated to film as "an instrument of highly *calculative construction.*[2]

The Workers' International Relief, which had been founded by the Communist International in 1921, had its American headquarters at 10 East 17th Street in New York.[b] Like other Party organizations with

---

[a] The American Prolet-Kino attempted a film on the struggles of Mexican workers in California's Imperial Valley, a film that was never completed and the only film attempted by the group.

[b] "An official Comintern publication gives the following explanation of its aims and activities: 'In the beginning, the W.I.R. was founded for the organization of aid to the starving people of Soviet Russia by the international proletariat. Later, the W.I.R. set its goal to: aid the strikers, the victims of an act of nature, and children of workers; [to give] social aid to women, invalids, and the aged; [to foster the] organization of Friends of Soviet Russia; [to organize] expositions of Soviet industrial products and art abroad; [and] antifascist propaganda.

A special field of activity of the W.I.R. is the production of proletarian movie pictures. For this purpose the W.I.R. has its own movie picture organizations in the U.S.S.R., Germany, Italy, Norway, America, France, Sweden and other countries. The

cultural goals, it was attracting artists in the early 1930s. The Japanese Workers Camera Club ("a group of progressive Oriental photographers," according to Sam Brody who "lent their fine-honed skills to left-wing causes")[3] was attached to it and had facilities and an office at the same location. In early 1930, someone suggested to the cameramen affiliated with this group that they form a companion film organization. Accordingly, Robert Del Duca, Lester Balog, Sam Brody, Brody's compatriot from the John Reed Club,[c] the brilliant young American film critic Harry Alan Potamkin, and others began to pull together the loose strings of left film activity.

On 7 July 1930, Brody published his "For Workers' Films" in the Communist Party newspaper, *The Daily Worker*. This article had been inspired by a communication from his comrade, Ralph Bond, who had written him from abroad about the Federation of Workers' Film Societies in England and its production of "newsreels of important revolutionary events" such as the National Hunger March.[d] Although the New York WIR had released short films, Brody found in them less political propaganda than what he sarcastically called "cultural activity." He argued that "if we have developed working-class journalists we can develop working-class cameramen and directors" and "if we can show to the foreign-born workers of New Bedford a film of striking native American textile workers of the South, we have transcended the limits of what we classify as 'cultural.' " According to Brody, there had been too much useless talk, and too many comrades with motion cameras were involved in amateurish individual efforts. He wrote that "the organization of an independent workers' film movement in America is the next step. In this work the co-operation of every class-conscious worker is imperative."[4]

Concurrently, in the July *New Masses*, the Party monthly, Harry

---

W.I.R. has national sections [affiliated organizations] in almost all countries.' " The executive offices were in Berlin.

It is not at all easy to find a description, or even mention, of the WIR in histories of the Communist Party written by people on the left, nor do histories of labor in America tell of it. I am indebted for this quotation to a research guide by Witold S. Sworakowski, *The Communist International and Its Front Organizations* (Stanford: Hoover Institution on War, Revolution, and Peace, 1965), p. 456. See also Russell Campbell's "Introduction" to "Radical Cinema in the 30's," *Jump Cut* 14 (1977): 23, and Bert Hogenkamp, "Workers' Film in Europe," *Jump Cut* 19 (1978): 36-37.

[c] The John Reed Clubs were organized by the Communist Party as places where leftist writers might gather.

[d] I believe the National Hunger March refers to the "parade" that began on 20 April in various parts of Great Britain and arrived in London on 30 April. It was organized by the National Unemployed Workers' Movement as a protest against the government's unemployment policy.

Potamkin reported the varied film activities of New York John Reed Club members. His list included the shooting and editing of workers' films, film criticism, talks at workers' clubs, cooperation with the WIR and the ILD, and support for meritorious pictures like Turin's *Turksib*. According to Potamkin, integration of effort was imminent. A film group was "to be mobilized for the study of the technique of picture-making and the education of workers in the cinema as an ideological and artistic medium."5

As the events of the ensuing months indicated, substantial film activity was, as they said, already under way. On 5 October 1930, the Department of Cultural Activities of the WIR showed Eisenstein's *Potemkin* at the Ukrainian Labor Hall in Newark, New Jersey. On 11 October at the John Reed clubrooms, Potamkin gave an introductory talk prior to the screening of Yakov Blyokh's *A Shanghai Document*. *Fighting Workers of New York*, a "revolutionary film" of the "March 6 and other demonstrations and the Katovis funeral demonstration,"e probably shot and edited by the film people at the WIR, was presented for the first time at the New York Coliseum on 7 November, one event in the thirteenth-anniversary celebration of the Russian Revolution. On 30 November, at the Hungarian Workers' Home, the WIR showed *Harbor Drift*, a film by a workers' group in Germany.6

Meanwhile, Balog, Brody, Del Duca, Potamkin, and the others were busy organizing. Early in December, the Workers Camera League had become the Workers Film and Photo League of the WIR. A housewarming party was held on 13 December to celebrate the League's new headquarters on the first floor of 131 West 28th Street, the new address of the local WIR itself. This was only the first of the League's many subsequent quarters. By late January 1931, it had the same address as the Labor Defender Photo Group studio at 7 East 14th Street. *Experimental Cinema*, a fledgling and promising periodical edited by Jacobs, Platt, and Stern, was quick to note that the very choice of this second location was a hopeful challenge to commercial American films and their low-cost escape for the masses: only two doors

e Steph Katovis was fatally wounded on 16 January 1930 by patrolman Harry Kiritz while organizing fruit and vegetable store clerks. The ILD and ACLU both protested the "police brutality," and the Communist Party organized a funeral demonstration, but Kiritz was absolved of blame by a Bronx grand jury. It is probable that *Fighting Workers of New York* also included all of the following: a newsreel of the New York May Day parade and demonstration; footage of 6 March unemployment demonstration leaders William Z. Foster, Harry Raymond, Robert Minor, and Israel Amter in jail (September); other CP-led demonstrations (September); activities at the WIR children's camp (October); a raid on the WIR camp at Van Etten, New York (October). See "Filmography," compiled by Russell Campbell and William Alexander, *Jump Cut* 14 (1977): 33.

away, at number 11, was the former brownstone home of the old Biograph Company.[7]

Statements of the League's intentions were not long in coming. Sam Brody issued a general announcement of its existence and purpose in January 1931, and Potamkin, now a member, published a "Film and Photo Call to Action" in the July *Workers Theatre*. In this article, he listed thirteen decisive goals of the WF&PL. According to Potamkin, the League was expected to aid in

1. The education of the workers and others in the part the movie plays as a weapon of reaction;

2. The education of the workers and others in the part the movie plays as an instrument for social purposes—in the U.S.S.R.;

3. The encouragement, support and sustinence [*sic*] of the left critic and the left movie-maker who is documenting dramatically and persuasively the disproportions in our present society;

4. The creation of a chain of film-audiences who morally and financially guarantee such films;

5. The regular publication of a periodical devoted to our purposes;

6. The fight against the class-abuses of capitalist censorship;

7. The attack upon the invidious portrayal in the popular film of the foreign born worker, the Negro, the oriental, the worker generally;

8. The opposition to the interests of the institutions like the church as they participate in the shaping of the monopolized film;

9. The use of methods of direct action, boycott, picketing against the anti-working-class, anti-Soviet film;

10. The distribution of suppressed films of importance;

11. The defense of artists and critics abused by reactionary elements (as in the Eisenstein case);

12. The re-discovery and presentation of neglected films of significance;

13. The education of the critic and worker by closer contact.
THE SECOND PART OF NUMBER 3 IS EVENTUALLY OUR MOST IMPORTANT PURPOSE! Our film-makers need more training, and that is got by more opportunity. THIS PURPOSE IS MADE MEANINGFUL BY NUMBER 13.[8]

These plans boil down to creation and support of an awakened working class through boycott, leaflet, meeting, film showing, and film production.

By June 1931, the League's still photographers had covered the Albany Hunger March and that year's May Day demonstration in New York, and their visual record of this proletarian solidarity had appeared in the *Labor Defender* and *The Daily Worker*. Now back at the WIR at 131 West 28th Street, the League boasted its own darkroom, its own still and motion cameras, and its own projectors.[9] Collaborating with the WIR and the ILD, cameramen had shot newsreels about the Albany Hunger March, the New York May Day demonstration, and the Scottsboro case, while projectionists with leaflets and lectures were screening films at workers' clubs in and out of the city. From January through March, they held their own film showings—the Soviet *Arsenal, China Express, Potemkin*, and *Two Days*, and the German *The Weavers*—at twenty-five cents, either to raise funds for their own activities or for the WIR, which commonly showed Soviet and other films as a source of income. On 10 January, following a showing of *Arsenal*, David Platt headed a discussion on "Film in the United States"; on 4 February, in conjunction with a showing of *China Express*, Potamkin lectured on "Film in the Class Struggle"; and on 15 February, a showing of *Potemkin* was accompanied by a symposium on American films.[10]

The League also established a film and photo school. At the outset, in addition to a class in film projection, there was a class being offered in still photography taught by Howard D. Lester, and members were envisioning future classes in cinematography, film and photo history, and the principles of criticism. The League also announced that they were in contact with similar bodies in other American cities, as well as with groups and individuals in England, Mexico, the Soviet Union, Japan, Germany, France, Holland, Denmark, and Czechoslovakia. As a section of the Union of Worker-Photographers of All Lands, the League's still photographers hoped to achieve sufficient organization to participate in the Union's first international conference and exhibition of worker-photographers in Berlin later in the year. In order to ferret out the best work for the show, they dedicated the final week of July to an exhibit of the Proletarian Photo. Under the auspices of the new New York Workers Cultural Federation (of which Potamkin was an officer), a traveling exhibit would follow.

In the midst of all of this activity, the League was going through a series of organizational changes. It had "sloughed off the self-centered ones who could not see beyond their own noses . . . who were more interested in their own enthusiasms than in the prospects of a mass organization of workers-photographers and workers-cinematographers," it had finally formed a nucleus of the "more responsible and more magnetic worker-members," and Potamkin reported in the July

Workers Theatre that it hoped "to achieve stability and effectiveness this fall."[11]

The WIR affiliate in the United States, originally the Friends of Soviet Russia, had been distributing films since 1922.[12] As a result, from the start the League's relationship with the WIR enabled it to distribute films from Weltfilm and Prometheus Films in Berlin and from Mezrabpom and Sovkino in the Soviet Union. By the end of 1931, the organization boasted forty-five full-length films for distribution, including Pudovkin's *Mechanics of the Brain* and *Storm over Asia*, Eisenstein's *Ten Days That Shook the World* and *Old and New*, Vertov's *Man with the Movie Camera*, Dovzhenko's *Arsenal*, Trauberg's *China Express*, Turin's *Turksib*, and at least two films that contrasted Soviet and American life, *From Volga to Gastonia*[f] and Esther Shub's *Cannons or Tractors?* In addition, they advertised eight short newsreels of their own making (*Albany Hunger March*; *Passaic Strike, 1927*; *A Short Trip to the Soviet Union*; *The New World*, a two-thousand-foot film dealing with the history of workers' Russia, 1914-1931; *May Day in New York, 1931*; *Workers News, 1931*; *W.I.R. Children's Camp, N.Y.*; *Coal Strike, 1931*), one longer film (*Strike Against Starvation*), and another film about the 1931 Hunger March[g] to be shown 20 December at the Star Casino, with "great mass showings" planned for Boston, Philadelphia, Pittsburgh, Cleveland, Detroit, Chicago, Milwaukee, and Minneapolis.

By the end of 1931, the League claimed a technical staff of forty-five still photographers and nine cinema photographers, including, they proudly announced, Lewis Jacobs, editor of *Experimental Cinema*, H. A. Potamkin, movie critic, and Hiram Longview, cinema engineer. It proclaimed that League branches now existed in Philadelphia, Pittsburgh, Detroit, Cleveland, "and in many key cities and towns," and it pointed out that cameramen were now out shooting scenes for an eight-reel production, temporarily titled *Winter, 1931*. Whittaker Chambers, Robert W. Dunn, Robert Evans, Hugo Gellert, Joe North, and Potamkin (the advisory board of the League) were at work on the scenario, and Jacobs and Longview were to do the final editing—if another $4,500 should materialize.[13] Although the wise reader then and now might have hoped for more evidence than en-

---

[f] I have no other information on this film, except that it was probably produced in Germany.

[g] Aside from local hunger marches on state capitals, there were two national hunger marches that arrived in Washington from cities predominantly of the East and Midwest on 7 December 1931 and 6 December 1932. They were organized by the National Unemployed Council, which was established in 1930 by the Communist Party and was meant to include workers of all political affiliations.

thusiastic promotional writing in the *New Masses* to substantiate the existence of these great mass showings, the fifty-four photographers, the "key cities and towns," and an eight-reel production, the promotion was less an exaggeration than one of the many indications of a feverish enthusiasm that bore little fruit during the League's existence.

The Members

Who were the film members of the Workers Film and Photo League, and what was it that brought them together?[h] Like many artists and intellectuals during the early 1930s, a good number of them had been drawn to the Communist Party, which they considered the only organization with a concrete, viable cure for America's critical social illness. Although the League was not a strictly official Party organization (despite the fact that *The Daily Worker* could announce its 13 January 1931 meeting under "Party Activities"), it was wholeheartedly a part of the Party's cultural front in its sympathies, relations, activities, and general political line. Among the most politically committed were Tom Brandon, Sam Brody, Leo Hurwitz, Irving Lerner, David Platt, and Harry Alan Potamkin.

Tom Brandon was born and raised in Philadelphia. After the Depression forced him to leave college, he drove milk trucks and overload trucks, joined the Teamsters' Local, boxed as an amateur and professional prizefighter, and actively engaged in a variety of social and political work. Although he became interested in film as an art while he was still in college, it was in this subsequent period that he began to see its potential as a political medium. His savings bought a sec-

[h] I have only sketchy information about several of them: Lester Balog, Robert Del Duca, Victor Kandell, and Julian Roffman. Balog, a charter member, left in 1933 for the West Coast, becoming a member of the San Francisco League during its brief existence and continuing to involve himself with the production and projection of workers' films until his death in 1976. Del Duca, who was older than most of the other members, worked as a freelance cameraman for MGM and Universal newsreels during the days of silent film, and also took part in producing a local newsreel series covering Westchester County. Kandell, born in 1910, opened a Columbia University catalogue at random, noticed a course on Photoplay Composition, and went on from there to become a filmmaker, joining the League around the time of his graduation. Roffman, an early, active member of the League, was born in Montreal, attended McGill University, and studied film at New York and Columbia universities. Information on Balog was procured from periodical notices and an interview with Balog himself. Information on Del Duca and Kandell was obtained from *Living Films: A Catalog of Documentary Films and Their Makers*, a 1940 publication of the Association of Documentary Film Producers in New York. Information on Roffman was found in Eleanor Beattie, *A Handbook of Canadian Film* (Toronto: P. Martin Associates, 1973), pp. 142-143.

ondhand model-T Ford, and he touched base briefly with the League early in 1931. Then, with Lewis Jacobs and a Russian friend, he drove south seeking film material on Southern racism and ended up beginning a film on the Scottsboro boys. It was during this trip that he met truly courageous Communists who were working in a pervasively hostile atmosphere in which lynch law was the order of the day. Pursued by a Scottsboro posse, the three travelers slipped away onto an alternate route and then headed north to Harlan County, Kentucky for footage of the long, tenacious strike by the hungry miners.

As the strike spread, Brandon traveled on north to the mines of western Pennsylvania and Ohio. He was joined by Joseph Houdyma, a working-class cameraman from Detroit who had studied at the Mezrabpom Studios in Moscow. He alternated for a while between the mines, where he was deeply moved by the frightening working conditions of the miners, and New York, dispatching or personally delivering the exposed film to the League. There it was edited into *Strike Against Starvation*, a film that was ready for distribution by the end of 1931. Talented at organizational work and enthusiastic about the idea of film support for workers' struggles, Brandon became active in the still-amorphous League in 1931, and, according to Sam Brody and Lester Balog, pulled together the loose threads. From 1931 to 1934, he served as League secretary, seeking funds, acquiring raw film and equipment, making travel and lodging arrangements, directing circulation of the films, and helping to determine priorities. As head of the WIR Film Division, he also had charge of the overall distribution of its film collection. Although he was not a filmmaker himself, Brandon was a key figure in left film promotion, production, and distribution for the rest of the decade.[14]

Sam Brody, witty, articulate, excitable, and fully devoted to the concept of the workers' newsreel, was born in London on 1 January 1907 of Russian-Jewish parents who had emigrated at the turn of the century. Paris was his home from ages four to thirteen, then briefly Richmond, Virginia, and finally New York City. His father—a follower of the anarchist Peter Kropotkin who turned Communist after the outbreak of the October Revolution—was, Brody recalls, "a trade union activist to the end of his life, a tailor who toiled his life away in sweatshops in London, Paris, and New York." With left-wing convictions from the start, an interest in writing, and a vocation first in still photography and then in film, Brody joined the Young Workers League in New York in the early twenties, became a member of the John Reed Club when it was founded, and worked for a time with the Japanese Workers Camera Club at the WIR. He was present at the first commercial showing of a Soviet film in America, Pudovkin's *The End of St. Petersburg* at the Hammerstein Theatre on Broadway, and the experience made him "overwhelmingly convinced of the power of film as a medium for bringing the Marxist message to American working-class audiences." Eager from the start to form the League and make it work, Brody was a strong figure at its nucleus, plying his camera on a number of fronts and writing film criticism for *The Daily Worker, New Masses,* and *Experimental Cinema.*[15]

Leo Hurwitz's father taught Hebrew in Russian Jewish communities but broke with the orthodoxy and became an anarchist and a devoted follower of Tolstoy. Seeking democracy and education for his children, the senior Hurwitz came to America in 1898 and, in Philadelphia and New York, labored at a series of jobs (among them pushcart peddler and garment shop worker) until he had enough money to bring his wife and four children to New York's Lower East Side in 1900. Four more children followed, and the youngest, Leo Tolstoy Hurwitz, was born in the Williamsburgh section of Brooklyn in 1909. Like his brother Peter Kropotkin Hurwitz and the others, Leo learned socialism at his father's knee. "I knew what surplus profit was," Hurwitz recounts, "I knew who Debs was, I knew what a strike was, I knew what the problems of capitalism were." Winner of a scholarship prize, he was one of the few students from his type of background at Harvard in the twenties. There he read with excitement Mencken, Eliot, and Hart Crane, probed the art of El Greco, Rembrandt, Goya, Blake, Van Gogh, Cezanne, and Picasso, discovered Brady, Atget, Stieglitz, and Strand, found inspiration in the teachings of Alfred North Whitehead and Robert Feild, viewed with awe the filmwork of Chaplin, the avant-garde, and the great Soviet filmmakers, and realized the indifference of most of his classmates who were headed for law firms or brokerage houses when he tried to sign them up to protest on behalf of Sacco and Vanzetti. Denied a Sheldon Fellowship (a year of study in Europe) despite his *summa cum laude* (his tutor and others attributed this denial to his Jewish extraction), he returned to New York after his graduation in 1930 to work as assistant editor of *Creative Art.*

Although he had resolved to make his way into the film profession, Hollywood's compartmentalization of filmwork and its bland product did not inspire him, and so the ill success of his half-hearted application for a job at Paramount in Flushing was not disappointing. He turned to still photography and then bought a Sept motion picture camera. Soon after, he met Jay Leyda,[i] who had recently arrived from Dayton,

[i] I believe Leyda was predominantly in the photography division of the WF&PL, although *Bronx Morning* was made independently. It was this film that helped him gain

Ohio and was filming his experimental *Bronx Morning*, and Paul Strand and Ralph Steiner; the latter gave him valuable lessons in still photography and became a fast friend. As he watched the Depression extend tragically into the lives around him, he became increasingly radicalized and was soon convinced that the Communist Party had "the best grasp, not always right, but the best grasp on the situation." Possibly at the suggestion of Leyda or Steiner, he visited the League in late 1931 and "thought it was absolutely great: they were doing important work that fit my own basic cinematic and social points of view, they had some pennies for footage and a place to show and were a very lively and very interesting group of people." He joined up and quickly entered the practical political filmmaking of the organization.[16]

Irving Lerner's socialist father, another Russian immigrant, found that it was difficult enough just making a living in the new world and thus gave up his political activity. But like Leo Hurwitz and other members of the League, his son grew up with the benefits of his father's considerable leftist sophistication. An anthropology major in the Columbia class of 1929, Lerner paid his way by compiling bibliographies for *The Encyclopedia of the Social Sciences*, edited by his not-yet-illustrious cousin Max Lerner, and by taking stills for the college's anthropology department. When a covey of Bahamas dancers moved into Harlem and Ruth Benedict wanted to record them on film before their art became modified, Lerner pretended he knew how to run a movie camera and got the job. A classmate, Margaret Mead, directed him to the photo studio at the Museum of Natural History for some initial practice. He shot and edited the film, which was ambitiously accompanied by music on an aluminum disc, and his vocation was established. Influenced by the Soviet film, still at its height in 1930, he began to equate Communism and progressive art. He signed up with the Workers Film and Photo League because he had heard that this organization would enable him to combine his leftist, progressive inclinations and also to "pick up a camera and start shooting film" without the prohibitive expense he would encounter elsewhere. Eager to learn, he helped cover the 1931 May Day demonstration at Union Square, and that summer, together with Sam Brody, he filmed the WIR Young Pioneer Camp where children were "taught solidarity with the children of the striking miners in Pennsylvania, with the children of the Negro workers of the South, as well as with the children of the workers of the world."[17]

David Platt was born in Philadelphia and lived there until the mid-

---

a fellowship to the Soviet Union, where he remained from September 1933 until late 1936.

twenties, another son of a Russian Jewish immigrant; his father was a shoemaker. An avid filmgoer from childhood, he saw nearly everything that came to the screen, but recalls that he "first became acutely aware of the power of the movie on seeing Griffith's *Orphans of the Storm* in 1921." At about the same time he met Potamkin in Philadelphia, and a little later he came into contact with Lewis Jacobs and Seymour Stern, his future coeditors on *Experimental Cinema*. The three were attracted to one another by their common interest in experimental films, especially the early Soviet silent masterpieces.

Until he joined the *Daily Worker* staff full time in 1935, Platt worked days as a stenographer-secretary and nights as a film critic for *The Daily Worker* and *Experimental Cinema*. His first editorials for *Experimental Cinema*, written in 1930, sought an aesthetic in which cinema would serve as the central force in a new humanism, one that could be responsive to the problems of mechanization. It was announced that he was at work on a book about the subject, *Cinema and the New Naturalism*, but the book succumbed to the Depression and to his commitment to socialism. He became active in the organized labor movement, and, having been taught by Potamkin "that film creativity and experimental cinema could not be isolated from the fight for social change," his film criticism took on a forceful new political quality. Although Platt did not join the League until 1933, he was by then able to endow it with a great amount of knowledge about film and with a full commitment to the League's dominant purposes; he became its executive secretary late in the same year.[18]

Other League members, whether they were accomplished in experimental filmmaking or simply novices with a hopeful feel for the camera, were less ideological. Ralph Steiner is a prominent example. Born in Cleveland in 1899 into a lower-middle-class family of Czech descent, he was a good half generation older than most of his colleagues. He picked up his first still camera as an early, mild form of revolt against his parents, neighbors to the Cleveland Art Museum who had never ventured inside. As one of a handful of Jews at Dartmouth, he led a somewhat lonely life and recalls that he was "one of the two soldier-students . . . in fifteen hundred who failed to get credit for military training." Nevertheless, he was content to be away from a large extended family in which his own parents were the poor relations, and it was during these years that he took up photography in earnest. When a local bookstore proprietor offered to buy a hundred or so copies of a book of his photographs of the college, he finally decided against a career in chemistry and in 1921 enrolled instead in the Clarence White School of Photography in New York. In 1922, he entered a photogravure plant, where his first job was to make plates to illustrate Robert Flaherty's *Nanook*, and then moved on to advertising photography, a career he disliked but was to stay in, to his regret, for too much of his life. He took what he calls "amusing little photographs" around the city, and gave a series of small exhibitions.

A meeting with Paul Strand in 1926 or 1927 brought Steiner to regard his own pictures as "something done through a bathmat," and led him to install himself for three summer months at the artists' colony at Yaddo, outside of Saratoga Springs, where he worked on texture, photographing such objects as old Ford automobiles and wicker chairs. Then he ran an advertisement appealing for funds, and through the recommendation of Edith J. R. Isaacs, the editor of *Theatre Arts Monthly* (for which Steiner had supplied free photographs), the Elmhurst Foundation granted him an extraordinary $14,000 for the making of films. With this money, over the next five or six years Steiner created some of the earliest and best American experimental films, including *Mechanical Principles* and his remarkable and enduring studies, *H_2O* and *Surf and Seaweed*.[j] Aaron Copland helped with the editing of these films.

His funds depleted, Steiner returned to advertising, joining the Workers Film and Photo League in time to point his camera at the May Day demonstration in 1931. Despite his WF&PL affiliation, he continued to draw income from periodicals like *The Ladies' Home Journal*, while seeking in the League a fertile collaboration in further cinema education and a practical outlet for his growing social awareness during the early years of the Depression. Although he was never to arrive at a fully developed political commitment, he hoped to help engender liberal reformist measures within the system that many of his Communist colleagues were determined to overthrow, setting his sights on new hospitals, new jobs, low-cost housing, and unemployment insurance. Like some others in the League, he was responding much more to the human suffering caused by the desperate Depression winters than he was to any specific ideology, and as a result his commitment to the Party program had its limitations. He can recall one bitterly cold evening when, working together with Leo Hurwitz on a project in his big studio on West 10th Street, he prevented Hurwitz from sallying forth to fulfill a pledge to sell his quota of *Daily Workers* by buying and then burning the papers in his stove.[19]

Lewis Jacobs, a very different kind of person, shared certain political similarities with Steiner. When he began to publish *Experimental*

---

[j] These two films are in the collection of the Museum of Modern Art.

Cinema in Philadelphia in 1930, his impulse was chiefly to reach out for personal contacts and to find his own way into filmmaking. As a sensitive but not very politically sophisticated critic of Soviet films, Jacobs saw that a concerted grappling with the demanding social issues of the day could exercise a profound effect on American film form. When he came to New York in 1931, he found that the League, which recognized his fine critical abilities, was both eager to vaunt him as one of its members and willing to provide him with film and facilities for his own camerawork. After accompanying Brandon and their Russian companion on the southern trip, he worked for a film trailer company, devoting his lunch hour to shooting the grim scene of life on Sixth Avenue, with its numerous employment agencies, gaunt apple sellers, beggars, and homeless men, women, and children. Much of his footage from 1931-1933 went to the League, although he always maintained his political independence from the far left.[20]

Leo Seltzer falls somewhere between those who were committed to Party ideology and those who were not, although he probably was closer to the former category. His parents came to Canada in 1908 or 1909, Jewish revolutionaries who fled Russia to save their lives. Leo was born in Montreal in 1910, spent his first years in Calgary at the edge of an Indian camp, and entered the States in 1918, attending public schools in Chicago and New York. His interests led him first to art school and then to electrical engineering college, which he left after two years because of boredom and a bulletin board that admitted that there were no jobs for students in private industry. Back in art school in 1931, he applied himself to the decision that his two major interests, art and technology, could best come together in photography.

> [I] heard about a cultural center where there was an art class taught, photography groups, and so on. And I started the art classes. This headquarters was just being built, and they needed lights to illuminate the model. I knew a little bit about electricity, so I installed the lights. Next door was a darkroom, and they needed someone to put in lights there. So I went over and put in lights, and the whole thing looked so intriguing to me, I stayed.

The darkroom belonged to the Workers Film and Photo League. It was the time of the first major hunger march, in December 1931, and everyone available was being sent out to cover the event. Seltzer received some quick instruction on the Eyemo, and went off with the others, holding a camera for the first time in what would be a long and notable film career. From that point on, the work of the League became a "way of life" for him, something he gave himself to completely. He spent almost all of his waking hours out with his camera, sleeping at night on desks at the WIR as Del Duca and Balog did, covering themselves with whatever they could find in the cellar, spending their evenings either editing the film that came in or "running those old Russian silent films through a viewer, looking at them by hand." He was not, Seltzer now recalls, either politically aware or socially conscious, which he believes is part of what enabled him to become the League's daredevil cameraman: he did not instinctively assume, as did some of the others, that policemen thought him a dangerous red. Yet thanks to his parents' past, he had the ideological base Ralph Steiner lacked, and he was comfortable in the League in a way that Steiner could never be. Progressive activity felt familiar to him, and when he passed adolescence, as he puts it, and looked for his place in the world, he naturally sought one on the left and was always to point his camera "with that inherited point of view."[21]

What is significant here is that whether they were politically sophisticated or merely troubled, whether they were Party members or fellow travelers, far left or left liberal, arriving from working-class jobs or from college, it was the human suffering of the Depression that united these men. Regardless of their individual backgrounds, it was the breadlines, the Hoovervilles, the suicides, and the starvation that drew them into a determination for social action. "Shortly after I graduated from college," Hurwitz wrote,

> there were 16 million people without jobs. They had been suddenly shaken loose from a much-publicized prosperity. The breadlines grew day by day. An army of apple sellers—who had previously been carpenters, garment workers, storekeepers—appeared on street corners and in front of subway stations. Homeless men built shanty-towns in Central Park and on the edges of the city. When you put your hand in your pocket and you can touch your total savings, your life is revealed as not the private thing it seemed before. It becomes connected with others who share your problem.

If the "work of the Film and Photo League was crude," Hurwitz stated,

> it had energy derived from a real sense of purpose, from doing something needed and new, from a personal identification with subject matter. When homeless men were photographed in doorways or on park benches, feeling guided the viewfinder. The world had to be shown what its eyes were turned away from.[22]

And it certainly was not shown these realities by Hollywood or by the contemporary newsreel.

The League members also felt themselves in solidarity with other young people in the arts, in literature and drama especially. They identified themselves as part of a mass of people who were eagerly taking part in an exciting new kind of cultural ferment. Edna Meyers (then Edna Ocko), whose husband Sidney joined the League in 1934, was a performer in the Workers Dance League and a writer and speaker on "The Revolutionary Dance Movement" (the title of a *New Masses* piece she wrote). She went on to be a founder of the New Dance Group and dance editor and editor-in-chief of left periodicals throughout the decade. She remembers growing up on New York's Upper West Side, the child of a radical cigarmaker from Russia and a member of a set of talented, sophisticated young people who attended all the concerts and performed in each other's homes. She recalls what happened to many of them as they entered the thirties:

> The thirties . . . everybody speaks of it as a period of great ferment and great excitement . . . but here we were, young people involved in the arts in one way or another. . . . Sidney had gone to City College, but he was a musician and he was interested in poetry and things like that. My brother was a musician. I studied the piano. I wrote poetry. I appeared in anthologies. We lived near each other . . . and we were excited about the times and we loved people. We thought that you get excited about what the world is like when you're young. Well, look what the world was like! People were starving. There was a lot of ferment in the unions. None of us belonged to unions, but there was ferment in the unions. And there were many left-wing organizations that wanted talent. [It was our desire] to be their pamphleteers, to be their writers, to express their point of view . . . and our beliefs were very ideal: we really thought the world was going to undergo a change and . . . that the revolution was close! . . . I didn't know when it would happen. I thought it would happen in my lifetime, but I didn't know. . . . But I remember going to the 42nd Street Public Library. Someone told me to read the Communist Manifesto. And I remember sitting down—you could take it out of the library then—and I burst into tears at the end of it. I thought it was the most beautiful thing I had read in my life.[23]

Just as a later generation of youth was to create both a new politics to combat racism and the war in Vietnam and a counterculture to defy the technocracy, the younger generation of the early thirties turned to the left to fight against capitalism and the Depression.

Film Theory, Production, and Product

One starting point for some of the young filmmakers was a formal revolt from Hollywood. As Hurwitz and Steiner wrote in 1935:

> During the twenties we grew disgusted with the philistinism of the commercial film product, its superficial approach, trivial themes, and its standardization of film treatment: the straight-line story progressing from event to event on a pure suspense basis, unmarred by any imaginative use of the camera, unmarred by any freshness in editing or any human or formal sensitivity. Our reaction, which we shared with the young generation of experimental filmmakers, was a more or less aesthetic revolt from the current manner of film production. The important thing, we felt, was to do those things which the film was capable of, but which the commercial film didn't and couldn't possibly do. There seemed unbounded possibilities for the use of the film as a visual poetry of formal beauty.[24]

With the coming of the Depression, the radical filmmakers came to view Hollywood as more than cinematically unimaginative or thematically trivial and stylized. They came to view it as the dream-and-propaganda machine of the establishment, and some of them were to trace for the uninformed the ultimate ownership behind Warner Brothers, Columbia, Paramount, and Fox. Hollywood newsreels, fast-paced with pet shows, beauty contests, and mummified diplomatic arrivals, carried no word of breadlines and evictions or of strikes in the coal mines, in the textile mills, and on the waterfront. Feature films either entirely avoided social issues or, on the rare occasions that they touched on them, merely emphasized the shallow knowledge and concern, the tendency toward sentimentality, and the often reactionary stance of their respective creators.

Sam Brody's description of the 1932 Hunger March film emphasizes the League effort "to unmask the lies and provocation of the capitalist press and screen" and to support and raise the militancy among their audiences:

> Whereas the capitalist cameramen who followed the marchers all the way down to Washington were constantly on the lookout for

sensational material which would distort the character of the March in the eyes of the masses, our worker cameramen, working with small hand-cameras that permit unrestricted mobility, succeeded in recording incidents that show the fiendish brutality of the police towards the marchers. We have records of workers writhing in pain from the after-effects of tear-gas. We have pictorial evidence of police terrorization in New England.

Our film also proves conclusively that in no case were the marchers intimidated by the unparalleled display of weapons and bombs. . . .

Our film also records the fact that the marchers were greeted and welcomed all along the line of march by Negro and white workers who saw in this March the expression of their own power and determination to fight against starvation and for unemployment insurance. . . .

The Paramount cameramen did not want to see all those things. They were too busy "shooting" Lord and Lady Astor on a slumming trip through the New York Avenue encampment. They were too preoccupied with photographing Commissioner of Police Brown in conference with his fellow-thugs.[25]

Six of the thirteen League activities that Harry Alan Potamkin proposed in *Workers Theatre* in 1931 were aimed directly at Hollywood, and a relatively large amount of League time would be devoted to a critical attack upon the industry film. Two reasons accounted for this: the League was composed of a small, unknown group of filmmakers in New York, with scant equipment and a narrow purse, and the industry they conceived of as their opponents was a multimillion-dollar operation with complete control, not only over every conventional channel of distribution, but over the minds and pocketbooks of the American working class. Accordingly, the assault was leveled not only out of a desire to disabuse that working class of its indoctrination and out of the League's own need to gain recognition for itself and its members but from a conviction of being in the right. Hurwitz recalls:

Competitiveness was not an important aspect of the relationships of people interested in film. We shared what we knew. We felt tied by a kinship of meaning and aim. Underneath was the latent feeling that we and unknown cohorts were preparing to storm the citadel of commercialized, meretricious, and dehumanized art. If "storming the citadel" is too romantic a metaphor, then at least we felt we were preparing to break through the narrow frontiers of the dominant attitudes toward film.[26]

Although it may also have been true that for some members of the League it was easier to criticize than to create either theory or film, in the end it was true that until the American audience was taught to penetrate status-quo soporifics, it would not be ready for the "truer" films, the ideally more advanced forms, and the League's sociopolitical perspective.

Their desire to make films, their anger over the Depression, and their contempt for Hollywood spurred them on. And always informing and inspiring them were the successes of the Soviet Union: the October Revolution, full employment, and the revolutionary content and techniques of the Soviet cinema. In the United States, as everywhere else in the world, their first viewings of Soviet films came as revelations to aspiring filmmakers. During one of our two hurried 1973 interviews in the dark living room of his West End Avenue apartment, Leo Hurwitz reminisced:

When I first saw those films, they hit me here [striking his chest]. They had a great impact, but it wasn't the montage. Their strength was that they had something of great importance to say, something that moved people and forced itself out into original film language. They revealed that past films could be transcended for something deeper and further reaching. They gave one a new way of looking at the world, a way of growing and working from that, and a way of giving specificity to the outlook and the growth. They made one believe the world could be changed.[27]

The very history of Soviet film energized the young, untrained documentarists. Seymour Stern acknowledged this by printing a piece by N. Kaufman after his own lead article in *The Left*. Kaufman related how, during and immediately after the Revolution, Soviet filmmakers had lacked raw film, studios, and modern equipment, and how, accordingly, they had taken to the outdoors to film the battlefronts, mass demonstrations, antireligious action, and the pioneering progressive projects of the new Soviet Union. He told of the brave and dangerous lives of these dedicated cameramen and of how the extraordinary discovery of the montage technique had been a result of the economic necessity for a low shooting ratio. He paralleled the triumph and the dialectical form of montage to the success and to the very nature of the new nation.[28] In such beginnings and such achievement, American cinematographers of unorthodox political and cinematic persuasion found crucial inspiration.

The League's most sophisticated theorist was Harry Alan Potamkin, who exercised a large influence, both professional and personal, upon his colleagues. Born in 1900, the son of Russian parents who emigrated to Philadelphia, a graduate of New York University, a member of the expatriate community in Paris during the twenties, and a visitor to the Soviet Union in 1927 where he had met Eisenstein and Alexandrov, Potamkin had one of the most acute, energetic minds of his generation.

Although his interest in Soviet film was purely artistic in the beginning, its influence gradually turned him toward social and political considerations in his film criticism during the late twenties; although he never joined the Communist Party, by 1930 he was an active cultural-front fighter.[29] One of the founders of the New York John Reed Club in 1929, he wrote poetry, short stories, and a great deal of criticism, mostly on film. During the early thirties, his work appeared frequently in *New Masses*, *Workers Theatre*, *Experimental Cinema*, *Hound and Horn*, *Close Up*, and other magazines. He reedited a Soviet film, *Jimmie Higgins*, for release in the United States, and he wrote a pamphlet on censorship and the social and financial nature of the Hollywood film (*The Eyes of the Movie*, illustrated by William Gropper), a biography of Lenin (*Our Lenin*, with Ruth Shaw), and an operetta (*Strike Me Red*)—the latter two for children.

With five other delegates from *New Masses* and the John Reed Club, Potamkin attended the Soviet Union's International Congress of Revolutionary Writers and Artists at Charkov late in 1930, and he was elected to the Control Commission of its International Bureau. In America he spoke at clubs and camps, served as editor of *Pioneer*, the Party children's magazine, and was elected to the presidium of the New York Workers Cultural Federation in 1931. He was a member of the National Committee of the Film and Photo League and of the National Board of Review,[k] and he gave a series of twelve ambitious lectures on film as art, industry, and social force at the New School for Social Research.

With all of this, Potamkin neglected his health, and on 25 June 1933, his abdomen, which had been ulcerated for three years, hemorrhaged. Twenty-six members from the John Reed Club, the Workers Film and Photo League (including Brody, Jacobs, and Seltzer), and the *Daily Worker* staff, as well as a number of total strangers, volunteered their blood. Only four of them, including the photographer Walker Evans, shared Potamkin's rare blood type, but their donations made no es-

[k] A "volunteer organization reflecting public sentiments and cooperating nationally with producers and city officials in the review and regulation of motion pictures on the basis of minimum standards." The National Board of Review made a strong effort to get good films publicized and shown, including most of the films discussed in Chapters II through VII of this work. See Lina D. Miller, ed., *Directory of Social Agencies* (New York: Charity Organization Society of the City of New York, 1930-1931), p. 598.

sential difference: his condition worsened, and he died on 19 July at the age of thirty-three. A red funeral was conferred for the first time on a non-Party member, the result, Irving Lerner reported, of Potamkin's devoted and understanding service to the cause of the working class. Shelley Hamilton, film critic for the *National Board of Review Magazine*, wrote of him that

> with all his artistic gifts and appreciation, he cared more for human beings than he did for art, he stood almost alone among writers in his passionate insistence that the great force of the motion picture should be used in the broadening and strengthening of human understanding and in helping build a civilization in which the lives of men and women and children would be better worth living.[30]

With his death, the left film movement in America lost its foremost activist and theorist, a powerful force who was just reaching full maturity.

A first premise in Potamkin's critical perspective was that the film must be politically effective—that it must expose, impel, and sustain. This was a premise whose general tenet was shared, if in varying degrees, by every artist on the left.[31] For Potamkin, political effectiveness hinged upon mature revelation of social and political causes, upon a point of view rising from the fully developed convictions and commitments of the filmmaker, and upon a provocative but unostentatious style.[32] The ideal film would be totally integrated, every frame fully subordinated and sensitive to the overriding social idea and its dramatization. Thus in *Turksib*, the piston gliding on oil, the spinning mechanisms, and the camera angles became "structural elements and social persuasions"; if *Kameradschaft*'s indictment might have been more pointed, the film was still important, for its "artistry is the complete submission of the technique—camera, set, lighting—and almost complete submission of the acting" to Pabst's socioethical intention.[33]

Like most critics rooted in Marxism, Potamkin opposed narratives like those of F. W. Murnau's *The Last Laugh* and King Vidor's *The Crowd*, where the individual is "caught pathetically in the social morass" instead of being "the concentration of the social force" as in Pudovkin's *The End of St. Petersburg* and in *Arsenal* and *Storm over Asia*.[34] Soviet film structure was dialectical, whether the dialectics were between the individual and society, as in the work of Pudovkin, or "expressed completely as structure and conveyed as idea," as in Eisenstein. "There is the THESIS—the status quo. The ANTITHESIS asserts itself—the proletariat (combatant, antagonist-protagonist) or the new force. The result is the SYNTHESIS—the new order," and in this as in other things, "the USSR serves the cinema of the world and becomes its mentor." The power of purely cinematic dynamics over an audience should work hand in hand with dialectical structure: filmmakers should take advantage of the fact that film is both "a progressive medium moving toward intensiveness" and that "it concentrates ecstasy, mystery, horror."[35] The impact of this "intensifying medium" can be used to spur the struggle for a more equal society, thus making film a very important political weapon.[36]

Yet Potamkin was far from agreeing with Stern's vision of "a motion picture as blazing as the blood of the 322 convicts who burned to death like animals in a caged trap" and of an "art of hammering image-ideas into the mentality of the spectator by the persistent ingenious manipulation of aggressive, violently emotional montage-forms." Soviet cinema itself had abandoned such once-useful muscular film for "inferences" and "implications," Potamkin wrote. It had moved, in Eisenstein's terms, from the "metric" to the "overtonal" in anticipation of "the development of the intrinsic cinema the world over," a development all in favor of political effectiveness. For *Storm Over Asia* seemed to ask, "How much immediate impact, how much after-effect? Cannot what drives in too forcefully, just as easily drive out? Is not propaganda the accumulation of what is implied?"[37]

All this represented a sophisticated goal that Potamkin hardly expected the League's eager, self-educating filmmakers to apprehend immediately. In fact, not everyone in the League or in the film movement at large was deeply aware of his writing. Although the early film criticism of Lewis Jacobs paralleled and benefited from Potamkin's more political essays, Ralph Steiner, who was not inclined toward theory, never read Potamkin and can remember no influence at all. Willard Van Dyke, who was to come East in 1935, recalls that Potamkin was scarcely known on the West Coast,[38] and it is true that his most substantial influence would not be visible until later in the decade with the work of Frontier Films. Those political activists in the League who were not filmmakers were probably impressed primarily by Potamkin's status and by his assaults upon Hollywood. And when the New York left-front cultural groups affiliated in 1931, these activists were pleased by his useful argument that "the pre-eminently important propaganda group" was the Film and Photo League:

> The Federation must relate the work of this group to every workers' club and to the entire revolutionary press. The League must be encouraged and supported in its showing of films, its agitational

work against reactionary movies, the making of proletarian film-documents and in the spread of the function of the worker-photographer.[39]

Where Potamkin sensed conflict between his ultimate goals for revolutionary film and the narrower notions of some of the other League organizers and filmmakers, he did not join battle. His attitude toward League filmmaking, Leo Seltzer remembers, was never pedantic but always encouraging and supportive. Irving Lerner and Leo Hurwitz, talented practitioners of the art and close friends of Potamkin, profited greatly in the early thirties both from his writing and from his personal encouragement concerning their own careers. He was the first to admire the dramatic scenes that Seltzer dared to capture close up, and both his warm, generous personality and his helpful criticism touched Seltzer so deeply that he felt, and still feels, Potamkin's death to be "one of my life's tragedies."[40]

One film, planned but never produced, bears the influence of Potamkin, who was at work on its scenario. *Winter, 1931* was an ambitious film: it was to be eight reels long, budgeted at over $4,500, and it was intended to dramatize the class struggle and to develop proletarian culture among American workers. Aimed at exposing "the misery . . . of the American workers and poor farmers . . . greater than it has ever been in the history of the country" and at emphasizing the "bitter struggle that will certainly take place this winter," the film was also intended to raise relief funds for the families of striking workers and to support the growing militancy of the unemployed. Its brief prospectus, possibly prepared by Potamkin, reveals an elementary thesis-antithesis approach, with perhaps an implicit synthesis and what appears to be a rather muscular progression toward intensification:

> It will be a unified structure composed of separate news events, each news item featuring some dramatic detail of unemployment and mass struggle. Sharply against the cold of winter will flash the flophouses, the tattered clothes, the bread lines, lonely men freezing to death, spontaneous strikes, suicides, the more and more insistent demands of the starving millions, their hunger marches and demonstrations. The leisure class will be contrasted with the underfed.[41]

Lerner and Hurwitz, both readers and friends of Potamkin, have remarked on the importance of the Soviet filmmaker Esther Shub's compilation films.[42] Her *Cannons or Tractors?*, a forty-minute film distributed by the League during 1931 and 1932, was for them an example of a more synoptic film than they were producing, a film that they considered to be based on true dialectical structure and cinematic dynamics. An outline of its content, published in 1936, will be useful in conveying the impact it made on the two filmmakers in terms of the kind of art they aspired to. In what follows, the phrases in quotation marks are captions in the film.

PART I—THE CAPITALIST WORLD

1. Pennsylvania—"No Trespassing, Private Company." Mining shacks.
2. "Harlan, Kentucky"—mining shacks; baby crying; a woman barefoot; babies and wives of miners; children picking and eating spoiled fruit discarded into an empty lot.
3. Mining scenes; miner entombed, "Why?"
4. Africa; Negro children under whip.
5. Coal mine—"Speed Up!"
6. "Unemployment"—on line for job; girls barefoot; breadline; park sleepers.
7. Issuing propaganda leaflets; oratory; marching under banners.
8. Police attack crowd.
9. "Upholding the Sanctity of the Home!" Man and children evicted from shack; a whole street of evictions; a rent strike; oratory.
10. Union Square; orations; police on motorcycles dashing through.
11. "Peace on Earth, Good Will to Men!" A bishop christening a war ship.
12. "5/6 of the World Prepares for War": launching a new battleship; cannons booming; army going over the top; laying of barbed wire in devastated field; gas attack.

PART II—ONE-SIXTH OF THE GLOBE
BUILDS A NEW CIVILIZATION: "U.S.S.R."

1. "From the Frozen North"—harnessing of water power.
2. "To the Semi-tropical South"—women working leisurely in fields.
3. "Collectivization," "Competition for the benefit of all!"; workers signing up.
4. Tractors working a Giant State Farm; plowing the soil.
5. "Livadia, a Worker's Rest Home, Once the Home of the Czar"; nurse reading to convalescents.

6. "1/6 of the World Gives Workers Opportunity for Study"; students watching a laboratory demonstration.
7. Nursery; nurses caring for babies left by workers for the day.
8. "Our Little Comrades Wonder Why Capitalists Dump Milk"; milk bottle under sanitary conditions; babies drinking milk.
9. Recreational centers for workers.
10. Giant Tractor factories.
11. U.S.S.R. being industrialized; "The Five Year Plan Succeeding in Four."

According to Solomon P. Rosenthal, even in its weak spots, in its overload of radical oration, *Cannons or Tractors?* was typical of radical newsreels, a film "well calculated to arouse emotion."[43] A Depression working-class audience easily identifying with Part I would find little transitional difficulty in warming at least a little to the secure and spirited scenes of Part II. The League reported that with no funds for high-priced publicity the film drew seven thousand people on its first day in New York, and in two subsequent showings it attracted a total of seven thousand more (the figures are probably exaggerated).[44]

Cannons or Tractors? is built largely on the contrast between political systems. Part I has its own dynamic, developing in scenes 1 to 6 the miserable conditions of the American (and African) laborer, conveying in scenes 7 and 8 an active struggle against these conditions, synopsizing scenes 1-7 in scene 9, and scenes 7-8 in scene 10: the larger, grimmer characteristics of capitalism are arrived at in scenes 11 and 12. While it is less structurally dynamic, Part II conveys by multiple examples the successful dynamics of a workers' nation, reserving an overview for its final scene. In the larger dialectic of the film, the thesis-antithesis of scenes 1-10 in Part I, which should ideally lead to the synthesis of Part II, is weakened by the structurally irrelevant scenes of war preparation. Ironically, the thesis-antithesis conflict portrayed in scenes 1-10 was leading inevitably to the deadly synthesis of World War II, from which Soviet Russia was hardly to be exempt.

The typical process by which League films were organized and put together was invigorating and exciting. It was either the financial source of the raw film—usually the WIR—or the executive committee's judgment of urgency or significance that became the decisive factor in determining the event to be filmed.[45] People would be notified to gather at the League. Tom Brandon would say, "We need footage from Kentucky" (or from Pennsylvania, or from West Virginia) or "We have to cover Scottsboro for the ILD" (or we need someone on the waterfront, or someone at Union Square, or we have to cover the National Hunger March, the Bonus Army)—"Who will volunteer?"And people would make time: Seltzer almost always, and others very often.

As a case in point, Brody, Del Duca, Hurwitz, and Seltzer offered to cover the 1932 National Hunger March in Washington. Sent to Boston to follow the march from its beginnings, and joined on the way by Brandon, Brody, Del Duca, and Seltzer, Hurwitz formulated a basic method of shooting and loosely directed the camerawork. Looking at the footage back in New York and realizing that they had failed to make a sufficiently "intimate and detailed record of what transpired among the marchers during their two-day internment in Washington," they decided to attempt a more synoptic form, one that would emphasize the indignities that had provoked the protest. They took to the streets and brought back for the first of their four reels some strong, sensitive footage of the improvised housing of the unemployed. Within the next few days, laboring under high pressure in a house unlicensed for the handling of flammable nitrate stock, they edited *Hunger 1932* in time for a scheduled showing at the Cameo Theatre at 42nd and Broadway.[46]

Tom Brandon described the exhilaration and tension they all felt as they stood with the marchers on a hill above Washington, knowing that before dawn they might need to wield their cameras as clubs. Indeed there was always great risk in their activities, coupled with the kind of commitment that could lead Seltzer (whom Brody has delightedly dubbed "the Evil Knievel of the Film and Photo League") to edge out on an overhanging flagpole to film a visiting dignitary for the left-wing screen. On another occasion, when word was out that cameramen would be banned from a Scottsboro demonstration at the Supreme Court so that the police could be free to use unrecorded force, Seltzer rose to the challenge. He joined the line of march, popped out to do some filming, and captured a memorable shot of a man whamming hell out of a cop who had grabbed his picket sign—before the seven-foot-tall, six-foot-wide chief of the local red squad snatched his Eyemo and threw him into the paddy wagon. Irrepressible, Seltzer continued shooting through the window until his camera was finally confiscated. ("People would look at my stuff and they'd say, how'd you get it? Did you have a zoom lens? No! and I used to have black and blue marks on my hands from being beaten.") In another incident, in Scottsboro, Brandon, Jacobs, and a third League member were confronted at a lunch counter by an angry mob that forced them to make a frightened, hurried escape. A year later, Louis Berg, Leo Hurwitz, and a still photographer turned up in the same town—a town, Berg reported, that

> does not take kindly to the presence of strangers from New York. The alien is made to feel a hostile ring being drawn around him, tighter and tighter. The townspeople form in small groups to discuss him; the air is charged with threats. Glowering eyes follow him everywhere, catlike moving as he moves. To walk down the main street is an ordeal.

Hurwitz, later to edit the 1931-1933 two-reel film entitled *Scottsboro*, had been forbidden entrance into the black section of town, and in order to obtain the footage he needed for his film carried a small DeVry camera with which he shot quickly and quietly from the hip. On another occasion, Brody, sent down alone to cover the textile strike in Gastonia, North Carolina, slept with guns at the side of his bed.[47] Their experiences in the South presaged by thirty years those which so many of their inheritors, the civil rights activists of the 1950s and 1960s, were to live through and sometimes die for.

The projectionists had their danger and excitement as well. Sent out in midwinter to cover striking western Pennsylvania miners who had been living in tents for over two years, Seltzer strung up sheets to serve as movie screens in the minefields. Once, with characteristic aplomb (he calls it naiveté), he improvised his screen in a vacant lot between the houses of the sheriff and deputy sheriff so that he could show the miners a film of their own picketing, a common tactic of the League to help build and sustain morale. On another occasion, in Modesto, California on 11 February 1934, when the League, on tour for the *Western Worker*, was screening *The End of St. Petersburg* and local newsreels on the El Monte berry pickers' strike, the antiwar demonstration in San Diego, and the Los Angeles County Hunger March, the American Legion first marched on the building where the film was shown, and then the fire chief was sent to inspect it but could find nothing wrong. Four months later, Balog was thrown into "the almost airless jail of Tulare, California" and held there for a couple weeks for projecting for agricultural workers the Soviet film *The Road to Life* and the film of the berry pickers' strike.[48]

If all of this was exciting, ground-breaking, and intense, it was also spasmodic and limiting. After a few weeks of concentrated effort on *Hunger 1932*, there was no film activity for several months. Members would come in on weekends and at night or would use the camera for a few days and then vanish for weeks at a time. Some films were never completed; others were demoralizingly delayed.[49]

The principal cause was that the League's small cashbox seldom could support full-time effort. League members were unpaid: either they worked elsewhere for sustenance, if they were lucky, or they were on relief. Although the WIR Film Department provided raw film stock and processing, it was up to League members to turn up money for rent, travel expenses, the purchase and maintenance of equipment, advertising, printing, and so on. They derived some of this money from dues and some of it from selling footage to commercial newsreel companies, to the left-operated Acme Theatre, and later to the Cameo, who often paid from twenty-five to fifty dollars each for the use of League newsreels. The playwright Sidney Howard consistently contributed funds, and in 1934 the brilliant Hollywood technician and filmmaker Slavko Vorkapich declared his support, contributed a substantial sum, announced plans to make a film with the Los Angeles League, and joined the League's National Advisory Board.[1]

According to Brody, Edward Kern, who worked on some of the films as cameraman and editor, was an excellent fund-raiser, contriving cash-raising screenings at parties. In April of 1934, the first annual Film and Photo League Movie Costume Ball was held. Brody reported in his "Flashes and Close-Ups" column in *The Daily Worker* that it was "intended primarily to finance the production of workers' films over a six-month period at least." With typical verve, he went on to encourage readers to attend this sparkling occasion:

> The fact of outstanding importance is that at least one thousand dollars must be raised to enable the young and growing Film and Photo League to continue its courageous struggle against reactionary Hollywood movies, against the release of Nazi films, against capitalist government censorship and for the production of workers' newsreel and documentary films. Remember that the dollar that you pay for admission . . . will be translated into long celluloid ribbons carrying the message of struggle against war, hunger and fascism to tens of thousands of workers throughout the United States—into leaflets denouncing films like *I Believe in You*, the NRA shorts, etc.—into cameras and projectors. Ours is a gigantic task, challenging the most institutionalized of all the

[1] Other members at that time were Berenice Abbott, Margaret Bourke-White, Erskine Caldwell, Lester Cohen, Robert Gessner, Langston Hughes, and Ralph Steiner. King Vidor, who endorsed their program, was invited to join in August. I do not know if he did so.

bourgeois arts with its monster monopolies and gigantic network for mass distribution

Lectures and screenings of foreign and League films brought from twenty-five to seventy-five cents from each spectator, although the money did not always manage to get as far as the League's coffers. Often it would go instead to help children attend WIR summer camps, or to purchase food, clothing, and medical supplies for striking miners, veterans participating in the Bonus March,[m] and the city unemployed. The proceeds from the League's experiment with a workers' newsreel theater went to the Communist Party.[50]

And so the League's film production was meager, especially during 1932 and 1933. In 1932, completed films included: *Hunger 1932*; *Bonus March*, a two-reeler; *New York Hoovervilles*; *Workers Struggle in New York* (1932-1933); *The Ford Massacre*; and several other newsreels— *Kentucky-Tennessee 1932* (April), a newsreel of the miners' strike; a newsreel of the New York May Day demonstration; *May Day Scenes*, a newsreel of May Day events throughout the United States; *Scottsboro Demonstration* (probably filmed on 7 May in Harlem); *Foster and Ford in Action*, a newsreel of the CP presidential and vice-presidential candidates; *Rent Strikes*; an August antiwar demonstration; September footage on the miners' strike, on a farmers' holiday, and on a Trade Union Unity League picnic; and a November demonstration on behalf of the Scottsboro boys held in Washington, D.C. In 1933, Lewis Jacobs made a short independent film, *As I Walk*, composed from his lunch-hour filming of city misery; and Barnet G. Braver-Mann in Detroit, in collaboration with Joseph Houdyma, made an independent film entitled *Sewer-Diggers*. The Detroit League made a one-reel film for the Macedonian Workers Club and sent it on tour through five states.

In California, the Los Angeles League shot newsreel footage of a San Diego police attack on antiwar demonstrators and produced *Cotton-Pickers Strike*, and Brian Foy produced an artless but powerful two-reel newsreel compilation film for the Tom Mooney Molders' Defense Committee, *The Strange Case of Tom Mooney*. Theodore Dreiser spoke the prologue, and Mooney himself concluded the film, speaking

[m] The Adjusted Compensation Act of 1924 provided about 3.5 million veterans with bonuses for their period of service. The bonus policies averaged one thousand dollars. When hard times came, the veterans demanded immediate payment of the face value of these policies and marched on Washington in June 1932 to present their demands in person. President Hoover called out the National Guard to evict the bonus marchers and to destroy their camp.

in the doorway of the San Francisco County Jail in April of 1933, seventeen years after his framing for the bombing at the San Francisco Preparedness Day Parade. The New York League sent Seltzer and Sidney Howard out to the Dakotas in 1933 to cover a farmer's trial and to organize a film around the farmers' conditions, but they could discover no dynamic material and returned empty-handed (this was two months before the penny auctions and milk strikes began). This left the New York League with only its productions of *Scottsboro, Tom Mooney Demonstration, Unemployed Demonstration, May Day 1933*, and a number of their *America Today* series. This number included: Farmers' Conference (held in Washington, D.C., 7-10 December 1932, by the United Farmers' League); Lenin Memorial at the Coliseum; Gibson Committee Protest; Anti-Jim Crow Demonstration; Antiwar Demonstration in Wall Street.[51]

Contempt for Hollywood, admiration for Soviet film, interest in a dialectical style through the influence of *Cannons or Tractors?*, and Potamkin: What were the League films actually like? A preponderance of their early films were newsreels. For one thing, the *agitki* (short agitational films or film leaflets) pieced together by Vertov and others in the postrevolutionary Soviet Union had had notable success. For another, a shallow till, a lack of experience, and the usual rush to capitalize on events made newsreels the easiest films to contrive. The newsreel was also a very popular communications form in America, one that was flagrantly misused by the established film industry. In fact, a footage exchange arrangement with friends in the newsreel industry often rewarded the League with outtakes that could never have arrived on the commercial screen—a perennial political situation that Emile de Antonio and his successors in the 1960s and 1970s developed into a method and aesthetic of "radical scavenging" among library material. League films would reveal the reality Hollywood covered over, from breadlines to police brutality, in an effort to enlighten and provoke their working-class and liberal audience. It was left film's business to make the pictures tell the truth, Potamkin wrote in 1932: "Let us show 'Erbert 'Oover handing out the gaff, and comment from the point of view of actual facts on what the President represents. Let us use the common newsreel item and make it speak the truth."[52]

League members would record specific events, edit them in more or less chronological sequence (Balog and Seltzer hit upon the idea of using the newspaper line on the event as a continuity line) and then run them through at parties, clubs, and camps for consciousness raising, attitude reinforcement, and the collection of funds. With some exceptions, these films tended to be formally unsophisticated, relying for their effectiveness on the *fact* of the event, on the basic power of sheer documentation. Although Seltzer recalls working instinctively for a variety of angles and distances, and although there was usually a pre-event strategy and an effort to use numerous camera positions, shots were often taken from anywhere, with no such preplanning or camera editing. Sometimes this was because the cameramen were under duress during the speed of militant and police action and were forced to film from where they could. Still, the fact remains, and the films demonstrate, that these competent and courageous young men lacked schooling: they were amateurs at battle photography, and Union Square and Scottsboro were the only teachers they had. The newsreels they shot, often patched together quickly to take advantage of the currency of the event, were neither informed by dialectical structure nor fashioned into elaborate Soviet-influenced montage. Editing conditions at the League made matters even more difficult. Seltzer recalls:

> It was not easy to get editing equipment in those days; it was expensive. We never had any moviolas. . . . We did our editing by feel, by intuition, and then we'd run it off and see if it looked right. We had no viewers, just rewinds and an old Griswold splicer, and a so-called portable projector, which weighed about a ton.[53]

The eight minutes of *The Ford Massacre* that Tom Brandon shows today is typical of the unsophisticated newsreel. All but the funeral footage of the four labor martyrs was shot by Joseph Houdyma, then a Ford employee;[54] the film was edited by the New York League. Although the pacing of the editing has some effective variation, the power of the film is derived not from the camerawork but from the grim events themselves.[n] We see in sequence the tear gas assault, the running demonstrators under attack by the police and other antagonists, a shot of an unemployed workman's shack, still photographs of the four murdered strikers in their caskets, then banners, placards, protestors parading against the murderers, and a strong, if somewhat conventional, concluding shot, taken at an upward angle from waist height, that catches the signs, the raised fists, and the aroused faces in near close-up as they move across the frame.

But there were other newsreels that were more devoted to a concerted effort at the sort of associative montage these filmmakers ad-

---

[n] Four workers were killed and fifty injured by police guns in a clash at the Ford plant gates during a large demonstration at which workers attempted to present demands to the Ford management.

mired in the Soviet films. The nights they spent bending over the hand viewer watching *Potemkin* and *Mother* had persuaded Seltzer, Balog, and Del Duca that the fundamental, exciting point of filmmaking was the editing. Through screening Soviet film and through devoted study of Pudovkin's book on film technique, Hurwitz and Steiner had also reached the same conclusion. Accordingly, as they confessed in 1935, they found only minor importance in specific shot content, and regarded the shot's effect as being "the result of what comes before and after, the elements that react with it." Power came to the film in the cutting room, be the film a newsreel, a collage of original and/or borrowed newsreel material, or the more synoptic "synthetic documentary," a film based on more careful planning and a wider variety of scenes in order to give a "fuller picture of the conditions and struggles of the working class."[55]

Thus the cutting that the League filmmakers did was aimed at achieving a type of associative montage, although at a relatively crude level because of their lack of both training and time. Hurwitz edited this way in the now lost films, *Scottsboro*, *Sweet Land of Liberty*, and *Harbor Scenes* (the latter destroyed by Jacobs at Steiner's request). One isolated newsreel example of Potamkin's 'Erbert 'Oover-versus-truth genre occurs in the 1933 League series *America Today*. Taking two unrelated library newsreel shots and cutting them into three separate shots, Seltzer juxtaposed Roosevelt signing a document, a fleet going through war maneuvers, and Roosevelt looking up from the document with a self-satisfied smile. Here, Hurwitz explained (although the explanation might as easily have come from Eisenstein), "a new meaning not contained in either shot, but a product of their new relation on film, is achieved—the meaning of the huge war preparation of the demagogic Roosevelt government."[56]

Another film, *Bonus March*, edited by Seltzer and Balog and shot in New York and Washington by Brody, Seltzer, and other cameramen, is relatively unsophisticated in much of its camerawork and weak in some of its transitions, although it, too, has some telling juxtapositions. A series of shots of Herbert Hoover greeting World War I veterans at a ceremony is followed by: a waving American flag; a shot tilting down a cathedral facade; a continuation of the tilt; a man on a park bench, his face in his hands; and a completion of the tilt. Then we see a minister on the street; a triumphant war statue; a sign—"Catholic Charities; St. Francis Xavier's parish"; an eagle above the clock on the Bank of America window; then the man on the bench. Then there is another sign—"The Salvation Army; Jesus for the Bowery"; a second devastated man on a bench, looking up; two shots of tattered unemployed men on the street; another sign—"The Salvation Army; the Bowery for Jesus"; a high-angle shot of "Hooverville" written out large on the ground, and then a pan over the shacks; a man standing between two shacks; then five shots of the Salvation Army emergency food line; and finally, all of this resolved into a series of Union Square orators organizing the Bonus March.

The fragment of *America Today* that survives typically includes waterfront combat between police and strikers and the tense, famous sequence of police firing into the crowd of demonstrating workers at Ambridge, Pennsylvania. It concludes, however, with an unusual and striking shot of an impoverished farm family. In contrast with the pathos of most contemporary photographs of regional poverty, the farmer is shown speaking strongly, angrily, about his situation. The League's stress here, as elsewhere, was to provoke identification and the potential for militant action and not simply to arouse pity for the oppressed, which would only succeed in maintaining class distance. But it is rare that a League film should linger at all upon a group of people.

These League newsreels were journalistic, strongly propagandistic, sometimes analytic, sometimes dramatic, often convincing, and seldom, if ever, profound. The level of presentation has a certain flatness, deriving, for one thing, from an unexamined assurance that mere documentation would suffice to engage the audience—an audience that unfortunately was assumed to be at least potentially in agreement with the films' politics. And the haphazardness and haste of the filmmaking allowed little time for the filmmakers to deepen and enrich their work. Accordingly, people in these films are usually little more than functional fragments of the propaganda, and the films do not reach major stature. One finds little of the fertile delight Vertov takes in human movement and physiognomy at work and play in *Kino-Pravda* and *Man With the Movie Camera*. And there is nothing (unless it is in the lost first reel of *Hunger 1932* or in Kern and Seltzer's lost *Workers on the Waterfront*) of the tough but compassionate quality of Buñuel's portrayal of impoverished Spanish villagers in *Las Hurdas* (1932). There is nothing approaching that most profound and painful moment when the canons of documentary are broken, when one of Buñuel's crew steps from behind the observing camera, his wristwatch indicating his alien world, to touch the girl who has been lying, and dying, by the side of the road for three days and to acknowledge that there is nothing he can do.

Some of the League filmmakers were acutely aware of the limitations of the League films. More ambitious projects, such as *Winter 1931* and a film long-planned and dear to League hearts on the misery of Depression children, succumbed to the continuous pressure for money and for on-the-spot journalism. The League members were learning their shooting and cutting techniques only, as Hurwitz wrote in the spring of 1934, "in the crucible of events, in preparing films of workers' struggles to be used in turn as a weapon in these struggles," rather than under calmer and more controlled conditions.[57] As the first years of the League's life passed, some of these aspiring young filmmakers began to feel burdened by the restrictions of such an education.

Other Activities

The League was not always occupied principally with film production: distribution was also an important, time-consuming and problematic business. The League undertook the distribution of its own and Soviet films because, although such films were readily shown at art cinemas or political theaters such as the Acme and the Cameo, they were rarely exhibited elsewhere, for obvious reasons.° League distribution improved this situation, but not by much. Leo Hurwitz complained that *Hunger 1932* was a very important film, yet it had been seen by only a few thousand people, mainly in New York, "despite the fact that the three thousand delegates on the [Hunger] march were eager to have the film shown to their organizations all over the country. Being a topical and timely film, it was necessary to distribute it quickly. This was not done, with the consequence that it has in a short time become so much celluloid." This failure meant fewer funds for future films and profound discouragement for the filmmakers. Writing in June 1935, John Gessner wanted to know why *America Today* "hasn't been more widely shown, especially to workers' clubs throughout the country."[58]

Although it is hard to say just how efficient the League's distribution apparatus was, available reports indicate considerable early work and a good amount of continuing activity. In October and November 1931, for instance, seventy-five showings were arranged for "social, literary and music groups, A.F. of L. locals, Y. Branches, liberal clubs and fraternal organizations," more than half in New York, but some as far away as the Mississippi; orders for December and January demonstrated increasing interest in the midwestern states as far north as the

---

° In January 1935, M. Radin of the Cameo Theatre announced the establishment, by International Art Cinema, Inc., of a chain of theatres in nine large eastern and midwestern cities, "to make regular showings of the latest Soviet Films available to workers in other cities, where the regular commercial exhibitors refused to book pictures from the Soviet Union." See DW, 8 Jan., 6 Feb., and 21 Feb. 1935.

Dakotas.[59] Early in 1932, the WIR Film Department organized a series of mass movie meetings in support of the striking miners in Kentucky and Tennessee. These meetings, fifteen of which had been held by late January, were intended to raise immediate funds, to mobilize strike relief volunteers, and to establish permanent film centers for future efforts of the same sort. They were to be coordinated with a 130-city, coast-to-coast film lecture tour by John Ballam, the Communist Party candidate for governor of New Jersey. Ballam would have with him *The New World*, the *National Hunger March Film* (a two-reel film of the winter 1931 hunger march), and *Strike Against Starvation*.[60] Although the tour took place, few, if any, film centers came into being.

By the end of 1932, Tom Brandon, who had "decided to concentrate on learning how . . . to build independent distribution so that independent film-makers working in the public interest could sustain their work," had founded Garrison Films, which shared with the Soviet Amkino Corporation the distribution of Soviet films. Brandon also took over the distribution of League films, and, a good businessman and promoter, he sent out some Hollywood films as well. Active on a number of film fronts over the next few years, Brandon aided organizations throughout the country in establishing programs and dealing with the local censorship problems they confronted.

Garrison Films generously estimated its audiences among American workers and farmers in 1933 at 400,000, and in 1934 Brandon went to work on establishing film guilds and circuits in the Midwest. During the week beginning 27 October, the talkie version of Pudovkin's *Mother*, written by Mike Gold, went the rounds of workers' clubs in Detroit, along with a commercial comedy and *America Today*. The program then departed for Flint, Grand Rapids, Ann Arbor, Kalamazoo, and Berkley—cities on Garrison Films' Michigan film circuit. From the field, Brandon reported to Gold that in the Dakotas Garrison had established "a circuit of some 90 farming villages and towns" where League newsreels and *Potemkin*, *The End of St. Petersburg*, *Mother*, and Friedrich Ermler's *Fragment of an Empire* had already made the rounds.

> The operator travels in an old Ford from town to town, but his 16 millimetre sound projector is new and does the job well. The farmers eat it up. They flock in from miles around, and see the pictures in barns, schools, town halls; once even in a big funeral parlor loaned by a friendly mortician.

Further circuits were being developed in Michigan and Illinois "for the auto workers, steel workers, miners and farmers." Brandon was ecstatic:

It's a great experience for me personally. It is really thrilling to see it demonstrated that the American workers and farmers are not what Hollywood says they are—morons. No, they want good pictures, they love good pictures. If this thing keeps growing at its present rate, we are going to give Hollywood some real competition soon in the way of audience-appeal. We have already given several hundred thousand real Americans a sample of our new world, and they want more. Let's all become more film-minded. Who knows but that this machine may prove to be the best organizing weapon in a machine country like America?[61]

Impressed, Gold went on himself to enthusiastically estimate the impact of film on such audiences. But this vision was to wane after the early stages of Brandon's pioneering work: the theaters were never to be cracked, the informal spectator groups turned out to be difficult to keep together, and Gessner's query in 1933 attests to an overall failure in the circulation of League films.

The film producers, then, were also film distributors and exhibitors. Similarly, the filmmakers were not only filmmakers, for on occasion, Brody, Lerner, Seltzer, and others also served as still photographers. The still section of the League was a committed, industrious group: they gave classes, held exhibitions of their work in 1933, 1934, and 1935, and furnished photographs to the workers' press and to other periodicals. This was also a way of raising the money that the League filmwork did not provide. As Seltzer tells it, League members would often have knowledge unavailable to commercial photographers and thus scoop them on political events and then sell the photographs.[62]

The League also continued to participate in events such as the *New Masses* birthday party on 5 January 1932 and fund raising efforts such as the WIR picnic at Pleasant Park on 21 June 1931 (for the WIR children's camp and miners' relief). It held its own Motion Picture Costume Ball in April 1934 and a November 1934 housewarming party at its new 31 East 21st Street headquarters to help send delegates to the antiwar congress in Chicago. To raise consciousness and funds, the League also ran a lecture bureau of sorts,[63] continued to give and sponsor symposia and lectures (by Harry Podolin, Slavko Vorkapich, Merritt Crawford, Nathan Asch, Nathaniel West), and between 1933 and 1935 held single-program film showings, as well as a five-program history of the Soviet film, two evenings of experimental shorts, and several series of "Distinguished Films."

Several League members, notably Nathan Adler, Tom Brandon, Sam Brody, Leo Hurwitz, Irving Lerner, and David Platt devoted considerable time to writing reviews, film-front news, censorship analysis, and, now and then, theory. Although they had no periodical of their own (except for *Film Front* for a few months early in 1935), the pages of *The Daily Worker*, *New Masses*, *Experimental Cinema*, *Workers Theatre*, *New Theatre*, and others were open to them. At various times, *New Theatre* served as the League's official voice, and League members ranked high on its editorial staff.

Potamkin had early urged the League to make a fight against censorship one of its priorities, and he had written his own careful analyses of the forces of censorship. League writers did thorough and intelligent research, and Brandon and Platt, especially, found formidable targets in Hays, Hearst, and an array of powerful church leaders. When the Legion of Decency and other groups lobbied for a federal censorship bill to supersede the strict laws of six states, the League enlisted the aid of noted filmmakers such as Vorkapich and Vidor, organized a letter-writing protest, held a symposium together with the ACLU's National Council on Freedom from Censorship, and sent to a meeting of the Association for the Preservation of Freedom of Stage and Screen a delegation that "succeeded in securing unanimous endorsement of its proposal for condemnation of the narrow perspectives of the Church Crusade and for a city-wide conference against federal film censorship." The League also published an official position paper on censorship that revealed one basis for its concern: "The guiding codes in all these censorship bodies refer not only to immorality, or indecency, but in the main to films that 'incite to riot,' [that treat of] 'capital vs. labor' [and] 'disturbing the peace,' [and] 'that show disrespect for officers of the law.' " And in a four-part *Daily Worker* piece tracing the history of censorship, Brandon fiercely drove home the League's interpretation:

> The great masses of moviegoers . . . will recognize in this program of "decency" a striking resemblance to the kind of decency brought into their struggles for unemployment relief and for the right to organize, strike and picket, by the representatives of the Church in the N.R.A. anti-labor "arbitration Commissions." Mayor Rossi and Archbishop Hanna of San Francisco, like Father Haas of Minneapolis, carried the Church's standard of decency into the great General Strike and into the Minneapolis strike—a standard of decency that was expressed in practice as a bloody aid to the savage fascist-like assault on the embattled workers.

Newsreels did not easily fit in under the established censorship laws, and the League, which had been hauled into court for showing its own films at its own headquarters, was quick to protest when someone like

Mayor Kelly of Chicago used local police power to ban from the city's screens all newsreel pictures of rioting or mob scenes (picket lines, demonstrations, mass meetings, evictions) because they "incite to riot."[64] Local censorship boards, especially strong, for instance, in Pennsylvania (as late as 1934, *Potemkin* still had not appeared in Pittsburgh), internal censorship in the industry itself, and tough right-wing opposition not only to Soviet cinema but to the mildest leftist perspective on the screen made it difficult and even dangerous for any candid presentation of the American social scene.

As Hitler's power grew in Germany[p] and the tendencies of Mussolini became obvious in Italy, and as, according to League critics, Hollywood began to increase production of militaristic and antilabor films, the League emerged from the periodicals into active protest. Potamkin's call to action had previously designated such efforts as another early priority, but it was not until 1934 that the League finally rose to consistent attack. On May Day of that year, members leafleted the workers at Fox Films in New York, charging that Fox newsreels carried more Hitler propaganda than any other newsreel company. At a special meeting on 27 June, they resolved to join the fight to win release of Ernst Thaelmann, the German Communist Party leader imprisoned by the Nazis, who was subsequently tried and executed. A delegation was sent to the German Consulate in New York, which the League also picketed, and immediate plans were made to go to work on a film about the case, which they began not long after when they received footage smuggled from Germany. They combined the German footage with footage of Georgi Dimitrov (who had fought off the Nazi attempt to imprison him for the Reichstag fire) in Moscow. This was then intercut with footage of international demonstrations for Thaelmann and with a talking prologue and epilogue by Earl Browder, general secretary of the American Communist Party. The result, *Ernst Thaelmann, Fighter for Freedom*, ran to large audiences in New York from 19 to 22 September, and then traveled to other cities. In addition, in July, the League, together with two Party-backed organizations, the Anti-Nazi Federation and the American League Against War and Fascism, actively took up the case of Herman Blander, a Jewish film worker at Cinelab, who had been fired by a superintendent with Nazi sympathies.[65]

[p] League people were alert and sensitive to events in Germany, as the following quotation demonstrates: "Within six weeks after Hitler came to power, and before a general boycott movement developed in the U.S., a warning in film was produced by Tom Brandon called *A Symposium on Hitler*" (Brandon Film Program, Pacific Film Archive, 13 May 1973). See also Hurwitz's review of *Hitler's Reign of Terror*, "Vanderbilt is Star in Phoney Anti-Nazi Film," DW, 7 May 1934, p. 5.

Protests in New York, Detroit, Chicago, San Francisco, and Baltimore by various groups, including the League, had succeeded in shortening the 1933 run of *Thunder Over Mexico* (the corrupt version of Eisenstein's *Que Viva Mexico!*), but it was with the appearance in New York in May 1934 of the Nazi film *S. A. Mann-Brand*, an idealization of the storm trooper, that the League itself first really flexed its muscle. By vigorous protest, the League and other anti-Nazi demonstrators prevented both a downtown showing of the film and the production of a version with English titles, forcing it uptown to a neighborhood theater in Yorkville, the German neighborhood in New York's Upper East Side. The same protest forced the Bavarian Film Company to excise most of the film's more blatantly anti-Jewish sequences, most notably the frequent cry, "Perish, Jews!" In Yorkville, shopkeepers and homeowners were persuaded by local Nazis to attend the film, but those who came to its opening night on 30 May were met by a mass picket line. Disbanded by police clubs, the line returned and marched unmolested during the succeeding nights, strengthened by outdoor meetings that exposed the film through leaflets and speeches, the latter given by Brandon and Hurwitz, who also jumped onto the stage and addressed the audience inside. Soon attendance was so low that the film was finally withdrawn. Bolstered by this success, the League, together with the American League Against War and Fascism, went on to demonstrate against the prowar films *No Greater Glory* (over twenty theaters were picketed and thousands of leaflets distributed by 14 September) and *Call to Arms*, and against the Hearst Christmas Fund's screening of the Mussolini film, *Man of Courage* (which was subsequently canceled).[66]

The Politics of the League's Demise

Mid-1933 brought the League a new forward impulse from abroad. Between 30 and 31 May 1933, under the leadership of Leon Moussinac and Bela Balazs, the Cinema Buro of the International Union of the Revolutionary Theatre held a film conference during the International Workers Theatre Olympiad in Moscow. Although Moussinac set the keynote by stressing the importance of revolutionary film organizations in capitalist countries, the delegate reports that followed revealed very little to be afoot. It was therefore voted that in each country the theater section of the IURT must build a film movement. Where a film league already existed, one league member was to keep closer liaison with the Cinema Buro. The conference closed on a rousing affirmation of intention to strengthen the film movement as a weapon in the class struggle.[67]

This prodding from Moscow and from men as well-known and active as Balazs and Moussinac spurred the sluggish national efforts of the League and led immediately to the foundation of the Organization Committee for a National Film and Photo League. In the final number of *Workers Theatre* (July-August 1933), the Committee published "A Film Call to Action," echoing the title of Potamkin's original call in the same magazine's July 1931 issue. Filmmakers, photographers, and the working-class audience were urged to engender movie and camera clubs, film forums,[q] and better production groups. It was hoped that a national network of such groups would counter the enormous influence of the Hollywood film by the foundation and growth of a "genuinely creative film movement based clearly and boldly on the realities of our struggle for a better society." Interested persons were asked to get in touch with the Organization Committee at 12 East 17th Street in New York; its members were David Platt, Theodore Black, and Irving Lerner in New York, Jack Auringer in Detroit, C. O. Nelson in Chicago, and J. Buchanan in Los Angeles.[68]

Organizational efforts gradually progressed. At the end of 1932, League branches existed in seven cities, including New York, Chicago, Philadelphia, Detroit, and Los Angeles. I have found evidence of only one new group forming during 1933—the Hollywood group. But by the end of 1934 there were organizations in Boston, San Francisco, Washington, D.C., Laredo, Texas, Newark, New Jersey, and Marquette, Michigan, and at the University of Wisconsin in Madison. In late September 1934, carrying with them nearly forty reels produced during the previous year, delegates from Chicago, Detroit, Boston, Los Angeles, and New York met in Chicago to hold the First National Film Conference of the Film and Photo Leagues of the United States. There they pledged "to devote themselves tirelessly to building and strengthening the workers film movement in America." The formation of a National Film and Photo League was agreed upon, and talk centered on the need for increased production and nationwide coordination.

Recognizing the potential of 16mm film later than they should have, the conferees determined that local leagues should use 16mm stock

---

q It was probably in response to this article that the Film Forum was founded in New York at about this time, with Sidney Howard as president. See Fred Sweet, Eugene Rosow, and Allan Francovich, "Pioneers: An Interview with Tom Brandon," *Film Quarterly* 26 (1973): 12-24.

for easier, cheaper production and screening.[r] The National League was given the go-ahead on four 35mm documents—on coal, steel, the farm question, and the South—to be reduced to 16mm for mass distribution. A National Film Exchange and a Photo Exchange Department were to be located in New York. As a result, Los Angeles films would be shown outside of California, and negatives might be held at the Film Exchange for the striking of prints for speedy distribution in answer to specific political needs. A monthly National Film Bulletin, useful for organization and agitation, was to be published. As one would expect, a good deal of time was spent on the frontal attack against Hollywood: the judgment was that the *S. A. Mann-Brand* and *No Greater Glory* campaigns, while effective, had taken too much time and energy and that such campaigns must be taken more in tandem with other antiwar and anti-Fascist organizations. The newly established National League was composed of a national secretary (David Platt), a resident national bureau (Tom Brandon,[s] Frank Ward, John Masek, and M. Green), and the executive secretaries of the Leagues, supplemented by advisors and sponsors.[69]

The conference proved a strong incentive at first. New groups soon sprang up in Perth Amboy and Paterson in New Jersey, in New Haven, Connecticut, and in San Francisco. The "Movie Front" in *New Theatre* was full of news about their activities, as was "League News" in *Film Front*, the long-planned periodical that finally appeared in the last days of 1934. Both periodicals devoted sections to technical advice. At this time, Tischler (whose first name is lost in the memories of my interviewees), a very efficient engineer who performed numerous small jobs around the League, was manager of the National Film Exchange and enthusiastically proposed a nationally coordinated weekly newsreel to be produced in each member city and sent to the Exchange for mounting.[70]

Film activity, which had already been stepped up a bit in preparation for the conference, continued at a good clip. The Chicago League announced in late December "a three months' plan of work calculated to make this organization a real factor in support of the struggles of

[r] Although the Moscow Conference advocated the use of 16mm film stock, there had been good reasons for sticking to 35mm: the Acme and Cameo theaters were eager for the films, and films were often screened in the meeting halls of ethnic groups with old 35mm silent projectors. See Sweet, Rosow, and Francovich, "Pioneers: An Interview with Tom Brandon," p. 22.

[s] Although Brandon is listed and had a great deal to do with organizing the conference, he did not himself attend and had effectively resigned to concentrate on innovative work in distribution. Interview with author, 14 Oct. 1973.

the Chicago workers." In the four months following the conference, they completed *Criminal Syndicalist Law On Trial*, a World's Fair film, and *Newsreel No. 3* (nos. 1 and 2 had arrived in early September), and they began work on several shorts to be completed before spring. They also founded a "Film Production Committee in consultation with doctors and child health specialists to make a film exposing the alarming effects of malnutrition among the children of Chicago's unemployed and employed."[71] By the end of the year, the Detroit League had two films under way: *Speed-Up in Auto Industry* (never completed) and *Workers' Health*. The Los Angeles League sent *Cannon Fodder*, *Living Wage or Death*, and *Tom Mooney* to the National Exchange, asking for criticism, which they received.[72] The New York League underwent "complete revision to facilitate planned film and photo production," initiated a three months' plan to end in February, and gave birth to separate units—a Harlem unit, a taxi unit (for the crippling New York taxi strike), and an enacted film unit.[73] In addition to their intention to complete two films already under way (*On the Waterfront* and *Waste and Want*), they set to work on a number of new films: *Cigarette* (by Nathan Asch and David Platt; never completed); *World in Review*; *United Front*; *East Side, West Side*; *Harlem Sketches*; *Taxi*; and *W.I.R.*[t] In late January they hosted a Quarterly Conference of the National League, which was attended by delegates from Detroit, Newark, New Haven, Paterson, and Washington.

But all of this activity was more a flare-up than it was the beginning of a continuing, permanent effort. Tom Brandon returned from his midwestern tour in March to report a dearth of production. *Film Front* faded after five biweekly issues, despite the decision to popularize it by focusing on Hollywood. Robert Gessner, while critically lauding recent League films in the June *New Theatre*, felt that "coordinated action for production—and money"—was needed; he called for reorganization and enlargement of the League "until it becomes for the workers in the field of cinema what the New Theatre League already is in the theatre."[74] In spite of the conference impetus, the National League was simply not germinating enough vital development, other forces were wearing away at it, and in 1935 the New York League lapsed quickly into a state of semidemise.

When Potamkin briefly reviewed the League's progress and identified its needs in late 1932, he had applauded the motivation of its members, calling them "self-critical, eager and, as a unit, suspicious of egotisms."[75] They were without doubt a lively, dedicated, combative

---

[t] *World in Review* and *W.I.R.* have the same initials, and it is conceivable that an error in my sources has led me to cite two films where only one exists.

group of young filmmakers, but they were not unaware, in both personal and collective terms, of some of the problems that were sowing the seeds of their organization's eventual dissolution.

They knew, for one thing, that they were neither fish nor fowl—neither Hollywood nor the Soviet film industry. They knew, along with Potamkin, that Soviet film had risen out of the success and the positive themes and energies of the Revolution. They understood, when the writer Kurella and others observed it, that "the development of art has at all times been closely related to the ideas and forms of life of the class ruling at a given time."[76] In opposition to that ruling class, they also glimpsed that they were not a participatory unit in an exuberant, a successful, or even an extremely potential revolutionary situation. They were haunted by the reality that the vast majority of the working class was far from class-conscious, and perhaps they wondered what would become of their art and of their support from the few genuinely class-conscious workers as Roosevelt broadened his base and promised economic recovery. And however firm their hatred for Depression suffering, not all League members were full-fledged revolutionaries. In fact, as Edwin Seaver argued in the April 1932 *New Masses*, most American artists were not revolutionary: they needed time for an internal revolution before they could adequately face the world revolution needed to "uproot a tradition that is already bred in the bone." And Philip Rahv felt that the Marxist critic in America had an urgent task to

> carve out a road for the proletarian writer, who, living as he does under the constant pressure of the prevailing ideas derived from the property-relationships of existing society, is faced with immense obstacles in his struggles to liberate himself from various bourgeois preconceptions which he still unconsciously adheres to.[77]

In addition to all of this, these radical young filmmakers were isolated: they had either left or never entered the well-weeded roads to acceptance and success in journalistic camerawork, in industrial or governmental filmmaking, and in a Hollywood that they had such good reasons to despise. And they had chosen to attack the major political and economic assumptions of their country—an attack that subjected them to harrassment by their neighbors, their employers, and their country's established law-making bodies. Feelings of uncertainty and isolation, real though they must have been, however, would not alone have spelled a virtual end to the League by early 1935, for such feelings could be overcome by youth, hopefulness, commitment, cooperative activity, and the comradeship that goes with an exuberant cultural-front movement.

It was another, more important factor, that accounted for the League's decline. Because of its highly sectarian organizational core, the League made serious mistakes in judgment. This was the "hard-line" period of Communist Party activity in America, and some League members were inclined to take very seriously such suggestions as the following, contained in a cable from the International Union of Revolutionary Writers and Artists in Moscow to the New York 1931 meeting to form a Workers' Cultural Federation: "We hope the federation will pursue the correct line in its fight against imperialism, against class, national and racial oppression, in the struggle for culture which is national in form, but proletarian in substance. . . . We hope the federation will bear in mind that the only condition for a truly national culture is the hegemony of the revolutionary proletariat."[78]

Recall that in the first months of the League's existence, some members had to be "sloughed off" for not seeing past their own enthusiasms to the need of a "mass organization of workers-photographers and workers-cinematographers." One such case was that of Isador Lerner. Brody recalls:

> We considered ourselves quite left, you know: there wasn't room for much dissent. It was very sectarian. Aaron Suskind, the still photographer, quit the League when he came to a meeting one night and one of our very, very dedicated members by the name of Isador Lerner had just returned from the Soviet Union with his wife, where they visited her relatives in a little village in the Ukraine. And he found that people were hungry, there was a lot of bureaucracy, people were sitting in the street asking him for money or candy or whatever, and he came back with a very, very negative reaction to the whole thing. Now we had invited him to report on what he saw in the Soviet Union—our North Star, you know. But he got up and told just what he felt and saw, a mistake, because we all jumped on him in a very virulent manner, and a vicious discussion ensued, and we voted unanimously to expel him from the League.[79]

A later instance of the virulent tone that could sometimes shape relations in the League appeared in 1934. In a bitter dispute with the WIR over his expenditure of their and Sidney Howard's funds for his would-be *Imperial Valley*, Seymour Stern published an apologia for his position in the editorial of *Experimental Cinema*. The same number carried Lerner's memorial tribute to Potamkin. Brody, writing for *The Daily Worker*, was not pleased:

Leaving aside for the moment the question of whether it is correct for a member of the Film and Photo League to contribute to a publication at a time when we are fighting it (remember that that same issue contains an editorial attack against us!), there still remains the fact that a request for a eulogy of Potamkin by a group that devoted a good deal of its energy in reviling him when he lived, should have prompted Comrade Lerner to hesitate, to say the least. Any comment on Potamkin in *Experimental Cinema* at this time should have analyzed the divergent roads traveled by either since the rift that occurred three years ago: Potamkin Leftwards, E. C. to the Right. Comrade Lerner's note has helped to create a little confusion on this score.[80]

Antiindividualist tendencies were certainly at work, and they could not help but be reflected in the filmmaking. When Lewis Jacobs went south to film in the straitened mining communities, he expected to return to edit his material and shape a film. Instead, he was asked to turn over the footage to the League, with no explanation of what was to become of it. Some of it was edited—supposedly under the eyes of those with the "correct" political savvy—along with other footage, into *Strike Against Starvation*. Jacobs, who had gained some valuable shooting experience at League cost, did not complain.[81] But in reserving such major decisions for those whose hard-line attitudes were considered correct, the League was failing to provide full training and opportunity for some of its best talent—training that might well have paid off in the long run in terms of both propaganda and art. And in so doing it was nurturing its own elite, creating, unwittingly, its own self-destructive class system. Ralph Steiner, perhaps the League's most talented cameraman, recalls that "the things they wanted to use as assignments just bored the hell out of me." He felt even more uncomfortable after the second session of a still photography class he was asked to teach. He had sent his students to the Upper East Side on Park Avenue, and to the Lower East Side around Orchard Street for a first lesson in observing people and gathering the feel of a place. Reprimanding them for seeing everything in these locations in stereotypical images of exploiters and exploited, he reported to his students his own experience:

Up on Park Avenue it's the strangest thing, it's like a desert; you can walk for four blocks and not see one person. You look up at the buildings you've called grand and palatial, and they're all blank, the windows stare down at you, the door beneath the porte-cochere is a black hole, and those children of the rich don't dare walk or skip into the street or anything: their nurses are handcuffs on them. And then they go into that dark doorway and disappear. It's as if a black mouth swallowed them.

Down on the Lower East Side were cockroaches, hungry people, danger, but it was teeming with life.:

> They're running out in the streets and playing stickball, and the women are buying things and arguing. Jesus Christ, where are the violinists and astronomers and great creative writers going to come from, up on Park Avenue? Those are going to be certified public accountants and stockbrokers living the dullest of all possible lives. That's death up there, if you really look at it.

That was the last class Steiner gave: he was out; he did not have the Party line. He saw too many advantages to the lives of the exploited.[82] In this and other instances of the perennial tension between dogma and art, an inflexible, doctrinaire League was alienating some of the best people who could keep it alive.[u]

Another ongoing, underlying tension in the League was not yet prominent in the excitement of its early years; it became so only in 1933 and 1934. Cautiously, I incline to describe it as its own kind of class tension, despite the similar working-class, Russian-Jewish immigrant family backgrounds of so many of the League's members. This class tension does not entirely fit into terms of college education, but many of those who were college graduates did aspire to higher art than their less formally educated counterparts, and they often demonstrated a more theoretical bent than the others, which was experienced both as a directional and social difference. A retrospective image of Leo Seltzer's is helpful:

> SELTZER: There's a table. There's a lamp hanging over the table. This is at the Film and Photo League headquarters. There's a group of people sitting around it . . . four or five. That same image. People talking, talking, talking. Hurwitz, Lerner, and a few others. And once in a while there would be a shout somewhere—'oh, there he goes again!'—as I would walk out of the back room with a camera to go somewhere to shoot. Practically all of the New York stuff was done by me and by Del Duca.
> ALEXANDER: So you really were not friends? You weren't connected?
> SELTZER: That's right. We almost spoke different languages, you see. There were a few people who crossed over. Maybe one. Lew Jacobs was one of those who kind of crossed over both sides.

---

[u] Lerner remembered other "very heated, angry arguments" between ideologues and artists in the League. Interview with author, 1 Oct. 1974.

Because he was a film person and a theoretician also. But no one else that I remember quite like him.

The table theoreticians were, of course, filmworkers too, and they do not admit to Seltzer's division on that basis, but his memory suggests the substantial gap that he felt.

Brody echoes him and, in the class-conscious terms Seltzer avoids, identifies Hurwitz and Steiner specifically as "middle-class intellectuals and artists," part of an "elitist group"; he remembers his sense that "they felt that the rest of us were the great unwashed," the "hoi polloi."[83] Although I have found no other evidence of such feeling, it is true that Hurwitz, Steiner, Lerner (to some extent), and some of the others did believe that Brody, Seltzer, Kern, Del Duca, Kandell, Roffman, Brandon (to some extent), and Platt held too limited an intellectual/artistic perspective on 1930s America, and accordingly there is no necessary reason that they would not see them as in some ways inferior. At any rate, the aspirations of the former were being frustrated by the latter, and the tension was deepening.

These artistic aspirations were very significant. An American delegate to the 1933 Moscow Film Conference would have found the report on Soviet montage interesting and useful but not entirely novel. More original was Comrade Rodenberg's recommendation that revolutionary film organizations collaborate with the Workers Theatre.

A good example of this was shown by a French educational picture (Pomme de Terre) "The Potato," showing the exploitation of the worker. He plants and cultivates the soil and when the goods come back to him he has to pay a high price for them. In that picture the acting was done by a French theatre-of-action.[84]

The Potato may have drawn the attention of the dissident League members who wanted to go beyond both their regular newsreel assignments and their hurried opportunities in synthetic documentary to the enacted documentary and dramatic film. It added to the impulse that had long been developing out of their own drives toward artistry.

Another more subtle stimulus may have come from the death of Potamkin, who in December of 1932 had assessed the filmmakers and pointed them along the road:

The sense of selection has still to be educated in the political references of an image and its combination with other images. . . . And, of course, constant training in technology and its application is essential. Yet, in these first efforts of the Workers' Film and Photo League there is the one potential source for an authentic American cinema.[85]

Nothing was clearer to these filmmakers than their need for constant training and practice, and they believed that dramatic films had higher cinematic possibilities and potentially higher political impact than anything they had yet been able to do. They agreed with the thinking that had transformed *Workers Theatre* into *New Theatre*, the "broader conception of the revolutionary workers theatre as the historical successor of the bourgeois theatre."

The workers theatre now understands that it must study the technique of the theatres of the past, adapting the best of the old to the service of the masses—experimenting-studying-criticizing itself. . . . *New Theatre* [sic] will welcome every sincerely progressive trend in the American theatre.[86]

The October-December 1933 issue of *Hound and Horn* carried Potamkin's original sketch of a proposal for a university film school. This proposal demanded thorough grounding in the total background and history of film as an accompaniment to actual technical training and production.[87] As a result, on 13 November 1933, the Harry Alan Potamkin Film School of the Workers Film and Photo League opened classes at the new WIR headquarters on Lexington Avenue.

In an article dealing with the new WF&PL School, Tom Brandon informed the January readers of *New Theatre* that

the repeated technical and artistic shortcomings in the workers' film productions of the past two years have been ascribed to the fact that this period has been in the main a period of *organization* in a field, attended by lack of equipment and the search for an adequate medium (question of newsreel, short and documentary forms; 16mm or standard size, etc.). There appears progressive improvement in effectiveness of the 1932 one reel National Hunger March film over the two reel 1931 Hunger March film, of the 1932-3 reels on local struggles of the workers of New York over the 1931-2 Western Pennsylvania and Kentucky Miners Strike film. Yet the workers film movement of America is poorly prepared to film the historic period in which we live.

The film school was a significant departure from "the sporadic methods of the past," Brandon wrote. "It is a declaration of the *necessity* for *organized practical study* of the problems confronting workers in the film movement." The *Hound and Horn* sketch, he said, testified to Potamkin's opposition to the narrowness and even the impudence of the old-guard critics, and the school that bore his name would provide courses, meeting two evenings a week, that would embrace a wider view. One course would cover the technological, economic, and social history of the motion picture. Another, a history of Soviet film taught by Nathan Adler, Joseph Freeman, and Joshua Kunitz, would concentrate on the theories of Eisenstein, Pudovkin, Dovzhenko, Vertov, Barnet, and Kaufman. Sam Brody and Irving Lerner, film critics for *New Masses* and *New Theatre*, would teach a course in film criticism. Study of camera mechanics, lighting, laboratory techniques, projection, and so on, was prerequisite to a production class that would cooperatively produce a documentary film. Other instructors listed in *Experimental Cinema* were Leo Hurwitz, Lewis Jacobs, David Platt, Leo Seltzer, Ralph Steiner, and Barton Yeager.[88]

Despite its intentions, the school was to reflect and emphasize the League's growing factionalism. Brandon's article about film quality was written in part because of pressure from League members who wanted to become artists, not simply propagandists, and he believes that he was asked to head the school because others thought that he and the school could reconcile the now fiercely differing factions of the League—the artistic versus the political. According to Brandon, the school was one proof of his and others' agreement with the two most outspokenly artistic-oriented members, Hurwitz and Steiner. And although Brandon attributes the slow beginning of the school's emphasis on quality to the usual divided energies and lack of resources, he admits that his own primary concern remained the immediate political purposes of the filmmaking. As a result, current political events tended to overrule the school too, as Brandon acknowledged recently by quoting Sidney Meyers' somewhat exaggerated remembrance:

> I wanted to work on films, either teach or learn, and I went to the Harry Alan Potamkin Film School, and every time I would go there and start to discuss the work or pull out some equipment, the head of the school would say sorry classes are called off, we're demonstrating in front of a movie up on Broadway, class will be conducted tomorrow. Night after night I went to make a film or to teach, and night after night they said no class, there is a Fascist film, or there was some kind of deadly film to counter, or some mass meeting. I never had a chance to work on any films.[89]

Like Brandon, Brody was among those Hurwitz remembers as "not passionately interested in film as a means of expression but primarily for its political value," and, like Brandon, Brody still argues that the political priorities were the right ones:

> You see, the fact is that we were a bunch of amateurs and a bunch of beginners who picked up inexpensive cameras and went out

and shot. Now it's very true that it wasn't done on a professional level, it's very true that aesthetically and from the standpoint of craft it left a lot to be desired. However, suppose we hadn't done that. Then nothing would have been recorded of that era, of the marches, the demonstrations, the struggles. And at the time the films were used immensely. We have a man right here [Balog] who spent his days and many nights projecting these films to workers' organizations, to unions, to clubs, to groups everywhere. . . . They helped to fuel and inspire all of those movements, against hunger, against unemployment, for welfare. They were part of the struggle.

Brody maintains that to work at length on scripts, staging, directing and redirecting actors or nonactors, editing and reediting, talking and talking was unwise when movements and organizers needed the finished films while their events were still current. He and Brandon tended to think of the artistic dissidents as having, as Brody puts it, an "approach that was too slow and precious."[90]

At any rate, the school was an effort to keep the League together, and on the surface this seemed a very positive development. Yet Brody's article in the February 1934 *New Theatre*, "The Revolutionary Film; Problem of Form," reveals the kind of doctrinaire limitations that would result in its failure. Repeating his 1930 position that working-class cameramen must learn a style of cinematic reportage corresponding to the writing of revolutionary journalists, he argued that three film forms were appropriate for League filmmakers: straight film reportage of events; the synthetic documentary, its effect dependent upon the editor; and the educational film made for direct political-economic instruction. And David Platt opened his 26 July review of *Unknown Soldier Speaks*, *Pacific Coast General Strike*, and *War Resisters Anti-War Demonstration in New York City* by remarking that these three newsreel featurettes "help to confirm your belief in the unlimited propaganda power of the simple, sound-documental film."[91] At this time, Platt was executive secretary of the League, and it was Brody who taught the production class at the Potamkin Film School, directing students on the making of a never-to-be-completed documentary entitled *Waste and Want*.

Frustrated by the rigid limitations of these positions and antagonized by what they experienced as the League's resulting and continuing restraint upon art and artists, ten to twelve instructors and students of the school—including Hurwitz and Lerner—organized an experimental group under the technical direction of Ralph Steiner, while still functioning as League members. They set themselves a number of basic but specific problems, "each involving the writing of a shot-by-shot continuity for the sequence to be filmed, photographing of the sequence and the final editing." By May, two of the problems had been completed:

> The first, to render the simple act of an unemployed man entering his room after an exhausting day of job-hunting, sitting down, tired, worn and without hope. The second, a continuation of the first, the landlord entering the room to serve the tenant with a dispossess for non-payment of rent. This group works wholly with non-actors in order to duplicate conditions which will occur in making films later. The great task is to learn how to make the camera eloquent, how to make use of the natural acts of an untrained actor to serve the needs of the scenario.[92]

Working with the same basic material and with the same sort of people as before, the experimental group was learning to dramatize their documentary base through a planned and controlled reenactment. From Jay Leyda, they began to solicit similar exercises from Eisenstein's classes at the Moscow Film School, where Leyda was studying filmmaking and Soviet film.[93] The plan, Hurwitz wrote at the time, was "to develop this experimental group into a production group within the Film and Photo League for the purpose of making documentary-dramatic revolutionary films—short propaganda films that will serve as flaming film-slogans, satiric films and films exposing the brutalities of capitalist society." Steiner suggested that the ultimate aim was "nothing less than fine workmanship. . . . Film makers must keep in mind that the statement 'there is no art without propaganda' is also true in the reverse: *there can be no effective propaganda without good art.*"[94]

In these articles written in May and September of 1934, and in Hurwitz's report to the National Film Conference in Chicago,[95] Hurwitz and Steiner were making a concerted attempt to influence the direction of Film and Photo League filmmaking as well as the direction of their own professional lives. They were troubled, they said, by the low quantity and poor quality of the films that the League had been producing. Such films not only came far short of achievements in literature, theater, and dance but they were also ineffective in enlarging the revolutionary movement: the photography and editing were not professional enough; a tendency to assume that the audience was already on their side had led to a limited audience and a lack of *persuasive* propaganda; and the general League approach to filmmaking was mechanical, schematic, and conventional.

Newsreels, Hurwitz conceded to Brody, whose article on revolutionary film form he had in mind at the time, were certainly important, but they were fragmentary and necessarily lacking in depth. And the synthetic documentary had inherent limitations that might have been transcended if the League had been willing to experiment with more powerful forms, such as the trailer, the enacted short, the combined enacted and documentary film, the animated cartoon, and the satiric and didactic film. At this point, both Steiner and Hurwitz were turning away from what they saw as an overreliance on montage toward what Hurwitz called "internal montage," where scene control, shot content, and the mounting around clear, accurate, and forceful takes assumed primary importance. They strongly advocated complete support from the Leagues for filmmakers like themselves and for an experimental group like the one they had formed, so that they might work full time to develop the effective and artistic potentialities of the medium. They suggested a "shock troupe" like that of the Theatre of Action unit of the Workers Laboratory Theatre: "Here a small group live in cooperative quarters and are financed by the theatre as a whole. They are thus able to spend ten to twelve hours a day accomplishing an extraordinary amount of excellent work."

Support for their position came from leading critics inside the Party. Joseph Freeman, whose ideas were important to them, published a long, historical piece in the 11 September 1934 New Masses, including part of a report he had submitted to the John Reed Club in November 1932. Freeman wrote that because of all the agitation and the organizational and editorial work in the early revolutionary movement, few writers had been permitted time to develop their art or to produce books. This was unavoidable, but unfortunate, for "everything which Lenin said about professional revolutionaries was equally true of the revolutionary writer." But the growth of the movement since 1932 had given writers and critics more freedom, and

> it is no longer necessary to convince writers who developed in the movement in isolation, during years when loyalty was the primary test, that the revolutionary writer must perfect his craft, that he must be not only revolutionary but a *writer*. . . . Today we have the beginnings of a vital revolutionary art rooted in American life expressed not only in manifestos, speeches and essays but in novels, plays and poems. Our standards must therefore be higher, our judgments sterner.

"Let our authors," Freeman went on, "be implacable in their demands for better craftsmanship."

Two months later, Mike Gold expressed his enthusiasm for Brandon's film circuits and the power of film but had nothing good to say about film craft on the left. The League, he noted,

> has been in existence for some years, but outside of a few good newsreels, hasn't done much to bring this great cultural weapon to the working class [nor has it] produced a single reel of comedy, agitation, satire or working class drama. Many bourgeois amateur film groups have produced dozens of such shorts. The cost is comparatively slight; we have writers, directors, and film technicians in plenty. And we have this great audience waiting for us. An organizer seems to be needed, perhaps, to gather all the threads together.

Gold thought that Vertov's *Three Songs About Lenin*, recently arrived in New York, was "film propaganda raised to the peak of the highest art" and hoped that "somebody in the Film and Photo League finally learns how to do a film a tenth as good for proletarian America."[96]

Hurwitz and Steiner were trying to learn. In support of their ideas, they had not only formed the experimental unit at the Potamkin Film School but had been engaged in separate independent efforts. Hurwitz's *Sweet Land of Liberty* (1934), which had been mounted for the International Labor Defense, was an independent film, a silent mixture of library newsreel and his own footage. A bitter, ironic view of justice in America, a film he now says was probably very lively but very crude, *Sweet Land of Liberty* was not a very significant step beyond League synthetic documentary. In March of 1934, however, together with Albert Prentiss, Hurwitz organized the Animated Film Group of the WIR, which went into production under the direction of Prentiss and Leonard Barnes in late August. On 1 October, they began shooting a cartoon rendition of Helen Kay's left-wing story for children, *Battle in the Barnyard*.[97]

In mid to late 1933, working with the Group Theatre, which had been organized in his large studio, Steiner began an antiwar film, tentatively called *Café Universal*; a film with stylized acting based on drawings by George Grosz. Elia Kazan and Art Smith were the major actors, with Morris Carnovsky, Harold Clurman, Robert Lewis, Clifford Odets, and Paula Strasberg in subordinate roles. Spring found Steiner and Irving Lerner, along with Group Theatre members Elia Kazan, Elman Koolish, and Molly Day Thatcher, experimenting with film sequences at a Long Island dump. Inspired by the location, they shaped an idea for an antireligious film, *Pie in the Sky*, a short film codirected by the group, and not, as it turned out, to be finally completed until early 1935.[98]

In a 25 September 1934 review of the "world premier" of Nancy Naumburg's and James Guy's *Sheriffed*—in which "almost every conceivable error of cinematography is evident"—Irving Lerner (writing under the pseudonym, "Peter Ellis") announced a further step by the dissident League members:

> Revolutionary films must have high artistic quality in addition to their message if they are to have the most popular appeal. But only continued production, or as Ralph Steiner points out in the current *New Theatre*, a school based on production is the only way we can train the necessary forces for the kind of films the revolutionary movement demands. Therefore it is good to learn that Ralph Steiner, Leo Hurwitz, and Irving Lerner have organized such a *film producing* group in connection with the Workers Laboratory Theatre.[99]

Although they had formed this group, they had not left the League; they were still hoping that it could be influenced to support their convictions. In fact, the group's formation in early September was probably an attempt to influence the debate at the League's National Film Conference at the end of the month. The conference's decision would be crucial, for the local organization held firmly to the three types of film Brody had proscribed. Hurwitz and Steiner had made their position very clear both in print and in person. In his September article, Steiner had defined the opposition in no uncertain terms:

> Organizational and structural faults have to a great extent held back film production. The leadership of organizations may have good political and organizational ability but their lack of understanding of the problems involved in production has contributed to no small extent to the backwardness of the revolutionary film movement in this country. The leadership may not have the qualities necessary for making good cameramen or directors, and never intend to engage in those capacities, but a certain amount of experience in film making would give them a conception of "what it takes" to make films.

Shortly before the conference, Hurwitz attended a League executive meeting to argue passionately against the limitations being placed upon his own artistic ripening and, ultimately, upon the political effectiveness of League films. Meeting adamant opposition to his call for a shock troupe, he went so far at one point as to say, "if you don't do it, we'll do it anyway," whereupon he was sharply and bitterly attacked as a "dual unionist."[100]

Although Hurwitz was not a delegate to the conference, his report, a "Survey of Workers Films," provoked a lively debate, and led to the following League affirmation of purpose reported by David Platt:

> The Soviet film began with the Kino-Eye [camera eye, a term used by Dziga Vertov for his newsreel documentary theory and practice] and grew organically from there on. The Film and Photo Leagues rooted in the intellectual and social basis of the Soviet film begin also with the simple newsreel document, photographing events as they appear to the lens, true to the nature of the revolutionary medium they exploit in a revolutionary way. Aside from the tremendous historical and social value of the reels thus photographed, they are also true beginnings of film art. The reels exhibited at the conference with all their weaknesses of lighting, photography, direction, are the only films in America that breathe a spirit of life and art. They are beginnings on the right track.[v]

Accordingly, the conference mandate was that the "major task . . . must be the continuous and widespread production of newsreels and documents of the class struggle in action principally, and secondly, whenever and wherever the occasion calls, semi- or wholly enacted film production logically developed out of the firm newsreel base." This decision to reaffirm the primacy of the newsreel was a slap in the face to Hurwitz and Steiner, two of the League's most talented film-

---

[v] The difference between Vertov, on the one hand, and Pudovkin, Eisenstein, Dovzhenko and others, on the other, was an important critical distinction to left filmmakers in this period. Paul Rotha pointed out the difference in his *Documentary Film* (3rd ed. [London: Faber and Faber, 1952], pp. 88, 92), and Seymour Stern announced that the American Prolet-Kino "seeks to make pictures, rather than *take* them as it finds them. It thoroughly approves of the fictive or 'reconstructed reality' film and turns to Pudovkin, Eisenstein, and Dovzhenko, rather than to Vertov, as examples of what can be done by the powerful film endowed with a reality of its own" (see "A Working Class Cinema for America?" *The Left*, Spring 1931, p. 71). When Vertov's *Three Songs About Lenin* appeared at this time, both sides seized it as their own. Brody, who was to translate Moussinac and Vertov on the kino-eye for *Film Front*, was very excited about it, seeing it as an extension of Vertov's premises (the film uses newsreel and straight documentary footage only), while Lerner could also praise it, pointing out that it went far beyond the rigid limitations of the original kino-eye theory (see Brody, "Dziga Vertov on Kino-Eye: Excerpts from a lecture given in Paris in 1929," FF, 7 Jan. 1935, pp. 6-8, and "Dziga Vertov on Film Technique," FF, 28 Jan. 1935, pp. 7-9; also, DW, 1 Nov. 1934, p. 7, and 6 Nov. 1934, p. 7 ["For many years now I have been repeating that Vertov is the most significant director and thinker in the Soviet cinema"]; Lerner, "Three Songs about Lenin," NM, 20 Nov. 1934, p. 30). Jay Leyda, writing from the Soviet Union for *New Theatre* (where Hurwitz was film editor), argued that Vertov had gone beyond *pure* documentary (see "*Three Songs about Lenin*: Film News from the Soviet Union," NT, Nov. 1934, p. 10).

makers. The shock troupe concept was adopted, but only in the sense that the "best film and photo forces" could be concentrated "on the field of battle, adequately to record the vital events of our times." Nothing was said about full support or time for experimentation.

The conference did adopt other recommendations by Hurwitz: each league was to institute a training school, and it was resolved that local John Reed Clubs were to be asked for help on scenarios and that local Workers Theatres were to be asked "to assist with actors, equipment, etc. in the event they are called upon to help an enacted or documentary film production."[101] But the basic emphasis of the National League was clear, and it was underlined with the election to its executive body of Brandon, Platt, and Ward, three of the New York League's most organizationally central members. A leadership of reasoned purpose but limited imagination was doing what the left-wing parties would later try to do to neorealism in Italy: they were restricting the formal and topical dimensions of art and thus undermining the vital growth in individual filmmakers and the true power of film as a method of mass communication. The result was the final separation of the Hurwitz-Steiner-Lerner group from the New York Film and Photo League. In the final months of 1934 they formed Nykino, which for a month or so was tokenly affiliated with the League but then became completely independent of it.[w]

The actual split became evident in an unobtrusive way in the technical advice sections of the November issue of *New Theatre* and the January issue of *Film Front*. In *New Theatre*, a periodical in which Hurwitz was playing a major editorial role, Steiner and Lerner advised the use of Eastman Panchromatic over Super-sensitive Pan because the former catches more realistic facial tones and textures than are to be found in the smooth and idealized Hollywood versions produced by the latter. In *Film Front*, which was under the editorship of Platt and was a breakaway from the more artistically oriented *New Theatre*, Leo Seltzer contributed separate articles on camera control and on negative film stock. Illustrating from newsreel situations, he relates how to follow a worker chasing a policeman and describes the tonal sensitivity of negative stock to banners and placards, especially to those whose slogans are printed with red paint.[102]

The split was also evident in the criticism of three films that appeared at this time, Naumburg's and Guy's *Sheriffed*, Irving Browning's and Manon Miller's *The New Legion*, and Ed Kern's and Leo Seltzer's *On the Waterfront* (variously called *Waterfront*, *Workers on the Water-*

---

[w] Nykino combines New York plus the Russian word for camera.

front, Marine, and *Marine Workers).*ˣ Lerner cited *Sheriffed* as evidence of the need for the full-time experimental unit that he, Hurwitz, and Steiner had formed. Ed Kern (writing as "Ed Kennedy") reviewed all three films for *Film Front* and *The New Legion* for *The Daily Worker.* Agreeing with Lerner's judgment on *Sheriffed,* he still preferred his own and Seltzer's *On the Waterfront* to either of the other two films. The one strictly League film of the lot, he called *On the Waterfront* "a pure documentary film, and the type of film that we firmly believe to be our most valuable weapon at the moment." He concluded the *Daily Worker* review with "a word to the comrades who produced *The New Legion,*" admonishing them for unclear thinking, irrelevancies, and dense theatricality.

> Neither our artistic development nor our financial situation has proceeded so rapidly that we can afford to lose such valuable time and energy by working apart. We must consult together. We must go ahead by a collective utilization of our forces, adding new ones to the center where they are most needed.

This was also covert advice to Nancy Naumburg, a League member who tended to work independently, and it was clearly a strong attack on the direction of the Hurwitz group.

According to Lerner's 4 December review of *On the Waterfront* for *New Masses,* "Seltzer has recorded the dreary waterfront; the despair of men begging for backbreaking jobs at low pay; the joy of the favored few who are given work; the dangerous jobs; the walk-out; work of the Marine Workers' Industrial Union." It was "a fine little film" in the Vertov mode, with "a couple of scenes of stirring film reporting; and . . . sequences where intelligent cutting (the agitation by the M.W.I.U.) creates a sequence that is highly dramatic." Perhaps, Lerner suggests in his concluding paragraph, the League was just beginning to see the light:

> One of the chief points contributing to the success of this little film was the fact that the producers limited their theme to one of extremely simple construction. They seemed to have realized, *for the first time,* that the documentary is perhaps the most difficult medium of expression in film. *It's a long and difficult school.* When it is mastered we get a *Three Songs About Lenin.* And thus *On the Waterfront* is certainly a step forward.[103] (Italics mine.)

ˣ According to Seltzer, this lost film "dealt quite completely with the life of longshoremen, from early morning to night," begging for jobs, "many of them . . . homeless, sleeping on the docks." See "A Total and Realistic Experience," an interview with Russell Campbell, *Jump Cut* 14 (1977): 27.

On the surface, the Film and Photo League did not appear disturbed by the departure of the Hurwitz group. David Platt composed "A Reply to Michael Gold," confessing League failings and explaining a low budget, a difficult medium, lack of good organizers and directors, "a membership not always technically or theoretically equipped or inclined to avail itself of the opportunities latent in the class struggle for film and photo production," and a lack of interest and input from cultural workers in the other arts. The National Film Conference had been called to remedy such weaknesses, Platt said, and the League had dedicated itself to the "major task" of "mass production of news-reels and documents of the class struggle." A "significant ferment" was under way, and quite possibly the coming year would "mark the turning point of the revolutionary film movement in the right direction."[104]

There was a spate of production. On 11 May the League premiered Guy's and Naumburg's *Taxi*, accompanying it with six new films of their own: *May Day '35* (parts in color, a combined effort of the national Leagues); *On the Waterfront*; *East Side, West Side*; *Labor's 'March of Time'*; *United Front* (Kern); and *Harlem Sketches* (by Brody and Leslie Bain—not a League member—with a musical score by George Antheil). They also completed *1934* and *H.R. 2827*.[y] This was a last flurry of production, however, for League members had begun to disperse, partly because they were demoralized by the defection of Hurwitz, Lerner, Steiner, and others, partly, as Russell Campbell argues, because the WIR, in deep trouble in Europe, became inactive in the United States, and partly out of sheer personal economic necessity.[105]

Tom Brandon had already left the League to concentrate on the importation and distribution of foreign films and on the occasional production and distribution of anti-Fascist and prolabor films. Sam Brody left in order to support himself and his family by doing still photography; soon he was doing camerawork for the *New York City Guide* of the Federal Writers Project, and he went on to work for the Federal Photographic Project, the Federal Theater Project, and finally the Federal Art Project, until the Dies Committee had him fired because of his suspected political affiliations. David Platt left to work full time as a critic for *The Daily Worker* and other periodicals, helping, he says, to "organize the fight against anti-social and prowar films,"

---

[y] A film on the Lundeen bill for unemployment insurance, a bill giving unemployment compensation to all workers at the average local wage; it was introduced by Ernest Lundeen, a Farmer-Labor congressman from Minnesota and was backed by the Communist Party.

his "most important activity" in the decade. Leo Seltzer left to draw a salary for his filmmaking, first in 1935 from commercial and institutional sponsors (for an educational film on the manufacture of airplane engines in the Wright Aeronautical Plant and a series of surgical films for New York's Mt. Sinai Hospital) and thereafter from the federal and city governments. For the New York City WPA Art Project, Seltzer filmed the very efficient and instructive *Technique of Fresco Painting* (1936) and then went on to head the Motion Picture Production Unit under the Federal Art Project. There, with Elaine Basil, he completed *From Hand to Mouth* and *Sculpture Today* (Sam Brody and Sol Libsohn have credits for photography on the latter), and then, in 1940, *Merit System Advancing* for the WPA and the New York City Municipal Civil Service Commission. He later became Chief Consultant in Visual Aids to the City of New York, a post he held until the war began.[106]

The League continued its official existence until late in 1937, with Del Duca, Kandell, Roffman, and possibly Kern as its depleted core. Now and then they screened foreign films, and occasionally they screened new films of their own. Some of the latter were edited from newsreel and documentary footage that came in: *Hands Off Ethiopia* in November 1935, *The Birth of New China* in May 1936, and the magazine film one of them evidently put together for the presidential campaign of Communist Party candidates William Z. Foster and James W. Ford. In June 1937, Del Duca, Kandell, and Roffman, with the help of the Consumers' Union, made *Getting Your Money's Worth*, a one-reel sound film "exposing false claims and fraudulent advertising" about milk, shoes, and lead toys—a film that, ironically enough, was praised by Lerner when it appeared at the Filmarte Theatre the following September. Late in 1937, the three became Contemporary Films, Inc., thus ending the official life of the Film and Photo League. The trio went on to produce three more one-reelers in the *Getting Your Money's Worth* series.[107]

The Nykino group, on the other hand, stayed together, and we shall be following their histories throughout much of this book. Nykino was Hurwitz's "dual-union" threat come alive. In December 1934, working as the film section of the Workers Laboratory Theatre, the group advertised itself as having begun full-time production of enacted films—an exaggeration. It also had a studio group for film training and was at work on a short trailer for *New Masses*. By March, it was the film production unit of the WLT's Theatre of Action. "People experienced in some phase of movie work and writers interested in doing scenarios for short enacted films" were especially needed, and they were invited to apply for admission. By February, Hurwitz had left his associate editorship at *New Theatre* to devote full time to Nykino, at fifteen dollars a week.

Taking stock, the group discovered four films on hand that might be completed and then used as fund-raisers. One of the four, *Café Universal* could not be saved: while it contained some excellent photography, they found the material tonal rather than developmental and could not determine how the intriguing stylization could lead to filmic integration of an antiwar idea. *Harbor Scenes* and *Granite* (or *Quarry*), both nonpolitical, both filmed by Steiner—the first a sketch of New York Harbor, the second a treatment of quarrying in Vermont—were completed. And an opening sequence plus a few more dump takes were added to *Pie in the Sky*, which became Nykino's first publicized product.[108]

Pie in the Sky, the opening titles proclaim, portrays "the experiences of two sad young men who finally realize their kinship with God and discover that hunger is no hardship when one has gained the refuge of prayer." Following the credits, the film opens upon the exterior of the Grace and Hope Mission. Someone flashes through the frame, passing quickly by the mission, a broad hint that one might do well to avoid it. The film, a semicomic, ironic attack upon privately supported relief measures, focuses upon those church charities that preach acceptance of one's lot and require exaction in endless prayer. The mission priest's haughty demeanor and behavior are contrasted with the down-and-out appearance and the sometimes comically defiant actions of his victims, one of whom is played by Lerner. When the mission's thin slices of pie run out early, Kazan and Koolish, unfed and unimpressed by Russell Collins's cold consolation (he points to a picture of Christ against the sky: "The Lord Will Provide"), stroll out to the local dump, where, with the help of the trash, they improvise imagined better lives. In conclusion, they act out a parody of religious charity and perform a stylized skit to the IWW song (in titles) "You will eat by and by in the glorious land above the sky. Work and pray, live on hay, you'll get pie in the sky when you die." A hallucination of pie appears on the body of the prone Koolish, but it vanishes when they grab at it. They shake their fists heavenward.

A related subtheme is introduced in the credits when Kazan is presented lying on the ground casually, his head propped on his hand, his shoes off, before a sign that reads "Private Property—Keep Out." The spoof, of course, is on contemporary American bourgeois values. The American fascination with fast cars is burlesqued in one skit in which Kazan and Koolish are bouncing rapidly up and down in an old car until they "crash" (some ruined film is mounted here to simulate the crash). They turn and see an elegant set of old clothes ironed out behind the car. They shake their heads, and one mourns, "Alas, poor Matthew, I knew him Woll," a slam (which still provokes laughter) at the conservative unionism of the A.F. of L. and at its strongly anti-Soviet, anti-Communist official, Matthew Woll, who (like other A.F. of L. leaders) reluctantly endorsed unemployment insurance after more than two years of the Depression had passed and only after intense mass pressure from union members. Other shots show the individual actors juxtaposed with a distant industrial chimney emitting smoke and with a network of telephone wires spanning the dump.

Cheaply made, containing much improvisation, *Pie in the Sky* is rooted in the nonrealistic, agitational, street theater skits and reviews of groups like the Theatre of Action. It is neither thematically nor cinematically sophisticated, yet it is a clear, well-communicated take-off on an obvious evil, a genuinely amusing film. It features a well-calculated pace, good shot content—uncluttered backgrounds that emphasize the acting and props—and some effective cinematic devices. In one instance, the camera tilts slowly down from a motto on the wall—"Christ is the Head of this House, the Unseen Host at every meal, the Silent Listener to every conversation"—to the bald pate of the young, white-collared, praying priest, his hands clasped below the chin, his eyes raised to the Lord. A later shot (the only other camera movement in this sequence) travels slowly upward at the same pace from the empty pie tin and plates to the unhappy faces of the disappointed protagonists, strengthening through cinematic association the disparity between them and the priest. What is most impressive is the film's spirit, which is realized cinematically in the pace and in some of the cutting and which is derived principally from the imagination, wit, and humor with which the two men again and again aid themselves and one another in resisting their hunger and despair. This spirit endows the film with its essential and bitter-sweet vitality.

Ray Ludlow wrote in *New Theatre* that *Pie in the Sky* failed to "solve the cinematization of a revolutionary point of view" because of its inappropriateness for mass audiences, and he was correct in his assertion that "the fierceness and baldness with which it ridicules the Church would prove antagonistic to an average working-class audience." The Party, of course, would not find it in any manner a revolutionary film, and in fact the leader of a visiting Soviet film commission took Steiner sternly to task for making a film that did not seriously analyze causes or suggest militant action.[109] Leaving that particular criticism aside, one may still argue that while the film may nicely serve its limited purposes for a limited audience, its connection to any general audience *is* severely limited. It remains a light, detached film, a skit, the result in good part of the nonpolitical, whimsical, humorous character of Steiner.

Like the League newsreels, the first acted films by left filmmakers (*Sheriffed, The New Legion,* and *Pie in the Sky*) represented raw beginnings. But like the newsreels, they also served a purpose, and their makers deserve credit. Not all were so directly useful as the Los Angeles League film whose documentation of a police attack on a demonstration in San Diego succeeded in disproving frame-up charges against arrested workers,[110] but they all raised funds and encouraged a feeling of unity and activity among motivated workers and the already politicized. It was clear to the Nykino filmmakers, however, that their films had not yet found the appropriate form or level, the persuasive propaganda, and the popularity to reach and move a large audience. Having long been limited by relative lack of training, by hit-or-miss production efforts, by inadequate support for technical and artistic development, and by a narrow concept of film form, these filmmakers had split off from—and in effect helped destroy—an organization that had become a hindrance to them. They were now interested in creating their own opportunities.

The Growth of Nykino: Newcomers, Theory, and Experience, 1935

Those members of the film and Photo League who were devoted to the production of timely, militant newsreels made significant arguments and were genuinely committed to a viable form of political film. But it was right for the Nykino contingent to break free when political decisions served to limit, frustrate, and deaden their artistic power. It was right, too, for them to argue that enhanced artistic power and range would better serve the League's social and political purposes.

If Edwin Seaver's powerful question, "What kind of tinker's damn does all your private vision amount to if the innocent Scottsboro boys are to burn?"[1] is a well-directed challenge, it still fails to recognize the necessity for growth and change that is vital to the human spirit. No matter how fervently the cause is supported, art makes poor persuasion if the maker's heart is not in it. And as James Agee wrote late in 1936, even the work of Auden and Joyce and "the materials of dreams and the . . . subconscious" can be "important whether it frees the Scottsboro boys or not," for "the full and fearless use of the brain, whatever kind you happen to have, is serviceable to Marxism." Agee argued that such materials were utilized by the best popular art, which was "intended among other things to teach and to excite and to please and to inspire working people." This included "the best communist art"—that of Orozco, for instance, and of the great Russian filmmakers of the twenties.[a] It is the fully developed and fulfilled artist, whatever his or her

---

[a] James Agee, "Art for What's Sake," NM, Dec. 1936, pp. 48, 50. Agee's plea, of course, is only one in a chorus of voices raised at the time against dogmatic limitation of art. Recall Joseph Freeman's article, "Ivory Towers—White and Red," which appeared

own political persuasion, who offers infinite possibilities to those who wish to persuade.

In announcing one theory, however, I wish to avoid identifying myself with another that I find troubling. Reading through critical comment on the thirties from Alfred Kazin to Richard Pells and William Stott, one finds again and again the observation that the art the period produced is narrow and sentimental, lacking in insight, detachment, rounded humanity, and a large and tragic vision. And there is no doubt that for the most part this is true. But these observers often stop there, as if all were said, and do so for reasons that may be termed political. One need not be especially astute, for instance, to recognize the tendency in the seventies—whether direct or through books on other eras—to punish the left of the late sixties as romantic, overly rhetorical, sentimental, chaotic, cowardly, and narrow, with scarcely a nod to the validity of its motivations, its perceptive, needling criticisms, and its vital contributions to art *and* to social change. But many of those who take this position now do so from the vantage point of a smug status quo, in order to rationalize and dignify their own lack of concern or engagement in the sixties or to tame their guilt over having overstepped their own rational bounds. This is a tendency, then and now, of which we must beware.

I myself fully subscribe to the need for large perspectives, for touchstones, for disinterestedness and critical awareness. Any era suffers without such qualities. When they are present and active, the most considered and far-reaching action can derive from them. But instinctive and uncritical anger over poverty, waste, and unjust wars has its positive functions as well. For one thing, it can jog the detached mind. And even when it fails to do that, it still serves as pressure upon those who legislate and rule. As we now attempt to justify or improve upon our behavior and attitudes during the sixties through our current work and action, we can heed the warning in the final paragraph of Daniel Aaron's book about the writers of the thirties:

> We who precariously survive in the sixties can regret their inadequacies and failures, their romanticism, their capacity for self-deception, their shrillness, their self-righteousness. It is less easy

in the Sept. 1934 issue of *New Masses* (see Chapter I). In *Writers on the Left* (New York: Harcourt, Brace & World, 1961), pp. 392-395, Daniel Aaron tells how Party pressures, personal compulsion, and the needs of the moment distracted younger writers in particular from aesthetic considerations. During the Party's so-called third, or hardpolicy period, from 1928 to mid-1935, that pressure was the greatest, and what we have witnessed so far is one version of the larger struggle for freedom of artistic growth. Had the League split not occurred, it is doubtful that the skillful, powerful productions of Frontier Films could have been evolved in the next two or three years.

to scorn their efforts, however blundering and ineffective, to change the world.[2]

And it is least easy to scorn them when so many of our own efforts toward change have been so groping, so self-conscious, so slow, and often so inadequate—if they existed at all.

Whatever kind of film they wished to make, and despite their developing hostilities, the members of the Film and Photo League shared this effort to change a world gone bad. Perhaps they blinked for too long at the rule of Stalin, perhaps they had too little faith in the possibilities of the American political and economic system, and perhaps they had too little knowledge of and even respect for the attitudes of the American working class—too great a belief in collective thinking coupled with too little a regard for the individual within the mass. And of course their motives were often imperfect, and their power struggles were tainted with personal ambition. But like their very different descendents in the 1960s, they burst out with their exasperation against the economic and racial crimes of an imperialist class society. And within the limits of their abilities, they risked their own careers and lives to act against those wrongs.

Although we are dealing here neither with popular art—with the work of Frank Capra or the Marx Brothers—nor with high art—the best of Eisenstein, Renoir, Bergman, or Resnais—we are dealing with art of purposeful social impact. What distinguishes the films of this book from most Hollywood films of the thirties is not better technical facility, superior direction, finer acting, or better stories but a quality that is *charged* with an effort to face injustice directly and with an intention of forcing the viewer to do something about it.

Paul Strand and *The Wave*

One case in point is Paul Strand's *The Wave*, filmed in the village of Alvarado in Vera Cruz, Mexico in 1934. When it was finally released in the United States in 1937, critics praised the "sincerity" and "authenticity" of Strand's conception, which did not succumb to romanticizing the struggles or the lives of the native fishermen who were its subject. According to Strand, the film "created a great sensation and was shown over and over again" in Mexico in 1936. In 1939, it received an award from the Council for Pan American Democracy[b] for its ef-

---

[b] Franz Boas was honorary chairman of this liberal group. In July of 1939 they sent a delegation to Mexico to study the state's recent expropriation of oil and other resources,

fectiveness in improving conditions among Mexican fishermen.[3] In 1935, Strand would be a key newcomer to Nykino, bringing with him the ideas and commitment behind *The Wave*.

Of Bohemian descent on his mother's side, Strand, whose father had recently changed the name from Stransky, was born in New York City in 1890. When he was three, the family moved from an East 73rd Street brownstone to the house on West 83rd, near Riverside Drive, where he grew up. In 1904, at considerable financial sacrifice, he was sent to the Ethical Culture School where his first photography teacher was Lewis Hine. Hine was then a young biology teacher, deeply involved in photographing the immigrants as they arrived at Ellis Island and as they struggled to make new lives in the slums and sweatshops of the Lower East Side. Hine took the small class to the Little Galleries of Stieglitz's Photo-Secession at 291 Fifth Avenue, and there the wide-eyed Strand committed himself to a career as "an artist in photography." Uninterested in college, he worked first as an office boy in his father's importing firm, then spent his savings on a trip to Europe in 1911, returning to become a professional photographer. He passed through many of the then-current photographic fads but was early pointed by Stieglitz toward the challenges of the objective world. In 1915, a member of the group at "291," he became a leading exponent and practitioner of pure or "straight," as opposed to trick or "artistic," photography, and an entire number of Stieglitz's famous *Camera Work* was devoted to him in 1917.[4]

A photographer of high and growing reputation throughout the twenties, he increasingly devoted his art to capturing the vital relationships between landscape and people. Late 1932 found him in the small towns of Mexico, where he recorded what he considered to be the impressive spirit of the Mexican people. It was there, in 1933, that Carlos Chávez, a strong left-wing intellectual, a noted composer and conductor, then chief of the Department of Fine Arts in Mexico's Secretariat of Education, asked Strand to become chief of photography and cinematography, and urged him to make a film, the first of a projected series on Mexico.[5]

Strand was no novice at motion picture making. In the early 1920s, using titles from Walt Whitman and his own very active eye for abstract

the Mexican government's present policy in health, education, agriculture and public works projects, the collaboration between organized labor and government, and Fascist penetration and the government's handling of it. The delegation included Maury Maverick, Mayor of San Antonio, Texas; Justice James H. Wolfe of the Utah Supreme Court; the Rev. Owen A. Knox, acting chairman of the Michigan Civil Rights Federation; George Seldes, journalist; and Frances Grant, president of the Pan American Women's Association.

patterns, he and Charles Sheeler had created *Manhatta* (released as *New York the Magnificent* at the theater owner's insistence), a fascinating, sometimes tantalizing, lyrical documentary on New York City, carefully built into exquisite variations of movement, angle, and pattern. This early piece earned him a substantial reputation, the result being that he invested all of the $2,500 that he had inherited from a wealthy uncle in an Akeley camera. Soon he was making a comfortable income as a sports cameraman for Fox and Pathé and as a maker of background shots for Famous Players and Metro-Goldwyn; he also did short films for Princeton commencements. Strand had some experience, too, with more directly tendentious filmmaking, having shot, for a group named Visugraphic, a silent two-reeler, *Where the Pavement Begins* (1928), which pleaded for more city playgrounds.[c]

The Wave's production became closely linked with the internal life of Mexico's government in 1933. At that time, the head of the Revolutionary Family, the elite group that has ruled Mexico since the second decade of this century, was Plutarco Elías Calles. As President of Mexico from 1924 to 1928, he had been a progressive leader, prolabor, anticlerical, somewhat proagrarian, propublic works, and outspoken in opposing excessive foreign investment into Mexico. By law unable to run for the presidency again, Calles had nevertheless retained his power, continuing to rule through puppet presidents such as Abelardo Rodríguez (1932-1934). After 1928, partly under the influence of Dwight Morrow, U.S. Ambassador to Mexico from 1927 until early 1933, Calles had become increasingly conservative, dropping progressive labor and public works programs, drastically slowing land redistribution, and encouraging the investment of foreign capital. In doing so he alienated people in the government such as Chávez, the state governors he had appointed when president, and others in the determined left wing of the Family.

By 1933, thanks to the growing unrest in Mexico, the Depression, the international focus on political change, and the regrouping of Mexican labor unions and peasant leagues, a forceful movement to the left was under way. Calles tolerated the leftward swing partly out of a sense of diplomatic accommodation and partly out of his belief in the revolutionary creed of intellectual freedom. In May of 1933, the left drew up a six-year progressive plan to guide the next president, and chose, with Calles' approval, Lázaro Cárdenas as their candidate and thus the assured victor. The year 1934 brought important legislative

---

[c] Strand did not write or edit the film and could not remember if he shot it all, but he did recollect one difficult dramatic scene where a truck smashes a doll carriage and knocks down a child. Interview with author, 18 Feb. 1975.

successes and, in July, the election of Cárdenas, who had campaigned vigorously on the six-year plan platform. Once in office, he proved even more radical than his supporters had suspected, and in a show-down forced by Calles in June of 1935, Cárdenas chased Calles from power.[6] It was these political developments that made the commissioning of *The Wave* possible (its tentative title was *Pescados*, The Fishermen) and that had much to do with the film's content.

Shortly after Strand's arrival in Mexico City in the late fall of 1932, Chávez had arranged for an exhibition of his photographs in the *sala de arte* of the Secretariat of Education, a long, awkward room that formed a natural passageway between two downtown streets. Through this room passed "Indian women with their babies, policemen, soldiers, workers, businessmen, all kinds of people," and they would stop and scrutinize the photographs. This Strand found

> very satisfying, because after all "291" was, I won't say consciously elitist, it wasn't consciously elitist. It welcomed anybody who came, but it was a small two rooms, way up on top of a brownstone house, and on Fifth Avenue, and mostly people who came were people already interested in art.

Strand was also aware of the effects of the recent revolution in Mexico, and he was fascinated by the way Orozco, Rivera, and Siqueiros, the great muralists, had committed their art to its service. Approached by Chávez to undertake the program of government film-making, he quickly decided that the films should be made primarily for the sixteen million largely illiterate Indians and that they should focus on exploring the problems that they encountered in their own lives when attempting to realize the objectives of the revolution. Chávez and his superior, Narciso Bassols, agreed, and they suggested a series of films treating the production of wealth in Mexico, "the raising of corn, cattle breeding, mining of silver, fishing, and so forth."[7]

Rejecting the road of instructional or merely factual filmmaking, Strand's mind turned to Robert Flaherty, a personal friend whose *Nanook* and *Moana* had strongly impressed him. As he specified in a statement to the Secretariat of Education, he would follow Flaherty's example, making documentary films that were also stories about human struggle. The struggle would not be against natural but against social and economic forces. The drama would engage the fishermen, farmers, and miners and make it easier for them "to find in the films some reflection of their own lives, and above all their own problems." The pattern would be such that in the lives of the fishermen, "the agrarian workers of the plateau," Strand later told David Platt, would find "their own struggles and aspirations." Strand also told Platt that one reason he looked to Flaherty as a resource was because Flaherty approached his subjects "as a fellow human being, not as a superior example of the white race who found them 'interesting, picturesque and acute.' " And Strand, concerned in his photography with capturing the authentic characteristics of a community, was keenly aware of the travelogue dangers inherent in his subject matter. "In a world," his statement reads, "in which human exploitation is so general it seems to me a further exploitation of people, however picturesque, different and interesting to us they may appear, to merely make use of them as *material*."[8]

Strand was also inspired by Soviet films, such as *Potemkin, Storm Over Asia*, and *Road to Life*, not only because of their subject matter but because of how they used all the elements of filmmaking. The breaking down of the fishing scene in *The Wave* into nearly one hundred shots was consciously derived from Eisenstein's revolutionary breaking down of the Odessa steps sequence in *Potemkin*. Through his own finely tuned photographic sensibility, through the most developed techniques of film montage, and through pace and the juxtaposition of shots of varying angles and movements, Strand intended both to convey a respect for the subject and to heighten the excitement and the intensity of the audience's participation in it. Thus his films would speak "to people about themselves in a way in which they are moved and activated to do something about their lives." This beauty was compatible with a certain bluntness of content.[d] "We assume," he told the Secretariat,

> that these pictures are not being made for subtle and sophisticated people or even very sensitive minds accustomed to follow the intricacies of esthetic nuance. On the contrary, we assume that these films are being made for a great majority of rather simple people to whom elementary facts should be presented in a direct and unequivocal way; a way that might even bore more complicated sensibilities, though we believe otherwise. We feel that almost a certain crudeness of statement is necessary to achieve the purposes of these films.

[d] "On seeing *Redes* [*The Wave*] you could understand the remark you had once heard Paul Strand make. 'How is it that one can look far and wide in films and seldom find photographic beauty? Good acting, yes, good writing, sometimes, but that's all.' " Sidney Meyers, "Paul Strand's Photography Reaches Heights in *The Wave*," DW, 4 May 1937, p. 7.

He was also, he said, gambling on a belief that people would not always simply accept injustice and that artists might play a part in the changing of attitudes.[9]

With Chávez' nephew, Augustine Velasquez Chávez, Strand plotted out an outline and then cabled a friend he had made recently in Taos, New Mexico, Henwar Rodakiewicz, to take on the writing and directing of the film. Born in Vienna in 1902, Rodakiewicz was a Harvard anthropology major whose experimental film with light and water, *Portrait of a Young Man* (1925-1926), had caught first Strand's eye and then Stieglitz's and Frank Tuttle's, landing the young Austrian a film job in British Guiana plus an invitation to Hollywood. Strand's cable caught Rodakiewicz on his return from British Guiana. Working with Strand in Acapulco and in Mexico City, Rodakiewicz wrote a definitive (although not a shot-by-shot) script around the outline and observation of life in Acapulco.[10]

When at the end of 1933 Rodakiewicz had to return to New Mexico for a previous film commitment, he contacted his friend Fred Zinnemann, who had been accruing experience in Hollywood since 1929, and asked him to take on what would be Zinnemann's "virgin effort as a full-fledged Director." Zinnemann was a good choice: an assistant to Flaherty two years earlier, he was also, he recalls,

> still very much under the influence of the Russian silent film, particularly Eisenstein and Pudovkin and their method of deriving flow, dynamics, and drama through the editing and juxtaposition of images (montage). Therefore I was very much in sympathy with Strand's method (deriving from still photography) of careful composition of each shot, often with a bare minimum of movement within the frame.

In the first days of February the crew moved into quarters in the tiny fishing village of Alvarado, taking a rickety streetcar ride there from Vera Cruz, Zinnemann remembers, traveling forty kilometers "through a bit of jungle and past a few scattered Indian villages." He had joined the crew understanding that the production schedule was for four months,

> but after a couple of weeks it became quite evident to me that it would take more nearly an entire year. The rigidly organized Hollywood way of production just didn't apply. There was absolutely no way of hurrying anyone: one could either adapt to the natural rhythm of life in Alvarado, or go berserk, or leave. After

some soul-searching I decided to stay, and as a result I spent one of the happiest and most peaceful years of my life.

The feeling was shared by other members of the crew. Rodakiewicz's other film fell through, and he returned to work on the script day by day as the shooting proceeded, bringing with him Ned Scott, who provided a series of extraordinary production stills.[11]

Except for the male lead, Sylvio Hernandez, a university student, and David Valles Gonzales, an actor who played the fish-buyer, the cast consisted of native villagers who were paid one and one-half to two pesos (between thirty-two and forty-five cents) a day, "more money than they could have possibly earned, except during the height of the fishing season." Aside from the slow pace of village life and the intense sun that necessitated an 11:00 A.M. to 3:30 P.M. break, production was hampered by a current that kept pulling the huge net in the fishing scene out of place and by a minor lead who, in temperamental protest against the importance Hernandez's role was taking on, shaved a three-month beard in the middle of the shooting.

Some secrecy was called for as well. According to Strand, in order to prevent the bosses, the fish-buyers of Alvarado, from gaining "the real idea—that it was a revolutionary picture"—punch lines and key shots "were taken when they weren't around," and Rodakiewicz recalls that they filmed "way out of sequence" for the same reason. Technical conditions demanded patience and ingenuity: rushes took three to six weeks to return from the Davidge Laboratories in Los Angeles; and fortunately for the initial cutting, since "often the electricity didn't work during the day," Rodakiewicz "had the bright idea of mounting the moviola on a sewing machine, propelling it by pedalling." When the electricity did work, "fluctuating voltage made the moviola and the projector run at erratic speed which in turn created difficulties in timing."[12]

Strand supervised the entire production and served as cameraman on all except the water close-ups, which were shot by Rodakiewicz with his spring-driven Eyemo. Zinnemann, assisted by Gomez Muriel (who wrongly receives credit as codirector), directed throughout, except when he was laid low by sunstroke. Then Rodakiewicz took over, filming the opening sequence, most of the dialogue sequences, and a part of the fight sequence. Gunther von Fritsch, a Viennese friend of Zinnemann, who was also located in Hollywood, came to Alvarado to do the editing, a slow job in the constant heat. Sylvestre Revueltas, a friend and pupil of Chávez, composed the score after living in the village, talking to the fisherpeople, and listening to the local songs and music.

When officials of the new Mexican government replaced Bassols and Chávez in December of 1934, they dismissed Strand and his crew, despite a request for further time and funds, and then sat down to decide what to do with the uncompleted film. Strand returned to the States in great pain over the uncertain fate of his work[13]—the editing had been completed, but, except for the music, all the sound recording, including the dialogue, was yet to be done.[e] It was completed, however, and when the film arrived in the United States late in 1936, John Dos Passos and Leo Hurwitz added the English titles.[f]

The story line of *The Wave* follows to some extent what is known in proletarian literature as the conversion formula. The fish have not come in, the pay is so low that there is nothing to tide one over from haul to haul, and Miro's son is ill and needs hospitalization that Miro cannot afford. There is no more work in town. Miguel has work on the dock, and, less-educated by circumstances, is naive enough to believe that Don Anselmo, the fish-buyer, will help Miro out. Miro, no more respected by the fish-buyer than Don Anselmo's parrot, learns what he already knew, that of course the fish-buyer will not help him. His boy dies, and the funeral follows. The fish finally come in, and in the excitement of the detailed and magnificent full-scale fishing scene, we both thrill to the beauty, skill, and vigor of the fishermen and learn how difficult and demanding their work is. Their joy in the catch vanishes when they each receive but seventy-two cents for the ten hours of work, at which point Miro explodes into an argument with Sanchez, the politician friend of Don Anselmo—an argument that the still-naive Miguel breaks up. Miro gathers the workers at the dunes and speaks to them about their exploitation. As he advocates united action, Miguel shakes his head in disagreement, and Sanchez struggles

[e] The sound recording is not as good as it might be. The overextension of applause during Miro's speech is unreal, for one thing, and I feel, as did James Shelley Hamilton, that the delivery of dialogue is somewhat slow, stilted, too based on the script, not quite natural. Strand had no control over this—it was done without communication with the filmmakers. When the film arrived in New York in 1936, among the somewhat distorted credits (which Strand corrected) was an unfamiliar name, Jose Marino, and Strand gave him credit for sound editing. Hilario Paullada was credited with supervision of sound. The cutaway shots during the dunes speech were added at this later date as well. Von Fritsch letter to author, 18 Aug. 1976.

[f] Although the United States did not receive the film until 1937 (and even then it was to be "the first full-length film made in America [sic] on a working class theme, embodying the aspirations of the great masses of men," as Sidney Meyers put it in his Nov. 1936 *New Theatre* article), we must remember that Strand made it in 1934 and that he was thus to bring to Nykino in 1935 the knowledge and experience he had acquired in Mexico.

through the crowd to make a divisive speech. Not hired onto a boat the next day, Miro joins his friends at the weighing-in to advocate dumping the fish in the river if the price remains low. Miguel and his companions, fearing that this will not work, refuse. The others call them scabs, and a fight breaks out. During the scuffle, Sanchez shoots Miro, a fast montage of coins and political posters mingling with Miro's collapse to the ground. Under cover of the combat, the bosses weigh the fish and then offer Miguel and his men the money for them. These events convert Miguel, who joins the protagonists in brotherhood and takes on the group's leadership, arguing that Miro's plan be carried out. The fishermen of Alvarado gather as Miro's body is carried to the boat. As the boats move, united, toward town, the scene is accented through numerous shots and some lingering dissolves with Miguel depicted against the clouds. The final shot (taken by Rodakiewicz) holds on a wave that piles up very slowly, forms, and then breaks, a perfect reflection of the film's pace and a moving symbol of the slow but inexorable rise of these people to revolt.

In the opening sequence, an establishing shot of sculpturesque driftwood among the waves pans slightly left to a medium long shot of Miro standing in the water with his net, his back three-quarters to the camera. A cut to close-up gives us his handsome, troubled, expectant face. Then a shot of glimmering water, as in a pool, a close-up of Miro leaning forward, another shot of the water, and a medium long shot of Miro casting his net. A shot of Miro watching separates two lyrical shots: the net goes up, spreads across the screen, and comes down toward the camera; it settles in the water. As Miro slowly pulls it in, a close-up details his full pleasure, then his disappointment, as we watch a small fish pulled up to his hand. He throws it back, the waves break in, he turns away, and we linger a moment as the water fills his footprint.

This opening clearly functions as a symbol of Miro's experience and as a foreshadowing of the larger rise and fall of spirits in the later fishing sequence and its aftermath.[g] Aside from its overtones of transiency and its hints of Miro's death, the image of Miro's footprint is strikingly beautiful and calls attention to itself, as do the two lyrical shots of the net. Yet neither these shots nor the frequent use of close-ups and studied portraiture are isolated images or merely unintegrated tendencies of the still photographer. Instead, they serve a number of thematic functions. These moments of relevant yet pure composition

---

[g] Foreshadowing is frequent in the film. As villagers run to the boat bringing in the first catch, the camera holds on a boy tripping and falling. Arriving at the boat, two boys break into a fight over the fish.

make us catch our breaths, draw us in, and move us toward the film, the village, its people. The slow sensitive, molded treatment of faces and figures—what Archibald MacLeish called Strand's eloquent and moving respect for his materials[14]—also absorbs us and creates sympathy and identity.[h]

The beauty also plays an ironic role. The waves, the palms, the boats, a kite in the air, the nets, the rhythms of agile men alive in their work *contrast* to the dying child, the ragged clothes, a bitter old man slashing at the nets, the exploitation of the people. Here Strand's visual imagery is even more subtle than Buñuel's use of Brahms in *Las Hurdas*. In *The Wave*, the viewer may become aware of how he or she and Paul Strand can appreciate this beauty while too often it must go unnoticed by the struggling villagers.[i] Strand's Mexican villagers are not the sick, broken people of Buñuel's villages, almost entirely ignored by Western civilization and by their own government; on the contrary at their best moments the villagers of *The Wave* have both the autonomy and the spiritual unity of the Ceylonese of Basil Wright's *Song of Ceylon*. However, where Wright is critical but ambivalent about the effects of Western commerce and allows himself to celebrate his untouched natives and their god in the final section of his film, Strand makes a very different film by directly indicting the local businessman, demonstrating the dire effects of his power, and showing the possibilities for revolt against the conditions he portrays.

As Miguel leads Miro away from his dispute with Sanchez, he observes with acquiescent, if bitter, philosophy that "the big fish eat the little fish." Miro replies, "Yes, but *we're not fish.*" They exit frame as the camera holds on the hook to which fish are attached for weighing. While this seems to undercut Miro's exclamation and to foreshadow his death, it also asks the direct political question, Will the fishermen allow the fish to be weighed under present conditions? and connotes men now being weighed in the balance, having to determine that they are not fish, nor bait for fish.[j] The consciousness of this issue and the explosiveness of the events in the film prepare the viewer both to *will*

[h] Ideally the music, founded in native experience and sensitive to the pace of the film, should do this too, and at its best, as in the fishing sequence, it does. However, although it is appropriate and supportive throughout and serves to help convey emotion and suggest the direction of the action, to my taste, it is generally too heavy in its symphonic terms and too dramatic. For a brief discussion of Revueltas's music in *The Wave*, see Kurt London, "Film Music of the Quarter," *Films*, Spring 1940, pp. 46-47.

[i] This is an irony I detect in the film. According to the filmmakers, it was not intended.

[j] "That was Zinnemann's idea. . . . This is where we were influenced by the Russians who taught us to create feelings with strong images that start the spectator thinking." Gunther von Fritsch, letter to author, 18 Aug. 1976.

the confrontation implicit in those boats heading toward shore and to be optimistic about the outcome.

The film is not perfect. The dialogue is inadequately delivered, but that, we have seen, was beyond the filmmakers' control. The fight between the rebels and the scabs is poorly acted, although effective parallel cutting to Sanchez's gun, the weighing station, and the feet of oncoming soldiers, as well as close-ups of the straining bodies, alleviate the artificiality considerably. As Joris Ivens has argued, there are limitations to the use of the nonactor: when one begins to work with intimate psychology or to require nonhabitual behavior, one enters a region, as Rodakiewicz and Zinnemann acknowledge they did in this case, where one might better work with professionals. The death of Miro's son has power as a motivating force, but the filmmakers do not draw upon all the emotional resources of their story by either showing Miro's son or by working closely with his family, something Herbert Kline in his Mexican film *The Forgotten Village* and Herbert Biberman in *Salt of the Earth* were later to do so well. That decision, however, might as easily have risen from the character of Strand, who was "not," as Rodakiewicz recalls, "the kind of person who would go in for anything that he might think was sentimental."[15]

When Strand speaks of the necessity for a certain crudeness of statement in the film, he is referring to the simplification of economics and motives. The weaknesses in delivery, direction, and acting, including what seems an inappropriate stoicism of expression—whatever the actual local habit—during certain dramatic situations, cannot, of course, be subsumed under such a necessity. However, the flaws that mar the picture here and there are minor in face of the overall impact of direction, photography, and content.

One problem is not easy to resolve. During the funeral procession, when the camera captures for a moment a woman standing in a doorway with her children, it is possible to feel that Strand is quoting his own still photographs of the Mexican people (his "Mother and Child" in the *Mexican Portfolio*, for instance) and implying that through movement and story he is now exploring what lies behind those still faces and buildings. True or not, one is consciously aware throughout *The Wave* of Strand's earlier still photography, for he composes with light, line, and frame very carefully, he lingers, and his actors move slowly. One frequent compositional method imposes upon the film a specifically static sense: many shots begin with a single, posed figure in close-up or medium close-up; movement in the shot then consists of a single movement of the head. Variations on this occur in shots containing two or three people and in shots with larger groups.[k] In reaction to this, most of the negative criticism of the film centers on its slow pace.

Where a critic like Mark van Doren seems mainly to miss the "snap" of thirties' Hollywood film, this criticism can be for the most part discounted, although there is certainly something to Shelley Hamilton's opinion that more of the trickiness and "deftly varied cinematic ease" that lure "audiences to far more trivial movies, would have brought *Redes* more of the widespread appreciation its sincerity deserves." But others, like Frank Nugent and Willard Van Dyke, have more cogently found that although the photography is praiseworthy, it damages the narrative.[16]

The point underlying this argument is that film is movement and that individual shots and scenes are built on anticipation, on thematic *and* visual suspense, so that in a large number of ways film is directional, and one concentrates on what is being moved toward as well as upon what is moving. The photograph, on the other hand, rests in the hand, is a captured moment that one probes and penetrates, noting nuance of line, texture, and object relations. While some filmmakers have created striking exceptions, the film (especially the story film) that sacrifices any of its dynamic to the photographic mode is likely to perplex.

Other critics of *The Wave* found no problem here. Marguerite Tazelaar, writing for the *New York Herald Tribune*, and Katherine Anne Porter in an enthusiastic letter to *New Masses*, countered that "the deliberate slow-paced tempo seems to match the innate dignity of this little group of stalwart folk who have never before appeared in front of cameras" and that "it is the handsome, deliberate pace of the Indians of the hot countries." For these critics, it did not for a moment "retard the suspense or lessen the interest."[1]

[k] Rodakiewicz told of the importance of the frame to Strand—any unexpected movement from the original set-up, and he would have to shoot it over again. Interview with author, 15 May 1975. Von Fritsch explains this compositional device as due in part to the difficulty of directing these non-actors beyond one-two movements or emotions in a single take. Letter to Author, 18 Aug. 1976.

[1] Marguerite Tazelaar, "On the Screen: The Wave—Filmarte," *N.Y. Herald Tribune*, 21 Apr. 1937, p. 18; Katherine Anne Porter, "On *The Wave*" (letter), NM, 18 May 1937, p. 22.

Gunther von Fritsch, the film's editor, wrote: "It is true that the film was paced rather slowly. I was aware of that at the time, and intended to trim and speed it up later as I expected a great deal more material. But only a part of it was ever shot as the continuation and completion of the film got into jeopardy because of the changing regime. The film HAD to be near an hour in length . . . so it was not possible to speed up the action very much. In the end, considering the kind of audience it was made for, many of whom had never seen a motion picture before and were not trained to understand the 'language' of cinema, the tempo was just about right." Letter to author, 18 Aug. 1976.

This is not an easy dispute to resolve. In my experience the pace-equals-character point has something to it, for the pace feels right, though not quite right enough, and I find Nugent and Van Dyke insightful in detecting some control of one art over another. However, in the end, Tazelaar and Porter seem to me to be the most perceptive. If the influence of still composition makes me view the film with a certain aesthetic tension, still it does not diminish my interest, and it tends to work positively and vitally as a sign of Strand's respect and concern for his materials and his people.

As Sidney Meyers remarked in his review of *The Wave*, there is no essential difference between Strand's still work and this film: "From his earliest works, like the blind woman in Stieglitz's magazine, *Camera Work*, to *Redes*, Strand has spoken of one thing predominantly—the dignity of human life and of the things man has made that reflect his image." Other critics of the film recognized Strand's capturing of the "strength and nobility and depth of character," the "physical beauty of the people, the dignity and forthrightness of their character," and his refusal to falsify, sentimentalize, or otherwise exploit his subjects.[17]

Strand returned to New York in December 1934, where several conversations with Harold Clurman and Cheryl Crawford sparked his interest in a trip to the Soviet Union. Before he left on his two-month junket in May, he sat in on several Nykino gatherings at Steiner's big studio. "They welcomed me to their group," he recalled in 1974, "and I was very glad to be close to them, because what they felt about filmmaking and what they wanted to do with films was very near to my own feeling, which had already begun to express itself in *The Wave*, although nobody, including myself, had ever seen it." Upon his return from the Soviet Union, where difficulty in obtaining a work permit frustrated his attempt to aid Eisenstein (at Eisenstein's request) with his newest film,[18] he joined Nykino, commencing an affiliation that would endure until 1942.

Strand brought to the group the concern that he shared with Flaherty and the Russians that documentary "have the highest possible aesthetic content and dramatic impact," a concern he found already active in the Nykino circle. Of equal importance, he felt, was his refusal to "film down" to the people of *The Wave*, "or to any other people." His keen aesthetic and thematic stress on human dignity continued in the work of the New York group, he observed, and it "was one of the reasons" he was part of that group.[19]

Strand also brought his prestige to Nykino. That he had for years been recognized as a major American artist, someone ranking with Stieglitz, Steichen, and Weston, meant, Irving Lerner recalled, a great deal. For one thing, as a more established artist with significant connections, he would attract donors and sponsors to the struggling band. Of higher importance, however, was his artistry, for the Nykino film-makers had recently reaffirmed a dedication to their own artistic growth. I have already noted that contact with Strand in the mid-twenties radically altered Steiner's work. It was not only the quality of the work that touched him but the *seriousness* with which Strand "took being a still photographer or a cameraman. This was a way of life. . . . I began to see . . . what it means when you have a camera in your hands, what obligation is placed upon you."[20]

Hurwitz first met Strand in 1931 when he was selecting some of Strand's prints for publication in an impressionistic piece that Lola Ridge was doing on him in *Creative Art*. Strand had looked over Hurwitz's photographs and lent him a lens for a newly acquired camera. His reappearance in 1935 was very timely, Hurwitz remembers:

> When Paul came into the group, he came in as an artist who had a kind of accomplishment that we didn't have, not necessarily in film, but mostly in stills. It wasn't that Paul was a film man, although he was experienced in film, but that he had met the problems of an artist, which were very important to me. I learned a great deal from him that basically had to do with responsibility to the life that you're creating, whether a photograph, a film, or a poem. And Paul had great stature, and his work was absolutely marvelous. Then he was also a very forceful person . . . and he had the feeling I had, that once you took an idea, you put your teeth in it, you worked with it, you took responsibility for all its corners. . . . I learned from Paul that you don't let the first, second, or third brilliant idea say it's done. You constantly question it, let it talk to you. . . . There is a marriage to the work you're doing that requires a real completeness.[21]

Nothing could have been more supportive of their impulse to leave the League in pursuit of time to make more perfect art.

That Strand also had strong political beliefs of the Nykino strain was reinforcing to all concerned. Once he saw film as a more powerful political means than the photograph, Lerner believed, Nykino became essential to him as an organization that would help him "put into practice some of the things he felt very strongly about."[m] It is clear

---

[m] Lerner had high respect in those days for Strand's political dedication and was interested when they met in 1973 after years apart to discover that dedication undiminished (Lerner interview). Similarly, Strand was one of a number of artists who helped arouse my own conscience in 1965 by refusing an invitation to the White House in protest against the Johnson administration's policies in Vietnam.

too—from my conversations about Strand with other Nykino members and from my hours with Strand himself—that Strand added a forceful and outspoken personality to the group, a personality that focused on a goal and then pursued it without swerving.[n] His own certainty solidified the sense of purpose, possibility, and politics in the others. That he was eager to join Nykino in 1935 must have helped them to feel their activity worthwhile.

Lionel Berman, Sidney Meyers, and Ben Maddow: The Making of Three Filmmakers

In March and April of 1935, Strand met three other recent newcomers to Nykino, Lionel Berman, Sidney Meyers, and Ben Maddow. A member of Pen and Hammer, Lionel Berman had not joined the Film and Photo League, but he had turned up at several of its functions, and now he was bringing his organizational talents and an interest in filmmaking to the forming of Nykino. The son of Jewish immigrants from Lithuania, he was born 3 February 1906. His father, a small-businessman and socialist who had left Russia to avoid military service under the Tsar, was "utterly dedicated to his belief in social and political equality" and a strong influence on his children. Lionel's sister recalls:

> When we were 15 and 10, Lionel and I visited in Washington, D.C., and rode on a street car there. As our own protest to the rule that blacks must ride in the back of the trolley, we deliberately walked to the back. We would not budge when the motorman insisted we come forward. Instead, I remember, Lionel made a quiet speech about equality, and I proudly stood my ground at his side. It was only when a black woman, who said she understood what we were trying to do, but thought we would cause difficulties for the blacks, urged us to move forward, that we finally did. My father's influence was certainly potent.

Brooklyn's Borough Park was Berman's home from shortly after his birth in Manhattan until nearly age thirteen, when his mother died. He spent two years at De Witt Clinton High School in Manhattan, where he met and was influenced by Countee Cullen (who was probably also behind that Washington speech), and then went on to Central High School in Newark. A student of advertising at New York University, he left early to enter public relations, first as a Bell Syndicate

[n] He described himself in these latter terms. Interview with author, 18 Feb. 1975. See also Calvin Tomkins, profile on Strand, *The New Yorker*, 16 Sept. 1974, p. 64.

columnist and then as a free-lance agent in charge of "handling advertising and publicity accounts for several large companies," including the Kidskin Tanners of America. Disliking the advertising world, he took a trip to Paris during 1928 and 1929, where he became a friend of Henri Cartier-Bresson, who strengthened his eagerness to leave advertising for film.

An attack of scarlet fever at age seven had severely damaged his kidneys, and consequently Berman was tormented by nephritis throughout his life. Nervous, a chain smoker who had to take to the hallway when working with flammable nitrate film, he was "a shy man who didn't easily reveal his feelings," whose "constant struggle with illness pushed him into himself, made him often melancholy and led him at times to pessimism," at least in later years. Yet he was also an avid learner, with a sensitive, finely-honed, conscientious, and generous intellect that filled him with "a hatred of imposture . . . of destruction, of unconsciousness or lack of conscience." He was also "a natural teacher," with whom no one could "come in contact . . . without experiencing an opening of the mind." He was to be an important spirit in this group, a fund-raiser, a participant and advisor on many of the films to come, a man alert and dedicated to the politics of the far left. [22]

Lionel Berman, Sidney Meyers said at Berman's funeral in 1968, "was a saving brother to me. The day he came to me and said, 'Sidney, put away your viola, from now on you're going to make pictures,' he changed my life, and fundamentally saved it." Meyers was born in 1906 to a Jewish immigrant family who lived at New York's 115th Street and Lexington Avenue. His father's parents had been dyers, and his father, who had been a skilled bookbinder in Poland, was now a highly reputed paper hanger. A socialist who wanted his son to become a doctor or a businessman, he was to have little sympathy with Sidney's politics during the thirties.

These politics had an early beginning, for Meyers habitually stopped to listen to neighborhood soapbox socialists, and, his sister recalls,

> became friendly with a blind man on our block who was the neighborhood radical, a socialist. Sidney was 11-13 years old then, it was 1917-1919. He helped his friend to get around in the evenings and attended many meetings with him. The day after a meeting he would come to school and repeat what he had heard and call the children in his class "Comrades." Mother was called to school and warned by Sidney's teacher that she had better keep him quiet or the whole family would be deported. Those were the days of the Palmer Raids.

He attended De Witt Clinton High School, in whose award-winning orchestra he played double bass while also studying the violin. In 1927, during his senior year at City College, he had a successful audition with Fritz Reiner and the Cincinnati Symphony, where he played violin for a couple of years. In 1930 he married Edna Ocko, whom he had known since his early youth, and took on a job with an orchestra subsidized by New York City. It was through Edna, who was a friend of Lionel Berman's first wife, the dancer Blanche Evan, that he met Lionel. And it was Edna, aware of his long-standing interest in photography, who bought him his first camera, probably before they moved to the East 17th Street building where Leo Hurwitz and his wife, the dancer Jane Dudley, lived. It was probably through Hurwitz that Meyers joined the League as a still photographer, and then, at the Potamkin Film School and probably in the Hurwitz/Lerner/Steiner unit, developed his love for film. From early 1935 on, he wrote as a film critic and editor for *New Theatre* and other periodicals, choosing "Robert Stebbins"—a variation on his old family name, Stabinsky—as a pseudonym to protect his other jobs. He stayed with the orchestra until early in 1936, when under the persuasion of Berman and the sympathetic encouragement of Edna, he left his violin and viola for filmmaking.

It is possible that among this very talented group of young artists it was Meyers who was the most talented. Many of my interviewees believe this to be the case. A man of great wit and character, an assiduous reader who was highly skilled in several arts, a man who could never be doctrinaire yet whose politics and loyalties were firm, a man who would edge into the background rather than seek recognition, he was greatly loved and admired. It is almost impossible to find a negative word about him from old friends, a fact far from true of anyone else about whom I am writing. It has been one of my regrets that I did not have the opportunity to know him. He died in 1969.[23]

At Steiner's studio, Strand also met a young poet named Ben Maddow, who had been put to work on Steiner's *Harbor Scenes* as the result of answering a Nykino advertisement.° Luxuriating in the use of film footage as illustrations for his poetry, he was also experiencing new excitement in his discovery of the modification that commentary could impart to an image.[24]

° Hurwitz has a different memory of Maddow's joining Nykino, a memory Maddow denies. Hurwitz recalls going to a meeting where Maddow, then working with a rival film organization [?], was reading a paper on film: "Ben was there talking, and I thought, this is really a mind, this is a sensitivity. Come and work with us." Hurwitz remembers Maddow as "a great talent": Hurwitz interview, 21 Nov. 1974. Maddow's denial: letter to author, 24 Dec. 1974.

Born in Passaic, New Jersey in 1909 to an immigrant Jewish family from the Ukraine, Maddow did not speak English until he was four. His father, who "came to America . . . to avoid the Russian draft . . . military service was particularly hard on Jewish recruits," was a social laborite, a devotee of Daniel De Leon, and a lifelong Democrat who always voted Republican but whose philosophically leftward posture affected his son's thinking. When he decided to give up a faltering shop and return to farming, the family split up. Ben stayed with his mother in Passaic and New York City, spending parts of summers on the farm. Because the Jewish quota system denied him admission to the Columbia College of Physicians and Surgeons, he switched from pre-med to biophysics in his fourth undergraduate year at Columbia, while still retaining his strong interest in literature; he briefly studied the foundations of mathematics after his 1930 graduation. Unemployed between 1930 and 1932, he recommenced his career by working "with the outside people." For three years he earned his living as a hospital orderly and from 1935 to 1938 as a social investigator (a case worker) for the Emergency Relief Bureau in New York City, his salary paid by the Works Progress Administration or some other federal agency.[25] Because the government was not anxious to employ radicals, in 1934 he assumed the pen name of David Wolff, which he thought a translation of his father's Ukrainian cognomen, Medvedev.[p]

His poems had appeared in *Poetry, Symposium, New Masses, Dynamo*, and elsewhere. In 1935, *The Partisan Review* had taken two and *Dynamo* had taken one, and in the same year three previously published poems were being anthologized in *Proletarian Literature in the United States*. These poems indicate how oppressive he found New York City tenement living, how stunned he was by the way its citizens were deprived of privacy, love, growth, and fulfillment. This and the deadening effect America had had upon his father he found stifling, debilitating, constrictive. The poems suggest an almost frantic need for a way up and out, for a personal vitality, for a career or commitment that would suffice.[q] Emotional, concentrated, biting, his poetry is sometimes almost too private. It was poetry that seemed to be the commitment he was looking for, at least for a while. "I swam," he wrote, "against the flaccid run/of cheap perverse events . . ."

[p] "The actual reason I changed my name was that I was publishing poetry and was too shy to have this known by my colleagues in the Bureau. After that, I was stuck with the name—though I used other pseudonyms as well." Letter to author, 18 Aug. 1976.

[q] Hurwitz remembers him as having "that kind of thing where one's inner qualities are not contained by the rigidities of the environment but burst through." Interview with author, 21 Nov. 1974.

or chafed at symbols to recover mine
among the pompous meters; or retraced
with fingers of the glance the hopeful walls
of colored oblongs to pluck forth the shape
of fruit descended from my own lost land;
or seethed to glimpse among the trivial swerves,
a kindred gesture in the dancer's head;
but most in music sought the adagio slur
of my hard accent in the orchestral chord
of Schönberg, or Skryabin iridescent;
or once, numbing the keys beneath my hand
cried brother in my heart to Beethoven dead.

Into this poem suddenly enter "the Unemployed," who cry to the poet from the "defeated barricades of the ribs," "Name us. We are starving." And the poet responds:

O comrades, speak to me; here are my naked
brains for you in my double hands; your own
eyes tore my bandages of festered calm
scorching off, while wild into
the textile of my dream, were thrust
your bony hands like bayonets.

The poet then names "our brother shut from the dark mill,/from the picket line broken with slugs," and the hard accent sought in Schönberg sounds with revolutionary affirmation:

O all our hands together, let us lift
our miseries to burn in the red banner,
whose scythe is toward the rotting limousines
not distant, but disastrous,—fell, not fallow;
whose hammer shall reprieve our famished arms
for the new time, for concrete swift foundations,
where, pierced with steel, afloat with light, shall rise
our homes unshadowed but of cranes that swing in the free air.

In the poem's final section, a jobless father, the "famine-blown" bellies of his five children in his mind, "leans his side upon the vacant air" at the edge of the tenement roof, and Maddow concludes:

Look, comrade: it is summer in the Square;
attentive now the shifting feet;
harangues flame in the sunlight; now
the shoes like stones stamp Internationale

to grind the streets into the single lens
of revolution, and converge their massing thunder
to the one pure bolt of proletarian red.[26]

The other poems, including memorials to Sacco and Vanzetti and to
Hart Crane, speak forth in a similar revolutionary vein.

Into his alienation, anger, and need, the far left brought Maddow
a cause, a way to fight. There he found focus and great personal stimulation. In another of his poems, "On Signing Up" (1936), the protag-
onist finds himself "among a double thousand subway eyes/twitching
at anxious headlines," but because he has "the red card flaring warm
at last" in his pocket he is able, "as in the first of evening the early
meteor skids/clearly down birdless heaven," to celebrate "the freshness, the first joy, the manhood of rebellion." The far left also furnished
him, as it did so many others, a substitute family—in Maddow's case,
Nykino. To someone like himself—from a broken family and of the
second generation, with no ties to the old country and some sense of
not quite yet being at home in America—the attraction of people who
worked together and shared resources in a common cause was immense.[27]

Maddow's poems have a common pattern, moving in a rather simple
dialectic from depressing moments (sometimes juxtaposed to scenes
from the lives of the rich) to points of strong affirmation. In "Images
of Poverty" (1935), the subway stops while a suicide is removed from
the tracks, and the poet asks whether all of those in the car "who
remember the distrust of affection, the morning when we were laid
off, the broken cup of gin, or the feverish child in the darkness
. . ." should join the victim. He answers, no—and "Anew! Ugly, shaking
with dialectic, the train plunges our metal force."

In 1974, rereading this poetry for the first time in forty years, Maddow felt "that it all seems to have been written by someone else,
though possibly someone intimately related," and that the poems
"suffer from the seductions of political rhetoric" but "do have the
quality of being struck off while the iron was white hot." In his opinion,
the poems and films he worked on during the thirties exhibited a
common pattern and were in the last analysis intended for an audience
of people like the artists themselves: "Depression intellectuals who had
gone to college in the late twenties and thirties, had been through the
mill, had been unemployed, had had various kinds of jobs and so on."

ALEXANDER: Then in making these films, in writing your
poems, what were you as a Depression intellectual trying to do
for yourself, or to yourself?

MADDOW: Number one, there was a tremendous amount of morbidity and inner depression from your experiences. Because you didn't know quite where you were going when you got out of college. There were no jobs, and it was very tough on you spiritually. And this emotion of sadness, of loneliness outside society, just built up a residue which, I guess, was inexhaustible finally. And I think that a lot of the morbidity that you felt is partly expressed in these poems [and films]. Now, since you were half-conscious of this, this last half stanza [or sequence] that I'm talking about, was supposed to take the curse off of us. You didn't want something that was utterly depressing, because then you might recognize it yourself.[r28]

Whether or not Maddow is fairly representing his fellow filmmakers, apparently this is the pattern of personal experience he brought with him to Nykino, and his was to be the strong hand in the commentary of nearly every film they were to make.

Film Theory and the Softening of the Hard Line

Among the Nykino group in 1935 there persisted a strong sense of the "present low level of the revolutionary film" and of the formlessness and poor quality of the Film and Photo League newsreels with the exception of "isolated examples" of achievement.[29] There was also a "feeling [that] something was missing." In an important article in the September 1935 *New Theatre*,[30] Hurwitz and Steiner traced the influences that until the winter of 1934/1935 had "warped our basic attitude toward the film medium." The most important and representative of these influences was the experience of the 1920s:

It was a period in which much was learned and explored about the technical resources of cinematography and montage, but the whole emphasis was on the beauty, the shock, the effectiveness of OBJECTS, THINGS—with no analysis of the effect on an audience. . . . The audience got next to nothing out of it. . . . The film had been depersonalised, inhuman; the THING, technique

---

[r] According to Maddow, a problem with Isador Schneider's poetry was that "Schneider has never had . . . to cauterize the infection of defeatism,—and run the risk of amputating his powers" ("Comrade and Master," *Dynamo*, May-June 1935, p. 30). Poetry, he said in the same review, should hold to an external class standard and admit "the actuality of the workers' life and struggle; the real, ugly, and exciting world; the biting necessity of revolution; [and] metaphors which are contemporary, true, and dialectic."

and formal problems were supreme. Even people were considered externally, as objects rather than as human beings.

Such experience, they now wrote, had made them all too ready to misunderstand Pudovkin's seminal *On Film Technique*. What Pudovkin intended as a study of techniques they took for a study of principles, which led them, as they moved to social-political documentary film in the 1930s, to concentrate on shot construction and especially on editing and montage.

> In brief this was our approach: you were going to do a film about the Scottsboro case, or New York Harbor. You knew what the film was going to say. Then you took your camera and attempted to capture [as] completely as you could the most meaningful visual aspects of reality. Then, to the cutting room, where you pieced the film together in a brilliant and cogent montage to make it a moving document of life. Only somehow it was never really moving.

In an attempt to discover what was "missing" in their films, Hurwitz and Steiner had enrolled in Lee Strasberg's course in theater direction at the Theatre Collective school during the early months of 1935. There was no Eisenstein film school in America, but it was their feeling that perhaps working with a stimulating teacher in a related area would be equally as useful.

Over Steiner's protestations, Strasberg had assigned them to write a director's script for *Romeo and Juliet*,[s] a script to be based on their reading of *Shakespeare's England* and another similar text. In so doing, they were to arrive at a method of determining "the basic idea of the script" by understanding what "effected and conditioned its contents." By extension, the two filmmakers now told their *New Theatre* readers, they had "learned that the film as a dramatic medium cannot merely concern itself with external happenings even though they be revolutionary happenings, but must embody the conflict of underlying forces, causes."[31] They had also learned that knowledge of the basic idea alone was insufficient if the audience was not *emotionally involved*, and if one can judge by repeated reference within the article, this was the crucial lesson. Emotional involvement would be created through *dramatic structure* ("suspense, build, dramatic line, etc.") and through a degree of human understanding, complexity, and realism that made

---

[s] Steiner remembers protesting: " 'Oh, Lee for God's sake not that soupy love story'; and [Strasberg's] very rabbinical, you know, wheels within wheels, and he said, 'so, how do you know it's just a love story?' " Interview with author, 19 Aug. 1973.

identification possible. It was essential to know, Hurwitz and Steiner told their fellow filmmakers in conclusion, that

> the making of a film involves not merely: (1) knowing what you want to say, (2) a scenario, and (3) shooting and cutting it, but the intermediate steps of theatricalizing the events through the invention of circumstances and activities which transform concepts, relationships and feelings into three dimensional happenings that are plausible, effective and rich in significance. Only in solving problems does it seem likely that a film conduit can be constructed which can carry our revolutionary viewpoint to an increasingly receptive audience, one that is really moved because in the life on the screen it finds its own aspirations and struggles, its own failures and successes, its own truths.

It should be noted that these words were remarkably similar to those of Strand when he was working on *The Wave* in Mexico.

These lessons were reinforced by a number of other developments in 1935. Early in the year, the Soviet cinema celebrated its fifteenth year of existence. This anniversary, together with a special Russian issue for the January *New Theatre* assembled in Moscow by Jay Leyda, the appearance of Sergei Vasiliev's and Georgy Vasiliev's *Chapayev* and Grigori Kozintsev's and Leonid Trauberg's *The Youth of Maxim*, and a two-day retrospective of Soviet films at the Fifth Avenue Theatre on the first and second of March brought Soviet cinema into unusual prominence. Influenced by Eisenstein's hopeful summary in *New Theatre*, critical comment focused on the developments of the past seven years. In his article, Eisenstein explained that after the initial period of organizational shaping and early production, a second, or "formalist" (to him "poetic") period of filmmaking, when "skill of presentation" and "cinematic expressiveness" had very high priority, had taken place in the twenties in the Soviet Union. This had evolved at the turn of the decade into a relatively narrow period of naturalism and then into socialist realism (what he called, with some antagonistic intention, the "prosaic," or third period). The evolution was due partly to sound but more to popular criticism and official Soviet policy. Now, with *Chapayev*, Eisenstein thought Soviet cinema had entered a fourth period, which would synthesize the best of the poetic and the prosaic periods.[32]

It was in the third period that the Soviet's official "disciplining" of Eisenstein began, as well as the frequent, niggling accusations of "formalism" and "intellectualism" that tormented and hindered the more adventuresome artists, including Pudovkin, Vertov, and Dovzhenko.[33]

If they were aware of such developments,[t] Lerner and the other critics on the left paid no attention. What engaged them was the fact that, in order to reach a wider audience, Soviet film had moved beyond formalism and a merely external naturalism to an exploration of individual psychology, a representation of rounded character.[34] *Chapayev* was hailed on all sides as a peak example of this, and it reinforced the Nykino incentive to move in such a direction. For Nykino, as for most American viewers, the cinematic expressiveness of the early Soviet period remained more exciting and seminal than did the more recent Soviet films, and they must have been encouraged by Eisenstein's wishful statement about a period of synthesis.

Nykino was not alone in its search for a more appealing style and a greater depth and broader range of content. Herbert Kline, the author of the one-act play "John Henry—Bad Nigger" (1934) and editor of *New Theatre* since July 1934, had for some time been criticizing sloganism and shoddy technique and urging the left theater to win over more competent artists and draw more fully upon major traditional works. Both he and Ben Blake, a founding member of the Workers Laboratory Theatre (by then the Theatre of Action, with which Nykino was affiliated),[u] favorably remarked in 1935 on the progress from the one-time useful agitational skits to realistic drama. *New Theatre* reported in June that, after reaching a high point of agit-prop[v] with Clifford Odets's *Waiting for Lefty* (January 1935), the Theatre of Action was "deepening its artistic work, concretizing its mass audience, and raising its standard to professional levels." In retrospect, John Howard Lawson saw a substantial shift between two nearly exactly contemporary plays:

> *Waiting for Lefty* was brought to us on a wave of spontaneous strikes and exposure of class-collaboration policies in the labor movement. Its romanticism, its acceptance of conversion as a final solution, its technique of direct audience participation, reflected a mood which was valid at the time. *Black Pit* represented a valid

[t] Leyda corresponded about this with friends in the States.

[u] Nykino auditioned actors from the Theatre of Action, but they were never used. Hurwitz interview 2.

[v] "Agit-prop, from 'agitation' and 'propaganda,' was as basic a form of theatre as can be imagined—not necessarily crude, for it could be done with great skill . . . but elementary. It could if necessary dispense with scenery and costumes and even a stage. Above all, it dispensed with the complexities of human character, being peopled by easily recognizable symbols. . . . The purpose of agit-prop was to make certain direct points and to make them as forcefully as possible." Jay Williams, *Stage Left* (New York: Charles Scribner's Sons, 1974), p. 36.

reaction against this mood, a recognition of the complexity of the forces which encircle the individual and make his choice difficult.[35]

Here was a result of the gradual ending of the Communist Party's hard-line era and the official opening of a soft-line era that had already gradually begun—the era of the popular front. The change is obvious in the difference between the Party's call for an American Writers' Congress in January of 1935 and its call for an American Artists' Congress in October of the same year. The former call was to "all writers . . . who have clearly indicated their sympathy to the revolutionary cause; who do not need to be convinced of the decay of capitalism, of the inevitability of revolution." The latter invited "those artists, who . . . realize the necessity of collective discussion and planning, with the objective of the preservation and development of our cultural heritage," who feel that "we must ally ourselves with all groups engaged in the common struggle against war and fascism." Nykino, which had been working in early and mid-1935 on "revolutionary films," was giving its time "to the production of progressive social films" in 1936.[36]

At the 1935 Writers' Congress, Malcolm Cowley argued that one stood to gain a large working-class audience by moving left, but he was mistaken. The Roosevelt administration had succeeded in allaying many of the fears engendered by the Depression. It had also competed with considerable success for the potential constituency of the radical left. To gain that constituency, in fact, and to make inroads into what there was of the susceptible bourgeoisie, the Party saw that the left writer needed to move to the right, adopting the terms and appealing to the particular experiences and traditions of his or her neighbors. From 1934 onwards, left-wing critics of the New Deal, and only gradually the far left critics, began to realize "that any radical movement would have to speak a reformist and pragmatic language," the language of the New Deal administration, in fact, if to different ends, "if it wished to be understood by the average citizen."[37]

One impetus toward the Communist Party in the early thirties had been the need of intellectuals and artists of the 1920s to overcome their political isolation and find an effective organization where their commitment would bear fruit. As the Party's hard line grew noticeably ineffective, and as anti-Communist bias increased, the same need directed them to seek ideas and methods that would be more consonant with the prevailing American outlook. Like playwrights and actors, filmmakers on the left were subjected to censorship and exclusion, and their sense of relative political isolation increased when Soviet films distributed in America came under hysterical attack in late 1934 and 1935 by the *Motion Picture Herald* and the Hearst press. Holly-wood, polite but antagonistic toward the Soviet film delegation headed by Boris Shumyatsky in the summer of 1935,[38] began producing that year a series of clearly anti-Communist films.[w] These and the Hearst *Metrotone News* generated serious and sometimes successful protests from the left, often on a popular-front basis. They also added to the impetus of left filmmakers to find ways, without essential compromise of their political positions, to win a larger American audience.

Another reason for turning to the politics of a popular front was the frightening growth of international fascism. Since Hitler's rise to power and the death of the German Communist Party in 1933, the Soviet Union had moderated its hostility toward the West. In 1934, it joined the League of Nations, and in the summer of 1935 the Communist International called for a popular front to combat fascism everywhere. In the United States this call helped to bring liberals and radicals together in various cultural and noncultural leagues in a "struggle against war and fascism." The Communist Party maintained a great deal of control in these leagues, but to do so moderated its expectations of a radical proletarian revolution. The need for such leagues was deeply felt on all sides, for there were Fascist stirrings in the United States, and by the mid-thirties war appeared to be very close. Hitler rejected the Treaty of Versailles in 1935 and was swiftly building his army, all the more frightening to Americans who were repelled by the atrocity stories that were coming out of Germany. The military faction in Japan was consolidating its power and continuing its aggression in China, a fact *The March of Time* accented—as it accented Nazi Germany—in its early issues of 1935. And the year 1936 was to bring the invasion of Ethiopia and the Fascist uprising in Spain.

The threat of war, Fascist dictatorships in Germany and Italy and near chaos in France and Spain, the gradually growing recognition, even before the Moscow Trials, of Stalinist repression in Russia, and the unifying effects of Roosevelt's New Deal rhetoric were beginning to make Americans look more assiduously at the virtues and traditions of their own country. William Stott has pointed out how, beginning in 1935, the "news about America" by traveling documentary reporters moved from a radical outlook that pushed drastic, Soviet-inspired change to a more conservative, New Deal tack. Still vitally interested in social change, these writers now emphasized what they found "constant and valid in American experience."[39] Artists who were further

---

[w] These included *Red Salute, Fighting Youth, Riff-Raff, Frisco Kid, Stranded,* and *Oil for the Lamps of China.*

left and more severely critical of American institutions and New Deal policies were similarly influenced by this impulse.

Pare Lorentz

It was in terms of its members' attitudes toward America that some dissidence was to be felt within Nykino, and especially between Nykino and a new figure, who, late in the summer of 1935, arrived on the filmmaking scene and entered the lives of three Nykino filmmakers. Pare Lorentz was born in 1905 into a West Virginia family that went back to the late eighteenth century there, and before that, to the Penn colony in Pennsylvania. Lorentz was deeply conscious of his background. In a letter to Richard Dyer MacCann in 1950, he recalled that

> my people settled northwestern Virginia before the Revolution. There used to be an old man named Roach who was superintendent of a lumber company and he used to come down on the B & O spur line on Saturdays and go in the barber shop and sit around and talk and I remember vividly his saying, "They are going to dig it and cut it and gut it and the whole goddamn thing will fall down some day." He added the fact that nobody cared enough to save some timber on the ridges or to stop polluting the river with chemicals. My father was that kind of man—fought endless battles trying to keep the bass from being killed off. I grew up among such people.[40]

It was precisely because of having grown up among such people that he found his first job as editor of a General Electric publication, the *Edison Mazda Lamp Sales Builder*, both very instructional and very troubling. Six years later, in 1931, he angrily portrayed the experience in an article he wrote for *Scribner's* entitled "A Young Man Goes to Work." If he and his contemporaries at General Electric "had any spiritual tradition," Lorentz wrote, "it was one of individual freedom."

> The old fathers, the pioneers, the forty-niners and then—the latest folk heroes—the Edisons, Garys, Hills: these legendary heroes were to us as American as pumpkin pie. They had with their own hands built something. While we had not swallowed these myths whole, nevertheless they had been so much with us it was an integral part of our ambitions.

Corporations now claimed that these myths resided in *them*, that it was through *them* that opportunities for creative endeavor and heroic struggle were available to young men, that it was they who therefore stood for the beneficial growth of the country. Accordingly, Lorentz and his new friends, with their "various varsity sweaters, honor society pins, and innumerable stories of our own capacity for liquor and last-minute touchdowns," were able to think of themselves as "two-gun men pushing back the frontiers of the world," and they serenely wrote "advertisements telling the public how our company was pioneering for humanity."

But when the tight discipline, the penalties for disagreement, and the plethora of company taboos dawned on him, Lorentz learned that "America is no longer the land of opportunity for a young man of honor and decency." Those who stayed on had in six years become over-whelmed with shame and confusion, victims of "intrigue, bootlicking, 'good-fellowship,' all the mores of clerkship, [and] mean advance-ment," in one of those entities that had "in one decade physically exhausted and financially overpowered the country." In the face of this, a young man who wished to "conduct his life . . . in the ways of the old freeman" would need unusual quantities of courage, agility, and toughness.[41]

This was deeply disillusioned writing indeed,[x] yet it also represented a stand, a warning, and an attack. When Lorentz left General Electric in 1927, one of his first acts was a fictionalized exposé of the subtle exploitations by utility companies who were buying out the old mu-nicipal power facilities and moving offices into communities throughout the country. This piece brought about a meeting between him and Morris Ernst, then a young lawyer with similar attitudes. Together in 1929 and 1930, they wrote *Censored: The Private Life of the Movies*, a caustic assault upon the state censorship boards, the Hays office, the National Board of Review, and the cowardly movie industry. The most dangerous trend they saw in 1930 was the growth of the powerful, opinion-dictating, myth-controlling corporation:

> When two hundred men direct corporations controlling a hundred papers, or ten million radios, or 40% of the world's movies—and with the sole thought of making their companies show a profit—you can wonder how far the modern leader has run from Horace Greeley, Tom Paine, or Jefferson.[42]

Lorentz is a familiar American type. Most of us grow up with a ritual schooling in the greatness of American history, American leaders, and

---

[x] As one statement in the article implies, the literature of the 1920s had some influence upon this disillusionment. A short story Lorentz wrote in 1934 exhibits a substantial Hemingway approach. See Lorentz, "Reunion," *Story*, Sept. 1934, pp. 19-23.

American dedication to the noble values of freedom, equality, and justice, and in many of our communities there are few to tell us while we are young how deeply contrary to the ideal the reality often runs. While many persist all their lives in believing the myths of the school books, and while others know better and simply take their own personal advantage of the realities, still others like Lorentz suddenly find themselves without blinders, surrounded by the jungle of racism, governmental and institutional corruption, consumer exploitation, military adventurism, and injustice that lies so closely behind the facade of our slogans about freedom and democracy. The resulting confusion and disappointment can either be devastating, incurring a lasting bitterness and cynicism, or, as with Lorentz, the anger may unite with both a pride in the high values many Americans nonetheless actively hold and a resolve to fight for those values. There is usually an edge in the work of these latter people, a tension between their own American pride and their troubling, sometimes overwhelming awareness of the victimization so many Americans so painfully undergo.

From 1927 through the early forties, Lorentz wrote film criticism regularly for such periodicals as *Judge*, *The New York Evening Journal*, *Vanity Fair*, *Town and Country*, *McCall's*, and in 1934 he wrote a political column, "Washington Sideshow," for William Randolph Hearst's national news syndicate, King Features. He also contributed fiction and nonfiction to publications such as *Story* and *Newsweek* and, quick to recognize in the progressive administration an affinity in class background and values, published *The Roosevelt Year*, a collection of photographs with text, in 1933. Lorentz could be pompous, scornful, and nasty, and he was not always interesting, but Sam Brody thought that he was "the only American movie critic writing for a bourgeois sheet [*Judge*] and reckless enough to write as he thinks at the same time." Consistently, he lauded anything that rendered contemporary actuality and faced up to tough contemporary facts, believing that if you showed people what was *there*, they would have both the opportunity and the propensity to decide whether it should remain. Maintaining "a strong love for the land and the people of America," as Arch Mercey later put it, he was antagonistic toward film sets, urging on-location shooting in different regions of the country, particularly the neglected farm and town areas.[43]

Lorentz's strong faith in the power of the medium led him to hold the usual industry product in low esteem and to continue his reaction against the corporation's standardization of America and its corporate repression of individual and local character and autonomy. In much the same way that General Electric diminished the lives and spirits of its employees, for instance, he found that Hollywood ruined talented actors, actresses, and directors with standard, cheap, and unimaginative roles and scripts. He encouraged independent filmmaking and attacked the film corporations for roadblocking nonindustry productions. And he was constantly on the watch for people in or out of the industry who showed real courage, who demonstrated the wish to conduct their lives, as he perceived it, "in the ways of the old freeman," who took risks, whose products were perhaps roughhewn rather than polished, but were "brisk" or "lusty" (a favorite word of praise), full of the high spirit and character he admired. Roland Brown, for example, "ignorant of many movie-making fundamentals" and therefore denied frequent production by Hollywood, had "a terrific dramatic power and a hair-brained technique that is original and exciting. . . . He's the Erskine Caldwell of the movies: he has the same gusto and shocking humor. . . . He's by far the most interesting director on the coast right now."[44]

Lorentz traveled the western drought area in 1931 and wrote that although even Thomas Paine "must have realized that his dream of a 'decent' nation was short-lived, that sooner or later the valleys would be gutted and the hills trimmed," it was still "appalling to see how the machinery of business has in one decade physically exhausted and financially overpowered the country." In 1934, he proposed a Dust Bowl film to Hollywood and, angry as he was, could not have been totally surprised by their cold shoulder. He stopped over in Des Moines to share his rage with James D. LeCron, a distant relative and assistant to Secretary of Agriculture Wallace, and then late in the year promised LeCron an outline of his "New Deal motion picture idea." On 30 April 1935, the New Deal's Resettlement Administration was established, its members aware from the start of the need for innovative public relations to convince a wary, sometimes hostile voting public of the necessity of its programs. Departing from conventional government practices, it produced radio transcription programs to dramatize the problems it was fighting, and it created its famous photography service under Roy Stryker to show "what America looks like." In June, Lorentz was called to Washington to talk with Wallace and then with Rexford Tugwell and John Franklin Carter of the RA, and he was forthwith named motion picture consultant to the RA information staff.[45]

In this capacity, he quickly transformed Tugwell's idea for a series of eighteen films into a plan for one film that would be worthy of commercial distribution. The Tennessee Valley Authority was suggested as a subject, but Lorentz opted for his Dust Bowl film, deciding to direct and produce it himself. With congressional approval in mind, the RA intended to keep film production cheap, so Lorentz had to make low-budget decisions: no professional actors, all footage to be taken on location, and so on. Convinced, however, that only good artists create vital films, he determined to hire "the best men available for the various technical positions on the crew."[46]

Lorentz and Nykino: On Location for *The Plow That Broke the Plains*

In March of 1931, at a Copland-Sessions concert, Lorentz had seen and liked Ralph Steiner's first three experimental films, *H₂O*, *Mechanical Principles*, and *Surf and Seaweed*, which he saw accompanied by music that had been composed for the films by Colin McPhee and Marc Blitzstein. More recently he had viewed and praised *Pie in the Sky*, and he knew the still work of Paul Strand. Soon Steiner, Strand, and Hurwitz were hired for the location camerawork at a new government salary of twenty-five dollars a day (plus travel expenses) that Lorentz wrangled for them. Past government films had been of low quality, but when these three were engaged, according to Irving Lerner, hopes ran high:

> It was impossible to maintain an air of detachment toward the venture any longer. Here was an opportunity for a group of talented young filmmakers to produce a film of social significance which would have government backing, and receive commercial distribution, something no film art group had ever attained before.[47]

In September, the three left for Montana to catch grass footage before the fall.

Lorentz had no sympathy with what he variously called "the radical school of critics" and "the Communist, or camp-meeting critical school." One March evening in 1935 he toured the Cameo, the Acme, and the Rand School theaters, finding only the relatively nonpolitical *Pie in the Sky* worthy of praise as "an irreligious but very funny picture, with some excellent pantomime." Reporting on the evening to his *Town and Country* readers, he announced that the Communists had brought uptown with them "one authentic Russian note. . . : the smell." He never specifically mentioned the Film and Photo League or Nykino, but his few vague references to far-left filmmaking are derogatory, accusing it of dogmatism and moralizing.[y] All of which makes it curious that he should turn to these particular men for his crew on *The Plow That Broke the Plains*. Steiner had already made a short government film, *Hands*, and from this Lorentz may have picked up the idea that the three were enthusiastic about the New Deal. He might also have felt that the three would be working in a purely technical capacity, and even amidst all of his bitter backward glances a year later, he could still praise Steiner and Strand as men "who had spent their whole lives trying to find out what a picture can do, and who perhaps are the finest and most sensitive technicians in the field."[48]

By all accounts, Lorentz was not an easy person to get along with. Richard Dyer MacCann describes him as "an artist, with a variable temperament and a keen desire to watch over every detail of production himself." J. P. McEvoy thought him a "study in controlled violence" and a "charming non-listener" attached to his own points of view. Ralph Steiner, both then and now highly sympathetic to the man's flair and creativity, recalls him as "neurotic" (the word is used vaguely): "He's got enemies, and people are always trying to cut him down."[49] The potential for conflict was high.

Upon Lorentz's request, the Nykino trio drew up an outline.[z] According to Irving Lerner, the outline was "forthright . . . its implications inescapable." It "embodied a concept of epic implications: capitalism's anarchic rape of the land, and—by extension—the impoverishment of all the natural resources of America: mines, forests, men." Lerner quoted from the outline:

> Great herds are driven in on the range. Countless heads of cattle feed on the sea of grass. Steers grow fat. The cattlemen grow rich. The range is free. More ranchers drive in their herds. The herds increase. Scramble for water rights and control of range, and speculation in cattle. More stock men! Each after what he can get—no responsibility to safeguard the great resource—*the grass*.

Because such emphasis seemed compatible both with the facts and with the way Lorentz and Tugwell, at least, often saw things, the outline met the initial approval of Tugwell, John Franklin Carter, and

---

[y] Lorentz was often short on interest in the social issues that racked other Americans: a later review shows him having only the vaguest knowledge of the Sacco-Vanzetti case, and a review of Hollywood's Spanish Civil War film, *Blockade*, finds him unable to determine which side is which. He was not alone in that difficulty, but it was not a difficulty for anyone with reasonable concern about that war. See Lorentz, *McCalls*, Feb. 1937, p. 93, and Sept. 1937, p. 12.

[z] According to Hurwitz, he first told them they would write the script as well and that Hurwitz would edit the film. Interview with author, 21 Nov. 1974.

Lorentz. Lorentz then wrote a shooting script, which he either delivered personally (Strand's account) or by courier (Hurwitz's) to the train that was to carry the three west.[50]

With "mounting astonishment," Strand says, they read the script in the car to Buffalo. "Wild and private," it was replete, Hurwitz remembers, with "elements of fantasy that didn't fit the rest." Interspersed with a mingling of poetic, musical, and some cinematic terminology, it provided them with no sure sense of what or how to shoot, no sense of a considered whole to which any shot should relate. Written by a man they hardly knew, who had never before worked on a film, the script, so far as they could see, was technically useless. They also began to sniff out compromises from *their* point of view. Left-wing members of a popular-front effort, they felt it their duty to hew the artistic product as closely as possible to the anticapitalist line. In one instance at least they found their outline's biting criticism remanded to poetic indirection, to fantasy:

> Lorentz had one scene in which a lot of men in top hats would walk across a field, get on tractors, and plow up the field. The idea was clear enough—that the rich who profited by grain deals were the ones who were destroying the land—but there was no way that we could see to make the scene work with the rest of the material.

From Buffalo they dashed off a telegram declaring that they couldn't understand the script, couldn't shoot from it, and needed another.[51]

No script visible in Montana, they went out to a ranch for the grass and cattle footage that so magnificently opens the completed film. They caught a dust storm too, then either ran out of stock (Steiner's account) or out of material to shoot (Hurwitz's). Still no script, they wrote "*forceful* letters" to Lorentz, which Hurwitz believes they all signed. They began to see, too, as Strand wrote to Stieglitz, that

> the chances of messiness are excellent—but we knew that when we started. The man we are working under is an imbecile.[aa] But we took the work to get enough cash to do other things, which *we* can control. At the same time make [*sic*] an effort to make a film as well as the "boss" permits.

In Sheridan, Wyoming, with time on their hands, they sunned themselves in an empty baseball and rodeo park and began to work up their own script. Steiner, by now anxiously marking out some dusty space

---

[aa] This notion of Lorentz as a "crazy man" was, according to Strand, a combination of Steiner's representation of him and their reaction to the script. Strand interview.

between himself and the others, had little to do with the collaboration. He straggled off to take target practice with a twenty-two rifle on some old tin cans, an act, Hurwitz recalls, not unlike his sudden retirements to a dart game in the corner of his studio in previous years.[52]

Working from their original outline, Hurwitz and Strand labored with intense excitement. Here they were on the crew of a substantially backed film that was to have wide distribution. Here was a chance to "put into practice the ideas [they] had been germinating" in Nykino, ideas about "dramatic structuring of a documentary film" "where you don't have a person within a plot to identify with," ideas about the problem of evoking "needs, a sense of empathy, a process of growth of feeling without these devices. Opposition, conflict and contradiction" were utilized "to create the equivalent of plot . . . rather than simple exposition, or declaratory statement." Those plump livestock would be contrasted with "cattle now starved by the lack of grass and made thirsty by the lack of water, their bones sticking out of their thin-skinned hides," creating in the viewer a strong need to have the former replace the latter. Once such a need was evoked, their dialectical theory went, "then, one could look at the structure of a film, and design it—with image and word and sound—as a chain of interactive needs progressing toward a resolution."[53] In a hotel in Alliance, Nebraska, Hurwitz formalized their design on a rented typewriter.

They must have hoped that the inexperienced Pare Lorentz would look up to their greater know-how and go along with it. But this was not to be. Somebody told Calvin Tomkins that there was "no direct clash of wills" when the crew joined Lorentz in Dalhart, Texas. But Steiner remembers that "Pare just out and threw [the script] away or tore it up, and he was absolutely furious, insanely furious at them." In Strand's words, he was "fit to be tied."[bb]

Lorentz learned from their script, he complained in 1939 to interviewer W. L. White, that "they wanted it to be all about human greed, and how lousy our social system was." He "couldn't see what this had to do with dust storms."[cc] In response, Hurwitz and Strand at first continued their refusal to work from his script, insisting "that he was

[bb] If Lorentz's constant angry brooding on these events in his talks with Willard Van Dyke over a year later and his slanted characterizations of his Nykino staff are any indication, he was indeed furious. Needless to say, the letters he had received prior to his arrival must have built up a good head of steam.

[cc] The reader may wonder why Lorentz took this position after his own indictments of corporate exploitation. For one thing, everything in his background made him hostile to the revolutionary position, and he was wholeheartedly behind the New Deal. He, Tugwell, and Carter also knew, of course, that a film directly indicting not the whole social system but simply local western greed and money would cook up for the RA the kinds of trouble it didn't need.

lightly skimming over the basic causes of dust storms to dramatize their immediate effects." Lorentz then gave them the choice of a paid trip home or of recognizing their subordinate position on the project. If they decided against the next Golden State Limited, as Lorentz later told it,

> they were to report in the dining room at six-thirty in the morning, ready to work. When Pare came down to breakfast they were already there, and as he entered they sang, "Good Morning, Dear Teacher" in unison. Pare thought they had been sincere when they said they couldn't shoot his scenario; that Strand had formed a really vast and great philosophy of life, [and] sincerely believed in it. Would rather quit than capitulate. From that time on Pare was bitter.[54]

They were all bitter; they had all (except perhaps Steiner) been challenged in their basic artistic, political, and even philosophical faiths and in their diverse needs to have charge over this key film.

At breakfast the three agreed to go on with the filming, explaining that they did not want to disrupt the entire project, but they announced that they would not acknowledge any responsibility for the conception of the film. They also suggested that they would refuse screen credits for the camerawork. As Hurwitz tells it, he and Strand still would not follow Lorentz's script, and they certainly would not film the fantasy sequences. From the other side of the story, Lorentz decidedly wanted nothing to do with Hurwitz and Strand. Since Steiner was less involved in the revolt and quite agreeable to working with the script, Lorentz rented Hurwitz and Strand a big truck and sent them off to film dust storms and their effects. He and Steiner teamed up, filming, Hurwitz remembers, even the top hat sequence, which mercifully did not break its way into the final print.[55] The dust storm filming completed, Lorentz dropped his crew and left for California to purchase some stock footage and to film his final sequence with the help of Paul Ivano (as cameraman) and Dorothea Lange out at migrant Camp Shafter on U.S. Highway 99.

Assisted by Leo Zockling, Lorentz did the primary, rough cutting in New York and found a composer, Virgil Thomson, who was willing to work closely with him. Lorentz himself had a strong background in music and had argued frequently for the intelligent integration of music with other film elements. He and Thomson held long planning sessions, working out the appropriate music and determining the final score, which Thomson developed in accordance with the rough cut and which Alexander Smallens recorded with about twenty members of the New York Philharmonic. Then, finding his vital inspiration in the music, Lorentz reedited the film to reflect the directions and nuances of the sound track. In the meantime he had written the narration himself and hired Thomas Chalmers, who shared, according to W. L. White, Lorentz's "detestation of professional narrators," to speak it in his "unforgettably mellow American voice."

The film completed, Lorentz asked Hurwitz, Steiner, and Strand if they wanted credits. "They didn't know, held meetings, finally asked to see it. Decided yes." Highly surprised to see how brilliantly it had been put together, they were quite willing to take credit for the camerawork,[56] though Hurwitz and Strand were still disdainful of the point of view. Lorentz recorded his own prejudices by arranging the camera credits in nonalphabetical order—Steiner, Ivano, Strand, and Hurwitz.

Private showings in the White House, in Hollywood, and in New York in early March 1936, and a 10 May Washington, D.C. official premiere, plus an enthusiastic United Press review by Fred Othman and then some dogged work to break Hollywood and theater opposition to general distribution led to a substantial audience for the film. Lorentz felt that, as a result, The Plow That Broke the Plains, along with the Lange photographs and the Steinbeck novels, play, and motion picture, had "done more for these tragic nomads than all the politicians in the country," leading, at least, to "transient camps, and better working conditions, and a permanent agency seeking to help the migratory workers."[57]

The Plow That Broke the Plains

The twenty-five minute "documentary musical picture," as Lorentz named it, sketches in ten dramatic sequences the history of the Great Plains. Following a prologue in titles, a map slowly outlines the total area in such a way as to make us concentrate on its vastness. The succeeding sequences portray the cattle-grazing era, the coming of the settler, the first drought, the new financial and patriotic incentives to plow and harvest during World War I, the golden harvests of the twenties and the increasing land speculation, the thirties droughts that coincided with the Great Depression, a dust storm, efforts to dig out and departures westward, and the California camps for the jobless refugees from the plains. An epilogue (shot by Hurwitz and Strand in Nebraska) told of the RA's work in relocating 4,500 families on new small farms in ten states. The latter was soon dropped, possibly for artistic reasons, but more likely because it became dated, and perhaps because critics on the left were quick to point out how little the government was actually doing at a time when 50,000 families each month were being forced off the plains.[58]

The cattle sequence opens with three beautiful, static shots of the tall grass. A fourth shot pans slowly left to right across a wide stretch, a fifth continues the pan, and a sixth reverts to the beginning shot. Against this eloquent opening, the remainder of the film is measured. We remember the beauty of the grass as we look upon the dust and the cracked, barren soil. The negative content of later shots is underlined by the counterdirection of pans and internal movements to the movement of the initial pans. For instance, the first camera movement over the herds of cattle and the movements of the dust in the dust storm and the truck of the departing, blown-out, baked-out family are all from right to left. The structure of the opening sequence is also repeated, resulting in a sharp emphasis by contrast. A long pan left over unfertile, rippled dust is followed by two still shots of clusters of weeds. The final shots of the film parallel the opening shots: a long pan right over the growthless land, ending in the framing to the left of a lifeless tree, then two static shots of other such trees, a telling comment on the tragic distance the film has covered.

Such parallelism informs *The Plow That Broke the Plains* throughout, subtly, forcefully building a sense of repetition in the history of the Midwest. New destructive forces first enter the scene on a diagonal from upper right to lower left of the frame, while forces that have been outmoded or defeated tend to exit on the opposite diagonal, quite small in the upper left distance: the cattle, the tractors at the conclusion of the war sequence, the truck with the children sitting among the piled-up family belongings. Parallel shots of a train, tractors and plows, combines, and harvesters moving along a horizon in the extreme distance equate those machines with the constant depletion of the soil. The clear, moderately used narration adds to this effect by repetition of words, by a varied refrain, and by constant use of parallel structure.

The pace is well-varied, perhaps sometimes too obviously so. The relatively peaceful cattle sequences are replaced by a fast banjo tune and the covered wagon race from the border to the new lands; this in turn is followed immediately by a single drum beat and the isolated first post and first plow cutting into the new soil. A spirited harvesting sequence of eleven shots concludes with a fast-moving train trailing across the distant dark horizon; this is suddenly—on the other side of a fade—replaced by the stasis of a broken wheel against the ground, unused machinery, and the slow shadow of a man crossing the frame. The final frenzy of the golden harvest sequence is similarly followed by a static arrangement of animal bones bleaching on the parched soil. Thomson's music is indigenous and gay, even humorous, in the more positive sequences (the cattle, the first harvesting, the war) and somber and dissonant in those that are grim.

Lorentz has a fine knack for structuring visuals to make their own comments. The narration pauses a moment in the second sequence, and three still shots, each held a little longer than normal for emphasis, move from extreme distance to medium distance until about twenty head of cattle, their bodies no longer tiny, fill the frame: they have come to dominate the plains and the minds of its inhabitants. Three shots of the fence post being driven into the ground are followed by three shots of the plow digging into the soil, the repetition calling attention to itself and to the dire significance of the action. And here Lorentz creates a feeling of dissonance and conflict: the first plow movement, to the right, is countered in the second shot by a leftward movement, which is followed by a third plow going right. Later, directional conflict is no longer necessary, for sufficient conflict exists in the clouds of dust thrown up by the plows. To emphasize this, one shot holds eight seconds on a patch of dusty terrain after the plow passes from the frame.

One goal especially distinguishes *The Plow That Broke the Plains* from *The Wave* and from the films that Hurwitz, Steiner, and Strand would go on to make. The use of lenses constructed "to get the largest possible spread" and to capture "the ominous changes in the land itself" was an attempt to justify "a plea critics have made to Hollywood for a decade—namely, 'Take your cameras into the country and show us what it looks like.' " With Hollywood and major theater distribution in mind, Lorentz wanted his location to be dramatic, and his thoughts centered on an epic of the land. It was in these terms that he tried to sell the film to his *McCall's* readers. *The Plow That Broke the Plains* tells

> the story of the Plains and it tells it with some emotional value— an emotion that springs out of the soil itself. Our heroine is the grass, our villain the sun and the wind, our players the actual farmers living in the Plains country. It is a melodrama of nature— the tragedy of turning grass into dust, a melodrama that only Carl Sandburg or Willa Cather, perhaps, could tell as it should be told.[59]

Hurwitz, Steiner, and Strand, whose alternative script had associated the dust storms with a corrupt social system, were interested in other sources of emotion and in other villains.

Accordingly, Lerner wrote that *The Plow That Broke the Plains* "is a pale imitation of what it was intended to be," and Strand told Lorentz that "it was a pretty picture, but . . . the guts had been taken out of it." As MacCann has argued, the film is certainly a dramatization rather than propaganda for social change; evidently even some RA staff members felt that it did not sufficiently demonstrate the work of the RA or point the way toward further positive legislation.[60] Despite all of this, however, it *is* a tough and a disturbing film. It makes its point: one feels the waste, the irresponsibility, the failure in planning, and, even if in doubt, is likely at least to be drawn toward support of New Deal remedies. In addition, there *are* indictments of greed, although without the force and specificity wished by the Nykino crew. Handbills move forward to the steady rhythm of the mechanical press until they fill the screen: they are forced out toward the spectator, who reads,

Bargains in town lots!
The heart of the wheat land!!
Prices tripled in six months!!
Round-trip inspection
Trip at our expense—
Write *now* while these
Bargains are still available.
    GREAT PLAINS REALTY COMPANY.

The golden harvest sequence ends in an orgy of pouring grain and flying ticker tape and a broken ticker on the floor: the market domination of plains development leads to drought and the bust.

Of course, the film might have been tougher and more disturbing. There *were* starving cattle and cattle massacres, there were, as a Mrs. Duke of Dalhart wrote Lorentz, "people dying from dust pneumonia . . . and BLACK dusters." And Lorentz knew this. In fact he had described it in a way calculated to move his reader in an article for *Newsweek* in June 1934: "Destroying property at the estimated rate of $1,000,000 a day, drought burned a hole in the heart of the great Northwest's wheat and dairy lands and blackened the great plains until they resembled Belgium's war torn fields." He told of grim Norwegians "with cocked rifles guarding lonely Dakota water holes," "haggard farm-wives" carting water long distances, and "500,000 head of cattle moaning and staggering crazily . . . too weakened either to be sold or eaten, and deputy sheriffs shot them down."

But Mrs. Duke wrote him that he had excluded from his film "the worst things that happened out here." Lorentz attempted to explain this in his *McCall's* review:

You will not see the full horror of the dust storms in the picture, a horror that drove men to kill their cattle because they could not stand their ceaseless bellowing, the horror of children choking and dying of dust pneumonia. You will not see it because we had limited funds and a skeleton staff, but you will see enough of the Plains and the Great Drought to make it worth your while.[61]

Of course Lorentz could have acquired such footage if he wished. The truth is that a government film could not show, and he did not want to apprehend, that things had gone so bad.

Lorentz told Van Dyke that the first drought sequence, with "the little kid in the sand, the plow and the dust, the man looking at the sky, the woman sweeping the porch," was "the whole essence of the picture."[dd] But five years later, in a short essay on Dorothea Lange, he confessed that "I was more concerned about Texas and the end of the grasslands than I was about people, for many reasons which I do not wish to go into. I mean," he quickly added, "they were technical movie-making reasons." Recurrently praising Lange for being "more interested in people than in photography" and for "the terrible reality of her people," he hoped

some day the government, or a museum, or university, will publish four or five hundred of her pictures that are on file in Washington. It will be a frightening collection; a terrifying experience to turn from group after group of wretched human beings, starkly asking for so little, and wondering what they will get.[62]

It was Lange's photography that had inspired Lorentz to include a California sequence in his film and to borrow the photographer as a consultant from Stryker's division. This is the only sequence in the film in which his text takes on a similarity to his later description of Lange's work.

Blown out, baked out, and broke;
Nothing to stay for, nothing to hope for.
Homeless, penniless and bewildered, they joined
The great army of the highways.
No place to go, and no place to stop;
Nothing to eat, nothing to do.
Their homes on four wheels, their work a desperate
Gamble for a day's labor in the fields along the
Highways—the price of a sack of beans or a tank of gas.

[dd] See pp. 133-135. It is possible that Van Dyke heard this the way he wanted to because of his own desire to do more with the people in *The River*.

All they ask is a chance to start over
And a chance for their children to eat,
To have medical care, to have homes again.

Yet cameraman Ivano's images in the California sequence convey almost nothing of this. The nonactors are poorly chosen and awkwardly directed, the camera does not move in for many close-ups or medium close-ups, and the relatively static shots scarcely illustrate the text in any way. Even if the handling seems better in the earlier sequence, the child, the farmer, and the housewife are still *merely* illustrative: neither their personalities nor their personal situations are rendered. One senses that Lorentz does not recognize the poignant irony of the housewife's attempt, amidst all that dust and loss and isolation, to arrange her hair so as to appear attractive to a camera that barely acknowledges her.

Perhaps Lorentz simply was not ready to direct actors. Or perhaps his failure to capture the human element was due to his own personal limitation, to some frightened narrowness that was related to his quality of "charming non-listener" and "intense personal outlook." His own uncomfortable awareness of this insensitivity is implicit perhaps in the title of his later, never-to-be completed film *Ecce Homo!* and in his angry reaction to Paul Rotha, when Rotha, recognizing the lack of "human qualities" in Lorentz's films, recommended that with the money remaining in Lorentz's budget for his next film, *The River*, "he should take a sound crew and go and record some of the real people to find how they reacted to the problems of soil erosion and lack of flood control."[63]

A tougher indictment of greed, a grimmer portrayal of its effects, and a compassionate, spirited focus on people did not fit Lorentz's deep-seated resolution to define his own attitude toward America. Thus, while *The Plow That Broke the Plains* has its dark side, it is neither wholly condemnatory nor wholly tragic. And therein lies its peculiar tension and appeal. The end credits spread over a drawing, not of barren tree and soil, but of pioneers traveling left to right up a gentle slope. The voice of Chalmers, intoning "up from the Rio Grande . . . down clear from the eastern highways the cattle rolled into the old buffalo range" sounds enthusiastic, even exuberant, over the vastness of it all. Even where Lorentz is more ironic, more critical, one still hears in the voice some of his familiar awe of the American land and his apparently unshakeable respect for the resourcefulness of American settlers, inventors, and industrialists. For him, those plows may be breaking the plains, but they are also winning the war. The range music, the spirited folk music of the early harvesting shots, the popular World War I song all warm the heart. And in effect, they say "this is good, these are our people, from them came the songs and the traditions that belong to us." As James Shelley Hamilton astutely observed, the film is thoroughly patriotic.[64] It has a celebratory pride in America, a tone that is completely alien to any of the far-left films thus far made, and it is this perspective that tempers its severe criticism and lends a positive edge, a hint that Americans can and will marshal their talents to beat the drought and help those still-proud refugees get back on their feet.[ee] The edge cuts both ways, however, creating in the film a tension between Lorentz's American pride and his troubling awareness of what Americans have done to one another and to their land.

In his review of *Anthony Adverse* and *The Plow That Broke the Plains*, Otis Ferguson argued that there existed an unchanging public taste: "People *want* to see the funny Italian mans, the darkness of Africa, youth triumphant and love in bloom, titled bitchery, ups, downs, swords in a tavern, ride Harry ride and the damsel is mine sirrah."[65] Filmmakers who wanted to rise above such tired stereotypes could do so successfully only by incorporating them, he said, and Lorentz had failed to do so, the proof being that the film was not holding long in New York theaters. Besides begging the question of merit in making films for those who do not share public taste, Ferguson seems unaware of what Lorentz *had* done to extend the audience range for the documentary. He had provided the excitement of melodrama and story and had appealed to another side of public taste—its pleasure in American events, songs, and traditions.

We have seen how the Nykino people were themselves working toward drama and story as well as in-depth characterization. But celebrating America was another matter, and behind all the other conflicts, it was this issue over which they parted ways with the filmmaker whose background, temperament, and political affiliation enabled his film to easily fit into the new wave of appreciation and celebration of America. Those who gravitated toward the Film and Photo League and Nykino had lived in a very different America than Lorentz. Most of them had suffered the realities of poverty, discrimination, and alienation,[ff] and they were far less likely than he to cherish America as

---

[ee] Chalmers' voice again is of service here. In his strong, clear words there is something almost fatherly; amidst all the disaster, he can see and explain what has happened and in so doing helps to control it and endows us with a degree of confidence. It was, of course, the almost inevitable intrusiveness and distortion of such narration that led the *cinéma vérité* filmmakers and, perhaps more relevantly, Emile de Antonio, Marcel Ophuls, and Peter Davis to drop narration almost altogether in the last two decades.

[ff] Alfred Kazin captures some of this in *Starting Out in the Thirties*: "For me, too, all

their country; rather, they were devoted to changing it in the interests of those who were oppressed. Like Lorentz, they used their art to struggle with what they disliked about America, but their backgrounds, temperaments, and political solidarity endowed them with slightly more cynicism, more bitterness, and a less wavering eye on evil. There was to be a different tone, a different edge, and a different form to the films that they would make.

Hurwitz, Steiner, and Strand: The Upper House of Nykino

According to Hurwitz, the formation of Nykino had given "new energy" to its members. When working on *The Plow That Broke the Plains* they found that their subordination to a sponsor and a director of very different sympathies and aesthetics, plus the excitement of creating their own script—even though it had gone unused—had made them all the more eager to put their ideas into practice. And so, Hurwitz recalls, "when we returned from the west, we set to moving Nykino into a new stage: an independent production company with day-to-day continuity and with a full-time staff."[66] This could not happen overnight, of course: their talent required further development, and financial support was necessary.

Nykino members shared facilities, ideas, and the income they received for their work. As far as I have been able to determine, Hurwitz was still the only recipient of a salary: fifteen dollars per week. Steiner provided the monthly color food photograph for the *Ladies Home Journal* centerfold, a three-day-a-month job paying $750—income that helped with materials and with his own support and left him relatively free to work with Nykino. Strand evidently had other sources of income. It was these three who were what Maddow calls the studio group, able to work more or less full time, and through 1936 most of Hurwitz's and Strand's and much of Steiner's energies would go into the organization. The others, the "lower house," had outside jobs, turning up to talk and work evenings and weekends; in 1936 they would produce two sections of a left-wing newsreel series.[67]

We have seen that the camera crew on *The Plow That Broke the Plains* was far from completely unified, and in fact on location a sig-

these critics in power—Cowley, the Van Dorens, Canby, Chamberlain—were outsiders, . . . for writers from the business and professional class could only interpret in an abstract and literary way the daily struggle that was so real to me in Brownsville" (Boston: Little, Brown and Company, 1962, p. 50).

nificant split was brewing, although it would not be finally acted out until the end of 1937 when further developments would bring it to a head. "When Strand was around," Lorentz told Van Dyke, "Steiner couldn't work." "One week you could mention Steiner to Strand," Roy Stryker told MacCann in 1949, "and the next week you couldn't."[gg] Certainly some professional rivalry was a factor here, with Steiner unable to function well in the presence of another artist with very high standards, a dominant personality, and a more established reputation. But politics and temperament were to blame as well. Strand was firmly committed to the far left, a position Steiner, relatively apolitical, was always uneasy with. Looking back with an admitted bias, he now ascribes to Hurwitz and Strand a constantly gloomy outlook: "They were saying everything's terrible in America." His own temperament was and is sunnier, more optimistic,[hh] and 1935 finds him beginning to grope his way toward a position closer to Lorentz's impassioned liberalism than to the committed radical politics of his colleagues. But most at fault was an intensely personal development: Hurwitz and Steiner had become not only collaborators but strong friends, and now Hurwitz was deeply interested in Strand's Mexican photographs (which he later helped Strand to publish) and in beginning to collaborate with Strand.[68]

According to Maddow, after the trio's return from work on *The Plow That Broke the Plains*, the important decisions in Nykino came from Hurwitz and Strand—Steiner, yes, to an extent, but the first two were clearly the more powerful. Hurwitz remembers too that he and Strand now "became the motor force of the group." His collaboration with Steiner had been vital to his development, he says, and important to Steiner, but his significant creative interaction now shifted to his new relationship with Strand. Just how deeply Steiner felt, and still feels, about the shift is apparent from what follows:

> And, see, not being a cameraman, he needed a cameraman, then he had Paul you see, he didn't need me any longer. I was his camera, you see. . . . I went years later to show films to the school that he runs. And, I think I told you this, afterwards he came up and held out his hand and said "Hello, Ralph," and in front of the whole class I put my hands behind me and walked away. The only time in my life I've ever done that, and I'm quite proud of the

[gg] In our 19 Feb. 1975 interview, Strand said that this was not true.

[hh] "One of my quarrels with photographers," Steiner wrote in 1940, "is that they don't take enough really humorous pictures" ("Why Don't More Photographers Take Pictures That Make People Laugh," *PM Daily*, 1 Sept. 1940, p. 49). One seldom finds humor in a Strand photograph.

fact that I did, because it isn't political, I just think that, you know, I never had a friend so close, I *thought*, you know, and to have in a couple of days, you know, to have him turn on me, because he didn't need me anymore, or for whatever reason.[69]

From all I could perceive during a long afternoon of talking and screening his recent films, Steiner is a lively, generous person with the same capability and the eagerness, curiosity, and wonder about life that his friends remember in him from the thirties. He is not easily hostile or bitter. His story as such is one example of the hurt, bitterness, and underlying tensions that were beginning to surface at this time.

The difference in Steiner's state of mind before and after Strand's arrival on the scene is mirrored in two photographs of the period. The *New Theatre* cover for April 1934 carried Steiner's photograph of a scene from the Theatre Union's production of Paul Peters and George Sklar's *Stevedore*—a workman against the sky, holding a hook up in his fist before him, his other fist, clenched, held out behind. In contrast to this untroubled photograph made for the militant theater is a stark, amusing photograph by Steiner in the *U.S. Camera* annual for 1935, which also published such socially conscious works as Dorothea Lange's famous "White Angel Breadline" and Lewis Jacobs's "Bronx Home News." In Steiner's photograph, a man in a suit, wearing glasses, sits astride a stool, his left side to us, against a gray background. His face resting in his left hand, he blissfully contemplates a rose that he is holding in his right hand. From his back pocket protrudes a revolver. Here we find reflected the spirited, good-humored, outgoing Steiner, with the anger and hurt building up inside, and we remember him going off to shoot at tin cans in Wyoming while Hurwitz and Strand collaborated on the new script.

In 1975, a reference to Strand by interviewer James Blue triggered in Steiner a sudden recollection of this very photograph. Asked what he had learned as a photographer from Strand, Steiner referred, in words I quoted earlier, to Strand's seriousness. Then, out of nowhere:

> It makes me think. . . . Once I was spending an afternoon photographing Perelman, doing just crazy crazy pictures, just wonderful nutty pictures, just for fun. While he was smelling a rose, he had a pistol sticking out of his pocket, just foolishness. And in the middle of this I said, Sid, this is a strange way for two grownup men to spend an afternoon, and although Sid is a comic, he said, Ralph, this afternoon we may be the only two grown men not doing any harm in the whole world.[70]

Puzzled at having come up with this and unable to connect it to the question about Strand, Steiner returned to Strand's seriousness. One impulse for the association must have been his sense of the differences between his own sometimes humorous photography and Strand's inevitably serious photography. But another impulse was surely the tension generated in him by the mention of Strand and by the events of that earlier time.

Earlier in this chapter I touched on Strand's importance to Nykino. What about Hurwitz? Along with Lerner and Steiner, he had seniority, and by now he was a considerably knowledgeable filmmaker with strong ideas and an eagerness to further explore the medium. His desire to create an independent, fully functioning production company was intense, and he brimmed with drive and confidence:

> Even before I knew what the hell it was all about in my head, I had a sureness about it and a feeling that we could make this out of nothing . . . *make* it out of people who didn't know anything about films. We were very open to people with talent who didn't know anything. We could teach them ourselves. . . . I was a kind of binding aesthetic, ethical passion.

This is not to deny—nor does Hurwitz today deny—the absolute importance of everyone in the cooperative. But it is to say that Hurwitz was the source, through time, energy, and commitment, of much of their forward movement. It is also to evoke the fine youthful confidence, the spirit, and the creative enthusiasm shared by this family of talented filmmakers. And it is to hint at the potential problems common to any such group in which power becomes a little too centralized, leaving some people feeling held back, shut out (as Steiner was feeling), or dominated. Such problems were still relatively minor in Nykino. Maddow, in fact, remembers very well "that very fierceness of decision" on the part of Hurwitz and Strand, and he feels that for a long while, for years, it "had its results . . . was all right."[71] After all, it was this leadership that helped bring them all together, find projects, and make films they very much believed in.

III ■ Nykino, Ivens, and Lorentz, 1936

Joris Ivens

Joris Ivens, who was to become an important influence on the Nykino filmmakers, arrived in New York City early in 1936 at the invitation of the New Film Alliance, a popular-front organization officially formed in September of 1935.[a]

Although Ivens was Dutch, his reputation as a progressive filmmaker had been known in America as early as 1934. He was born in Nymegen, Holland in 1898, and his family had been linked to photography for two generations before his birth. His grandfather was a daguerreotype portraitist, and his father was a purveyor of photographic materials and the owner of a chain of camera shops; Ivens was expected from

[a] Its president was Merritt Crawford, a film historian who was interested in the early years of film; its vice-president was Shelley Hamilton of the National Board of Review. Secretary and treasurer were Edward Kern and Frank Ward of the Film and Photo League, while "Peter Ellis" (Irving Lerner) of Nykino had charge of film exhibitions. Its advisory board featured prominent people whose politics covered the radical/liberal range of American theater, literature, and film. John Howard Lawson and Albert Maltz were firmly identified with the far left, while others, like Otis Ferguson and Harold Clurman, were of more liberal persuasion. Others among the twenty-odd-person membership of the board were Margaret Bourke-White, Cheryl Crawford, Kyle Crichton, John Gassner, Robert Gessner, Langston Hughes, Leo Hurwitz, Clifford Odets, Herman Shumlin, and Lee Strasberg. Modeling itself on the new theater movement, the organization intended to coordinate independent film producers throughout the country, to provide sponsorship, distribution, et cetera, to build a strong audience organization, and to present a lecture series, screenings of nondistributed classics, and a magazine—all in competition with a Hollywood it despised. Its vital phase lasted for about eight or nine months, and only the lecture series and the screenings were as successful as had been anticipated.

the cradle to continue in Capi, the family business. Accordingly, he was sent to the Rotterdam College of Economics in 1917, his education there interrupted by service in the military reserve forces during World War I. He continued at the college until his need for the technical knowledge of photography took him to the University of Charlottenburg in Berlin in 1922. Funds ran low after a year or two, and he went to work on camera and lens construction in the Ica and Ernemann factories in Dresden, where he

> began to understand physically what it meant to be a worker, living within a small salary and working within a huge organization. In the state of Saxony the labor unions were having a tough struggle for existence. The justice of their minimum demands was clear to me. I marched in demonstrations in the streets of Dresden when the protesting workers were shot at by the police. I knew and felt strongly that the workers were in the right. They were fighting the first German battles against fascism.[1]

In his next job as an apprentice at the Zeiss factory at Jena, "doing scientific work on optics and the mathematics of lens construction," he found a more attractive capital/labor pattern, a "sort of paternal cooperative in which the workers were involved in the responsibilities and the profits" (p. 18).

Back in Holland in 1926, and restless in his managerial positions at Capi, he spent his spare hours in the lively young artistic and intellectual circles of Amsterdam. He found that the young artists were fascinated with cinema and that they envied his technical knowledge of photography. They went to commercial films together, engaging enthusiastically in critical discussion and some of them brought back from Paris glowing reports of independently made avant garde films. Soon after arranging a private screening of Pudovkin's *Mother*, which was banned in Holland, Ivens and his friends went on to form the Filmliga, which was devoted to the presentation of French, German, and Russian avant garde films, lectures, and discussions. The organization attracted a large, enthusiastic audience, and Ivens, as secretary, found himself spending more and more of his time there. During this period, relations with his father and business "cooled considerably" (pp. 18-23).

His technical knowledge was taking creative direction. At home on a rewinder, he examined *Potemkin* and *Arsenal* shot by shot, charting "the editing of the most important sequences" to learn "elementary visual continuity" (p. 24). In the spring of 1928, Dutch and other continental artistic circles responded enthusiastically to *The Bridge*,

Ivens' study of the movements of a railroad bridge over Rotterdam's Maas River, "a laboratory of movements, tones, shapes, contrasts, rhythms, and the relations between all these" (p. 26). *Breakers* and *Rain* followed, and then, in 1929 and 1930, *We Are Building, Heien, New Architecture*, and *Zuiderzee*. *We Are Building*, commissioned by the Dutch building workers' trade union, was a chance "to give my work direction, purpose, fighting qualities" (p. 43). It was not only a project in which he "would be participating in the growth of the country and enjoying the integration of an artist in society" (p. 44); it was also his first opportunity to make his art a part of the dynamic efforts of exploited working people to take pride in their work and to better their conditions, a preoccupation that was to define his work throughout his life.

The Filmliga invited Eisenstein, Pudovkin, and Vertov to speak at showings of their films. In the forty-eight hours that Dutch officials allowed Pudovkin to remain in the country in January of 1929, he managed personal talks with all the filmmakers in the group. Especially impressed by *The Bridge, Breakers*, and an uncut version of *Rain*, he invited Ivens to the Soviet Union to show his films and to lecture. The three-month, expense-paid visit, a fabulous dream for any young filmmaker of the era, came in early 1930. Ivens lived first in the absent Eisenstein's apartment, and then traveled the country, delivering more than a hundred lectures, receiving a reel of *Earth* as a gift from Dovzhenko, and gaining invaluable criticism from the eager Soviet audiences (pp. 49-61).

Back in Holland, still a manager at Capi, he made two commercial films in 1930 and 1931, *Philips-Radio* and *Creosote*, working now as a team with Helen van Dongen, Johnny Fernhout and others, and finding "the conditions and restrictions conflicting more and more with my own convictions" (p. 62). To evade the danger of slipping into a career as a slick, successful advertising filmmaker, he took up a standing invitation, returned to the Soviet Union, and under great physical hardship and a tight budget made *Song of Heroes*, the story of the building of a new blast furnace at Magnitogorsk. It was

the first time in my life that I felt integrated with my work, a part of my environment. Our film crew was not an isolated, strange group temporarily attached to a big industrial project, but part of the project. I was sure that many workers in Magnitogorsk felt the same way about us—felt that it was just as important to have a good film about the blast furnace as it was to build the blast furnace. That made up for all the hardships. (P. 72)

Back in Holland again, he found an offer from Henri Storck that contained "exactly the film subject that I wanted and needed" (p. 82), a documentary of the miserable situation of the Borinage miners in Belgium. The film was intended to "help the workers there by acquainting the rest of the world with their real conditions" (p. 82). The film was completed in 1933, and another new film, *New Earth*, his dramatic presentation of the reclamation of land from the Zuiderzee—a vast project which he and his crew had been recording since 1929—premiered in Amsterdam in 1934.

Arriving in New York, Ivens gave a lecture at the New School on 12 January 1936, another on filmmaking in the Soviet Union for the New Film Alliance on 13 March, and a third on "The Development of Independent Film Art" at New York University on 16 April. The New Film Alliance American premiere of his films was 22 March at the New School, with a repeat performance there on 28 March. A "last chance" showing took place at the 58th Street Theater on 19 April, and Ivens presented the films before the National Board of Review in mid May.

Rain, *Borinage*, and *New Earth* appeared in their entirety (except for a few annoying excisions from the latter two by the New York censors), along with two episodes from *Song of Heroes* and four brief fragments from *Philips-Radio*; the fragments emphasized Ivens' handling of people at work and included the now-famous sequence of the disastrously strained and weakened glass blowers. This last, a powerful sequence that made his sponsors squirm, is rather dwarfed in the corporate context of the film as a whole. Ivens' decision to accent it indicates both what he thought valuable in the film and how he wished to be known in the United States. The film was shown under its other title, *Industrial Symphony*, in New York, and Lerner reported that Ivens referred to the film as his own version of *Modern Times* in documentary form—a wishful but inaccurate analogy. Although *Rain* touched them with its sensitive poetry and with the personal quality of its perspective, the local filmmakers found *New Earth* and *Borinage* the most striking and the most significant for their own art.[2]

Most of *New Earth* was shot between 1928 and 1932. Ivens condensed the footage into final form during 1933 and 1934, adding an angry montage of archive and original material. Three-fourths of the film records the process of land reclamation: the building of mats to support the clay foundation of the new land; throwing stones to sink the mats; swinging bargeful after bargeful of heavy clay into the water at the separation point; fitting the stones; constructing the dikes; the dramatic locking out of the water; settling the land; digging the irrigation canals; plowing, seeding, and at last, the first harvest. Out of this basically instructional material, Ivens created a great film. Although lacking in the artful photography of *The Wave* and *The Plow That Broke the Plains*, it is much more gripping than either of those films, demonstrating the qualities that moved Pudovkin to invite Ivens to the Soviet Union, qualities, Pudovkin said, "which many of our documentary directors lack—qualities of tension and emotion that are very valuable in factual films" (p. 50).

For one thing, the sheer immensity of the landfill task creates a powerful dramatic tension, and that tension is reinforced by Hanns Eisler's score, which often works from a slow, measured, lyrical, workmanlike rhythm to another and much faster movement, a development that emphasizes both the enormous length of the undertaking and the quick energy it required. Sometimes these musical developments are counterpointed with the editing rhythms, as in the mat-sinking sequence. The first sixteen shots, in which men survey the land, motion the boats out, pull ropes, and begin to cast the stones onto the mats, average forty-two frames. The next ten shots, in which more men, moving faster, throw more stones, average only thirty-one frames. The final six shots, distant ones that follow the empty boats as they are towed away, average one hundred and twelve frames. The music, on the other hand, builds quickly to a fast rhythm that it maintains throughout, first reinforcing the editing and then functioning as counterpoint to the slower, heroic pace of the overall work symbolized by the distant shots and the less frequent cutting. A sustained dramatic tension also pervades sequence after sequence through the acute timing of man and machine and through the strain of men's bodies as they pit land against sea. Now and then the editing operates to create uncertainty and suspense by moving from detail to establishing shot, and the constant variation in length, distance, angle, and direction of shots in a film with a high shot ratio serves to maintain intensity.

The first time we see the clay in close-up, the camera holds in five or six shots from different positions while we watch the mud, wet and full of sunlight, lifted onto conveyor buckets to be dropped onto a barge: these are beautiful, almost caressing shots.[b] *New Earth*, indeed, is a celebratory film, the first three-fourths of it lovingly made. And

---

[b] In the cooperative French film, *Far From Vietnam*, Claude Lelouch's beautiful opening and closing shots of cranes sweeping American war materials to shore, together with the carefully positioned inclusion of Ivens' own footage of North Vietnamese farmers passing bright soil from hand to hand to a new spot on the earth, consciously echo *New Earth* and link the goals of the landfill to the motives behind the Vietnamese war for independence. They also serve as a tribute to Ivens as an uncompromising father to political filmmakers of the sixties.

it is this loving attitude toward object, work, and the creation of this land that is characteristic of Ivens.

The most striking sequence in *New Earth* is one of the most striking sequences in all of film: the final closing of the dike. As we watch the gap narrow, the water moves more swiftly toward and through the diminishing opening, threatening to wash away every shovelful of clay as soon as it falls. Ivens' decision to have each of his three camera-people—John Fernhout, Helen van Dongen, and himself—*identify* with one of the contending forces, land, sea, and man, had brilliant results. The camera moves dramatically with the flying crane, it is held in close on the plunge of clay into the water, and it catches in close-up the power of the machinery. In sharp diagonals, it catches the driving speed of the water as it sweeps by and submerges the soil. It picks up the swift, concentrated, efficient pull on his lever by the man in the cab of the crane. Three hubs were provided for the editing, and the intense struggle between land and sea is woven in quick shot after shot, with swift music and no voice, the generally constant speed enhanced by the sharp contrasts in the direction of movement and of line within the shots. The shots identified with the crane operator and his machinery increase toward the end until the title *GESLOTEN* (closed) appears on the screen, followed by a shot of water rushing to but halted by the land, and then a shot of a poised, fully opened shovel hanging triumphantly in the air, a visual and musical symphony that has seldom been surpassed (pp. 95-96).

Again and again in *New Earth*, as men pull at ropes, carry long lines of bound twigs, strain at rocks, toss planks, and carve out ditches, as fathers walk with their children and as a girl swirls past on a makeshift merry-go-round, Ivens chooses angles and frames that, no matter how they fragment the body or ignore the physiognomy, capture the motion and energy of the people, as of the machines, at work. Often the people are not centered, and even when the human image is large, the overwhelming focus of interest is on the movement of body and tool through the frame. This is done not in the service of depersonification but as the key element in Ivens' hymn to humanity's commitment, energy, and effectiveness in pursuit of a great end.

Yet Soviet audiences had rightly criticized him for ignoring the full dimension of people, and Ivens began to respond to that criticism in *Borinage* and in the final fourth of *New Earth*.[c] In the latter, Ivens

[c] A posthumous piece by Potamkin in the April 1934 *New Theatre* ("Hollywood or Lenin Hills") cited with approval Ivens' declaration upon his return from the Soviet Union "that he is through with preoccupation with 'things' and experimentation with forms alone, and will now concern himself with 'people'" (p. 9), a citation that surely caught the eyes of the dissident group within the Film and Photo League.

wanted to convey the bitter irony of an overspeculation that had forced the casting of new wheat into the sea and deprived the dike builders of work during the years of a world depression. He edited stock-library footage, mostly newsreel, into an idea-montage of contrasting shots, accompanied by a biting narration and a final satirical ballad. With powerful effect, shots of wheat blown in the wind and shots of harvesters, stacks of wheat, and piles of grain are intercut with shots of grain pouring into the sea, milk dumped from trucks, coffee burnt, derricks inactive, children hungry, laborers homeless, and crowds marching in protest. The dearth of narration in the first three-fourths of the film renders doubly effective the constant, shouted narration here, and the effect is also deepened when the camera holds for the first time on people, notably on child-victims of the Depression.

Ivens clearly supports the protesting marchers. Fairly early in the sequence, a shot of a crowd taken from a high angle fills the frame. Following a shot of stacked wheat come two more shots of marching crowds, each taken from a higher angle than the one before, so that each time more marchers fill the frame. The same three shots conclude the film: the camera tilts downwards through the smoke of burning wheat and, through an almost unnoticeable cut, into a repeat of crowd shot two, which is followed by repeats of shot three and finally shot one, the individual marching figures becoming larger. The burning of the wheat by the capitalist social order thus symbolically creates the fires of the revolutionary destruction of an economic system responsible for so much misery.

Much of the anger in that final editing of *New Earth* derived from Ivens' experience with the Belgian miners in the Borinage. He and Storck lived in the homes of the miners, sometimes jumping from house to house to keep a step ahead of the hostile authorities. The blacklisting that had followed the miners' recently compromised strike, the near hopelessness, the filthy living conditions, the disease and hunger, forced what Ivens later called a revolution in his style. The result was a prolabor film but of very different character from, say, *The Wave*.[d]

As he and Storck grew closer to the people of the Borinage, their need to report what they saw became more urgent, and Ivens made some decisions.

[d] It is difficult to talk about *Borinage*, for the print at the Museum of Modern Art is in 35mm and viewing conditions do not allow very close study, which is not the case with 16mm prints. The Museum of Modern Art has the Russian version, which Ivens, van Dongen, and Hans Hauska made in 1935; Russian material is intercut with that from the Borinage, with commentary in Russian. This is the version that was shown in America in 1936. See James Shelley Hamilton, "Joris Ivens," NBR, May 1936, pp. 9-10.

The approach used in *Philips-Radio* had to be dumped overboard. The urgency in which this film [*Borinage*] was made kept our camera angles severe and orthodox. Or one might say, unorthodox, because super-slickness and photographic affectation were becoming the orthodoxy of the European documentary film. This return to simplicity . . . was right because I felt it necessary to resist communicating personal pity for these people—what had to be stressed was the harshness of their situation without being sentimental or pitying. Every sequence should say I ACCUSE— accusing the social system which caused such misery and hardship. . . . We felt it would be insulting to people in such extreme hardship to use any style of photography that would prevent the direct, honest communication of their pain to the spectator.[3]

Ivens and Storck fought any false picturesqueness that their cameras might have caught in the exteriors of the miners' barracks, they broke the edges of a shadow that gave pleasant effect to dirty rags and dishes on a table, and they eliminated anything "that would undermine our purpose for a moment" (p. 88). The idea was not to capture the whole but the essential truth, by whatever means was necessary short of losing documentary's prime quality of authenticity.[e] Their purpose comes clear in the following statement:

> The film maker must be indignant and angry about the waste of people before he can find the right camera angle on the dirt and on the truth. I saw enough in the Borinage to encourage me to want to make more than a sentimental film about the miners. I wanted the spectators of the finished film to want to do more than send these workers money. This film required a fighting point of view. It became a weapon, not just an interesting story about something that had happened. (Pp. 88-89)

The film reflects this purpose. Neither the camerawork nor the cutting are very striking; they are a world away from that of *Philips-Radio* and even *New Earth*. The shabby interiors of the miners' barracks, the filth, the rags, the polluted water, the empty light socket, the drawn faces, the nine or ten people huddled in four beds, the swollen pelvis of the infant, all speak for themselves.

Yet *Borinage* lacks some of the strength of *New Earth*. Ivens was right to work out his anger and indignation in new cinematic terms,

[e] Ivens opposed the Vertov school's veto of reenactment in documentary and argued for tactical distortion of reality: "As in Music, there is often a need for dissonance in saying (or yelling) what you want your audience to hear." See "Collaboration in Documentary," *Films*, Spring 1940, p. 35.

for a part of his indignation was directed at his own earlier cinematic practices. But the strength of his emotion may have caused an aesthetic overreaction, the result being that he neglected his greatest area of talent: his rare ability to feel and to work out with his camera and his editing the physical force of an action, a stance, even a mood. This quality is certainly separable from the slickness he feared and rejected, and it is consonant with his theory that the documentary filmmaker must have a certain amount of stylistic license in order to convey his observations and ideas with the most impact. Had Ivens drawn more upon this talent, he could have used lighting and angle for *emphasis* without sacrificing his basic straightforwardness and without diverting the viewer from the conditions he was so determined to show. His film might then have been more unified, containing the continuous sense of involvement and conviction that sustain *New Earth* so well.

In discussing his films, Ivens stressed a number of points that absorbed the interest of the Nykino filmmakers. He told how the Soviet audiences had criticized him for his cinematic treatment of people and thus had raised "questions" that, Lerner reported, "were crucial ones for Ivens, as they are for every documentalist." And surely he also argued against an all-sides-of-the-question "objectivity" and for a *felt*, clear social point of view that determined form and content and carried *conviction* to the audience—a position that he was to present again and again throughout the course of his career. He discussed his search for alternatives to the hero and the plot that bind the viewer to the fiction screen. He spoke of the high importance of editing skill necessary in order to create rhythms that would catch the audience— something he and Helen van Dongen had concerned themselves with intensely in recent years. And he explained how the sensitive cameraman might work to the same end. According to Ben Maddow,

> one of the strong impressions I had was his intuitive knowledge of what cinema was about. He told this story of how anybody who does something [work] is very beautiful at it, particularly if it's a physical movement. And if you follow the movement with the camera, you will then get the essence of this course of beauty, and so on. This was an eye opener.[4]

Ivens' presence in New York had a major impact. The importance of his films "to the independent filmmaker cannot be underestimated," Lerner wrote in an enthusiastic review. "We were very interested," Strand recalled, "extremely interested in his films, especially in *New Earth*, which was the most dramatic film he ever made." It was the final filling of the land-gap, the juxtaposition of the final montage to the first three-fourths of the film, the editing and its counterpoint with the music and words that now stimulated the maker of *The Wave* and the Nykino theoreticians of dialectical structure, these artists looking for compact, telling art. Lerner's review hastens to communicate his impression that "no documentary films ever shown here before have been as exciting, stimulating, dynamic, tense and as brilliant in execution of their purposes." Non-Nykino reviewers were not far behind. Shelley Hamilton found Ivens' documentaries "far more creative than mere reporting . . . far more exciting and enriching than mere fiction." Otis Ferguson, struck by the fact that the audience broke into involuntary applause when the land-gap was filled, thought *New Earth*, "like the rest of Ivens' films, . . . more exciting than rapid fiction, and twice as beautiful."[5]

Equally important to the Americans was the nature and the certainty of Ivens' perspective. "What enormously aids him as an artist," Lerner wrote, "is that he has found his place in society." It was not simply the Marxist perspective that was attractive, it was also that that perspective was part of a broad outlook on life. His personal grace, his warmth and generosity, his rounded manner of addressing himself to ideas and situations, and his ability to perceive and to recreate "the beauty . . . under the surfaces of life by sensitiveness and sympathy" were aspects of what Hurwitz recalls as "the large area of his sensibility." In an appreciation of Ivens that he wrote with Jay Leyda in 1938, Sidney Meyers put it most cogently:

> The film . . . holding within itself the potentialities of rendering actuality most truthfully, has known an endless abuse since its invention by the failure to bring to it a valid viewpoint. Yet Joris Ivens, even in the heat of battle, has known no such failure. In him we encounter a complete socially integrated artist, one whose great craft is stimulated by a deep sense of unity with his fellow human beings.[6]

Ivens' arrival in America was what Lerner in 1974 remembered as "a turning point . . . a shot in the arm. . . . It was assistance from a recognized filmmaker who confirmed the theories of Nykino." Hurwitz recalls that they saw him as a real model for what they aspired towards: Ivens had taken the risk of completely devoting himself to independent filmmaking and "had made it, achieving work of very high standards." He was not only an example but a real spur to Nykino's budding effort to arrange "conditions for full-time production of independent films in America." His spirit and dedication and his "enthusiasm and determination" paralleled and sparked their own. Ivens took a strong interest in Nykino and characteristically generously shared his political and artistic experience with its members. In succeeding years, "in every way he could," Strand remembered, "he helped us to survive and make films." It was important, too, that he was articulate but undogmatic on political questions. Willard Van Dyke remembers that if a political question arose, Ivens was often the one who was consulted about its validity.[7]

The impact of Ivens was paralleled by the impact of Dovzhenko's *Frontier*, which arrived in New York in December of 1935. Hurwitz remembers that they all "had a tremendous feeling about that film"; Lerner, Maddow, and Meyers all wrote about it, and Strand thought it "a majestic work." They celebrated it as a poetic film of great intensity. It is a vast film of great size and high visual and verbal rhetoric. In the enormity of its landscape, the intensity of its larger-than-life characters, and the passion and commitment of its dialogue, the radical young filmmakers saw new ways to affect the minds and deeds of their audience. *Frontier* was a film, Meyers told his readers, that constantly "bursts through the hard resisting shell of necessary exegesis to uncover essential truths." It is

> not a film that one sits back and views complacently with but half an eye and no mind. It is a film that demands absolute and even strained participation, but afterward we feel rewarded by a fuller capacity to view and understand life in its wholeness.[8]

Here, as in the films of Ivens, was the integration between the personal and the social to which the Nykino filmmakers aspired.

In November of 1974, Leo Hurwitz and I shared a screening of *Frontier* at the Film Study Center of the Museum of Modern Art. Afterwards he talked expressively of the magnificent scene in which Glushak leads his friend, the traitor Vasil Kudiakov, into the forest for execution. Hurwitz pointed out the time Dovzhenko takes to watch them going, with Glushak in front not turning, Vasil stumbling, looking about him, looking back, then, standing before Glushak's rifle, hurling forth the enormous cries that echo through the forest, feeling his native environment one last time, feeling his aliveness, feeling the full brunt of the death that is now upon him. It was this wedding of a political event—the execution of the traitor—with a profound personal sense of the human condition, this ability to rise through and above the merely political film, that enabled the New York filmmakers to see the potential in their medium for political *and* major art. For them, Dovzhenko and Ivens justified the artistic direction they themselves had been taking.

At the end of May 1935, Ivens left for California, showing his films to enthusiastic audiences along the way. In July, his films were screened at Hollywood's Film Art Theatre for a crowd comprised primarily of actors, cameramen, directors, and writers who filled the 1,200 seats. The event was a small sensation in Hollywood, Hans Wegner says, for such turnouts were normally accorded only to "der grossen Stars." The occasion had its irony too, for Ivens' work had been spurred throughout his career by his reaction against the usual film product of his laudatory audience. He stayed in Hollywood for a couple of months, studying the latest technology and methods of production and observing several directors at work,[9] but discovering no desire to stay in the place that would later lure Ralph Steiner and eventually become a permanent home for Irving Lerner and Ben Maddow.

From the Hollywood experience, Ivens wrote a tough critical article for *New Theatre*. With "rich, full life at its door, life in which a Balzac or a Zola would revel," Hollywood creates "an endless row of variations on boy meets girl or the Cinderella story." He had seen a fruit-pickers' strike—

three thousand Mexican workers—which offered material for at least two *Viva Villa*'s. In La Habra I was present at the birth of a fighting song, the circumstances of which, if incorporated in a film, would have had ten times the strength, and directness and optimism and probably have been more of a popular hit than the usual Hollywood epic. Yet how many Hollywood film workers were aware of this heroic primitive struggle in the fruit orchards, where trees seem to be better cared for than men?

Ivens went on to say that Hollywood's marvelous technical apparatus in fact "only produces four or five good pictures a year," and "one becomes furious at the thought that such" "complete masters of their art, their craft," as Capra, Mamoulian, Milestone, and Vidor have not "the freedom necessary for the further development of the filmic art." Hollywood writers dry up and go soft after a few years, actors lack discipline and are forced continuously to play standardized roles. Fan magazine pursuit and the Hollywood social life "make the atmosphere . . . deadly for true talent." And censors and financiers hover over the films from "the very birth of the idea," while essentially decent human beings create distorting, exploitative works that constitute "a moral disarming of the masses."

Ivens did not merely mean to curse and deplore Hollywood. He called for audience organization to support more films like *The In-*

former, *Modern Times*, *Mr. Deeds Goes to Town*, *Fury*, and *Pasteur*, and to fight Hollywood's antilabor, fascist, and war tendencies. He called for an experimental studio where writers, directors, and actors could study film art and "give new vitality to their work." Outside Hollywood, the successful new theater movement should spur a young film movement to produce films with the "power, the artistic level and the social function of books like *Don Quixote, Uncle Tom's Cabin*." Independent film groups on the left already "are engaging in courageous pioneer work with . . . excellent professional quality: Nykino's *Labor March of Time*,ᶠ American Labor Films' *Millions of us*.ᵍ It must go on."¹⁰

The World Today

Before Ivens had started west, several members of the Nykino cooperative had put into production the first number of a newsreel series intended to be an antidote to *The March of Time*. The latter had taken American audiences by storm since its inception early in 1935, and it was one of the most popular, influential, and inescapable items on the American screen. Like others on the left, the Nykino critics praised it for revolutionizing the American newsreel by abandoning its frivolous "entertainment" tidbits, for adding dramatic punch, and for proving the validity of reenactment for news purposes. But they abhorred what they saw as its "flirting with Reaction," and they knew its reenactment was "wooden and unreal" and that its editing, whatever excitement it mechanically stirred in the viewer's bosom, was generally unimaginative.¹¹

According to Lerner, in mid-1935 the left had not, to this point, produced anything better. The Film and Photo League "subject matter was exciting and dramatic in itself," but their newsreels had been "formless and as poorly made as the commercial reel."¹² There was much to be done, and late in 1935 or early in 1936, Nykino decided to produce its own newsreel, "a kind of progressive *March of Time*," "a pro-labor film with the frame-work of *The March of Time*," a "*March*

ᶠ This is a projected title for *The World Today* and should not be confused with the Film and Photo League's film of early 1935, *Labor's 'March of Time.'*

ᵍ This film was made by American Labor Films, Inc., a group of left-wing Hollywood film technicians, directors, and actors who anonymously worked at left film on the side. The story is simple but effective: a roofless, unemployed worker goes through several attempts to find relief, almost takes on work as a scab, but is convinced instead to join the strike. A good film, it suffers a bit from the milieu in which it is made—the hero is Hollywood handsome and too well-groomed for someone in his condition.

of Time with a labor slant."[13] The connection with *The March of Time* was overstressed, however, for as Lerner wrote after Nykino's rival film, *The World Today*, appeared, Nykino thought it "would revolutionize the method of dramatizing actual news events and happenings."[14]

Lerner is not specific, but one can guess his meaning. Nykino rejected *The March of Time*'s imposition of a trademark style upon all subject matter and would collaborate with its subjects to devise a script that would accurately express the subjects' sense of their own situations. They proposed an authentic style that would "deduce both pace and drama out of the real scene and real protagonists." And they intended to present a more complete background to the events they covered than *The March of Time* did. Finally, by "dramatizing" the news, Nykino meant "projecting the basic dramatic *meanings* implicit in the documents." Lerner argued in 1936 that the documentary film could not be neutral, whatever statements *The March of Time* and others made to the contrary. Its "whole structure [is] . . . basically propagandistic, . . . More than any other form of the cinema, it demands an uncompromising point of view." No hedging, no avoiding reality, no mere provocation. Commentary, angle, music, pace, and editing would labor to convince the viewers of the basic meanings and to move them to action. Such conviction and action would come from emotional involvement, as Hurwitz and Steiner had argued in 1935, and so the film would attempt to get close to, into, and behind its subjects, its people, and "theatricalize events through the invention of circumstances and activities which transform concepts, relationships and feelings into three dimensional happenings."[15]

Although *The World Today* was plotted as an ongoing, if irregular newsreel series, the lack of adequate distribution potential and Nykino's development in other directions made this impossible. Only two sequences were completed:[16] one on homeowner resistance to evictions in a middle-class residential area in Queens, and the other on the Michigan Black Legion and its murder of a WPA worker.[h] The Sunnyside Gardens residents of Queens took part in the scripting and provided most of the acting in the first sequence, which was shot in the spring of 1936 with Willard Van Dyke, a new member, on camera.

[h] The Black Legion was a white terrorist vigilante group whose membership possibly numbered well over 40,000 in Michigan, with much smaller numbers in other states. Its members—from the South and reputedly all ex-KKK—wore black robes and hoods. Seven members confessed direct participation in the "ritual slaying" of Charles A. Poole on 13 May 1936. The literature of the organization "sets forth that it is anti-Catholic, anti-Jewish and anti-Negro and that it was formed to oppose communism and uphold the Constitution." *N.Y. Times*, 23 May 1936, pp. 1, 3.

The second sequence, "Black Legion," was filmed completely with actors ("in spite of that," Lerner wrote, "it looks like a documentary film and functions like one") during the summer of 1936, with Steiner and Van Dyke doing the camerawork. While both sequences were done collaboratively, with much discussion, Ben Maddow had the responsibility for the shooting script and commentary, Mike Gordon[i] directed the actors and probably provided the voice, and Irving Lerner took production stills (which *New Theatre* printed in July and September) and served as editor. Sidney Meyers acted the part of a policeman, and Lionel Berman and Henri Cartier-Bresson, temporarily a member of the group, also contributed. All of the other Nykino members were otherwise employed, and so they could work only part time on the film. Hurwitz and Strand did not take an active part, although Hurwitz recalls participating in consultations over the scripts, the shooting methods, and the rushes.[17] The two sequences were in final form by October.[j]

According to the narration, Sunnyside Gardens was "a peaceful development twenty minutes from the glaring towers of New York City," a paradise in 1926 when young professionals moved there with their families. It is soon established that although the interest payments of the twenties are no longer possible during the Depression, the complex's mortgage company has replied to a request for rate reduction with writs of foreclosure. In response, the families unite to fight for their homes. At a community meeting, the sheriff announces his good intentions, but he has eviction orders "in his inside pocket"—and the camera conveys his impersonality and his covertness: at three separate distances, we see him in his dark suit and only from the back. From here on, cutting, voice, and music are fast and urgent. The sheriff arrives to evict the Thals, and the word spreads as neighbors rush to the house, a few making their way in through the back door. After six arrests, the eviction takes place, despite the neighbors' storming of the house.

The World Today is not a revolutionary film; it is a film of the popular front, a film looking for an audience among those who are renewing their belief in America. The protagonists of "Sunnyside; the

[i] Born in 1909, Michael Gordon had been assistant director and an actor in George Sklar's and Paul Peters' *Stevedore* (1934) and director for Friedrich Wolf's *Sailors of Cattaro* (1934) and Albert Maltz's *Black Pit* (1935). He was now with the Group Theatre, and between 1935 and 1937 he would be stage manager for four of their productions and lighting designer for still others.

[j] Because I have been unable to see "Black Legion," or even to determine whether it still exists, my analysis must of necessity be confined to the "Sunnyside Gardens" sequence.

Second Battle of Long Island" assert themselves in "the traditional spirit of the American pioneers, who transformed a wasteland into farms, cities—and homes." But where *The March of Time* has a "militantly alert capitalism," *The World Today* has an alert populism. The narrative voice identifies with the people. It *becomes* their voices at one point: "Quick! the eviction has begun! Neighbor to neighbor, house to house, spread the word. The eviction has begun." And the narrative voice withdraws in the end to allow the Sunnysiders, in a final long-held static shot on Mrs. Thal, to assert their continuing resistance in one of their own voices. Nor does the film disguise the villains: it is the "billion dollar usurers, the mortgage companies, the insurance corporations" who are clearly at fault.

Lacking the polish provided by *March of Time* equipment, "Sunnyside" nevertheless demonstrates the kind of imaginative camerawork, cutting, and creative juxtaposition of words and image that are generally absent in *The March of Time*. Choices of distance, angle, and movement express attitude and event. High angles on the evictees and on the protestors inside the house convey the vulnerable position of the Sunnysiders. Our response to the narrator's question, "The American home or 6 percent?" is reinforced when the camera simultaneously holds on a woman and her two daughters being thrust from the house by two deputies and being walked straight toward the camera.

Yet, while "Sunnyside" avoids the a priori stylistic control over its subject so noticeable in *The March of Time*, and while it evolves its form from its suburban setting and people, it is infected with *The March of Time*'s resonant "dramatization" to the extent that it loses control over its dramatic elements. The pacing up of voice, editing, and music becomes an imposed technique that pushes the material a little too hard, consequently losing some of the nuances of the situation—and thus a certain amount of verisimilitude and truth. In contrast, in *Borinage*, Ivens lets people mill about more during the eviction reenactment, holds on the awkwardness, gets closer to the real feel of the situation. The music in *Sunnyside* is problematic too. As mere emotional backup in a Hollywood symphonic style, it makes one uneasy and seems especially false for a group that calls itself, as Nykino did for this film, Labor Productions. Nykino was still a considerable distance from the finer control and higher art of its subsequent creations.

But the film is spirited. Its reenactment is better than anything I have seen in *The March of Time*, it is responsive to an actual event and to its people, and it avoids the combed-hair kind of slickness that attaches itself to *Millions of Us*. It rings with strong commitment, and it takes a stand on something that normally did not touch a movie screen during the 1930s. According to Lerner, when they saw the film, the Sunnysiders could scarcely believe that it was not a depiction of the actual event. And Lerner also reported that with all its faults, it was still "strong enough, fresh enough, and exciting enough to amaze many members of the *March of Time* staff when it was shown to them." Hurwitz was not completely happy with the finished product, but he recalls that everyone felt that, "considering the circumstances, considering the fact of experience, the part time," it was "a remarkable achievement" and "very stimulating to people who saw it."[18]

The World Today and *The Wave* were previewed together at the end of the year for an audience interested in progressive films. The enthusiastic response they roused brought enough money and moral support to get Frontier Films off on a fine footing.

Willard Van Dyke with Nykino and Pare Lorentz

Willard Van Dyke was at the camera on both numbers of *The World Today*. When he came from California to New York in July 1935, he was twenty-eight. Born in Denver, he had grown up on a Colorado farm. Thanks to his father, a photographer, he had learned by age thirteen to develop and print his own pictures; since that time, although his primary interest was acting, he had devoted himself seriously to photography. His idea of photography was transformed when he saw an Edward Weston print, and as a result he moved to Carmel, California to study and work with Weston. Under this influence, he abandoned special effects for straight photography, and in the early thirties, along with Weston, Ansel Adams, Imogen Cuningham, John Paul Edwards, Sonra Noskowiak, and Henry Swift, founded Group F/ 64. The California group—named after the smallest stop on the lens, which gave the greatest depth of field and thus the sharpest image— was to both resemble and be somewhat competitive with the straight photographers at 291 in New York. Significantly, Dorothea Lange, who lived in the Bay area, was not a member. As Van Dyke recalls,

> our feeling was that the whole documentary thing was so different from what we were doing. We were looking for the beautiful print, the beautiful photograph. The subject material was of no importance to us at all. As a matter of fact, the farther we could get away from any literary content in the photographs, the better we felt about it—the more abstract, the better.[19]

It was not Van Dyke's family background that politicized him, but rather an experience that occurred during his college years. Working at a Shell station and attending classes at Berkeley[k] during the Depression, his hours flexible enough for his photography and his F/64 activities, he suddenly found himself faced with the choice of either a sixty-hour week or no job at all. He looked around and began, very naively, he recalls, to organize a union of Shell's mistreated employees. Once he had sent out the notices for a first meeting, he was promptly summoned by the Shell management, which pointed to a stack of applications for his position, notified him that Shell controlled the local Teamsters, and left him to work out the personal and political implications: "Well, this kind of opened my eyes to some facts of life that were more than rocks and shells and peppers, and I became a militant young radical at that point." Lerner, who felt that Van Dyke has never been very politically sophisticated, recalled that when he arrived from California he was politically "sort of red-hot."[20]

When *The Cabinet of Doctor Caligari* came to Oakland in 1922, Van Dyke "saw it almost every day for two weeks." *Variety*, *Potemkin*, and *Ten Days that Shook the World* also "made a tremendous impression," and he saw nearly every Russian film that came to California. Inspired by *Un Chien Andalou*, he and Preston Holder at some point in the early thirties attempted a film together in which they used rubber gloves, sheeps' eyes from a slaughterhouse, and a man on a cross on a hilltop. Entitled *An Automatic Flight of Tin Birds*, it was never completed. In 1934 they jumped at a chance to make a film on Californian self-help cooperatives, an opportunity that provided them with a chance to learn more about filmmaking, to open new career possibilities, and "to deal with the problems of people trying to help themselves." The film took nearly a year. In making it, Van Dyke recalls with amusement, "we remembered all of the German expressionist films and all of the Soviet films, and we were making those California workers into peasants right out of *Chapayev* [sic] or something."[21]

His new political orientation manifested itself in several ways in 1934. For one thing, sometime during that year he and Ella Winter went down to Hollywood in an unsuccessful attempt to interest industry people in their own version of the Film and Photo League.[l] For another, under his direction, F/64 exhibited Dorothea Lange's work

[k] At the end of his junior year, he left to concentrate on photography.
[l] This effort was unconnected with the official Film and Photo League branch organized in Hollywood in 1933. "It seems to me we met with John Howard Lawson and John Wexley." Interview with author, 12 May 1975.

that year, and the October *Camera Craft* carried a Van Dyke article on her. Appreciating her "deeply personal sympathies for the unfortunates, the downtrodden, the misfits," her ability to capture the people who most keenly reflected contemporary conditions and problems, he also praised her refusal to bring to her subjects a particular social philosophy or editorial bias.[22]

In the same article he also twice noted an unavoidable incompleteness in Lange's work, which he attributed in part to the still camera itself: "It must make its record out of context, taking the individuals or incidents photographed as climaxes rather than as continuity." This observation reflects both Van Dyke's experience on the self-help cooperative film and a decision that reflected his new political orientation. While he had considered adding extended texts to still photographs to make up for their limitations, he quickly realized that that meant denigration of the visual image. That option blocked, he had chosen to leave still photography "because it could not provide the things that I knew films could provide. I was excited and interested in film as a pure medium of expression, but I was more interested in using it for a social end." Hollywood was not interested in films of social problems, so "documentary was the obvious way to go." In retrospect, Van Dyke now believes that the decision to go documentary and to go film also may have been motivated, at least unconsciously, by an uncomfortable sense of competition with his mentor Edward Weston.[23]

He interested Nina Collier, an official in the Soil Conservation Service, in the film on cooperatives. She asked him to outline a possible film on soil conservation and then invited him to bring his cooperatives film to Washington for a screening. Dropping his job as cameraman for the new Federal Art Project, he set out for the East in early 1935. The primary factor in this move was the government film possibility, but a second reason for it was an effort to free himself from Weston's artistic influence. He was also deeply disillusioned about the current political strife in the West. Although the New Deal had brought him some confidence regarding the possibility of change from inside the established political structure, the violence of the 1934 San Francisco general strike, especially on the part of vigilante groups, had shaken that confidence and helped sour him on the Bay area.[24]

After the cooperatives film was screened in the early summer of 1935, Van Dyke was told to wait a month or so for word on the soil conservation film, and he took this occasion to head up to New York, where he met Iris Barry of the Museum of Modern Art and Ralph Steiner. As he had not yet given up an ambition to become an actor, he subsequently departed for the Soviet Union to take in night after night of the great Soviet theater. Although he had hoped to meet the famous Soviet directors, as Strand had done earlier in the summer, he found them all gone off to the Crimea. Upon his return to the States, he learned that Lorentz was making the soil conservation film and was to take on three Nykino members as his camera crew. He then joined Nykino, doing his bread and butter work as a photographer of cosmetics, gloves, luggage, and shoes for *Harper's Bazaar*.[25]

It was during production of *The World Today* that Pare Lorentz had asked Ralph Steiner to join Horace and Stacey Woodard as camera crew on his next government documentary, *The River*. Because Nykino was a cooperative, Hurwitz and Strand refused to release Steiner unless Lorentz rehired the entire *Plow That Broke the Plains* crew. Steiner, not yet ready to break from Nykino, "reluctantly told Lorentz no," and then, with the concurrence of Hurwitz and Strand, recommended Van Dyke.[m] Lorentz took him, Van Dyke says, "just as a kind of experiment, and he gave me a station wagon, with about 50,000 feet of film . . . and said, 'go shoot cotton.' And this was the greatest thing that could ever happen to me . . . a young cameraman . . . all the film you ever needed, and the director says shoot it your way." It was an opportunity, too, to work alongside and to earn the respect of two of America's finest cameramen, Stacey Woodard and Floyd Crosby. He began work in September, leaving Nykino as the final touches were being put on *The World Today*.[26]

During this time, Van Dyke's on-location letters home to his wife, Mary, tell a good deal about himself, his attitudes toward Lorentz's film, and his relation to Nykino.[27] The letters describe his excitement about new places and new and challenging work, his pain over the conditions of the southern poor, his difficulty understanding their enervation and lack of motivation, his tentative optimism about the curative powers of a paternalistic government and of the Southern Tenant Farmer's Union, and his almost uncontrollable rage over the treatment of blacks. He insisted that John Bridgeman, the crew's government fiscal agent, pay the black boy who assisted them as much as the white one was being paid, instead of a dollar less, as was the southern custom. He describes his pleasure in the variety of the work: shooting from a hired airplane over a flood disaster area; attempting both static, abstract shots as well as shots that captured the power of the dams; making "a series of things of leaves trembling in the tiniest breeze, covered with dew shining in the first rays of the morning sun"; applying his

[m] Dorothea Lange also recommended him to Lorentz. Kent Harber, "Photography and Film through the Eyes of Willard Van Dyke," *The Daily Californian* 10, no. 3 (1978): 3.

skills in still composition to moving subjects and a moving camera; working with people, especially on the film's levee scene.

> There is one scene in silhouette against the most marvelous sky you could imagine, all of them wheeling their wheelbarrows across the top of the levee, another of their singing faces coming right into the camera, details of the barrows being dumped, against a bank of cumulous clouds. . . . In fact, everything has a swell "singing" quality, with nice movement in space and nice tempo. I feel more sure of it than anything I have ever done.

The letters convey a sense, too, of passing time, a pondering of death, ambition unfulfilled ("what a lot there is to do in the short time that is left"), the perception of a career not yet fully determined—he turned thirty that December. At the end of his trip, a snowstorm hit as his car rounded a curve,

> but the sight I then saw hit me harder than the storm: there, ahead of us, was a cemetery on a hilltop surrounded by bare trees, its tombstones like bones in the one path of sunlight in the land-scape. Following a coffin up the hill were the mourners. The bare, newly opened earth waited for their burden. And then we were around the curve, and I'm not even sure that I saw it, so quickly did it appear and pass. But more real than I can tell you. It will always be as strong as I can see it now.[n]

Perhaps it is not too much to conclude that the graveyards that were to turn up constantly in his films over the next decade are his personal *memento mori*—symbols of the pressure against which he felt he was creating, reminders of the bones, the impediments in his path of sun-light.[28]

As a result of rumors he had heard from Nykino members, Van Dyke was surprised, he wrote home, to discover that Lorentz knew "more of what he wants than he has been given credit for." He liked Lorentz and found Lorentz's praise highly supportive. Yet, like the crew on *The Plow That Broke the Plains* and like Horace and Stacey Woodard,

---

[n] "Ben Maddow once described my photographs of the period as morbid lyricism. There were lots of gravestones, I guess, and yet they were done in a lyric sort of way. I always have had a sense of time. Pathological is too big a word. But I'm very aware of even seconds passing, and I've always worn the most accurate watch I can ever get. It's a neurosis, no doubt about it. But I have no fear of death. On the contrary, I think it's the most natural thing. . . . But there is some feeling in me that makes me like [certain parts of] T. S. Eliot's poetry. For instance, [I'm attracted to lines and titles like] 'saw the skull with nothing but the skin,' 'The Wasteland,' 'April is the cruelest month,' 'the dead earth.' " Interview with author, 12 May 1975.

he was distressed over Lorentz's vague, flowery instructions. Stacey Woodard, Van Dyke reported, was "disgusted":

> All this talk about "motifs, song of the river, symphony of cotton" and all the rest of the phrases Pare uses mean nothing at all to him. . . . All he can see is that Pare has no clear idea of what he wants to do, and as long as that is the case it is boring to him to shoot thousands of feet of film on a sequence that could be done in five hundred, simply because the cutter will have to have something to "cover up" with.

Woodard had two Academy Awards for best one-reel picture to his credit, but Van Dyke, with little previous reputation, saw the film as a personal steppingstone and knew he "must try to make Pare's fumbling words have meaning." Yet he too found himself having to upset Lorentz by explaining to him that "a lot of his ideas were literary, not translatable into visual terms." As time passed, his rating of Lorentz dropped, to rise "500%" when, under pressure of the 1937 flood, Lorentz gave them a "really cogent script" and organized and managed the situation with intelligence.

Still, because of Lorentz's vague instructions, he found himself shooting footage only in the hope that it might fit somewhere in the film, and he learned that he did not like the newsreel style. He needed "a starting point, some point of view," without which

> my technique goes sour, I get fussed, and I pass up stuff that I know is good, but I don't shoot it because I don't know how or why it will be used. . . . I keep thinking of the drama of this situation, but I think of it in *personal* terms, in terms of kids and women, and men, and the heroic things they are doing. I can't think of water over cities and have it evoke any response. And then, when I want to do the people, they aren't doing the dramatic thing. It has to be *controlled*. There is no other way to do documentary stuff and have it mean anything.

Wishing to get appropriate drama and to practice direction of non-actors, Van Dyke at one point asked Floyd Crosby to hire a family for him to work with. But Crosby suddenly "assumed the psychology of a newsreel man," insisting that their footage must be straight documentary.

The latter attempt is significant in several ways. Whatever drama Lorentz might make of the miscellaneous footage, Van Dyke was detecting in him a weakness that the editing room could not disguise: a lack of interest in people. Van Dyke's affinities with Dorothea Lange, his work on *The World Today*, the talk around Steiner's studio, the words of Ivens, and his own painful awareness of the conditions in the South had prepared him for such a judgment. When the floods came, he hoped they would force Lorentz to add "the human thing that this film needs," and when Lorentz assigned him "levee repairs, refugee rescue, and portraits of refugees," he felt that Lorentz was again showing confidence in him by giving him "the most important footage,"° for "of course, this is the crux of the story."

After discussing his need for the personal elements in his filmmaking, Van Dyke went on to talk of how the slow, freezing levee defense work might be filmed, and he also began to articulate his own increasing desire for control over his work. This desire becomes a refrain in the letters, which speak of his most exuberant moments as those in which he was working with nonactors on the levee-building scene and of his hopes to make enough money to attend the Group Theatre summer course in 1937. This ambition and this wish for control over his own filmmaking suggests that he had little interest in sticking with Nykino, little real commitment to its politics and its collective loyalties. Should *The River*, possibly "a stepping-stone to a great deal more importance and advance," be a good film, he wrote home early in the trip,

> it will mean a big step toward the ultimate establishment of a film producing section in the government. . . . But that is all a long story. . . . One thing you can be sure of—if there is a permanent program, and if there is a guy named Lorentz connected with it, there will be a cameraman who will soon be a director and whose name is Van Dyke also connected with it.

Van Dyke admired Lorentz as "a guy who had been one jump ahead of all of us, who knew the score," and he basked in Lorentz's divisive compliments, no doubt because they reflected the personal discomfort he already felt about Nykino. Lorentz had every reason to compliment Van Dyke, but he bore some grudges from *The Plow That Broke the Plains* experience, and wanted no Nykino-style trouble on the new film. He told Van Dyke that Steiner and Strand "wouldn't have had me around unless I was good, because friendship was unknown in their league, and that when they said I was a capable man, that meant more than it said [coming from artists of such high ability], and that I was young, ambitious, obviously reliable." In a rather sinister remark,

° Here is one of many reasons to pay tribute to Lorentz: he hired talented, ambitious artists, and both intentionally and inadvertently encouraged them by his style of direction, which was both trusting and inscrutable.

Lorentz told him "that he had . . . told his wife that he had found a young gentile, a youngster who wanted to work . . . that he was going to make him number one man."

Van Dyke's tendency away from Nykino, however, comes from more than an artist's own urge for independence and control. Although all Nykino members had a strong political conscience about social injustice, their politics as individuals ranged from Communist to the moderate brand of liberalism that could still be comfortable on the popular front. Their attitudes toward the New Deal varied too, and not always in strict consonance with their respective places on the general political spectrum. But Van Dyke says today that his 1935 visit to the Soviet Union had disenchanted him about Communism and the glory of the' Revolution, and there is no doubt that on that subject he sat considerably to the right of the group's other members, most of whom still fervently admired what he had found wanting.

In addition, Van Dyke's Colorado and California background was sharply different from that of the other members. His father, an itinerant photographer on the Texas-Mexican border and a wet-plate photographer in Oklahoma when it was still a territory, had photographed Buffalo Bill and Annie Oakley in the frontier towns. When they brought their Wild West Show to Fort Collins, he had introduced them to his son.

> I had malaria when I was a kid, and when I was sick in bed, my father used to come and talk to me and tell me long and very moving stories about his life and about the early days in the West. . . . He was an extremely good pistol shot and he'd lived through a period when the West was very wild. His older sister went out to California in a covered wagon. It was very close to me when I was just a little boy. . . . So there was this marvelous feeling that I was living through a part of the development of the country, in a very real sense.

Certain exclamatory statements in his letters could never have come from other members of Nykino. For instance, studying maps and finding the "names that my father knew and loved" taking on new meaning, "American names, rich with the color of hard men and patient women who built a country," he runs them off, as Lorentz was to run them off in the narration of the completed film: "long rolling names for the great plains and wild sweet rivers." And Van Dyke asks:

> How are we to make real the dreams of the men who made this country? What can we do to justify their heroism? How shall we

carry on the work of John Brown, Bill Hickok, Daniel Boone? This is no country for scheming merchants and grocery clerks. We have a bigger destiny. Our lot crawls not between dry ribs, but past them, over desert to a rich land where the sun shall rise forever. How to recreate the vision of the pioneer?

When he arrived in New York in 1935, his memories of growing up still "very, very strong," he felt that New York "was somehow a little effete, a little too intellectual, that the true source of American strength lay in the heartlands."[29] If he shared with Berman, Hurwitz, Lerner, Maddow, Meyers, and Strand a very critical stance toward American values and behavior, the vast difference between his and their experience is clear from this 1937 letter, which might have been written by Lorentz of West Virginia.

The River

Lorentz himself, in private acknowledgment of the relation between his work and his roots, shot the first footage of the film overlooking the land that was his grandfather's at Tygart's Valley, West Virginia, in the country where his father had fought to keep the river clear of bass-destroying chemicals. The filming, which began in early October, appeared to be over on 16 January; Lorentz expected to find stock footage for the flood scenes he would need to add. But on the twenty-first, Lorentz recalled Crosby and Van Dyke (Horace Woodard had left the film early in the shooting, and Stacey had gone at the end of December) and sent them to Memphis; there they began coverage of the great flood of 1937, following it and its terrible destruction up the Mississippi and Ohio valleys until 1 March. Lloyd Nosler, an experienced Hollywood editor who had been recommended by King Vidor, came to New York to work closely with Lorentz, delighting in the chance for experimentation. Virgil Thomson once again composed the score, mingling original with folk music, beginning with piano sketches of each large sequence, and then, when Nosler and Lorentz had the sequence down to a preconceived time, developing further ideas; the final cut resulted from a continuous negotiation between film and music. Lorentz's poetic narration was then written and added, and again, as in *The Plow That Broke the Plains*, Thomas Chalmers did the voice.[30]

Postproduction took almost six months, interrupted by the fatal heart attack of Lorentz's father on 1 June and the confusion that arose from the closing of the Resettlement Administration. The film unit was transferred to the Farm Security Administration,[31] and the film was finally completed in September 1937. Secretary of Agriculture Wallace was unenthusiastic, but after a White House screening, Roosevelt offered to help in any way he could, becoming a key impetus in establishing the United States Film Service that Lorentz would soon be heading. *The River* was tactfully premiered in New Orleans on 29 October to forestall possible southern misconceptions that the film indicted the South, and then screened in other river cities before its 7 December Washington premiere. It met with almost universal praise, and reports of spontaneous audience applause are numerous. Shelley Hamilton accorded it the high compliment that among the documentary films he knew, "one has to go to the best work of Joris Ivens for anything to compare it with, and Ivens has not done anything with the expanse of *The River*." Denied a screening in the Academy Award competition, the film won the J. Emanuel Plaque for best three-reel dramatic film of 1938, and it triumphed over Leni Riefenstahl's *Olympiad* and all other entries to take first documentary film prize at the Venice International Film Festival the same year.[32]

As *The River* opens, shots of clouds and mountains give way to water dripping and spreading over patches of land, to tiny rivulets speeding through indentations in rocks, to a pool across which leaves sail, to small brooks and streams, to rivers flowing through forests, to larger rivers with more distant banks, and finally to the Mississippi herself, her widening shores, and the Gulf of Mexico. The camera varies in stasis and movement, although the flow is almost always toward the camera, and panning shots move left. Lorentz's narrative, which James Joyce called "the most beautiful prose I have heard in ten years," and which was quoted in review after review, summons forth the beauty and history of American names.

> Down the Yellowstone, the Milk, the White and Cheyenne;
> The Cannonball, the Musselshell, the James and the Sioux;
> Down the Judith, the Grand, the Osage, and the Platte,
> The Skunk, the Salt, the Black, and Minnesota . . .
> Down the great Valley, twenty-five hundred miles from
>   Minnesota . . .
> The Mississippi runs to the Gulf.[33]

Words, names, and shots rhythmically accumulate, mounting to an awe-inspiring sense of the movement down a continent of America's great and powerful river. Much more extensively than the opening grass shots in *The Plow That Broke the Plains*, this powerful beginning remains a touchstone for the film's subsequent images and events.

Historical sequences follow. After the Louisiana Purchase, Americans construct a one-thousand-mile levee from New Orleans to the mouth of the Ohio; they plant cotton in the now-protected land, and river commerce greatly expands. Lee's farewell message to his troops moves up the screen in titles, and images of decayed houses and eroded land reinforce the allusion to the "doubly stricken" South, impoverished both by war and by a quarter century of single-crop cultivation. But, we are told in a sudden, dramatic transition, "there was lumber in the North. Heads up!" Axes fly into trees, giant trees fall in long arcs, and, to the tune of "Hot Time in the Old Town Tonight," logs speed down sluices and move in masses down the rivers. "Hot Time" and "The Eagles They Fly High in Mobile" carry on through the industrial sequences that celebrate the rise of American cities, the mining of coal, the production of iron, and the development of the huge foreign markets for American cotton.

In the sequence that follows, clouds gather over stump-strewn, burntout hillsides, the narration pauses, and a shrill dissonant chord sounds as beads of water drop from icicles clinging to rotted trunks. The opening sequence then recurs, but with a disastrous difference: water drips and flows over patches of ground in the rain of an early spring, taking pieces of mud along, moving on to the turbulent swelling streams and rivers whose names are sounded once again as they flow to the Gulf, creating the great floods of the past and then the flood of 1937. Men fight the river, as the names of the towns along the levee that we heard in the second sequence resound again, and the river claims its victims. Another sequence views the aftermath, not only of the floods, but of the year-by-year attrition, the worn-away land, the terrible poverty of a sharecropper's cabin. As we look at a map, the dread statistics are repeated, flood control is mentioned, and the Tennessee Valley Authority is introduced. The film's final sequence presents the dams, the houses, the land, and the electrical power that have been brought into the valley by the TVA.

Chalmers' narrative performance cannot be sufficiently praised. His very tone sounds the exact vibrations of awe at the beauty of the rivers, of pride and spirited enterprise in the logging, industrial, and commercial years, of sorrow touched with anger over the land's devastation, of unsentimental compassion for the sharecroppers, and of resolution in the concluding New Deal sequence. His modulation is always perfect, reinforcing the shifts in mood carried by images, music, and words.

The prologue echoes that of The Plow That Broke the Plains. However, whereas that film was "a record of land . . . of soil, rather than people—a story of the Great Plains," this "is the story of a river; a record of the Mississippi." And the Mississippi is Lorentz's epic hero. It is a force, as Van Dyke noted on location, that offers itself to cinematic possibilities much more than do "dust storm stuff" or land. The river's movement dominates and unifies the film, giving it a forward impulse that carries through every sequence and to which Lorentz skillfully matches music, images, and narration. The citations of miles, bales, cities, and even flood victims, the pride in size and in successful enterprise voiced almost everywhere in the film seem to emerge from this vast body of water flowing through its great valley. The photography is often so brilliant, especially in shots of trickles and small streams, of eroded land, of lumber spinning down the sluices, and of cotton bales rolled by hand and conveyor on and off the ships, and the river's unifying force and the film's imaginative editing so powerful that the critics failed to note the existence of several undistinguished shots—and there are more here than in *The Plow That Broke the Plains*. Such flaws, however, are simply drowned out by the preponderance of striking images, the voice, the music, the pace, the film's sheer movement.

Unlike *The Plow That Broke the Plains*, which in its amended version[p] concludes with dust storms, Oakies, and barren trees, *The River* does not end with flood, sharecroppers, and eroded soil, and the difference in final effect is substantial. Even though it was sometimes condemned during the 1930s, as it is sometimes condemned today, the adulatory TVA sequence fits the film in a coherent fashion that was evidently lacking in the original epilogue of *The Plow*. *The River* is essentially about power. The vast body of water sweeping down the continent, the building of cities and industries, the shipping, logging, and steelmaking, the great flood, and the whole accumulating driving movement that affects even the slower sequences are redolent with power, and the film is always at the very least subtly celebrative of these forces. When the two great, unbridled powers have done their damage, they themselves are not destroyed: American enterprise and the great Mississippi remain.

As we watch the map, we begin to learn of their potential and mutual transformation, and our learning is reinforced by the repetition of words signifying power and control:

> Flood control of the Mississippi means control in the great Delta that must carry all the water brought down from two-thirds the continent

[p] The epilogue was removed sometime in the second or third year after *The Plow*'s appearance.

And control of the Delta means control of the little rivers and the
  great arms running down from the uplands.
And the old river can be controlled.
We had the power to take the Valley apart—we have the power
  to put it together again.
In 1933 we started, . . . when Congress created the Tennessee
  Valley Authority, an authority[q] commissioned to develop
  navigation, flood control, agriculture, and industry in the
  Valley . . .

Then the sound of an explosion: a dynamited hillside blows outward.
A steamshovel digging the earth and swinging up; an extreme low
angle of a man against the sky jackhammering stone; dams under
construction; more blasts; more jackhammers. Fast-moving legs, fast-
moving heads, the Civilian Conservation Corps youth on the march;
axes swing through the air, feet pound the soil around newly planted
trees on flat land and in deep gullies. New communities, new houses,
large still bodies of water contrast with earlier shots of the flood and
its aftermath. Then the final, fast, thirty-four shots of the film: dams,
power lines, towers accented by low-angle and tilted-camera positions,
valves, levers, engineers, water streaming and rushing from the dam,
all culminating in a frame-filling shot of pouring turbulent water acting
at man's bidding. Over these final thirty-four shots, Chalmers intones:

But where there is water there is power.
Where there's water for flood control and water for navigation,
  there's water for power—
Power for the farmers of the Valley, cut off for years from the
  advantages of urban light,
Power for the villages and cities and factories of the Valley.
West Virginia, North Carolina, Tennessee, Mississippi, Georgia,
  and Alabama,
Power to make a new Tennessee Valley for a new generation,
Power enough to make the river work!

Thematically, then, the conclusion is consistent with the rest of the
film, and it represents an answer to a vividly recorded problem. One
may feel considerable unease over the bell-ringing propaganda for a
New Deal program. One may also remain unconvinced that the solution will prevail. Yet one must admire the sense of conviction that
is conveyed in the final sequence, a conviction that is lacking in the

---

[q] The repetition of "authority" was added to reinforce the assertiveness here—it is
not in the *Film Comment* manuscript.

conclusion of Steiner's and Van Dyke's later, and in some ways rival film, *The City*.

The River has the same peculiar tension we found in *The Plow That Broke the Plains*. There the credits appeared across an illustration of pioneers on the move. Here the title is backed by a drawing of steamboats lined up at a busy wharf, smoke pouring from their stacks, an evocation and celebration of American commerce and of the great romance of the Mississippi River. Here again we hear exultation over the size of America and the prowess, inventiveness, and resources of the American people. Here again the viewer is warmed by the spirit of local folk songs and popular ditties based on American traditions. And here again such pride and hopeful spirit coexist with the images of the devastating flood and the negligence and greed with which Americans have used their land. They coexist in creative tension because Lorentz is no naive optimist plumping for national greatness. A tough-minded artist, he captures much of the worst that nature and human inadequacy can do and have done. He captures it in a way that hurts, but with a style that also asserts a love and a faith in national qualities that, if they are far from triumphant, remain potent and moving.

I have criticized the handling of people in *The Plow That Broke the Plains* and have recorded Van Dyke's on-location suspicion that *The River* would also be weak in characterization. And I have mentioned Rotha's suggestion that Lorentz take his remaining funds and "record some of the real people to find how they reacted to the problems of soil erosion and lack of flood control." Praising the film, Shelley Hamilton said, "As *The Plow* told about the land and the dust storms, *The River* tells about the water and the floods. The third part of a natural trilogy would be about the people."[34]

Essentially this is correct. In this epic of the river, people are dwarfed; they are illustrations, and neither they nor their situations are lingered over. During the flood, whether piling up sandbags, being helped from boats, or being evacuated in cars, the people are not carefully observed. There is only one exception: two juxtaposed shots in a relief camp of two boys in close-up and a woman feeding her baby, where the voice-over is effectively absent. Otherwise the film, driven by the force of the flood, passes over the people who, along with the upturned houses are simply part of the wreckage of the raging water.

This lack of human perspective is not entirely a flaw. Had Lorentz added Rotha-inspired interviews, it would have fatally undercut the film's singular poetic unity and thrust. When Van Dyke wanted to direct a family scene and to structure the film around personal dramas, he was thinking of his own needs and sympathies. Lorentz's purpose was different. Concerned with natural power that needed harnessing, he had to develop in the audience a desire for that control in addition to a feeling of affirmation and support for a government that was ostensibly acting to answer that desire, and acting in harmony with the spirit of a great nation. Any accent upon victims or individual portraiture would have clashed with these goals.

And yet one sequence to some extent undercuts the criticism and looks ahead both to Lorentz's next project, *Ecce Homo!*, and to his future film, *The Fight for Life*. *The River*'s longest shot (aside from the Lee titles and the map) holds for twenty-five seconds, the first eighteen free of narration. On the screen appears a cotton field with sparsely scattered bolls. As we watch, four pickers, dragging white bags along behind them, slowly enter the frame on a diagonal from the lower right hand corner. Lorentz holds and holds on this at a sharp overhead angle, and the pickers' weary motion across the profitless land, with those wormlike appendages, takes on a sad, disturbing quality unlike anything else in the film. Then the narration begins:

And poor land makes poor people.
Poor people make poor land.
For a quarter of a century we have been forcing more and more
    farmers into tenancy.
Today forty percent of all the farmers in the great Valley are
    tenants.
Ten percent are share croppers,
Down on their knees in the Valley,
A share of the crop their only security.
No home, no land of their own,
Aimless, footloose, and impoverished,
Unable to eat even from the land because their cash crop is their
    only livelihood.
Credit at the store is their only reserve.

Five more shots of the cotton pickers accompany these words: one for thirteen seconds from one side; two accentual close-ups, one low-angle, the other profile, the face far left in the frame; one from the other side; and one of the bags from behind, tilting up to catch the pickers. A young boy in rags is playing with tin cans, then we are inside the sharecroppers' cabin with the dirt, rags, miserable food, and crowded sleeping conditions—the shots tough, caring, concerned, Chalmers' voice compassionate with a touch of bitterness:

And a generation growing up with no new land in the West—
No new continent to build.
A generation whose people knew King's Mountain, and Shiloh;
A generation whose people knew Fremont and Custer;
But a generation facing a life of dirt and poverty,
Disease and drudgery;
Growing up without proper food, medical care, or schooling,
"Ill-clad, ill-housed, and ill-fed"—
And in the greatest river Valley in the world.[r]

Accenting the irony of the final words, the sequence concludes four shots later with a repeat of the final two shots of the opening sequence, the river mouth opening into the Gulf and the water of the Gulf itself.

People who write about *The River* seldom mention this sequence. It remains relatively unnoticed by the viewer because, like all the other sequences, it too is overwhelmed by the river's cinematic and narrative domination of the film. Had the film ended on this sequence, however, it would have had much more force. Unfortunately, the map and the TVA take over. The film is not Buñuel's *Las Hurdas*, nor is it Storck's *Les Maisons de la Misère*, nor Strand's *The Wave*. The victims of the conditions it describes are not woven into the film's texture from the start, nor does the major body of the film move toward these sharecroppers. But it does, unexpectedly, dwell on them for some strange moments, and a sensitive viewing of the film will inform the viewer that for Pare Lorentz their existence is, after all, very significant.

[r] Lorentz's original script for the ensuing narration (which is heard in voice-over while the map is shown) states that the sharecroppers were "living in a state of squalor unknown to the poorest peasant in Europe." Someone found this an unpleasant thought, and it was dropped from the film.

IV ■ Frontier Films and Ivens:
Fighting Fascism, 1937

Frontier Films

Returning from *The River*, Van Dyke found to his discomfort that Nykino was now a large-scale production company under a new name. During his absence, *The Wave* had been completed and, after a stop in Los Angeles's Spanish quarter where Rodakiewicz, von Fritsch, and Zinnemann first saw it, it premiered in New York in the fall of 1936. Hurwitz and John Dos Passos supplied subtitles, and after a year's planning, Nykino was ready to invite seventy-five writers and film-makers to a screening of *The Wave* and *The World Today*. George Sklar was there and recalls Clifford Odets "getting up, all impassioned, and shouting, 'This is it! This is the future! And I volunteer all the talent I have to contribute to it!' " Vera Caspary offered to write a script and asked Sklar, who had five plays and some film experience with Paramount to his credit, to collaborate with her. An enthusiastic Donald Ogden Stewart promised a second script. According to *New Theatre*, all skepticism was accordingly "brushed aside" and plans . . . immediately launched for the solidification of all progressive film forces in the East." In March, "the successful reorganization of those forces into Frontier Films"[1] was reported.

Both films went to public theaters, and Frontier Films published a brochure, its cover graced with a still from *The Wave*, a quotation by Archibald MacLeish ("a bold new step in the field of American movies"), and a description of Frontier as "an independent, nonprofit motion picture organization devoted to the production of realistic films of American life."[2] Within appeared a statement of purpose, stills from

The Plow That Broke the Plains and "Black Legion," strongly supportive statements by Catherine Bauer, Harold Clurman, Malcolm Cowley, Lester Granger, Eleanor Herrick, Gardner Jackson, Max Lerner, Lewis Mumford, Clifford Odets, Herman Shumlin, Sylvia Sidney and Rose Terlin, and favorable comment on the photography of *The Plow That Broke the Plains* and *The Wave* by Waldo Frank, Arthur Kober, Eleanor Roosevelt, George Seldes, Frank Tuttle, *Time*, the *Baltimore Sun*, and *The National Board of Review Magazine*.

The brochure listed the new organization's board of directors: Paul Strand, president; Leo Hurwitz and Ralph Steiner, vice-presidents; John Howard Lawson, secretary; Bernard J. Reis, treasurer; Lionel Berman, executive director; and Kyle Crichton, William O. Field, Elia Kazan, Mary Lescaze, Anita Marburg, Philip Stevenson, and David Wolff (Ben Maddow), associate directors. In addition to some of the above, the staff included Joris Ivens, Louis Kamp, Herbert Kline, Irving Lerner, Albert Maltz, Margaret Murray, George Sklar, Robert Stebbins (Sidney Meyers), and Willard Van Dyke. Advisory board members and technical consultants were: Catherine Bauer, Albert Bein, Bruce Bliven, Vera Caspary, Carlos Chavez, Aaron Copland, Malcolm Cowley, Paul de Kruif, John Dos Passos, Waldo Frank, Lester Granger, Lillian Hellman, Josephine Herbst, Gardner Jackson, Arthur Kober, Max Lerner, Archibald MacLeish, Lewis Milestone, Clifford Odets, Sidney Perelman, Edwin Rolfe, Muriel Rukeyser, George Seldes, Irwin Shaw, Claire and Paul Sifton, George Soule, Virginia Stevens, Genevieve Taggard, and Leane Zugsmith.[a] The names alone proclaim a left-wing organization of fellow travelers, liberal adherents to the popular front, and Communist Party members. It was the latter group (he names Lawson in particular) that made Van Dyke uncomfortable.

In the brochure, a long quotation from Rose Terlin's *You and I and the Movies* zeroed in on Hollywood's misuse of the power of film. Hollywood avoided depicting poverty, celebrated individualism, and glorified "the racial barriers, militarism, imperialism and nationalistic chauvinism" that "have succeeded only in bringing us to the brink of another world war." In contrast, Frontier would wield film's power "consistently on the side of progress." It would reflect truthfully "the life and drama of contemporary America" and incorporate the "great new mine of material" Hollywood neglected. It would draw, Cowley

[a] Few of these people were very active with Frontier, and not all knew of the use of their names here and on official stationery. It was "totally unknown" to Vera Caspary, for example, "until 1952 when I was questioned in Hollywood about my participation with the group." Letter from Caspary to author, 22 June 1975.

suggested, on sitdown strikers marching behind brass bands and on the struggles of an ordinary working-class family. Underlying these declarations, Hurwitz remembers, was a sustaining sense of conviction: "We were young and confident. The confidence arose from two things: the existing constriction of the medium which asked for new ideas, and the generating power imbedded in having something important to say, deeply felt and deeply needed."[3]

Initial film plans? At the outset, five playwrights and some members of the board donated production rights to well-known plays, but Frontier never translated them to film. Having vowed to be at the disposal of "trade unions, educational institutions, social welfare groups, farm organizations, co-operative societies, peace organizations, etc.," Frontier quickly contacted key labor organizations and set Vera Caspary and George Sklar hard to work on a script for *Pay Day*, a three-reel dramatization of child labor. In April, Frontier announced "plans for a full feature on farm life and its problems as represented by the lives and times of the sturdy farmers of the early days of Bucks County, Pa." Nothing came of this. They also conceived *Labor Spy*, a film on the findings of the LaFollette Committee on Civil Rights. By fall, they had summoned Bill Watts, who had experience in the left theater, from Hollywood to collaborate with Hurwitz and Strand on the child labor film and to direct actors on the civil rights film. In October they dispatched a crew to a farm near Poughkeepsie to shoot the first sequence of *Labor Spy*. A film "portraying the unionization of John Doe, automobile worker" was also on the sketch board in the fall, and, in what seemed a stroke of financial luck, a group of city planners asked Ralph Steiner to produce a film for the 1939 World's Fair. Accordingly, Lionel Berman told John E. Devine that Frontier would "make a film on the need for town planning and some of the methods of its accomplishment."[4]

The group also imagined two fiction films. The first exists only as a vague recollection in the minds of the filmmakers. Van Dyke says Hurwitz, Steiner, and Strand collaborated on a script about an architect who could not find a place in society. Hurwitz barely recalls the script, which means, he says, only that he was not close to it. Steiner recalls showing Lee Strasberg a Hurwitz/Steiner script that "started with a man who was thinking of committing suicide." Strasberg exclaimed (and Steiner cites this to substantiate his view of Hurwitz as a gloomy person), "My God, you start way down at the lower depths, and then you keep on climbing farther and farther and farther down." He was probably referring to the architect script, which was most likely written in the late Nykino days and never filmed. The second film was Steiner's brainchild, born of Frontier's need for money and Steiner's own unease with the content of *Labor Spy*. He suggested to Dashiell Hammett that Hammett write a left-wing labor mystery film to be acted and directed by Group Theatre people. Delighted with the idea, Hammett nevertheless kept Steiner hanging for weeks, until Lillian Hellman counseled Steiner to drop the idea.[5]

Of all these potential films, only one, *Labor Spy*, expanded and renamed *Native Land*, was to be produced by Frontier. As usual, circumstances as well as money played a part here. Because their independence was crucial to them, the Frontier organization avoided all links with Hollywood, the government, and the corporations. This meant that they depended instead on individual donors and on sponsors who might act as collaborators and consultants and provide funds out of faith in the filmmakers' artistry and in endorsement of their politics. Even with the filmmakers themselves working for little and sometimes no salary, such sponsorship was not easy to come by, nor would film income suffice to finance new films. Blockbooking in the commercial theaters was a bar to distribution, and they counted on quick expansion of the 16mm market. In their early months, they told Ben Belitt, they "appealed . . . to the 'subway circuit' of motion-picture houses, for the most part independently owned and exhibiting the finer foreign films throughout the country." They also intended "to utilize the channels" of unions, public forums, schools, churches, and other groups favorable to their films. They had ambitions, too, for "a program of organized roadshows which will tour the farming communities and mill towns of the nation."[6] In fact many such sources were tapped but never on the full and regular basis essential to financial success.

Why "Frontier Films"? While on location on *The River* on 1 February 1937, Van Dyke posed a rhetorical question common in the latter half of the decade to people of many political persuasions: How, in a country of "scheming merchants," was one "to recreate the vision of the pioneer?" For the newly formed film group, this vision was to be recreated in labor's struggle for equal rights and in the discovery, through that struggle, of cooperation as a way of life. Accordingly, they would make films on the frontier of the labor battle, in support of industrywide unionization under the CIO. And they were, after all, film pioneers: left independent production had never before succeeded in America; the industry had barely touched their material and point of view; and, scornful of Hollywood art, they were devising an original film aesthetic. Dovzhenko's *Frontier* influenced the name as well, for they aspired to the poetry and depth of his political art. Finally—if one ignores a possible allusion to the popular front—the name was in part a response to the increasing anti-Communist attacks against the left. As Hurwitz has explained in relation to *Native Land*, the name asserted vitally American roots and was meant to challenge the assertions of those who were eager to brand them "un-American."[7]

Ivens' *The Spanish Earth*

A staff member and always a close friend and advisor, Joris Ivens was never to work on a frontier production. At the time of the organization's official founding, in fact, he was caught up in an international event that was to alter Frontier's plans. Back in July of 1936, while Ivens was studying the Hollywood milieu, while "Black Legion" actors were moving before Nykino cameras, and while Lorentz was gathering his crew for *The River*, the Spanish army rebelled against the five-month-old popular-front government and established its own government in Burgos, commencing the civil war that was to last nearly three years. Popular-front intellectuals and artists in America regarded the Spanish Civil War as a crucial combat between the forces of socialism or democracy and fascism, the first European testing ground of a struggle that America herself might not escape. The Communist Party was very strong in the Spanish Loyalist government and grew stronger, in part because the Soviet Union was the single nation actively supporting the Loyalists. In order to maintain its stance of "cooperation and compromise" and to overcome dissident anarchist and Communist groups calling for the spreading of the revolution and for workers' control of government and army, the Party in Spain resorted to repressive tactics that some associated with Stalinist Russia.[8] While anti-Stalinist Marxists in the States protested, most American leftists were either unaware of such tactics or preferred to ignore them. They knew the war was not, as some compatriots urged, merely a local struggle between Communists and Fascists, and they did not want admittedly significant internal Loyalist struggles to obscure what they saw, rightly, as a war against a growing international evil. The poverty of the Spanish peasant and worker was well known, as was the brutal stifling of liberties and the rising militarism among Franco's Axis allies, while the nature of a triumphant Loyalist government was not yet determined. Against those who cited Communist involvement as an excuse for not actively supporting the Loyalist side, Archibald MacLeish countered:

It is the familiar argument advanced by the hypocrites and the
cynical and frivolous who do not wish to understand what is happening in Spain. . . . It is the cheap and easy argument of those
who wish not to think. What gives it importance is merely this:
that its proponents use it to attack the intelligence if not the
integrity of those who, not themselves communists, stand with
the communists in active opposition to the menace of fascism.
They imply that those who find themselves in this position are
dupes: that they are being "used," and "used" without a proper
understanding of the "use."

The answer is, of course, that the man who refuses to defend
his convictions for fear that he may defend them in the wrong
company, has no convictions. . . . Why *should* a man be "used"
unless he pleases? Why should he not himself become the "user"?

It was "a war," Joris Ivens wrote not many years later, "where ideas
of Right and Wrong were clashing in clear conflict," a war that fully
engaged the emotions and many of the actions of the intellectuals and
artists on the left.[9]

By late summer of 1936, seeking new experience in editing, Ivens
and Helen van Dongen were at work on an educational film project
for the Rockefeller Foundation. Their job was to cut down to twenty
essential minutes a series of Hollywood story films that involved problems in human relations, including—once van Dongen expanded the
definition—such racial and economic subjects as lynching and housing.
The twenty-minute film was intended to trigger discussion in schools
and colleges.[10]

While van Dongen was thus employed, a group of Loyalist sym-
pathizers asked her to edit Spanish War newsreel footage into a documentary film that would detail the war's background and clarify the
issues for an American audience. Available footage was mainly from
the Franco side, making the job difficult and expensive. Ivens, who
since the outset had sought means to aid the Loyalists, suggested it
would be better in every way for the group to produce their own film.
Accordingly, John Dos Passos, Lillian Hellman, Ernest Hemingway,
Archibald MacLeish, Clifford Odets, Dorothy Parker, and Herman
Shumlin became Contemporary Historians Inc. to sponsor and finance
Ivens in the undertaking that was to become *The Spanish Earth*.

After raising two or three thousand dollars, Ivens flew to Paris in
December to arrange processing facilities there and to pick up Johnny
Ferno,[b] who had agreed to serve as a cameraman. Like everyone else

[b] This is Johnny Fernhout of *New Earth*; he adopted this spelling for *The Spanish
Earth* and his subsequent work in America, and I will use it henceforth.

involved with the film, Ferno and Ivens were to receive no pay. Van Dongen would stay in New York and edit material Ivens sent her, reporting to him her sense of what footage was still needed. Meanwhile, she continued shortening the Hollywood films and also completed the editing of the other film, *Spain in Flames*,ᶜ which appeared at the Cameo Theatre late in Janaury, where it was introduced by Fernando de Los Rios, the Spanish Loyalist government's ambassador to the United States.[11]

Ivens had carried with him to Spain a scenario prepared by one of the writers in the Contemporary Historians group. The citizens of a village on the road between Madrid and Valencia were to reenact their experience from the abdication of King Alfonso to the present. The film would center on a nonpolitical family that was gradually educated to the meaning of the great struggle, a story that would both involve and educate the American viewer. But when he reached Spain, Ivens found that its people were so engulfed in the fight that the efforts at reenactment obviously had to be junked. In the chaos that was Spain, he could find no Ministry of Information, no organized propaganda center to assist him. He dropped the scenario, began to ask questions, went to Madrid to film some fighting, and soon developed as a line for the picture the connection between land reform and the war. He and Ferno selected Fuentidueña, a village on the Madrid-Valencia road, as the site for their agricultural link. Caught up in the confusion and the excitement of the war and thus unsure of the nature of his footage—was it more than newsreel material?—Ivens took what he had shot to Paris for processing and advice. The results were encouraging.

At this point Dos Passos, who had been working on the film, left

ᶜ *Spain in Flames*, a film I have not been able to see, resulted from a collaboration between Amkino Corporation (the New York distributors of Soviet films) and Film Historians, Inc., the group who had earlier turned to van Dongen. The film was in two parts: a three-reeler entitled "Spain, the Fight for Freedom," composed of footage by Spanish cameramen from both sides, and a four-reeler entitled "No Passaran!," made up of Soviet footage. Dos Passos and MacLeish wrote the narration, evidently with some advice from Hemingway. "Spain, the Fight for Freedom" first presented the sociopolitical background for the war, stressing the long oppression of the peasant and working classes in Spain. It then "exuberantly [chronicled] the revolution and the establishment of a Socialist republic and [hurried] from there into the counterrevolution," attacking the German and Italian support of the rebels without which the rebellion would collapse. "No Passaran!" had much combat material and included the siege of the Alcazar, the bombings of Madrid and the Soviet food and supply ship, and speeches by La Passionaria and José Diaz. *Spain in Flames* ran into censorship suppression in both Philadelphia and Ohio. Information from film manuscripts at the Film Study Center, Museum of Modern Art, New York, and from: N, 27 Mar. 1937, p. 340; Frank Nugent, "The Screen: *Spain in Flames*, Depicting the Spanish Revolution, Opens at the Cameo—*Holy Terror* at the Palace," *N.Y. Times*, 30 Jan. 1937, p. 21; and Irving Lerner, NM, 9 Feb. 1937, p. 29.

A Madrid Document, a three-reel newsreel from Madrid screened for the first time

Spain in bitter disillusionment over the political developments in the popular-front government, and Hemingway, whom Ivens met in Paris, joined the crew of *The Spanish Earth* as an integral, hardworking member. He carried the camera, helped with arrangements, and out of his own past war experience prevented Ivens and Ferno from taking unnecessary risks while filming on the Morata de Tajuña and Jarama fronts. All the while they never forgot that they were in a hurry:

> Our job was not to make the best of all films, but to make a good film for exhibition in the United States, in order to collect money to send ambulances to Spain. When we started shooting, we didn't always wait for the best conditions to get the best shot. We just tried to get good, useful shots.

Covering shellings and bombings, men at work on the land, and battles, they found themselves instinctively seeking "the significant human detail," the "human way" of representing war to the human beings whom they were determined to inspire to react against it.

Ivens returned to New York in May. There he worked intensely on the editing with van Dongen, who "put all of her professional skill into this work" and merits a great deal of credit for the finished film, as she does for all of Ivens' films of the twenties and thirties. Van Dongen and Irving Reis developed effects for the sound track, while Marc Blitzstein and Virgil Thomson listened to record after record of Spanish folk music in order to prepare the score. Ivens and Hemingway agreed to keep comment to a minimum, to use but "a few words . . . at the beginning of the sequences as a sort of springboard, from where the audience starts to be involved in the action . . . a sort of awakening of the public's active relationship with the film." They also decided to avoid tendentious material, thus forestalling "any of the expected accusations of purveying red propaganda[d] . . . providing, instead, a base on which the spectator was stimulated to form his own conclusions."[12]

at the New School on 14 February 1937, ran into similar censorship suppression in Philadelphia. The film contained an appeal for funds, appeared at the New School under the auspices of the Medical Bureau of the American Friends of Spanish Democracy, was confiscated after one showing by the New Theatre of Philadelphia, and was advertised as "a great epic film—Actual Bombardment—International Brigade in action—Writers and authors from Madrid as commentators." See NM, 16 Feb. 1937, p. 26, and 6 Apr. 1937, p. 21; NT, Apr. 1937, p. 18.

[d] Governor Earle of Pennsylvania branded *Spain in Flames* "pure communistic propaganda. . . . We Pennsylvanians are not interested in the propaganda of a government largely made up of Communists, Syndicalists, and Anarchists who butcher priests" (N, 27 March 1937, p. 46). Ivens' and Hemingway's care paid off. The Pennsylvania Board of Censors banned the film, but after a special showing, Governor Earle overruled them (*Film Survey*, Oct. 1937, p. 4, and Nov. 1937, p. 3).

For narrator, MacLeish suggested Orson Welles, a name that would both attract viewers and bring in money. And in fact, those who previewed it—Franklin and Eleanor Roosevelt and Harry Hopkins at the White House on 7 July, the celebrities at the Ambassador Theatre in Los Angeles on 11 July, the guests at Fredric March's home on 12 July, and a capacity audience at the Los Angeles Philharmonic Auditorium on 13 July—viewed a Welles-narrated film.[e] Ivens, unsophisticated when it came to the nuances of English, had thought that the narration was excellent, but Hellman, Parker, Shumlin, and van Dongen felt that Welles' rich tones were inappropriate. In accordance, Ivens agreed to drop Welles, and the film opened in late August at New York's Fifty-Fifth Street Playhouse with Hemingway reading the narration. For the same reasons that had turned Lorentz to Thomas Chalmers, reasons vital to the sense of reality in documentary film, Ivens found this change an improvement:

> His commentary sounded like that of a sensitive reporter who has been on the spot and wants to tell you about it—a feeling that no other voice could communicate. The lack of a professional commentator's smoothness helped you to believe intensely in the experiences on the screen.[13]

The setting of *The Spanish Earth* is the town and the fields of Fuentidueña, the city of Madrid, and battlefronts along the key highway that connects Valencia and the besieged capital. Madrid and the highway must be defended, and a Fuentidueña irrigation project is crucial to that defense: on lands once withheld from farmers by Spanish landowners, farmers are now able to cultivate the wheat, potatoes, grapes, and onions that will feed the defenders of Madrid. Maps, dissolves, parallel action, and scenes of a Fuentidueña son fighting in Madrid stress this central connection between the work on the land and the defense of Madrid. As *The Spanish Earth* draws to a close, peasants hold high in the sunlight the last link of sluice that will insure the irrigation of the precious land, soldiers prevent Fascist rebels from taking the Arganda bridge, and, in a final montage, a single soldier pulls his rifle trigger as the water floods into the fields.

As the film opens, we see the vast land, with mountains rising in the distance and the figures of men and animals tiny in the frame. Then the angle is low, the men large in medium close-up, dry soil

[e] Evidently, the Welles print still exists at the Museum of Modern Art, for although they have no record of it, Helen van Dongen saw it several years ago (van Dongen Buffalo interview). Jean Renoir narrated the French version, in which a great deal of the effect that Hemingway gave the words was lost (see Robert Grelier, *Joris Ivens* [Paris: Les éditeurs Français réunis, 1965], p. 48).

sifting through their hands. Later, scattered soldiers move into attack positions, small against the battlefield and the sky, knowing the "ultimate loneliness," before them "all the great unknown." At other moments, with their rifles, guns, and field-phones, they dominate the shot. It is established that the earth and the universe are huge and powerful, the war destructive and its fortunes uncertain, yet that people assert their spirit and their humanity nonetheless.

Whereas in Ivens' *New Earth*, the motion of spoon to mouth dominated the rare pause on a face, in *The Spanish Earth* the camera lingers on a soldier eating fruit and moves down with him as he bends to reach something. This is one of five such tender camera movements that are dedicated to human activity in one short sequence. When Julian's small brother shouts to his father in the distant field that Julian is home, the father does not hear and moves on in his work to another spot, the camera at medium distance moving with him. Another shout: the camera tilts up with the father as he straightens in response. In the careful shots of men constructing the irrigation canal, it is not the dynamics of straining bodies that receive the emphasis but the individuals themselves. Between the shooting of *Borinage* and *The Spanish Earth*, Ivens' inclination to *locate people* had developed, and so had his technique for doing it. The relatively relaxed cutting pace and the constant camera movement with and over individuals, drawing us to them, convey a warm involvement with the nature and the character of the Spanish people, a high respect both for them and for their noble engagement against the Fascist rebels.

As fresh bread emerges from the ovens in the morning and women sweep the streets, as donkeys are mounted and horses haltered and a loose procession of men, boys, and animals make toward the fields, as women lay out the laundry and bunch up at the bakery window for their union-labeled bread, there is implicit in the camerawork and cutting a willingness to linger, to let movements and attitudes reveal themselves, to support the calm, deliberate rhythms of the village. This cinematic tactic, this effort to reflect the reality of place or event, permeates the film. It dictates the approach to soldiers who are at leisure and to soldiers who are undramatically, uncertainly, slogging up the road to an active front. And it dictates the handling of death. In Madrid, a shell has found a bookkeeper on his way to work in the early morning. The camera discovers him through a long tilt down a tall building to the street, continuing in a pan right to his body isolated on a curb. Then there is an agitated series of shots. Camera position is gradually closer to the bookkeeper, but the camera pans away from the body, pans from nearby rubble back to it, sketches the curious, unsure onlookers, pans up the dead man's body from his feet, cuts from side to side as the men from the municipal service place him in a coffin and the coffin in a truck. All the awkwardness and tension and difficulty of dealing with his death—for both filmmakers and citizens— is sensitively communicated.

As MacLeish astutely pointed out, this tactic may be compared to the art of the realistic novel.[14] Avoiding romanticization and overdramatization, Ivens attempts to get at the casual, normal, everyday, minimally edited contents of a way of life, of what it is really like to live socially, culturally, politically in a given environment. We are not very much farther into the inner character of individuals than we were in *New Earth*, but we have a significantly fuller awareness of who they are and how they live. The strategy of the realistic approach is as follows. We learn the faces, the habits, the jobs, the environments, and the rhythms of a people in their daily lives, and we make an association: whatever the differences, they live from day to day, casually, as we do. And *then* we realize that these daily lives are being lived in a state of crisis, that these people are engaging their habits, skills, and rhythms in a war. At the end of the first long Fuentidueña sequence, for instance, after the many shots of activity in town and field, we watch at a distance the farmers laboring on the irrigation project and hear *for the first time* the guns in the mountains beyond them. That these people with whom we are in considerable empathy are so willingly engaged in the battle against the Fascists makes us feel that the Loyalist cause is deeply worthwhile. *The Spanish Earth* seeks both the normally experienced reality of an environment and the truth of human experience, and it presents both in the service of a cause.

A key sequence further defines the integrated purpose of the Spanish people. Troops come together to elect representatives to a meeting celebrating the formation of the United People's Army. One small group of these troops is linked through a dissolve to raised fists at the meeting itself. There Enrique Lister, Carlos, José Diaz, the German writer Gustav Regler, and La Passionaria deliver spirited, passionate speeches to a militant, cheering audience. The viewer is strongly moved by the engagement and by the nobility in these working-class leaders and in the German writer "who came to Spain to fight for his ideals." As La Passionaria speaks, a wipe takes us to a sound truck that projects her words over a loudspeaker to troops in the field, just as earlier, internal montage had linked barber and sound trucks, and the loudspeaker had sounded over troops both at leisure in the trenches and at a rifle-assemblage session. The daily activity, the soldiers, the leaders and representatives—all of these connections underscore the fact that the proud mood at the meeting permeates both soldiers and peasants, as day by day they lead their wartime lives.

With this film, Ivens became conscious of three levels of editing, the first being the "simple visual editing, as in . . . the closing of the dam" in *New Earth*. On the second level, "this limited sensual aim is broadened to include psychological factors": Julian's homecoming is "aimed at an overall emotional warmth, rather than at any story point that could be isolated and identified." On the third level, the emotional aim is raised to "the personal, social and political point of view of the filmmaker." This is "empathic cutting, pulling the spectator by his emotions from stage to stage of an idea's development." It derives "mostly from a wish to deepen the relation of real things—to show what is below the surface." Here Dovzhenko was as important to Ivens as he was to the members of Nykino, who spoke of him in the same terms. *Earth*, *Frontier*, and especially *Arsenal* had influenced Ivens' work "more than any other so-called 'non-factual' films." To demonstrate this third level, he takes an example from *The Spanish Earth*:

> In the fourteen shots that compose the core of the sequence of the bombing of the village, the editing directly follows an emotion-idea line: tensions before the bombing; the threat; the fright; the explosion; the destruction; the horror of not knowing what it's all about; the running around of the women; the start of activity, searching for victims; the slight happiness of a baby; then the horror of corpses and the accusation against the enemy—ending on a feeling of young life, a preparation for the counterblow, and then the blow itself.[15]

Nothing angered Ivens more than two frequent arguments from critics of *The Spanish Earth*. Where the film became strongly propagandistic, John McManus suggested, it was not art. Other critics argued that a film on Spain should be "objective," presenting both sides. In an unpublished reply to McManus, Ivens indicated that artists might, as they always had—and he cited Goya—reveal their personal, social, and political points of view, might urge a cause, and remain artists nonetheless. The call for "objectivity" was based, he later wrote, on a misunderstanding of the difference between a document and a documentary: "Do we demand objectivity in the evidence presented at a trial? No, the only demand is that each piece of evidence be as full a subjective, truthful, honest presentation of the witness's attitude as an oath on the Bible can produce from him." *The Spanish Earth*, Ivens told Gordon Hitchens years later, was certainly propaganda, but "propaganda on a high level—it is more a *témoignage* or what you call

. . . testimony, testimony of a man, where you know how he stands—
I don't hide myself."[16] One recalls Jean-Luc Godard's statement in *Far
From Vietnam*—a film Ivens took part in in 1967—that French film-
makers should make the scream of the Vietnamese their own.

The Spanish Earth has its weaknesses: Hemingway's narration, ad-
mirable for its sincerity and restraint, sometimes undercuts the Spanish
Civil War with its Hemingwayesque generalizations about war itself;
the use of Julian as a transitional device between city and town creates
an artificiality that distances the viewer, thus counteracting somewhat
the power of the music and the cinematography; and the film provides
insufficient background on the war.

Those are minor weaknesses. Archer Winston's comment that "perhaps a theme so large and diffuse will not prove exciting to the general
public"[17] touches the film's major weakness. What I have been calling
the realistic method is a highly viable, valuable way of creating sympathy with a cause. The danger inherent in a method that attempts
to depict the normal rhythms of life is that the pace of the film may
seem slow and diffuse in contrast to the tighter pace that drives a
propaganda picture forward and engages the viewer's emotions, intellect, and subsequent behavior, as Ivens himself argued that a militant documentary film should do. While *The Spanish Earth* draws so
much from the realistic method, it falls prey a little, just a little, to
its dangers, and it may, on first viewing at least, seem to go a little
dead.

With *Borinage*, Ivens decided to keep his angles straight, to make
plainer, starker, and what he called more honest films. But this decision, born in his reaction to the Belgian mining district and against
the slickness of his *Philips-Radio*, deprived his style after *New Earth*
of an intensive cinematic poetry, as both Hurwitz and Maddow point
out with regret.[18] It is my regret too, for I believe the earlier poetic
style could have been combined with the realistic method. Ivens'
greater artistic engagement in the individual shots and scenes of *The
Spanish Earth* could only have increased for the viewer the sense of
his conviction and concern. Still, however much we may regret this
failure to combine the intensive cinematic poetry of the early films
with the realistic method, the elimination of the former was a personal
necessity for Ivens, and he replaced it with another form of lyricism
in the relaxed pace and in the camera's respect for people. As a result,
The Spanish Earth is one of the best nonfiction films of the thirties.

Ivens and his sponsors hoped that the film would have some effect
upon Roosevelt's foreign policy and that it would raise substantial funds
for direct aid to the Loyalists. The immediate results were mixed.
Roosevelt's reaction to the film was positive, but he ventured no further

opinion on either the U.S. policy of nonintervention or on the neutrality act. The seventeen guests remaining at Fredric March's after Errol Flynn escaped a donation by fleeing through a bathroom window, gave $1,000 each to the Loyalist cause, and Los Angeles screenings netted over $20,000. The money went to the Ford factory in Detroit to purchase ambulance chasses, which were shipped to Madrid for completion.

It was crucial to Ivens and his sponsors that the *reality* and the significance of the war be brought home to Americans and to the United States government. MacLeish put this eloquently in a speech to the second American Writers' Congress early in the summer of 1937:

> Spain is no political allegory. Spain is not, as some would have us think, a dramatic spectacle in which the conflict of our time is acted out. These actors are not actors. They truly die. These cities are not stage sets. They burn with fire. These battles are not symbols of other battles to be fought elsewhere at some other time. They are the actual war itself. And in that war, that Spanish war on Spanish earth, we, writers who contend for freedom, are ourselves, and whether we so wish or not, engaged. . . . The military prestige of the fascist powers . . . is engaged in the Spanish war. We know that a fascist success in the Spanish war would mean a tremendous increase in that prestige and an almost certain end of democratic institutions in France, which means, in Europe. We know that a fascist failure in the Spanish war would mean a decline in that prestige and a possible collapse of fascist forms.

It was discouraging to Ivens and his sponsors that, despite titanic efforts and supportive telegrams from Hollywood artists, *The Spanish Earth* could not break through the tenacious power of the theater monopoly and the fears of the distributors into major theater distribution. But it finally did find a distributor—Prometheus Pictures of New York—and, after a long run to favorable reviews at the Fifty-Fifth Street Playhouse in New York, it was eventually booked into more than four hundred theaters in up to sixty American cities. In 16mm form, it played to many nontheatrical organizations as well. All the profits went to the assistance of the Loyalists.[19]

Frontier Films' *Heart of Spain*

One day in Madrid during the making of *The Spanish Earth*, Ivens had been visited by Herbert Kline, who solicited his comment on a film script he had just written. The script was a new departure in the already considerable career of the twenty-eight-year-old Kline. Brought up in Davenport, Iowa, in a middle-class Jewish family, he had stretched out his high-school years by bumming around the country and briefly going to sea, all the while reading widely in both classical and contemporary authors under the guidance of his older brother, Mark Marvin. Reacting against the Depression's extension of the "misery and poverty I had seen on the road," Kline began to write for transient midwestern publications of the John Reed Club, serving as associate editor on *The Left* in 1931 and as a contributor to *Left Front* in 1933 and 1934. He also "helped organize and wrote sketches for labor theaters," completing a one-act revolutionary play entitled *John Henry—Bad Nigger* in 1933. He mailed it to a Broadway producer who had advertised an interest in plays on social problems; the producer brought him to New York to ready the play for production. Before it could be produced, however, the producer went broke.

But *New Theatre* sponsored a dramatic reading of *John Henry* at the Theatre Collective on 18 March 1934, where Kline answered questions, and a number of labor theaters picked it up. Eager, highly competent and committed, Kline became managing editor of *New Theatre* in April, and by its July-August issue he had become editor. In January 1935, he signed the militant call to the First Writers' Congress, and along with James T. Farrell, Nathaniel West, Edward Dahlberg, and others, he joined the employees in their picketing of Ohrbach's Department Store on Union Square. In April he raced up to Boston to give the audience a preshow, anticensorship speech, when the Boston New Theatre group decided to violate the ban on Odets' *Waiting for Lefty*. The sixteenth of March found him participating in a critical symposium on MacLeish's *Panic*, the twenty-seventh of May found him lecturing on "Playwriting for the Revolutionary Theatre," and on the twenty-first of November he spoke in a symposium on the Soviet play *Squaring the Circle*, for which he also helped make some changes. During August and September, he took a trip to the Soviet Union as the head of a *New Theatre* tour that was to be welcomed by Tretyakov, Eisenstein, Friedrich Wolf, Jay Leyda, Leon Moussinac, Chen-I-wan, and Irwin Piscator.[20]

During these years, Kline skillfully guided *New Theatre* from the Communist Party's hard-line period into the era of the popular front, drew on a wide range of excellent writers, and managed to keep subscriptions up during difficult times. Within the magazine's pages, he strongly advocated the unified growth of workers' theaters and constantly pushed for higher artistic standards in revolutionary art, for

less agitational and more realistic productions, for increased participation by major playwrights, and for awareness of dramaturgical tradition. An article that he had composed in the Soviet Union urged
artists of the American left to draw upon native dances, songs, and
legends, upon vestiges of "old country life" brought over by immigrants, and upon such heroes as Daniel Boone, Nat Turner, John
Henry, Abraham Lincoln, Eugene Debs, and the Haymarket martyrs.[21]

Kline resigned his editorship on 1 January 1937 in order to join the
Loyalist cause as a radio propagandist and to share with James Haw-
thorne the war correspondence for *New Masses*. He went first to Paris,
where he spent several evenings with the Hungarian still photographer
Geza Karpathi, fantasizing over the documentary film they would like
to make in Spain. In February he began work for station EAQ in
Madrid, his voice issuing over the shortwave air in America late in
March and carrying as far west as Kansas. EAQ carried Loyalist propaganda behind the Fascist lines, and the message was communicated
in Italian, German, and Moorish to the hostile forces lodged in University City on the outskirts of Madrid. As the "Voice of Spain," it
broadcast "an honest interpretation of the Spanish issues" to "the land
of . . . Valley Forge and Long Island . . . of Wat Tyler and Milton
. . . of Robespierre and the Paris Commune . . . of Karl Liebknecht
and Heine, and . . . of Garibaldi's red shirts." So Kline explained in
a piece for *New Masses*, for which he also wrote a moving memorial
on John Lenthier, the twenty-two-year-old Communist and New Theatre member from Boston who had acted in *Waiting for Lefty* and had
been killed in action with the Abraham Lincoln Battalion. He also
wrote an article about the young leftists of the Lincoln and Washington
battalions whom he had interviewed in the trenches at Morata—men,
he reported, who saw their presence there as an extension of their
presence on picket lines at home.[22]

Late one night, Karpathi arrived at Kline's door, announcing that
the Canadian doctor Norman Bethune had commissioned him to make
a film to raise money for the Loyalist medical service. The film was
to describe Bethune's new techniques for transfusion and blood preservation. Would Kline write a script? After traveling a few days with
the mobile blood unit, Kline set to work, creating a "crude thread of
a story showing how one of Madrid's mothers who gave her blood as
a volunteer donor meets the young soldier whose life was saved by
her blood," a story for nonactors. Who, Kline asked Ivens, could he
get to direct the film? Anyone who can visualize as well as you have
done in this script, Ivens replied, should do the directing. Impressed

with the story idea, Bethune and Karpathi agreed that Kline should take on the job.

Neither Kline nor Karpathi had had any previous experience as filmmakers, a fact that they kept to themselves. They learned to operate their Eyemo under the pretext that it was broken, watching carefully as the lab technician took it apart and loaded it. And so they began shooting what was to become *Heart of Spain*. They filmed in hospitals, on the front, and in Madrid before and during bombardments, and they lived with the blood unit, sometimes helping to unload the ambulances. The work was dangerous: Karpathi, who did most of the camerawork, was wounded while he was covering a bombardment in Madrid. But their artistic ambition was high, and they were sure that the cause was worthwhile. From the beginning, Kline wrote later, their aspiration was to go deeper than the newsreel, to achieve in film the distinction attained in writing by "the great foreign correspondents."[23]

No one in the States knew what Kline was up to except Leo Hurwitz, a good friend whom Kline describes as a "very good film editor on *New Theatre*." Kline and Karpathi had expected to edit in Paris, but they accompanied Bethune to the States in midsummer and took their footage to Strand and Hurwitz at Frontier Films. Strand and Hurwitz thought it an excellent basis for a film, although they believed that it needed additional material. They revised the scenario, and Maddow, in collaboration with Kline, began work on the narration. They all labored intensely, hurrying to bring the film to the theaters. The narration came to Hurwitz late the night before mixing was to begin, and he sat into the small hours going over it, paring it down. According to Strand, the footage presented problems:

> We had a lot of very ordinary images from Herbert Kline and Karpathi, both of whom were novices. . . . They did some very good things, very good work that could be used. . . . Without the excellent footage of the donors' arms going down we probably couldn't have made the film at all. . . . And they did other things that were the devil to cut, almost impossible. For instance, Karpathi did what all beginners are apt to do: they pan the camera on almost every scene. . . . So you were always faced with a pan and what to do with it. Then there were ordinary shots that visually were good but not very handsome to look at in any way.

These shots, Strand thought, were redeemed and vitalized by Maddow's "absolutely great" discoveries that "are a part of the aesthetics of filmmaking."

Maddow himself recalls sitting at the moviola with Kline and sometimes Hurwitz, "going over the footage. . . . And I would say, What about this idea? Here? And I would make a little note. And I remember getting very excited by this combination of word and image." In his eyes, the image became a noun for his words to modify: the viewer would see that image within the meaning and timing of his words. The excitement over the film was clearly general: although it was not the labor film they had planned, *Heart of Spain* was Frontier Films' first film. It was not only their first chance to enact their theories about cinematic structure but also an opportunity to bring money and volunteers to the Loyalist cause. Assisted by Jay Leyda, Alex North made a masterly arrangement of Spanish music, and Joris Ivens contributed some footage shot for *The Spanish Earth*, at a point, according to Strand, "when we were just scraping the barrel." Irving Lerner worked on sound effects, and John O'Shaugnessy was asked to narrate.[24]

Heart of Spain, perhaps the finest Frontier film (although it must compete for first place with the later *People of the Cumberland* and *Native Land*), is very carefully structured. In the static opening shot, which depicts a rather scenic evening setting, the camera is placed across the street from a house punctured by a huge shell hole. Succeeding moving camera shots of ruins are modified by Maddow's telling narration: "Silent: blood has been spilled here" and "This is Madrid" (spoken over a tilt down a single broken wall). The successive images reinforce the negative implications of the words. Several men sit on large rocks while a large empty cart goes by: "They eat what little there is to eat." Other people stand by other rocks while men and women walk the street in the distance: "They sleep where they can." Ten static shots follow, exposing the everyday movements of people through the streets of Madrid. Then the notion that "sometimes on the surface everything seems normal" carries over three shots in which things pace up a little: a tram approaches the camera, looming large in the frame; the camera, now in a car, moves quickly down the street past a group of people, a brief shot; a boy on a donkey crosses in front of a tram approaching the camera, a conflict shot. Two quick shots of long-range guns firing first screen left then screen right; a short shot of a tram crossing in an "x" directly in front of an oncoming tram, the frame filling with its side and windows; then a shot filled with exploding noise and fragments. Cut to a body, and the sound of a voice screaming, smoke racing up a doorway, more screams, people running, a body being carried, sirens, and so on, quickly cut, striking, for fourteen shots. The commentator lets us watch, *then* takes advantage of our horror: "We must give them credit: this is the kind of thing the fascist dictators do very well." This sets into our consciousness as we view smouldering ruins, a stack of fresh, unfilled coffins, and two rows of dark, open graves.

A similar and more powerful development takes place in the second major sequence. The countryside; harvesting shots; water for the Spanish earth; adults and children by a town wall; lively, lilting music over jump-ropers around whom citizens and soldiers are gathered; the sound of airplanes; then the sight of airplanes in the sky flying left to right; people scrambling for shelter right to left; bombs released; two quick clips of Hitler and Mussolini speaking and gesturing; then three shots of exploding bombs; and, as we watch the desperate townspeople fight the flames, we learn that "Germany and Italy want Spanish steel for guns, Spanish coal for warships, copper, lead, mercury, zinc" (the last four words over four shots of buildings in flame). Another explosion, and then, with the absolutely heart-rending crying of a woman in our ears, we watch the crowds and watch with the crowds as the bodies of children are extracted hurriedly from the rubble. The commentator's voice returns over four shots of bodies in the fields at extreme angles: "Hitler wants iron, Mussolini wants coal." The camera pans over coffins, neighbors attempt to soothe the grief-stricken woman by the doorway, and her crying fades over two final shots of ruins. The pointed economy of both editing and narration in these early sequences is powerfully telling.

The visual dialectic of a short sequence between these early sequences established the film's key motif: against Franco, against the wealth and privilege that support him, and against his mercenary troops are pitted the essential humanity and human kinship for which and on which the Loyalists are basing and sustaining their struggle. Here and throughout the film, parents with children, sons and brothers building barricades, international volunteers, Lister delivering his beautiful speech on Spain and brotherhood to his listening and marching troops, together with the frequent linkage of ambulances and battlefield, the record book that joins blood donor with wounded beneficiary, and the lyrical montages of people giving blood, all dramatize this humanity and kinship.

The music in the first hospital sequence is a Spanish folk air, two mellow-toned guitars, tender and poignant. After eight shots of the wounded in the courtyard, we view a head-on shot of a woman and man in adjacent beds: "Side by side, the mother bombed in her home, the son shot at the front." On "mother" comes a cut to camera placement at the side of the mother's bed and a pan right to the foot, where a nurse is aiding the mother, another assertion of the humane, caring stress of the film. But then we move immediately to an answering, leftward pan over several men against an outside wall until we reach another nurse, black and clothed in black, dressing a soldier's wound: "This man was struck by an Italian explosive bullet." On "-ive bullet" we cut to his mangled, bloody stump of an arm, partially framed by the black hands. As we look, stunned, the commentator states: "Don't turn away. This is neutrality. This is non-intervention, Italian style." The pan and close-up are of unusually long duration for this film, comprising its strongest moment. Through the extraordinary direct-ness of image and address, the uncommitted American viewer is forced to confront both Fascist intervention and his own and his nation's neutrality toward these events. The sequence ends with four shots— a nurse helping a man walk, a nurse feeding a man, men walking and talking together through the courtyard in twilight (two shots)—all in some degree using leftward movement, responding in their essential tenderness and humanity to the pan that ended on the armless man. The contrasting cuts on "mother" and "-ive bullet" are part of a general tough complementariness through which the film asserts a truth: peo-ple *are* akin and they *are* being maimed by Italian bullets.

The final movement of the film begins at one of the six front hospitals established under Dr. Edward Barsky of the American Medical Bu-reau. Accompanied by the blood-donation music, ten shots portray a life-or-death transfusion performed by Doctors Barsky and Bethune. A beautifully optimistic cut then takes us from the bed and the drained bottle to a position beneath the high right arm splint of a wounded soldier, a pan right to close-up of his laughing face, then further to close-up of the happy woman he is talking with. With this shot begins a "woman's throaty voice singing an heroic *fandanguilla*.[25] Six cheerful women wash the hospital linen by a pool; a separate shot shows re-covering patients sitting on a wall; a third shot pans right from the women to the patients on the wall with whom they are gaily talking. An exactly parallel series of three shots follows: Ero Escavedo enters a hospital room; while we hear *her* name being spoken, we are shown a separate shot of a wounded soldier in bed; then we hear *his* name, as the camera pans right with Ero, bringing the two together: he is the soldier who has received her blood. The *fandanguilla*[f] ends. A close-up of him, her hand on his brow, and we hear the beginning of a light, gay dance music, almost as if the dance we then cut to exists in the soldier's imagination.

For nearly twenty seconds we observe the dance, and then the final

[f] A *fandanguilla* is a type of fandango with an introduction on the guitar, a vocal part, and accompaniment on the castanets.

montage begins. At first we hear the donation/transfusion music. Shots of a bottle filling with blood alternate with a shot of marching recruits, three shots of donors' arms in very fast succession going down on the table, two shots of a long-range gun firing, another arm. Then three fists shoot up into the frame, two percussion thuds break into the sound track, the music alters to a slightly swifter and a more definite beat, the melody alters too, but the instruments and pitch remain the same. This change brings with it the final images: marching men in Madrid with raised fists; a truckload of soldiers, their fists in the air; a frame-filling crowd of men from high angle, some fists raised; perched on another truck a man holding a proud flag; the bottle, three-fourths filled and still filling, holding the screen and then dissolving at length into the marching shot used earlier while Lister spoke of brotherhood. The entire final movement, from transfusion into celebratory shots that unite people in dance and then lead into the final affirmation of the blood giving, the brotherhood, and the battle against fascism, create a striking, moving conclusion. On opening night, some of Hollywood's leading actors and directors wired that *Heart of Spain* was "unanimously acclaimed the most compelling document ever shown of war-torn Spain."[26]

The film is in some ways both a tribute to and an outcome of *New Earth*, to which it relates much more than it does to *The Spanish Earth*. Thanks to their preparation over the years, to the example of Ivens, and to the pressure of international fascism on their hearts and minds,[g] the filmmakers of Frontier Films made their first major film. It does not try to tell a story in sequence or to compose a linear essay—something Hurwitz says he passionately opposed—nor does it attempt to develop fictional or real characters either dramatically or in depth. Instead, like *New Earth*, it dynamically utilizes appropriate fragments of cinema—shots, scenes, sequences, commentary, and music—to dramatize a situation in a telling, convincing, powerful way. It raised, Hurwitz recalls, a hell of a lot of money.[27]

The decision to remain close to *New Earth* and the characteristics of the early Soviet cinema and to eschew the more relaxed pace of *The Spanish Earth* was a considered one. In his advocacy of sociopolitical content and dialectical structure in films of high art, Harry Alan Potamkin had remained a source of critical inspiration to Frontier Films. But they parted company when he urged an art of implication. Maddow spelled out the difference in a February 1936 article on Potamkin:

---

[g] "The documentary film," Sidney Meyers wrote, "found in antifascism its reason for being." *TAC*, April 1939, p. 14.

It is vital at our stage to disagree. Not only is it necessary for contemporary film-makers (especially amateur, non-commercial, left-wing groups) to theatricalize their productions, but they should not even begin to think in terms of "intensive, not extensive" cinema, until they have produced a series of living, even if "muscular" films, interesting by the sheer force of impact.

The aesthetic of impact was thought to be a crucial method of gaining access to the Hollywood audience: subtlety would not do. This position was not to alter in the five years of Frontier Films' existence. Early in 1936, they had praised Dovzhenko's *Frontier* for its poetic intensity. In August of 1936, Maddow criticized Alfred Hayes for his willingness "to indulge himself in length and skimp on intensity" in his poetry, but praised him for his "skill and passionate organization." In 1938 and 1939, Meyers applauded certain films for their "overwhelming quality," their "genuine impact" and passion, their "crude physical impact" and their "force," and in a review for *Films* in the spring of 1940 entitled "Film Intensity; *Shors*," Maddow praised "the marvelous tension and the continuous, driving excitement" of Dovzhenko's new film.[28]

Heart of Spain's essential similarity to *The Spanish Earth* lies in the film's attainment of *temoignage*, the quality Ivens defined in his interview with Gordon Hitchens as the mature and deeply human testimony of a particular group of artists. Women and children in *Heart of Spain* have an obvious propaganda thrust: negative emotions are most easily roused by showing the enemy's destruction of the traditionally helpless. Also, the volunteers' graveyard and the Canadian/American medical work are intended to stimulate in the American audience a spirit of international giving. Yet these things do not remain starkly propagandistic, principally because they are *personally* felt by the filmmakers who translate their feelings into cinematic correlatives. Woven into the emotional texture of the film are the filmmakers' own sense of contribution to the cause, their feelings of kinship with the wounded, the donors, and the soldiers, and their efforts to learn how to make connection with people who are doing what is noble and right. This is precisely why when the mother uncontrollably cries, when the soldier and the woman laugh together, we experience some of the deeper grief and joy of human existence.[h]

A good number of Americans saw the film that fall and during the

[h] According to Hurwitz: "Our underlying belief was that the penetration of real experience and a substratum of real feelings were prime energies for art." See "One Man's Voyage: Ideas and Films in the 1930's," *Cinema Journal*, Fall 1975, p. 14. See also Paul Strand's "Letter to *Art Front*," Feb. 1937, p. 18.

following years. It premiered in Hollywood early in September, and on 10 September, advertised as "pictorial dynamite," it opened in New York at the Fifty-Fifth Street Playhouse for a run of seven weeks. On 28 October, it opened for a week at the Century on 2nd Avenue and 12th Street, and although "the main distribution was non-theatrical," it eventually reached "maybe 30-40 first-run theaters in the country," according to Tom Brandon. It also accompanied two ambulances destined for Spain on a two-month tour of major cities and towns from California to New York. Martin North, a Hollywood writer, and Albert Kahn ran the tour, addressing meetings and performances along the way.[29] My guess is that *Heart of Spain* did make, as Hurwitz remembers, a good deal of money. Probably most of that went to the Canadian Committee to Aid Spain and the American Medical Bureau to Aid Spanish Democracy, some of it to Garrison Films, and some small portion into the meager coffers of the filmmakers at Frontier Films.

China Strikes Back

Frontier welcomed the opportunity to aid a cause dear to them and as a result made a film of which they were justly proud. Yet *Heart of Spain* was a diversion from their plans to conceive, write, and shoot their own films, and they knew that another diversion was in the making. Before *Heart of Spain* opened, Kline had returned to Spain, this time sent by Frontier to make a film with Henri Cartier-Bresson. Frontier would supervise from afar and write, arrange, and edit where necessary once Kline returned. But that was in the future; for now, they could turn their full attention to the farm film and *Labor Spy*. Or so they thought. Almost immediately Harry Dunham appeared with some footage he had shot and smuggled out of China. One look told them that it was "obviously a sensational film," containing the first footage ever shot in Yenan, or Soviet China, the first footage of the Eighth Route, formerly the Red Army.[30]

The footage was in an entirely raw state. Dunham, a newsreel cameraman, had shot without scenario or documentary scheme of any sort. Yet it was "too hot for the newsreel to handle," and a Frontier crew set to the enormous job of shaping the random material. They worked out a concept, found needed stock footage, and disappeared into the editing room. Hurwitz and Strand served as advisors—as did all Frontier members in one degree or another on all films—but the writing and editing were essentially a collaboration between Meyers, Lerner, Maddow, and Leyda, who appear in the credits under the pseudonyms of Robert Stebbins, Peter Ellis, David Wolff, and Eugene Hill, in that order. Van Dyke and Meyers created an opening sequence that Hurwitz edited, and Alex North again arranged the music, with O'Shaughnessy doing the narration. Years later, Lerner still recalled their enthusiastic spirit and their dedication to the Chinese cause, while in his moving memorial to Meyers, Leyda described both that spirit and some of the problems that such projects posed: "Point and effectiveness would have to be carved out of semi-satisfactory materials. In most cases the well-intentioned persons who had originally filmed these materials would resent this 'interference,'[i] but we were now a confident cuttingroom staff that realized the powers waiting in that tiny room." The film, *China Strikes Back*, premiered at the Squire Theater late in October, continued there several weeks, and eventually appeared as a short in 204 of the 700-odd theaters in the New York area. This meant little money—the theaters paid only $2.50 or $3.00 a week for rental of the film[31] but it provided good visibility and publicity, which should have meant good money and eager sponsors for future projects.

In *China Strikes Back*, an opening montage of radio news voices and headlines recalls and challenges other cinema and radio coverage of the war; for Frontier, *The March of Time* would have provided the most offensive model for this type of coverage. In its first issue in March 1935, *The March of Time* did not greatly repress its eager anticipation of strife and sympathetically characterized Japanese military growth as the poisoned fruit of international racial discrimination against the Japanese. Avidly opposed to Japan in subsequent issues, the newsreel series devoted its footage to the procapitalist Chinese nationalist forces and fretted aloud over the safety of American interests. In contrast, *China Strikes Back* was highly supportive of the new united front in China, depicting the growth, the spirit, and the courage of the Red Forces.

China Strikes Back develops in the simple dialectical pattern that was common to the work of Frontier films. First the destructive forces are dramatized, often explosively: in *Heart of Spain* the bombings ripped into the normal lives; in *China Strikes Back* the Japanese peace-and-harmony rhetoric is confronted with Chinese corpses, hands

---

[i] It is difficult to say whom Leyda had in mind. Possibly Dunham, but Lerner remembered Dunham as working in unusual compatibility with Frontier, and Lerner agreed with Leyda that few people "seemed to be able to work with us very well." Possibly Leyda referred to the people who did direction and camerawork on *People of the Cumberland*. He may have also had in mind Kline—though I have no indication that Kline's experience was dissatisfying, unless his eagerness to move out and make his own films in 1938 was a sign of abrasion.

bound behind them by their executioners, left on the street for the horrified, curious eyes of citizen onlookers. Second, we see the counteractive forces, here the young soldiers of the northwest provinces. The camera presents their university and military training and explores their fruitful relationship with the villagers, who donate food and bedding and receive education and medical assistance in return. We are introduced to their officers, Mao Tse-tung and Chu Teh, and learn of their new union with the nationalist forces under Chiang Kai-Shek. Third, the destructive forces are reinvoked but in a manner that emphasizes the strength of the counteractive forces as well. Finally, an optimistic upbeat: rally speeches by a student leader, by Chu, and by Mao, the latter accompanied by shots of the new weapons and planes of the army.

The editing in *China Strikes Back* builds situation, idea, and feeling out of the juxtaposition of fragments and has a dynamics that is superior to any newsreel—and to much of the Hollywood cinema—of the day. The cutting is always kinetic: a nurse vaccinating a peasant is presented in medium shot, close-up, medium shot. In stronger moments, short shots are broken up and intercut for force: Japanese troops moving forward in attack; Chinese civilian bodies; troops in attack; bodies; troops in attack; bodies. Shots of bodies, burning buildings, and ruins are often accented, unrelieved, like those in *Heart of Spain*. And the juxtapositions are sometimes devastating: the stylish American news montage is undercut by three drum beats and the undeniable reality of three dead Chinese civilians. O'Shaughnessy's voice, far from the melodramatic, overly empathetic voice that some of the same filmmakers had chosen for "Sunnyside," does not dominate like the aggressive voice of *The March of Time*, and its relation to these stark images and to the other images is far more subtle.

The finest sequence in *China Strikes Back*—and one of the finest sequences in the work of Frontier Films—occurs with the reintroduction of the destructive forces. Their strength is now modified by what has preceded in the second sequence (the university and the young soldiers, a unified, eager China) and by the context in which they now appear. Before bedding down on their borrowed straw, several Chinese soldiers, standing against a brick wall in medium closeup, sing a poignant, lyrical song about China and the Japanese invasion, a song accompanied by a montage that depicts the effects of that invasion. Simultaneously we hear the words of an evocative poem by Ben Maddow:

Brothers, it is midsummer, the hours are still warm,
And the fields are gathered in the North.

I remember our life, the shining grain in the sunlight,
The dogs in our village quarreling far off.
The dogs are silent, greedy and fat in the ruins;
The village is dead in the summer sunlight.
The crop is gathered in the black barns, the crop of ashes.

We have no homes, the Japanese stand on Manchuria,
The men without mouths, that speak out of guns.
Where their voice is heard, there are many peasants already
    dead.

With words and tears we assailed the enemy,
The Japanese, the locusts with human faces;
Brothers, the wind as we fled was bitter with smoke.

Scattered are the families, the children without care,
The homeless people scattered like leaves,
The children like dead leaves on the freezing stream.

I have heard that many are locked in the Japanese mills.
Where are you, O younger sister, where are you?

The families walk in slavery,
Toiling till moonlight for the cup of rice.
Hunger moves them—hunger makes them weak.

Stand up, brothers, do not stoop.
As you bend, the Japanese climb on your backs.
Stand up, look, a lion roars in the sky: it is me flying.

Look up, I am armed.
My hands are friends to the rifle.
Look up, brothers and sisters.
I am coming with planes to defend you.[32]

The images are a lyrical montage of grain, men at work, Japanese
soldiers, explosions and burning buildings, refugees, children at work
in the mills, the running feet of a rickshaw driver, people drawing
wagons, people bowing to worship, and people, bowed over, pulling
a canal barge by rope. The latter two images are twice juxtaposed in
the last four shots, which correspond, roughly, to the final seven lines
of the poem. This is the tightest, most striking, most moving portion
of a beautifully filmed, finely constructed work. We are frightened by
what we see of the Japanese military handiwork and warmed by what
we see of the growing, spirited defenses of the Chinese. It is an

excellent historical document of what was then underway "in the secret interior of China."

Pie in the Sky, China Strikes Back, and the future *People of the Cumberland* each involved at least three of the following people: Elia Kazan, Irving Lerner, Jay Leyda, Sidney Meyers, and Ralph Steiner; it is interesting that these films differ significantly from the two films in which Hurwitz and Strand figured prominently, *Heart of Spain* and *Native Land* (Ben Maddow was chief scenario writer on *China Strikes Back* and the two Hurwitz-Strand films). *China Strikes Back*, for example, manifests a relaxed, easy-going humor and warmth, an interest in the mundane, in local sports, in the courtesies and manners that condition much of the treatment of the Eighth Route Army. These qualities allow for jests such as the following—"Sports are popular in the army. Even the president of the university plays—usually left guard"—and communicate a particular sense of sympathy that is absent in, say, *Heart of Spain*ʲ where the feelings conveyed are very much different. In the Hurwitz-Strand films, Spanish country children jump rope, an American farmer plows his land, a city girl washes windows and sings. In each case one feels warmth toward the people, feels how beautiful it is to do such things and to be happy, but always there are ominous undertones, for these scenes are almost inevitably permeated with dramatic tension: the bombers will come, the thugs will drive up, the corpse will be found, and the movement to such events is implicit in the presentation of the happier moments.

Since everyone at Frontier contributed to each project, these individual attitudes modified each other to some degree, and on the whole the film crews worked with enthusiasm, confidence, and a minimum of friction. Yet personality differences were also taking their toll. According to Van Dyke, he and Meyers had worked out an opening for *China Strikes Back*. He remembers

a sort of montage sequence—a series of shots that linked together in a specific way with specific movements related to each other. We knew exactly how one shot moved into the next. The newspaper was put on the closet floor, the closet closed, the newspaper brought into focus, and then that cut to another movement where something went away. It was all planned down to the inch. We shot it, the rushes came back, we came in to assemble it, and Leo had already broken it down and started putting it together without even discussing it with us. He didn't put it together the way we

---

ʲ This sympathy is reinforced by Dunham's camerawork, which has a large percentage of medium close-up and close-up shots that bring the viewer nearer to the people.

had shot it. Maybe it wouldn't have been as good. But the kind of contempt in that gesture: this was fellow workers working together! In effect, we had shot some stock footage for Leo to put together.

Vera Caspary and George Sklar also felt taken advantage of. Eager to begin the filming of *Pay Day*, Hurwitz and Strand put great pressure on them to complete the script, "a sad little story about a boy whose family made umbrellas," Caspary recalls. On the stipulated date, sometime in late December 1937, the two writers delivered a script that pleased them both and gained them high praise from Donald Ogden Stewart. Sklar recollects:

> There was no acknowledgment—not a word for over a month. Then one day Hurwitz called us into a conference. They had, he said, turned it into a "shooting script." What that meant, I don't really know. As far as I was concerned, ours was a shooting script; shots were indicated in detail. Not that we didn't expect them to be changed. The director's authority is clear in that area. What we didn't anticipate was rewriting of lines of dialogue. Hurwitz and Strand knew the language of film but were totally unaware of the sound and rhythms of human speech. They made piddling changes, converting natural speech into stilted expository lines.

Caspary and Sklar both remember an angry, "slam-bang fight." They quit, and the film was never made. One senses here, as well as in the *China Strikes Back* incident, that somewhat too much self-assuredness on the part of Hurwitz and Strand led to a failure to communicate and collaborate.

Consonant with these two instances, though perhaps more subtle, was the motivation behind the crew assignment for *People of the Cumberland*, Frontier's first labor film. Strand recalls that he and Hurwitz were finding *Heart of Spain* "a very rough, tough job." As a result, they gave this new film to Ralph Steiner because they thought that it would "keep him happy" and also because they "thought he'd do it all right."[33]

People of the Cumberland

In 1925 and 1930, two resident labor colleges had been founded in the South, Commonwealth College in Mena, Arkansas, and the Highlander Folk School in Mount Eagle, Tennessee. The latter was headed by Myles Horton, a graduate of Union Theological Seminary who had attended the University of Chicago and spent a year in Denmark studying Danish folk schools. Both institutions trained mainly southerners to be labor organizers within their home regions. Both had stretched their influence into their immediate communities. Highlander had started cooperative stores and canneries, served as a community center, and housed the area's best library. Both had become targets of intensive anti-Communist attack, although they protested in their advertisement/editorial in *The Nation*, "all the false charges of their enemies to the contrary, the aim of these labor schools is single: to teach workers how to force better living standards through higher wages and increased purchasing power." As northern industry came south to profit from low labor standards and salaries, the importance of the combined yearly graduation of one hundred activists increased. Both faculties had been unpaid from the beginning, and faculty and students kept costs low by doing all manual labor and growing most of their own food. But money was needed for maintenance, scholarship, and faculty subsistence, and in early 1937 a finance campaign committee was organized in New York to raise $35,000. It must have been as part of this campaign that Ethel Clyde, a sponsor of Highlander, came to Frontier Films with the money for a fund-raising labor film on the Highlander Folk School.[34]

Steiner and Elia Kazan drove down to Mount Eagle that summer, Kazan to write and direct the script, Steiner to do the shooting. It was Kazan's first film. Like earlier trips by others to Harlan, Gastonia, and Scottsboro, it had its risks. Joe Dobbs, president of the Chattanooga Central Labor Council, had been shot and critically wounded two days after leaving conferences at Highlander; Matt Lynch, a Highlander alumnus, had been kidnapped during a recent strike; and four other organizers had been killed by local vigilantes in recent years. To show how the school, in the face of such murders, went on with its work, Kazan and Steiner required footage of a meeting with lime plant workers. "We were chased off the plant ground [by the management]" Steiner recalls.

So I said, "Well, let's do it out here," and [the management] came after us with guns and said, "We own this whole town." . . . This was a company town: everything was owned by the plant—the stores, . . . the houses, everything. So we shot the meeting right in the middle of the road . . . because the road is county. Then, after we got through shooting, [the lime plant workers] said, "They may stop you on the way back up the mountain, where the road climbs around, so we're going to go with you. Wait here." And they [went off and came back with] six cars, three in front and three in back, and they all had hoss pistols, you know, just tremendous pistols. Well, when we got to the top of the mountain—it was terribly dangerous—Ethel Clyde bought all of them ice cream cones, and if I only had a still picture today of these tall mountaineers with all their hunting rifles and their big hoss pistols . . . all licking ice cream cones—it was just absolutely wonderful.[35]

Meyers and William Watts accompanied Steiner on a second trip, and the filming was completed by late summer or early fall. People at Frontier thought the murder sequence too brief, so Strand took his Akely to a Greenwich Village backyard and broke the event down, both lengthening it and quickening the pace.[36] After someone dug up stock footage of union rallies and parades, Erskine Caldwell, assisted by Maddow, set to work on the commentary.[k] Alex North came in again on the music, and Earl Robinson composed the choral arrangements and the introductory music. Meyers and Leyda edited the visuals and Helen van Dongen the sound. Released in the spring of 1938, *People of the Cumberland* acquired a good reputation and was frequently screened by progressive and labor organizations in subsequent years. Myles Horton sometimes appeared at showings as a guest lecturer to speak about the school.

People of the Cumberland follows the pattern of other Frontier films. The first fourth of the film constructs the impoverished Cumberland environment, the following third presents Horton's answer to that environment. An unusual downbeat dramatizes the murder of a union organizer—a downbeat modified by juxtaposition with a continuation of the presentation of Horton's work and the following commentary: "Americans are too tough to frighten. The school went on with its work, went to the men at the lime plant, men with hands as hard as shovels, showed them how to make a union. A new saying came to the mountains: 'Don't mourn, organize!' " Approximately the next one-fifth of the film depicts an Independence Day labor rally on 5 July 1937 in LaFollette, Tennessee. The reintroduction and control of the

---

[k] Maddow writes: "I have no memory of ever meeting Erskine Caldwell, but I am quite certain that if he wrote any narration, there was very little of it left in the final version. My listing as assistant to him was another curious instance of collectively enforced self-negation" (letter to author, 24 Dec. 1974). Strand remembered all of them having lunch with Caldwell but had no idea who wrote what. I suspect that Caldwell wrote an initial commentary and Maddow revised it to fit closely to the images. Since, during his blacklist period in the fifties, Maddow did screenwriting for which others were given credit, it is possible that he projected this situation back onto the thirties.

1. Sam Brody and Irving Lerner (with camera), clowning on location for *W.I.R. Children's Camp*, N.Y. (1931). Courtesy of Sam Brody.

2. *Pie in the Sky* (1935). Elia Kazan and Elman Koolish shake their fists at the sky when their hallucination of pie vanishes. Courtesy of Joel Zuker.

3. *The Wave* (1935). Miro's body is carried to the boats by the finally united fishermen. The Museum of Modern Art/Film Stills Archive.

4. *The Plow That Broke the Plains* (1936). "The tragedy of turning grass into dust." The Museum of Modern Art/Film Stills Archive.

5. *New Earth* (1934). From a distance, the immensity of the landfill task. The Museum of Modern Art/ Film Stills Archive.

6. Paul Strand at the camera on *The Wave* (1935). The Museum of Modern Art/Film Stills Archive.

7. *The River* (1937). The cotton pickers "down on their knees in the Valley." The Museum of Modern Art/Film Stills Archive.

8. Joris Ivens and Ernest Hemingway on location on *The Spanish Earth* (1937). The Museum of Modern Art/Film Stills Archive.

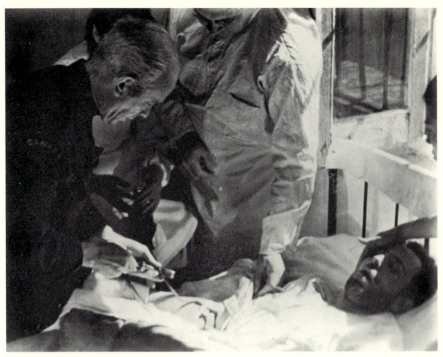

9. *Heart of Spain* (1937). Doctors Barsky and Bethune perform a life-or-death transfusion. The Museum of Modern Art/Film Stills Archive.

10. *People of the Cumberland* (1938). "Lonely and forgotten people." The Museum of Modern Art/Film Stills Archive.

11. Lionel Berman, sometime in the early 1930s. Courtesy of Hortense Socholitsky.

12. Sidney Meyers, sometime in the 1940s. Courtesy of Edna O. Meyers.

13. Herbert Kline, 1938. Photograph taken in Prague by Rosa Harvan (Kline). Courtesy of Herbert Kline.

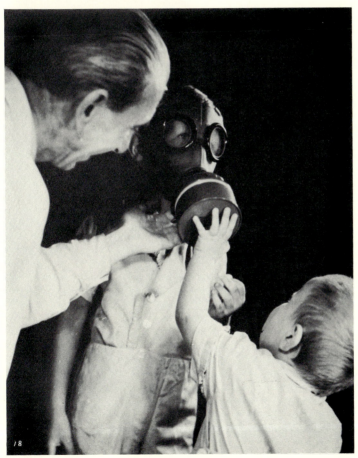

14. *Crisis* (1939). Anticipating the war that didn't come. The Museum of Modern Art/Film Stills Archive.

15. *Native Land* (1942). Sharecropper (Lewis Grant) wounded by sheriff's posse: "Few knew, and few remembered." The Museum of Modern Art/Film Stills Archive.

16. Leo Hurwitz, shortly after the opening of *Native Land* (1942). Courtesy of Leo Hurwitz.

17. Ben Maddow, William Watts (applying makeup), and Fred Johnson (farmer) on location for farm sequence in *Native Land* (1942). The Museum of Modern Art/Film Stills Archive.

18. *The City* (1939). Pittsburgh cityscape: "this no man's land, this slag heap." The Museum of Modern Art/Film Stills Archive.

19. Ralph Steiner at the camera on *The City* (1939). The Museum of Modern Art/Film Stills Archive.

20. Willard Van Dyke with DeBrie camera on *The Children Must Learn* (1940). Courtesy of Willard Van Dyke.

21. *Valley Town* (1940). "Why should these men be thrown away as if they were obsolete? As if they were broken machines?" The Museum of Modern Art/Film Stills Archive.

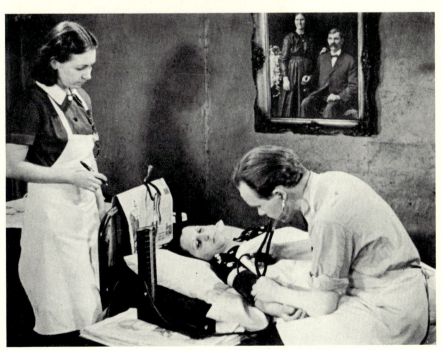

22. *The Fight for Life* (1940). Intern O'Donnell (Myron McCormick), nurse and patient: "young doctors . . . bringing modern science to the poor women of the city." The Museum of Modern Art/Film Stills Archive.

23. *Power and the Land* (1940). A still of the barn-burning sequence that Ivens could not include: "There was sometimes also fire, you know, provocations." The Museum of Modern Art/Film Stills Archive.

24. *Men and Dust* (1940). "Dust in the ground, dust in the mills,/Dust in the towns and on the window sills." The Museum of Modern Art/Film Stills Archive.

hostile forces then occurs: a final montage first recalls the impoverished soil and citizens, then dynamically mingles United Mine Worker oathtakers with shots of water pouring through TVA dams, an interior of a TVA power plant, and members of the "new generation" at the rally competing in the shot put, all an affirmation of the school's reply to Cumberland destitution.

The opening narrative underscores the "forgotten" condition of the people of the Cumberland, the related barrenness of earth and population, the feelings of isolation, waste, loneliness, and decay. It touches, subtly, the viewer's own fear of such a state. Static shots parallel the narration: the camera scarcely moves, and within individual shots, movement is minimal. Everything else in the film reacts against this opening. The commentary, for instance, hammers home the emotional and practical results of Horton's return to the region: "They're not alone anymore. They've got a union. . . . The people of the Cumberland are not alone. . . . The schools and the unions working together. . . . A new kind of Independence Day, no more terror, no more insecurity, no more gangsters, no more fear in the streets." The proportion of moving camera shots does not increase, which is to good effect, for their static nature is now superseded by the purposeful and increasingly active movement within the frame, by the expressiveness, intentness, and happiness of the people.

As a result of this emphasis on stasis, the rare uses of the moving camera are highly effective. In the opening sequence, we hear "no food for the people," while a father and four children stare out a cabin window. A rightward pan over the earth then breaks the camera stasis, but in so engaging us with the land, it actually increases the strain, for the land is bare and the voice intones "stones and weeds, forgotten land." In the same panning shot, the words that follow, "Lonely and forgotten," first modify the land and then its inhabitants, as the word "people" accompanies a cut to the beginning of a group portrait. In a leftward pan over a family on their porch, both camera and comment run counter to growth: "the middle-aged, the young, the newly born." If the pan involves us with the people, a succeeding medium-distance shot of them from the other side of a fence again fixes them in their static pose and position ("the years of hard work and hunger"), and we move to three shots of primitive graves ("and nothing left of their lives but these bits of crockery on their graves, decorations of broken glass").

The voice pauses several seconds on the third shot, a poignant banjo chord that focuses our emotions on the grave. Still over the grave, we hear "the earth," then cut to a mother and baby, extremely thin, the long upward lines of a doorway accenting their thinness—and hear the words "that failed to keep them alive." Silence on them for several seconds, a cut downward to a ragged daughter eating from a tin can, the banjo chord again, then cut back to the mother and baby and two more chords. Skillfully and subtly, voice, sound, and image convey the death in these Cumberland lives and provide memorable material for later counterpoint. The next pan over a group, a pan right, shows students hoeing the ground and answering questions from their instructor on the benefits of unionization. Later, moving shots follow racing youngsters at the Independence Day rally.

Even in the light of popular-front politics and the late thirties' celebration of American life, the degree of American patriotism in this Frontier production comes as a surprise. It is most blatant in the presentation of the American flag, which first appears on a chart demonstrating the need for labor unions. It moves toward us in the final marching shot, with the "U" of "Union" visible on the flag behind it, the juxtaposition symbolizing a unionized America. A gun being loaded to commit murder in one shot is directed toward the point in the frame where the flag appears in the next shot on a low podium behind the organizer who is swearing men into the United Mine Workers Union. Two rally shots catch the flag waving in the breeze. Add to this: the traditional dance and square dance at Highlander and the folk tunes on the sound track; the combination of Independence Day with a labor rally; the band playing "Columbia"; and "Dinah," "Mary Had a Little Lamb," and other such tunes accompanying the games. The chart explains that the government, the Wagner Act, the Constitution, and the Supreme Court back unionization, and the final montage refers favorably to the TVA. The rally is not at all depicted as a militant labor rally but as a spirited, fun-loving American holiday, complete with a boy up in the rafters of the stands, people doubled over in laughter, and a tug of war. These people and their unions are as American as apple pie. More than any other film by the far left, *People of the Cumberland* is a concerted effort to engage its audience by appealing to its basic American experience and instincts.

In sensitive coordination with the patriotism and the spirited good humor that is endemic to a Kazan-Leyda-Meyers-Steiner film are the more militant overtones. The parade to the rally grounds is primarily composed of bands, children, and banners, but one noticeable shot shows marching men, determined and muscular, taken from a slightly low angle at medium-close distance. The speeches are brief, heard over some casual shots of a relaxed audience, and they are ended quickly by the commentator: "But no more speeches: this is a holiday." Yet there they are, conveying the necessity for organization, vowing the Folk School's intention to remain and to continue to be answerable only to the people. It is the strong and courageous "children of union men in a union town" who vie with one another at the rally games.

At some level, the filmmakers intended a response to Pare Lorentz's two films. In 1936, Irving Lerner complained of the lack of forthrightness in *The Plow That Broke the Plains*. At the end of *People of the Cumberland*'s opening sequence, as we learn how people moved hopefully to other mountain towns and into the industrial valley, three slow pans over the mountain and towns lead to static shots of sordid houses and factories. In the last of these shots, a distant train crosses the frame from left to right, an allusion to a similar shot in *The Plow That Broke the Plains*, and we hear about the "greed" that Lorentz refused to focus on in his film. The commentary over these static shots is direct:

> Plenty of work! Eleven hours a day, six dollars a week. The trees torn out, the mines ruined to make a dividend, the people drawn down into the town and robbed there. The same greed ruled the valley and the mountains.

In the concluding sequence of *The River*, a series of dam shots juxtaposed with other shots stress and praise the federal government's flood control activities and other improvements in the Tennessee Valley. In *The Roosevelt Year: A Photographic Record*, Lorentz had juxtaposed two photographs: an old, worn "Tennessee cabin, Jackson period," and a modern "mountain cabin, Roosevelt style."[37] Although he was by no means unsympathetic to unions, he innocently placed his faith in federal programs to improve the conditions he depicted. In *People of the Cumberland*, on the other hand, we are shown interior and exterior shots of TVA dams and rushing water, while at the same time being reminded that TVA is "a good beginning, but only a beginning." And in the film's concluding moments, both commentary and images reaffirm the crucial importance of unions. Three quick close-ups of miners taking the union oath are framed by water pouring from the dam, their accompanying words: "The people stand together, their union is their power." A shot of the waving flag follows, then a shot of pouring water, and then an intense young man, a member of the new generation, puts the shot at the rally, and *he* frames four TVA shots: the final shot of the film is his follow-through, his fist dominant on the screen.

The film is not perfectly unified. The gangster/murder sequence, with its Hollywood staging and dialogue and its dramatic lighting, is out of place. Also out of place (although to a lesser extent) are some of the episodes within sequences, the coast-to-coast marching shots following the study of the chart, for instance: one feels ever so slightly the contrivance, the planning. *People of the Cumberland* does not have the same pressure of necessity in development, music, or narration, quite the same compactness as *Heart of Spain*. Still it is remarkably tight, engaging, and warming, and I think perhaps the best gauged of all Frontier Films to reach its audience. It remains a film of subtlety and high skill, one of the best progressive films produced in the thirties.

The Split

Several months before *People of the Cumberland* appeared, Steiner and Van Dyke left Frontier Films for reasons that will shed more light on the nature of the organization, on the filmmakers, and on the politics and the development of documentary film in the thirties.

When he returned from *The River* in February 1937, Van Dyke caught up on his still photography assignments for *Mademoiselle* and then seized an opportunity to join Peter Stackpole on a trip to California for *Life*. On the way out, and during a "marvelous" swing up the coast with his old mentor Edward Weston, in which he spent some time working out new relationships of light and texture in his landscape photography, Van Dyke did "a lot of thinking" about his situation in New York. The stimulation of his artistic rapport with Weston, backed by the independence and trust he had experienced under Lorentz, refocused his sense of what had been lacking for him with Nykino and Frontier. Instead of entering into colleagueship with the artists who were more developed in their craft than he as he had in California, he had been thrust by Hurwitz, Steiner, and Strand into the junior group, among people he admired but who could not offer him as much as the senior members of Frontier. He was a subordinate. Still, Frontier had asked him to do the camerawork on *Labor Spy*, a central project. Possibly things were changing: he was "very much" looking forward to the job.[38]

Although his experience with Hurwitz on *China Strikes Back* had angered him, the "breaking point" came on this new film. He and Michael Gordon were to shoot the first story sequence on a farm outside Poughkeepsie. Committed to other jobs, they could not stay on location. It was late fall. Up at 4:00 A.M., riding an unheated station wagon, they would arrive for the right sun at 8:00. It was "so cold that the camera would slow down and stop, and I tried to crank it and get the motor going at the same time and get the stuff done." After several days of shooting, they screened the rushes for Frontier.[1] Hurwitz thought the concept too mild and schematic, the camerawork only fair. "We decided we needed a new script and new production unit," he remembers: "A much longer film was necessary, on a more serious basis." It was not easy, evidently, but exercising his prerogative as president, Strand took a firm position, announcing that he and Hurwitz would take over the film. Accordingly, he, Hurwitz, and Maddow began rewriting, and the next summer the three and Bill Watts settled in on location on the farm. Deprived of responsibility and confined to the lower ranks once again, Van Dyke had reason to be angry.[39]

Steiner recalls a somewhat similar experience. The second trip to Tennessee during the making of *People of the Cumberland* was for material he and Kazan had thought unnecessary, and he felt that the stock footage was being added for the wrong reasons: it "didn't belong there, and I was such a weak-kneed, weak-spined idiot, that I didn't scream and holler."[40] Thus, although *People of the Cumberland* was made collectively, with a great deal of discussion, it was clear that, like Van Dyke, Steiner had felt relegated to a somewhat secondary position by Hurwitz and Strand.

Sometime during the summer or early fall, Clarence Stein of the American Institute of Planners contacted Steiner. The Institute had $50,000 from the Carnegie Corporation of New York to make a film on city planning for the 1939 World's Fair. Steiner screened some of his films for Stein, and Stein asked Steiner to make the film.

> And I said [to him], "Well, I'm still part of Frontier Films, [but] I'm getting out." And so I went back and resigned and [then] called up Clarence Stein and said, "I've resigned, and since I negotiated with you as a member of Frontier Films, I'm resigning [from the film]." [Before all this happened] I'd asked Willard [Van Dyke] to work on it with me. [A short time later] Clarence Stein called [me back] and said, "Whether you work on it or not, Frontier Films is not going to work on it." I said, "Well, in that case, if you put that on paper, we will work for you."

But Steiner telescopes events. Before October, Berman had told the writer John Devine about Frontier's projected film on city planning, and it was not until December that Van Dyke and Steiner resigned from Frontier. In the meantime, two other members of Frontier

---

[1] During this period, Van Dyke also shot a separate short sequence for *Labor Spy*, with Kazan directing, Strand playing the head of a spy agency, and Van Dyke's younger brother playing the part of the goon who intimidates a worker; a shot or two, of Strand, remains in the finished film. Van Dyke interview 2; Strand interview.

conferred with Stein, agreed to submit a scenario, and discussed their plans with Steiner.[41] Frontier Films had some reason, it appears, to think the film theirs. Nevertheless, the American Institute of Planners wanted Steiner, and when Van Dyke and Steiner formed American Documentary Films, Inc. in December, they took *The City* as their first film.

Furor resulted. Some members were intensely angry, and Frontier threatened Steiner with a lawsuit. A betrayal. A violation of the co-operative's spirit. Steiner and Van Dyke had carried away an important project at a time when projects were hard to come by, when good films were needed to keep Frontier people in shoes and beans and to help pay for *Labor Spy/Native Land*, a film of increasing importance to the organization. According to Steiner:

> There was terrible trouble with Frontier Films. Rocks were thrown through my window. People I had known intimately for years and years didn't know me when they saw me on the street. And there were all sorts of things written that I was a Trotskyite, and I finally had to say something. I knew who Leon Trotsky was, there was such a man, but what is a Trotskyite? You know, I was that brilliant politically. So finally I got a really wonderful person, a person I worked with [later] when I was in Hollywood, really one of the fine left-wing writers, Albert Maltz, and he was the Communist party's, I guess, top artistic guy, and there was instituted . . . a kind of a trial . . . to stop some of the *Schrecklichkeit* that was being thrown my way by the Communists, and he listened to me, and he listened to them, and he said, Ralph is not getting out for political reasons, that I was a political idiot.[42]

It was a very unhappy time for Steiner, and a bitter period for all. On the one hand, Steiner and Van Dyke felt badly treated by Hurwitz especially, and also by Strand. On the other hand, the people at Frontier believed, and still believe, that it was redbaiting that prevented them from keeping *The City* and from acquiring later projects, although I have found no hard evidence to defend this position. Nevertheless, the split was a searing one, and the wounds it left were, in some cases, permanent ones.

From Steiner's point of view: "What I think happened to both of us [to him and Van Dyke] was that we saw they wanted to say everything's terrible in America." And according to Van Dyke, Strand's world view held an undemocratic bitterness.[43] This should call to mind the distinctions I previously made between Lorentz's outlook on America and that of his crew, especially Hurwitz and Strand, on *The Plow That*

Broke the Plains, and it should also reassert my association of Van Dyke's ties to the country with those of Lorentz at the time of *The River*. Steiner's vital, good-natured cheerfulness and Van Dyke's American romanticism grated sharply against the tougher, more caustic way in which Hurwitz and Strand regarded the ills of contemporary America. It is not surprising, therefore, that *The City* and *Native Land* are very different films.

Everyone agrees that money played a role in the split. Weeks would often go by without the income to pay their thirty-five dollar weekly salaries—income derived from "richer individuals who felt what we were doing was important" and from the few sponsored films for which they obtained commissions. Willing like the others to live on very little, like the others Steiner and Van Dyke found doing so unpleasant. In retrospect, both agree that deprivation was a motivation for their leaving Frontier, and according to Lerner and Maddow, it was a significant one.[44] It is my belief, however, that money played a minor role: had their political perceptions been closer to those of Hurwitz and Strand, and had their creative activities been regarded on a more equal and thus a more rewarding basis, the financial strain would not have taken its toll—at least not so soon.

Agreeing that money was a significant issue, Hurwitz supports the position that the political differences were more important.

> Frontier Films was starting something new. It was a collective, with people working together, individual strengths being very important. It was a collective venture based on the idea that much was wrong with American life which required radical change socially, and that much was wrong with the movies which required radical change. And things were getting hot. The Dickstein Committee, the Dies Committee nearly formed, the right-wing unions: there was much in the air. The ACLU was reluctant to sponsor *Native Land*: they feared it was too left, too labor conscious. And Steiner and Van Dyke felt it all was too dangerous, too left, too scary.[45]

And even Steiner and Van Dyke would grant, if not in Hurwitz's terms, that politics was an important factor: Frontier Films was a popular-front organization, and many, though far from all, of the staff and the advisory board were Party members and fellow travelers.

Van Dyke often explains that his trip to the Soviet Union in 1935 disenchanted him with the Soviet system. He was dismayed, he says, when the formation of Frontier Films brought the Nykino group under the influence of Communist Party members like John Howard Lawson.

Upon invitation, he attended a meeting of the theater section of the Party, but under the advice of Maddow ("The kind of discipline, the necessity of following an intellectual path that is laid down by somebody else is not something that is easy for you handle. Why do you want it?"), he decided not to join. When Van Dyke talks about Frontier, he suggests strong Party control over the films; Steiner does the same: "Everything had to be approved by the Party." The extra footage required for *People of the Cumberland*, he says, consisted of "revolutionary shots" insisted upon by the Party, an assertion that enraged Strand when I questioned him about it.[46]

Perhaps Steiner and Van Dyke attribute to the Party a degree of influence it did not have: for one thing, Lawson took no actual part in any Frontier film; and when I asked him for evidence of a heavy political hand in the films, Van Dyke confessed it was not there. He was clearly less troubled by the films than by the politics of some of the filmmakers and their friends.

Hurwitz offers an entirely different perspective on the nature of Party influence.:

> I needed to have a center from which I could understand the world on more than an event-to-event basis. And my feeling at the time was that the Communists had the best grasp of the world, the fight against fascism, and so forth. This didn't mean I was not critical of various things, as many Communists were. So having a central set of political values to estimate things was an important part of *my* work at Frontier Films. . . . On the other side, in terms of Party politics and control, there was no external influence or manipulation. I knew of such manipulation on magazines like *New Masses*. . . . We never had that. And one of the reasons was that we never asked for it. . . . The work of Frontier Films became highly valued in Party circles. In reviews in *New Masses, The Daily Worker*, and so on. But we were rather severely left alone. All our films were finished before they were shown to the Party people. And I considered that a very important factor in terms of the independence of the artists. . . . I remember wanting to show the finished *Native Land* to Browder and Foster, and we got them into a screening room, but that was the finished film. I had heard and knew enough about the danger of politicoes invading an area which they didn't understand to know that was a very important factor. At the same time, that didn't lessen my own feeling of responsibility to the political wholeness.
>
> Art was not simply another form of stating a political program.

Joseph Freeman writing in *New Masses* at the time reflected what a lot of us were thinking. The motivations behind a work of art have to do basically with human experiences. They don't involve the kind of summarization and generalization that can define a political program. Art and politics are two different ways of dealing with that same reality and of course there is a significant connection between them. . . . With the film . . . you're trying to alter people's consciousness by dramatizing real experience, clearing away distortions so that they begin to see events in a way that has some truth to it. Action may then follow in the specific contexts of people's lives. You have to allow your artists and intellectuals to grow from within. You must have democracy as well as centralism.[47]

All of the members of Frontier Films (including Van Dyke) shared with the Party a commitment to a Loyalist victory in Spain, a Chinese victory over Japan (although interest in the eventual control of China by the Red forces would vary among members), the growth of the militant trade unions, and other general domestic struggles against social inequality. Because of this commitment, the Party valued the work of Frontier. But the same commitment was also shared by many anti-Communists (like Van Dyke), who also valued the films. Although Party member John Howard Lawson's name was on the Frontier roster from 1936 to 1941, so was Archibald MacLeish's. The fact that the films were not hard-line politics and the fact that they were admired by a wide spectrum of people on the left suggests the relevance of Hurwitz's statement that, at the time, the Party seemed to offer the best grasp of the world. This appeared to be so especially during the early thirties, when the Depression politicized these filmmakers, and it continued to appear so throughout the late thirties, especially for those who were able both to ignore reports of Stalinist repression and to separate Marxist-Leninist philosophy from Soviet practice. Practically speaking too, the Party was attractive. Arthur Garfield Hayes of the ACLU tried to explain this to the House Un-American Activities Committee in 1948:

I think . . . the Communists do one thing valuable in this country: that is they are gadflies. Whatever their purpose may be, they have been fighting the cause of all mean injustices in the United States, starting with the Sacco-Vanzetti case, then the Scottsboro case, then cases of workingmen all over the country, fighting against Negro oppression in the South—and all the way through they have done a job that the rest of us ought to do and, so long as we ignored it, we give the Communists arguments. I think it is very fortunate that we have some people in this country who do wake up the public mind to these injustices. I wish these people did not go to the Communists.[48]

But clearly, Steiner and Van Dyke were troubled by Frontier's relations with the Party. Van Dyke rejected communism and, whatever his own desire for significant change, wanted no part of Party politics. How much he thought affiliation with Frontier might make trouble for him in the future, I have no idea, and surely such a motivation for leaving the organization cannot be ruled out as a possibility for either him or Steiner.[m] But most important in Van Dyke's case is the fact that he wished to become a director and to work at the highest level in Frontier; as a result, he felt profoundly thwarted and frustrated when he lost *Labor Spy*. And although Hurwitz argues that Van Dyke should have stuck, that he would have received further assignments,[49] precious few other films actually turned up, and on this basis Van Dyke was right to jump. My guess is that this was his primary motivation in making the split and that the political and financial were simply the significant factors that supported the larger decision.

The same factors are significant for Steiner, but certain personal issues also come into play in his case. It harks back to location on *The Plow That Broke the Plains*, where it first became clear that Hurwitz was drawn to Strand's way of thinking and to Strand as an artist and that Steiner found himself more in sympathy with Lorentz's ideals. The same type of anxieties that plagued him then were at work now as Steiner looked over the *Labor Spy/Native land* script and found it gloomy. Having failed to substitute the left-wing labor mystery film he had solicited from Dashiell Hammett, he may well have wished to break rather than to stick with something so incompatible.

But it was more than that. By every testimony a person uninvolved in politics, Steiner was startled to find himself both a subject in the

---

[m] Hurwitz: "This activity . . . did provide material for blacklists before, during and after the McCarthy period" (Michael and Jill Klein, "*Native Land*: An Interview with Leo Hurwitz," *Cinéaste* 6, no. 3 [1974], p. 15). In his testimony before HUAC on 10 April 1952, Kazan mentioned Frontier Films as an organization "since . . . listed as subversive" (Eric Bentley, *Thirty Years of Treason: Excerpts from Hearings Before the House Committee on Un-American Activities, 1938-1968* [New York: Viking Press, 1971], pp. 488-489). Also in 1952, Vera Caspary was questioned about her "participation with the group" (letter to author, 22 June 1975). Hurwitz was a victim of the blacklisting during the fifties (interview 2), and Van Dyke too found himself on a "grey list" (Kent Harber, "Photography and Film through the Eyes of Willard Van Dyke," *The Daily Californian* 10, no. 3 [1978]: 12).

rancorous Stalinist-Trotskyite exchanges of the period[n] and the target of a threatened lawsuit. It hurt him deeply that these attacks came from the man who had been his closest friend. In name, he, Hurwitz and Strand had been the top triumvirate of Frontier Films, but since the days of Nykino, it was actually Hurwitz and Strand who had been the dominant figures. Steiner had been assigned to *People of the Cumberland*, while Hurwitz and Strand worked on *Heart of Spain*; Steiner was a cameraman, and *Heart of Spain* had already been shot, but he did not work with Hurwitz on *People of the Cumberland* either, and *Native Land* made it even more eminently clear that Hurwitz preferred to collaborate with Strand. And now the bitter attacks. Although Steiner was resilient and was soon at work on *The City*, there is no doubt that this "very unhappy period of my life" was a traumatic one.[50] And the trauma was primarily and enduringly personal: Steiner now honestly warns interviewers that his statements about Hurwitz are informed by dislike and bias.

A very talented artist in photography and film, Steiner was highly respected by most other documentary film and theater people in New York. His inventive personality delighted in life's surfaces and amusements, and the small films he controlled, such as *Pie in the Sky*, *Harbor Scenes*, perhaps *Café Universal*, and a film he made for the dress designer Elizabeth Hawes, ran to the funny, the whimsical, the vitally eccentric. But he did not find his way, somehow, to great and substantial art, most likely because he did not possess the driving passion of a Hurwitz, a Strand, or a Lorentz. In Hollywood he "didn't produce anything, I wasn't aggressive or brilliant enough, you know," and he spent most of his years, until recently, in commercial photography, something he regards as having been debilitating.[51] The interpersonal results of his lack of full artistic and political commitment were most likely the key to his final departure from Frontier Films.

[n] Having returned to England after a stay in New York, Paul Rotha learned from Steiner, among others, that he too was caught in this controversy because he had advised the Museum of Modern Art to purchase a print of the Max Eastman (Trotskyite) film, *From Tsar to Lenin*, for its historical value, and because he had considered making a film with John Dos Passos. Steiner and Van Dyke had previously enlisted Rotha in setting up American Documentary Films, Inc., and Rotha quotes a letter Steiner wrote to him on 13 May 1938: "The Frontier Film boys have been going around town denouncing you as a Trotskyite. In the *Daily Worker* there was a short piece that was nasty. It is said to have come from England. It ran like this: 'It is on very good authority from England that we hear that Paul Rotha is a thoroughgoing Trotskyite. In view of this, the infant American Documentary Films Inc., might have been more careful in its choice of directors.' " See Rotha, *Documentary Diary: An Informal History of the British Documentary Film, 1928-1939* (London: Secker & Warburg, 1973), p. 211.

Kline and Ivens Preview
World War II: Films of Warning,
1938-1940

Kline in Spain: *Return to Life*

In April 1938, Herbert Kline arrived from Paris with his new film, *Return to Life*. Henri Cartier-Bresson, who had never used a movie camera, had assigned the shooting to Jacque Lemare to assure the film a professional quality. Kline and Cartier-Bresson had written the script and directed, and together with Lemare and Laura Sejour, they did the editing in Paris. There Charles Koecklin wrote a score, and Spanish refugee children sang the children's song. The film was given a French commentary and titled *Retour à la Vie*. In New York, according to Kline Frontier made some changes, although he cannot remember what they were. Maddow wrote a commentary that Richard Blaine, the voice on *People of the Cumberland*, narrated. The Film Division of the Theatre Arts Committee, a lively popular-front organization that ran a brilliant cabaret to raise funds for Loyalist Spain, arranged a premiere for *Return to Life* in the Grand Ballroom at the Waldorf Astoria on 20 July. Among the notables present were Donald Ogden Stewart, as master of ceremonies; Villaplana, a prominent Spanish jurist; Luis Quintanilla, the Spanish anti-Fascist artist; and Ralph Bates, the English novelist who had fought in Spain. The proceeds of more than $1,000 were contributed toward the supplying of a relief ship for Spain.[1] The film then went on to what was probably its only theater run in New York; appearing at the Cameo from 3 to 8 August.

Produced to raise funds for medical supplies, ambulances, and hospitals, *Return to Life*, like *Heart of Spain*, makes medical activity its principal subject. An initial sequence affords some idea of current life in Madrid: the bombing and shelling, the defenses, the blockade, the rationing. Following sequences show the Republic's care for its children, people working night and day to make bandages, farmers planting and harvesting close to the front in order to feed the cities, refugees, hospitals and soldiers, the training of a stretcher crew, soldiers entering battle. Beginning in the second third of the film, ambulance crews go into action, bearing wounded soldiers from the field of battle, giving first aid, operating on an emergency case in an ambulance donated by the Artist's Union of America. Then come two major sequences in which we watch at length while the wounded are unloaded from a train and then witness their sometimes agonizing recoveries in the hospital. A village fiesta in honor of wounded servicemen at an American hospital is followed by an oddly placed, rather lyrical sequence on war orphans. The third major sequence is set at convalescent hospitals by the Mediterranean, where the "wounded make their way back to life," where machines return flexibility to their limbs, where they learn to read and where eventually they wrestle, swim, play soccer, and prepare to go back to the front "to stop the fascists before they attack the world."

Essentially *Return to Life* attempts to touch us with the condition of the wounded, with what is being done for them, and with what they are fighting against. It is a film of missed opportunities. Let me take two examples. In the opening sequence, for two shots the camera sweeps over ruins while Blaine effectively evokes the human losses. Music then covers three powerful but short shots of four pieces of ruined church statuary: a crucifix and three saints, all at extreme angles, three in close-up, the last with a black hole through its eye. These are followed by a long shot of the destroyed building, and we learn that "Franco smashed a church, but he couldn't destroy a people." We are then confronted with a propaganda poster depicting two muscular men, the arm of one over the shoulder of the other, UNIDAD printed across. Succeeding shots continue to make this upbeat point. The faces of the statues have extreme symbolic value, for with all the overtones of stylized religious artifacts, they signify both humane values and humanity under attack. But because the filmmakers rush to the more facile propaganda point, the power to be gained by holding on the statuary is lost.

The second example: after an abundance of shots of the wounded coming off the train and of bedridden men—men in gangrene-induced delirium, men bored, despairing, tormented, in terrible pain—a full-frame close-up confronts us with a soldier's face, incredibly drained, incredibly sad, full-eyed, motionless, terrifying in a way, propped on a pillow and staring directly at the camera. This shot should have been accompanied by silence. Instead, the narrator intones: "Whom does this man accuse?" The camera cuts back to capture the soldier, his face unchanged, from the waist up, then further accenting this startling, troubling image, cuts back even more in order to frame the entire body, the head shifted a bit, the expression unaltered, and then the voice intones again, this time the intrusive, ruinous, generalized question: "Who brought death to the Spanish people?" An uncalled-for fade intervenes, and we gaze on a man walking the ward on knee-length stumps, while the commentary offers the following reply: "Reich-chancellor Hitler, il duce Mussolini, Generalissimo Franco, the Rome-Berlin axis." This unnecessary spelling out, this awkward inability to leave the images alone, undercuts the deeper messages they hold.

The film contains many excellent, imaginative shots, like the one that holds on the stumped man approaching on his new, artificial legs until the legs fill the frame and momentarily falter. Yet the cinematography is too often simply unengaged. The work is sometimes unprofessional: amateurish quick tilts and certain pans reveal set-ups that are too obvious and contrived. Images are sometimes unclear: the commentator *must* tell us that survivors are taking firewood from their demolished houses, for we don't really *see* what they are doing. Most importantly, far too many shots are simply uninteresting. There is little creative selection of angles and distances to fix the vital significance of people and locations.

Editing and commentary reflect the same creative failure. A few sequences are well built, but nearly everywhere too many shots (and many bad shots) are retained, and shots are unimaginatively juxtaposed. Possibly the filmmakers thought accumulation would bring power—as it does in the train-unloading sequence—but the general result is diffusiveness and some boredom. While we confront the three shots of the soldier's unaltering stare, a lack of compactness in the film prevents us from associating these shots with the three parallel shots of the bombed-out statues, an analogy that adds such powerful dimension to the suffering.[a] I suspect that Maddow tried through nar-

---

[a] A comparison is helpful here. *Hiroshima-Nagasaki, August, 1945* is a film by Paul Ronder, composed twenty-five years after the bombing from recently released on-the-spot footage. At Nagasaki, three shots take us from a distant look at a cathedral to a close-up of the charred broken foot of a statue; a tilt then moves slowly up to the extended hand, to the painfully sad blackened saint's face, the Catholic symbol ineffably registering all the implications of the bomb from the West. Later, as high and piercing Japanese notes sound over silent shots of the radiation victims, the film cuts from burned and skinless feet, to hands and arms, to the ruined faces of the Nagasaki victims,

ration to make insignificant shots and sequences become significant, an effort almost inevitably doomed to failure. This attempt also rendered him incapable of allowing the forceful images that do exist to assert their own implications.[b]

I have something particular in mind when I say that the cinematography is often "unengaged." I have no doubt that everyone who took part in the making of this film cared deeply about the events in Spain; I have no doubt that they hoped to make a film that would both register their own care and recreate it in others. But we have all listened to the renowned person who is unable to communicate his or her intense interest and involvement in a subject. Such a person reads in a monotone from a paper, addresses the podium or the ceiling, glances nervously at the clock, is deferential, apologetic, keeps coughing, becomes lost in a point, trails in irrelevant examples, and so on. The result is the same when filmmakers have not put the full pressure of their concern for the subject into the making of the individual shot and into its relations to the shots around it. We lose a little of our concern, carry some of the looseness, the haste, the indifference with us to the succeeding shots, and we are not engaged. Had the awareness of suffering, resilient humanity and the great, artistic skill that we find combined in the best of Cartier-Bresson's still photography been dominant in this film, *Return to Life* might have been superior to *The Spanish Earth* and *Heart of Spain*.

My criticism of *Return to Life* caught Leo Hurwitz by surprise, for in 1938 he had been moved by it. Similarly, Paul and Hazel Strand had seen Cartier-Bresson's French print of the film in 1974 and found themselves very impressed, especially by the dramatic idea of rehabilitation and return to battle. Lewis Jacobs's brief review of the film for the September-October 1938 issue of *Direction* suggests that he too found it powerful.[2] Other reviewers were less enthusiastic, more pointedly critical, but generally found it at least informative, which it certainly is. But in 1938, Hurwitz and Jacobs brought to the film their intense, current concern over the fate of Spain, the rest of Europe, and China, and very likely they invested the images with more emotion than they now carry. Nevertheless it should have been evident

---

concluding as instruments pry open an empty eye socket. The striking relation between statue and victims, so cinematically and subtly established, is unforgettable.

[b] In response to my query about this, Maddow stated: "Cartier-Bresson's film *Return to Life* was completely edited in Paris before I saw it. I don't recollect what instructions I was given, but I do recall being extremely pressed for time, a situation where rhetoric . . . takes the place of judgment." Letter to author, 24 Dec. 1974.

to them that the film fell far short, as other works by Frontier did not, of fulfilling the need for telling, anti-Fascist art.

Ivens in China: *The 400 Million*

Not many weeks before the 7 July 1937 White House premiere of *The Spanish Earth*, the Japanese undertook a new and intensive invasion of China. Hellman, Hemingway, MacLeish, and Shumlin reconstituted themselves as History Today, Inc., and along with Louise Rainer, who had recently played the female lead in *The Good Earth*, conceived a second Ivens film, which was to become *The 400 Million*. Negotiating delicately, Rainer raised considerable sums from Chinese-American businessmen in New York, and other contributions flowed in, predominantly from the Hollywood community. Ivens flew to Paris to appear with *The Spanish Earth*[c] and to make plans with John Ferno and Robert Capa, the noted battle photographer whose wife, a photographer too, had been killed by a rebel tank in Spain. Ivens, Ferno, and Capa agreed to meet in Hong Kong in February, and Ivens returned to the States for equipment and for consultation with Paramount Laboratories over film problems in subtropical climates. In January, his friends at Frontier saw him off.[3]

Ivens was gone for more than eight months. Upon his return, he and Helen van Dongen made a first cut in footage—from 40,000 to 6,000 feet—in Hollywood in September and early October. They then completed the editing in New York, where editing and recording costs were lower. Dudley Nichols, who had been unable to accompany the crew to China, wrote the commentary with subsequent assistance from Maddow.[d] Fredric March narrated, and other voices, including those of Adelaide Bean, Morris Carnovsky, and Sydney Lumet were used. Hanns Eisler was brought in to do the score, his third with Ivens. No one was paid: receipts were to go for medical aid to the Chinese Army. After a premiere at the Esquire Theater in Hollywood, *The 400 Million* began a short run at the Cameo on 7 March 1939, and had another short run at the Thalia, also in New York, in May.[4]

[c] Jean Renoir gave this film a French commentary that lacked the Hemingway touch. Its theater premiere in Paris occurred on 14 April 1938. See Robert Grelier, *Joris Ivens* (Paris: Les éditeurs Français réunis, 1965), p. 48.

[d] In my interview with Maddow, he remembered that he, not Nichols, had written the commentary: Nichols had turned in an unsatisfactory commentary, and Maddow rewrote it, but they had used Nichols' name because he was well known. In a later exchange of letters, after I had quoted Ivens' account of Nichols' doing the commentary, Maddow became less sure about this.

On 1 April 1938, at the base of a bare hill near Taierchwang, Joris Ivens and John Ferno had met a refugee family. The father, who had been forced to carry Japanese munitions, had been wounded by a grenade tossed at him by a Japanese officer. In telling his tale, he mimicked the officer's voice and look, and Ivens found himself making a connection. "It is the hard guttural sounds of a Nazi officer or Hitler's speech," he wrote in his diary:

> I detest such strained, fanatical ways of talking and the mentality that goes with it; I detest both military and moral aggression. And people everywhere who share the same feeling know they must unite to destroy these cliques. The lines of the battlefield of Taierchwang are longer than you think. They reach out into each country. . . . A man sitting on the ground in the middle of China becomes the symbol of what is happening to millions of other people. A symbol bearing the slogans of the reality of freedom, sorrow and the will to live.

To Ivens and his backers a film about China was a logical extension of the film about Spain. It was the same fight. And to put both on the screen was, they hoped, to drive home the need for a worldwide struggle against fascism. "We have a mission," Ivens noted on 12 April, "we are here for the sake of American audiences."[5]

By 12 April, the Fascist rebels were winning key victories in Spain, the *Anschluss* had overrun Austria, and Czechoslovakia was the new focus of world anxiety. Accordingly, Ivens endeavored now even more than before to touch the American viewer. In *The 400 Million*, many minor and several major connections are established. The Chinese university has coeds, "just as in America"; Sun Yat-sen is depicted as China's George Washington; China is now a democratic land with growing industrialization, national pride, and a great desire for independence; Madame Chiang Kai-shek endorses a check from New York: a fund-raisers' parade marches through New York. On the other hand, the United States ships enough scrap iron to Japan to supply 54 percent of Japan's munitions needs. Yet Japan's military plans extend to California. Painful shots of civilian victims of Japanese bombings provoke a personal reaction: "These are not easy things to look at, but as Americans, we had to see them." Would Ivens be able to make Americans look?

His hopes for the film were high, but his purposes were constantly frustrated. While at the same time appealing to Americans, the film was also to show, through Chinese art, history, and landscape, through the depiction of officers who had been produced from among the people, and through the portrayal of leaders like Madame Sun Yat-sen, whom Ivens greatly admired, the deep sources of the Chinese instinct to defend their homeland. But thanks to the many patronizing and humorous Hollywood treatments of the Chinese, the Chinese officials were suspicious. They could not comprehend Ivens' devotion to their cause nor understand how his films might help. He was not permitted to work with members of the Chinese motion picture industry, he was prevented from reaching the Taierchwang front lines, could not go to the northwest where the former Red Army, with whom he had more sympathy, was more aware of the value of documentary film. General Tu, their "liaison and censorman" did all he could to keep Ivens and Ferno away from the officers and forbade the shooting of certain scenes and equipment.[e] In Hankow, every shot was duplicated in 16mm film, which was developed in Hong Kong, returned to Hankow, and viewed by the censor before the 35mm film could be sent on to Hollywood. Ivens finally found the source for some potentially exciting footage in a small city:

> Four students stood outside a small Buddhist temple. They had a primitive sound relay system and soapboxes for a home-made loudspeaker. They were singing songs agitating the people in the fight against Japan. Men, women, soldiers, children, pigs comprised the audience. The whole market place was alive. The elementary latent force in these people—found all over China—was being brought to life by these students. It was a great manifestation. But we were not allowed to film it because it would give the impression that the Chinese mass was dirty and not well organized! We argued with the censor. No luck. The arguments became stronger. The censor put his hand in front of the lens. A very conclusive argument.

Back in Sian the next day, officials presented them with a nicely arranged demonstration of ten thousand people perfectly lined up, shiny loudspeakers and all. Against their desire, they filmed the rally, and it appears in the film. Nothing could have been more contrary to the spirit in which *The Spanish Earth* had been made or to Ivens' notion of documentary as personal discovery and witness to reality.[6]

Nevertheless, some of their goals were realized. In *The 400 Million*,

---

[e] Ivens did outwit his guardians in one case. He pretended to have lost a camera in the Yangtze River, then slipped it to an officer of the Eighth Route Army who carried it to the Communist forces. Their only camera from 1938 to 1945, it is now in the Revolutionary Museum in Peking. Ivens, "Joris Ivens Interviewed by Gordon Hitchens, November 20, 1968, American Documentaries," *Film Culture*, Spring 1972, pp. 194-195, and Georges Sadoul's preface to A. Zalzman, *Joris Ivens* (Paris: Editions seghers, 1963), p. 12.

Ivens and Ferno do evoke the deep, cultured past and the ancient land of China. Graves of the old kings form hills amidst waving wheat. Aged stone lions and the stone statues of great philosophers stand in the open country. The camera moves, adding graves, lions, philosophers to the frame, cinematically stressing their number and their importance. The balanced structure of each scene, the careful slow pans and tilts communicate a deep and implicit respect. Then camels approach the camera as we learn of the remarkable findings of Marco Polo. From a distance we see people plowing and working in rice paddies, and we admire the great river and the mountain landscapes. Elsewhere are instances of Ivens' effort to picture the resistance as an outgrowth of the spirit of the Chinese people—in the rally, the street theater, the singers, the ceremony dedicating the tomb of the unknown soldier, in various scenes with national leaders, including Chiang Kai-shek and Madame Sun Yat-sen.

It is in this approach to the cultural context of the war that one can see the difference between an Ivens and a Frontier Films production. I have already mentioned the relaxed, good-humored attitude that permeates the films dominated by Kazan, Leyda, Meyers, and Steiner. Ivens' films have yet another style of relaxation. Their fundamental, consistent seriousness of tone approximates the Hurwitz/Strand films, but in their effort to feel out lives, rhythms, culture and country, they are looser and less compact, and they have less immediate impact. Where the attempt is successful, there is clear gain; where it is not, there is a diffuseness that diminishes the film's intensity.

The 400 Million is less than successful. It has well-timed, sensitive narration, a high information level, professional use of sound effects, and music beautifully composed to carry some of the piercing tonality of Chinese music. But the overly long sequence of children donating coins for the war and the continual return to uninteresting shots of the military council after scenes illustrating the matter of their deliberations slow it to the point of boredom.

The shortcomings may not be wholly attributable to the relaxed style, however. On 13 April, Ivens noted his growing indignation against the Japanese army after filming "the wounded soldiers, and the terrible things that occurred in the villages." This indignation was part of the tension "you recover many months later in the cutting-room in New York alone with all this film material." And that indignation functioned very powerfully in the editing of bombing, battle, and refugee sequences, as well as in the scenes of the ancient land and culture, although in the latter it has been remarkably transformed. My guess, however, is that other indignations—over censorship, over his "impression that Chiang Kai-shek did not want to fight this war to the bitter end"—caused a tension that kept him from fully integrating the material and presenting it with complete conviction. This may be what was behind Ivens' despairing wish, after the cutting, to abandon the film and destroy the negative. Although work with Nichols on the narration made him feel better, the sense of frustration continued, and it was communicated to other members of the crew: Eisler, for instance, wanted the film to be named *Notes Toward a Film on China.*[7]

But despite all of these problems, the film has excellent camerawork, a vital score, and dedicated narrative, and it is both informative and to the point. For the sake of propaganda, Ivens effectively suppressed his frustrations and his doubts about Chiang Kai-shek: in fact, the film expresses a belief in the growing unity and dynamism of the Chinese armies. And although the film was clearly limited by censorship, no viewer can miss Ivens' feeling about the war and his passionate appeal against Fascist international aggression.

The 400 Million had enough bite to hit censorship troubles in Pennsylvania, London, and France (which had recently signed a commercial treaty with Japan). Yet in spite of some friendly reviews, Ivens was bitterly disappointed:

> It was just that the potential audiences for whom the film had been intended stayed away and didn't give the film a chance to tell them anything. The Nazis had just marched into Prague and the public didn't realize that this was the same war as the one we were showing in our film—or they didn't want to realize it. The only group who came en masse to the first New York theatre showing was the Chinese-Americans—who didn't need to be told.

In the face of the current European developments, China may have seemed too remote. Possibly some of the fault is also attributable to the viewers themselves—to their predictable apathy to what lies outside of conventional fare. But it is also likely that audiences sensed that *The 400 Million* lacked what both Ivens and the artists who left the Film and Photo League in 1935 believed most necessary in a film. In Ivens' words: "Our way of helping is to make a good film. To move people by its professional quality so they will feel and understand that the wounded soldier needs a good stretcher for his very life."[8]

Kline in Czechoslovakia: *Crisis*

While Ivens was in China, Herbert Kline, a great admirer of his films, arrived in New York with *Return to Life* and then characteristically

did not await its American premiere. With financial backing from Arthur Mayer[f] and others, he was in Czechoslovakia in April to film the
beginning, he thought, of World War II. For "various reasons," he
did not wish to make this film for Frontier. Perhaps his backers were
leery of Frontier, or perhaps he was aware that while Ivens, Meyers,
Steiner, and Van Dyke had encouraged him as a filmmaker, Hurwitz,
Maddow, and Strand had not.[9] Clearly Kline was an energetic, independent young man who now knew filmmaking and was ready to
go it on his own, a common source of separation in the decade. I
suspect, too, that he felt it was *he*, like Ivens, who was going to the
war fronts, and therefore that he, like Ivens, should be allowed to
shape the film according to what *he* was finding there. His Czech film,
Crisis, was billed as "an eye-witness exposure of 'the Nazi Way,' " a
reflection of Ivens' *témoignage*.

Furthermore, Kline knew the sort of film he wanted to make. From
the outset, he had aspired to become, according to Kline, one of the
great "foreign correspondents of the screen." Now he hoped to create
"a classic of the conflict between fascism and democracy" and to avoid
the kind of political film that would alienate his audience: "a human
film," he told me in our swift, vibrant talk amidst half-packed bags in
his New York hotel apartment, as opposed to "a political film." According to Kline, a human film expresses the experience of a people
in a critical situation of wide importance.[10] And although his friends
at Frontier were similarly opposed on principle to narrowly political
films, they might have shaped such a film differently: they might, for
example, have been more inclined than Kline to play up the role of
the Czech labor unions.

Before he and his wife, Rosa Harvan, left New York for Czechoslovakia, Kline wrote ahead to a Prague friend who was active in the
Czech theater. Consequently, Hans Burger went quickly to work and
greeted Kline with a screen treatment for a documentary about Czech
minorities. The subject would be important in any contemporary film
on Czechoslovakia, but Kline wanted to cover political developments
from the *Anschluss* to whatever was ahead—the betrayal at Munich,
as it turned out. Accordingly, he wrote a new script, one that would
be subject to repeated alteration, for, as he later explained, the film
was produced by two crews working from the same scenario: *Mein
Kampf*. One crew was his own, and the other was composed of "Hitler,
Goebbels, Henlein and their associates," who "shifted our climaxes,

---

[f] Mayer, born in 1886, had been director of publicity and advertising for Paramount
Pictures from 1930 to 1933; he was now operator of the Rialto Theatre in New York and
president of the Mayer-Burstyn Film Corporation.

rearranged our finales, etc., so that in the end we had nothing to follow but the skeleton of the original idea."[11]

It was an extraordinary experience. Permits to film the Czech army came easily, but Kline needed to record Nazi activity in the Sudeten, a northern, largely German-speaking region where Henlein was based. Flattering Henlein's cohorts, pretending to be pro-Nazi, writing fake letters, taking risks not even his companions knew of at a time antagonists were sometimes murdered by Henlein stormtroopers, Kline got the crew into party rallies, parades, and funerals, and received the cooperation of stormtroopers for scene set-ups and retakes. He had less trouble passing than another Jewish member of the crew and, despite his *"verboten* and despised racial origin,"* had the "strange" experience of having "a troop of SA men to do my bidding, and march, and *heil* and shout as they were told." A constant challenge was to recognize and understand significant events as they broke and to have the camera in the appropriate place. It was also a challenge to penetrate the lies of their Nazi guides concerning, for example, why the factories were shut down and why men and women were out of work in the Sudeten.

The film was edited in secret at the Bata Shoe Film Department, and absolute secrecy regarding its contents and the presence of its Czech crew was maintained. Two days after Munich, the crew left the Sudeten, then hid their film for five weeks in a Prague basement, fearing its confiscation under the new censorship laws. Six weeks after Munich, they smuggled the film out: how this was accomplished remains a mystery that I hope Kline will divulge in the memoirs that he is currently writing. Afterwards, Kline helped Burger, his brilliant young cameraman Alexander Hackenschmied (later, in this country, Hammid), the comedians Voscovec and Werich, and other Czechs who took part in the film to escape Czechoslovakia before the film was released.[12]

Kline brought the completed film to New York in December, where it was premiered on 13 March 1939 at the 55th Street Playhouse. As "a striking and tragic piece of film journalism," it was, according to *Living Films*, "among the most widely distributed of American documentary films," and it was named by the National Board of Review as sixth among the "Ten Best Films of 1939,"[g] a reception in some part

---

[g] Unfortunately, this does not mean as much as one would like it to, for according to Arthur Mayer: "although it won sixth place for merit, it was not six hundredth at the box office, for it took in less money than the average travelogue. Do not unjustly attribute this to indifference or hostility on the part of exhibitors. Both Warners and Loews tried to show the picture in their theatres and only withdrew it after obtaining very unsatisfactory results." See Mayer, "A Plea for Unpopular Films," NBR, May 1940, pp. 6-7.

due to its painful relevance to the dark subsequent events in Europe.[13]

In its documentation of the growing strength of Henlein's Deutsche Party and the efforts of the Czech democracy to stem the tide, *Crisis* derives from *The Spanish Earth* the concept of *teimoinage* and the use of an individual (here, the Czech girl, Mirka) to link locations. But, unlike the work of Ivens, it has a newsreel quality: it is a news film, controlled by events. The commentary, in fact, has something of the pace, aggressiveness and dramatic tone of *The March of Time*, and sometimes, like the latter, its words are insufficiently illustrated by its images.[h]

But, despite the remarks of some reviewers, *Crisis* is superior to both the newsreel and the travelogue.[14] For one thing, the accomplished people whom Kline found for cameraman, narrator, and composers (H. W. Susskind and Jaroslav Harvan) produced a high artistic quality not commonly found in either of those types of film. Although it lacks *Frontier's* tight, impressive, kinetic, and symbolic editing, in its juxtapositions directed at a consistent, significant point, in its awareness of subtle meanings and themes, in its sense of tragedy, and in its insistent purpose, it is a moving documentary film of high character. If we define the documentary film as film that is dedicated to change, and if we argue that a good documentary film is artfully constructed and reaches substantial human depth, then *Crisis* is a major documentary film of the thirties.

The opening images stress Czech pride, Czech love of peace, tolerance, and democracy. We are given to understand the presence of the engaged, admiring American filmmakers, who have been drawn to a country whose constitution is modeled on that of the United States and whose general national policy is founded on the ideals of the League of Nations and collective security. In immediate contrast, we learn what the Nazis make of such unity. Unsettling shots of citizens awkwardly fitting gas masks and receiving instructions on bomb and chemical burns and a discussion of Nazi book banning are followed by a sequence on refugees from Austria and from German concentration camps, a sequence distinguished by remarkably sensitive close-ups supported by the sound of a single cello. Such juxtapositions, often accented by sharp clashes in music, again and again emphasize this difference between Czechoslovakia and her predators. A blonde Czech

---

[h] The problem of how to capture on film the entire story you wish to tell is common to the news media. *The March of Time* ran into this difficulty with its famous *Inside Nazi Germany* (Jan. 1938), in which the images were so unsupportive of clear and strong anti-Nazi indictments that some accused the film of supporting the contemporary German regime.

child and a dark-haired Jewish refugee child swing in a Czech father's arms. The dulcet music-over gives way suddenly to flaring, vibrant martial horns, while marching youth of the Deutsche Party occupy the screen and *Mein Kampf* titles-over explain that the German youth must be trained to think themselves superior to all others. Morbid, heavy music sounding over the pageantlike Nazi funeral for two men shot by Czech border guards yields to a serene music over a close shot of a single, cigarette-smoking Czech guard on watch at the frontier. For Kline, then and now, the film centers around this one shot of the calm resolute Czech ready to defend his homeland against a massive, brainwashed, goosestepping military force.

Both Kline and Burger were theater people, and as a result, the film has many performances. At a theater where Voscovec and Werich mock the Nazis, we first meet Mirka, who works for a solidarity organization dedicated to achieving better understanding between Czech and German citizens through their children. We see folk singers and dancers of many nations come together in a packed Prague stadium for the Congress of the Sokols. At the solidarity summer camp where Mirka counsels, the children rapturously take in a traditional puppet show. Later, in the film's most moving sequence, Voscovec and Werich accompany the children in a song entitled "Against the Storm" that the children know by heart. As they sing, the striking disharmony of martial horns suddenly rises over their song; this new sound continues as, in a shocking juxtaposition, we cut to Hitler, high on his podium, spitting invective at the Czech government. Here theater, music, and song are shown to have the power to unite a threatened people both physically and emotionally. The film itself, as a work of art closely affiliated with the performances it depicts, was the filmmakers' own attempt to bring to the world what they admired in the Czechs: their solidarity against Nazi Germany.

But in Czechoslovakia, as the film recounts, that solidarity was betrayed from the outside. Throughout *Crisis* we hear reference to the support sworn by Czechoslovakia's allies, England, France, and the Soviet Union: the Czechs, including President Benes, were willing to mobilize not because they expected to defeat the enemy but in order to hold him until the allies joined in the fight. From the sound track:

> When the results of the deal at Berchtesgaden were imposed on the Czech nation by ultimatum, hundreds of thousands of people turned out in protest. It was a bewildered people, singing and weeping by turns, but we who were in Prague that night can never forget it. The women in the Parliament Square shouted to the Government, "We give you our sons. Give them arms!"

It is against this kind of spirit that the film's pathetic denouement occurs. The filmmakers, who had risked their lives to tell this story, who had expected to film the beginning of the war as the allies finally rose united against Hitler, who had saved the last of their film stock to capture that uprising, were left to record their bitter sorrow at the world's failure to live up to the Czechs. The narrator speaks:

The last demonstration of the brokenhearted people of Prague after the surrender at Munich showed that thousands still had the will to resist, but in vain. Leaderless and betrayed, they could not stand against the Munich powers. . . . The Western democracies have sacrificed their prestige. The human race itself is impoverished and humiliated by these events.

Here was still another warning film for Americans. The voice-over tells us that while the latest refugees

trudge up and down the wind-swept road or huddle in rags and straw to keep themselves warm, the only hope life has to offer is that in other lands may still be men who do not tremble and obey when Adolph Hitler cracks the whip. Peace and freedom and the right to live: they can only be possible in countries where men are determined that the swastika shall not be raised in triumph, where the pages of *Mein Kampf* can never become our supreme law.

From some quarters came praise for Kline's clear and single propagandistic intent and for his avoidance of specific political lines. For instance, writing for *The National Board of Review Magazine*, Shelley Hamilton thought he had played his American audience perfectly. But from other quarters came less satisfied comment. During previews of *Crisis*, Kline had resisted pressure from the sectarian left to make changes. James Dugan's *New Masses* review, favorable until this final paragraph, describes what was found wanting:

Crisis does not answer Hitler's murder with the cry to fight back. . . . The picture should present a plan of action: a strengthening of every fight in Spain and China, a unity of the democracies against fascist aggression, every step that can be taken to strangle Hitler—boycotts, embargoes, vigilance against the Bunds, the spies, and the traitors in the democracies. . . . *Crisis* has failed to . . . show the anger of the democratic people of London and Paris. It failed, too, to show the strength of the Czech working-class parties—the Communists particularly—who fought then and are still battling against capitulation.

In a review of *The 400 Million* and *Crisis* in *TAC*, a popular-front theater arts periodical, Sidney Meyers had other criticism. He praised the film for its notes of "warning" and, characteristic of a Frontier filmmaker, admired "the remarkable force" of most of Kline's images.[i] However, it was also characteristic of a Frontier filmmaker to wish the kind of wholeness of vision they had found in Dovzhenko's *Frontier* and in the films of Ivens. In fact, just the previous summer, Meyers had lauded Ivens for his "integrated version of life," his "deep sense of unity with his fellow human beings," and his "instinct for thoroughness, for order, and . . . profound social alliances." By comparison, *Crisis* now fell short: "the 'world-view' of the director of *Crisis* was subservient . . . to his great desire to 'bring back the story.' There was an overbalance of the 'trouble shooter' to the neglect of the 'world-thinker' that a true documentary artist must always be." In response the next month to a challenge from Albert Maltz that he was advocating artistic constrictions and formulaic endings, Meyers replied that he had been misunderstood and explained further that by world view he meant "the completest absorption of reality in terms of an integrated personality."[15]

Meyers' criticism of *Crisis* is both astute and just, although I hope my treatment has made clear in a way that his does not the considerable degree to which a heartfelt world view and sense of unity with fellow human beings does permeate *Crisis*. It is true, however, that the journalism, the shot, and the incident do predominate in the film, and

---

[i] The quality of his descriptions suggests the sort of sensitive, humane influence that the future maker of *The Quiet One* (1949)—a tough compassionate study of the saving of a troubled Harlem boy by the Wiltwyck School—exerted when he was consulted at any stage on a Frontier production:

> They are the bone of the bone thereof and marrow of the marrow. The terror and misery that overcomes one in the gas-mask station; the unforgettable image of the white-haired attendant screwing a chemical filter on to a child's mask and trying to make a joke of it; the face of the refugees, of the old Jew whose neatly brushed bowler and glazed-over eyes will always say "refugee"; the Austrian child who looks up at her mother as she receives a handful of bills from the Czech relief depot. Nor is it possible to drive out of one's mind the first Nazi we see, his hands clenched behind his back, his nose screwed up in frozen hatred, a compound of all the loathed excrescences of life; the lovely children and the tragic uniqueness of the afternoon with Voskovec and Werich at the solidarity Camp—the footage of the Nazi outbreaks at Eger which someday a liberated humanity will look at and wonder, so strange and detestable will it seem.

In another review, in 1938, Meyers urged Jean Renoir to make a film on a greater theme even than that of *Grand Illusion*, on "the tragedy of the violence done to the human soul by those who would wreck the world" ("One Man's Contribution," *TAC*, Nov. 1938, p. 6). In 1968, Meyers' assistant editor on Walter Reade's production of *Slaves* found him weeping in his Shreveport, Louisiana motel room, before the television set that was showing the police violence at the 1968 Democratic Convention in Chicago (letter written by John Kaufman, 8 Apr. 1974; in the possession of Edna Meyers).

although this did not prevent the extensive distribution of *Crisis* during 1939 and 1940,ʲ perhaps it does explain why *The Spanish Earth* remains in distribution today while *Crisis* does not. Nevertheless, as high journalism, a perennial warning, and a major documentary film, it deserves to be redistributed.

Kline in Poland: *Lights Out in Europe* and the Soviet-Nazi Pact

His desire to film the Arajevo of 1939 undiminished, Kline knew his next destination. Back in Paris in May, he had his cameraman, Alexander Hackenschmied, released from jail (where recently entering Czechs were being kept under surveillance) and smuggled him over to England. There they were joined by Rosa Harvan and by Arthur Mayer's son, Peter, who was to serve as associate producer on the new film. Hackenschmied could not move about much with his invalid Czech passport and so was assigned to record England's gradual awakening to the implications of Munich. The Klines, together with Douglas Slokim, an Englishman taken on as still photographer, left for the first of two trips to Poland. A Polish cameraman was sent to Danzig to capture Nazi activity there, and others worked with Kline, filming the tardy, inadequate war preparations of the pretentiously confident Polish leaders. On location when the invasion struck, the crew retreated with refugees and soldiers, learning to freeze flat beneath the strafing, dive-bombing German planes. Two Polish cameramen were killed, and Slokim had a close call. Two Eyemos were lost.

According to Kline, the other cameras kept running, proving for any doubters who the invaders were. Evidently, then, at some risk, the Klines made their way out of Poland via Riga, Latvia with their film and equipment. Back in England, they studied their footage and Hackenschmied's, while he continued to film the English mobilization. Kline and Hackenschmied then traveled to France to capture the look and mood of the western front as a cap for their film but "were disappointed at the lack of interesting material." Permitted to visit the Maginot Line, they were asked to leave their cameras behind, and the French wartime censor lifted all their close-ups of camouflaged allied guns.[16]

The film edited, the crew returned to the States, and Kline crossed

---

ʲ "When the B'nai B'rith Lodge in Seattle wrote, asking for advice on a film to be shown at a meeting, we suggested *Crisis* and told them how to get it. They showed it on October 12th—and broke all records for attendance in the lodge's history. Over a thousand people jampacked the hall." See *Film Survey*, Dec. 1939, p. 13.

the country to record the sound in Hollywood. There, in another instance of Kline's emulation of Ivens, he chose Fredric March, the narrator of *The 400 Million*, to speak the commentary, which James Hilton, author of *Goodbye, Mr. Chips*, had been assigned to write. Werner Janssen composed the score. *Lights Out in Europe* opened to mixed reviews at a time of all-out European war, on 11 April 1940, at an independent New York theater, the Little Carnegie.

It is not as good a film as *Crisis*. The problem is that here the trouble-shooter side is even more dominant than in Kline's previous film, and because of the parallel pictures of Poland, Danzig, and England, the newsreel base shows more clearly. This in fact caused some critics rather too quickly to find it "a compilation of newsreels," "a newsreel pastiche without reference or control." *The Nation*, however, in a not entirely friendly review, thought, with more accuracy, that *Lights Out in Europe* had

> the same relation to the general run of newsreels that the inside stories of really informed correspondents have to mere news dispatches. . . . Here these events are seen and reported by somebody who knows what they mean and who shows their relation to the great drama of which they are a part.[17]

Siege, another film of the time on the same subject, had no such perspective. Its one-man crew, Julien Bryan, took a train from Switzerland when fighting became imminent, incorrectly figuring that drawn-out trench warfare was ahead, and so arrived in Poland too late to film the retreat. But he stayed on in Warsaw after the Polish government, almost all foreign representatives, and all other correspondents and photographers had left, and he captured the bravery and the pain of the Poles under daily bombardment. Masquerading as a Swedish embassy official, he smuggled his film out during a three-hour truce on 21 September, and quickly produced *Siege*, a ten-minute newsreel report that was released to a stunned world. *Siege* has moments that only a sensitive news photographer would record—fire upon fire burning away in the night, close-ups of the faces of "a nation besieged"— but it is nonetheless simply a newsreel: the shots show less care than Kline's and are accompanied by constant voice-over narration. In contrast, the selection of images in *Lights Out in Europe* reveals attentive, imaginative shaping and an intention of depth. It is surely more effective than *Siege* but not sufficiently so to be viewed as an outstanding film.[18]

Crisis had fully acknowledged the German opposition to peace, and it concluded by calling out for people and nations to rise up against the swastika. *Lights Out in Europe* has a very different thrust, a thrust that becomes evident in the words spoken toward the end of the film in conscious allusion to Erich Maria Remarque's famous antiwar novel and the film based on it: "All was quiet on the new western front." And it also is evident in the film's final narration, as we watch soldiers backed by beacon lights that search the skies:

> Europe of today knows now it was not a war to end wars, that the great promise was unfulfilled, and now once again the lights had gone out in Europe. All over this darkened Europe, the soldiers stand on guard, watching for the sky raiders with their loads of death. But behind many a uniform is the heart and mind of the average man, asking why he cannot quietly get on with his job, why he cannot be allowed to watch his children grow up in a decent world. And in this troubled heart of man there must sometimes come the thought that though a way to end wars was a failure, a peace to end wars has never yet been tried.

The filmmakers' purpose, then, as the prologue tells us, is to convince us of "the futility of war." And so the toughest scenes record the horror of war: a baby is forced into a gasproof container, its tiny hand pressing desperately at the window from within; a Polish woman writhes in her final agony on a train bench, a victim of German strafing, machine-gunned through the throat. In on-the-scene circumstances, such images lend themselves naturally to the camera. But the scenario also sent Hackenschmied searching for victims from the past. In a London street, signs sadly adorn three groping men: "partially blind," "totally blind." A hand follows a rail, another traces braille letters, then two close-ups precede a hand-on-shoulder file of men slowly trailing through a home for the blind. Then comes a powerful World War I clip of the "same" men, newly blind in ragged battle fatigue, lined up hand-on-shoulder for the first time. Another clip shows the horror of their last sight: wartorn corpses strewn together on the ground. The millions of Europe, March's voice tells us in introducing this chilling sequence, "have good reason to hate war."

And war's ironies and injustice receive special note. Civilization's first job for the unemployed in many a year is to build frail bomb shelters. The London slums finally give up their children—evacuated under the imminent threat of war. And pilots all over Europe are

> being trained to rain death on those whose names they would never learn and whose whereabouts they could only identify from a map. . . . Shells by the million were now fashioned for the army

as throughout all Europe man's struggle to clothe and feed and house himself decently was suspended, and his whole strength turned to the machinery of destruction and death.

Franz Hoellering of *The Nation* felt that the shift in emphasis between the two films made *Lights Out in Europe*, which he called "easily the most dramatic, most eloquent, and most revealing picture yet made about contemporary events," finally "hopelessly confused." The opening statement on war's futility and the bland closing statement are "empty." And Hoellering had no doubt about what had happened:

> There is in the picture itself a . . . contradiction. It begins quite naturally as a militant anti-Nazi film, but suddenly vague pacifist overtones are accentuated; the graves of the soldiers of the war of 1914-1918 are shown again and again. The reason for such forced inconsistency is not difficult to detect. It lies obviously in the Soviet-German pact.[k] Its effect on the people of England and France is, significantly, not shown, but its effect on the producers of the film is clear. They became, to say the least, confused and began to censor reality. Starting out in May, 1939, to fight fascism, they found themselves suddenly in August propagandists for an "imperialistic war"—this is the impression given by the omissions and the accents in the second half of the picture. Fortunately their material remains more impressive than their confusion.[19]

That the filmmakers were shifting ground along with the American Communist Party's refusal to condemn the pact and its implications is certainly one interpretation. No reader of *New Theatre* and no follower of Kline's career could avoid knowing of his large sympathy for the Soviet Union. The news of the pact had to affect Kline as powerfully as it did everyone else on the left, and it must have caught him as completely off guard. It is certainly possible that a reluctance to dissociate himself from the Soviet Union somewhat tempered his interest in strongly confronting the Nazis, and perhaps at the time of the film's completion he was still experiencing considerable ambiguity about his own position in the left's bitter division over the pact.

But my own interpretation assumes a very different perspective. *Crisis*, in its profound sympathy for the Czech people and their situation, is a deeply human film. So is *Lights Out in Europe* in its own way. While in Danzig, Kline's cameraman filmed swastikas posted

[k] This notorious mutual nonaggression pact occurred during the making of the film and is referred to there as shocking and confusing to everyone.

everywhere, store window signs crying "Die Juden sind unser Un-
glück," and the razing of the synagogue, and March tells us of the
dispossession and the expulsion of Polish and Jewish minorities. This
material might easily have been tamed at the editing and writing stage,
which came after the Soviet-Nazi pact. It was not. Two of Kline's
cameramen were killed in the invasion, while he clung helplessly to
the earth and listened to the cries of the wounded. It was not his first
war experience, but my guess is that it was this trauma that motivated
his "pacifism"—which came from the same personal sources that created *Crisis* and was now being formed into an awareness of the tragedy
tied to massive war. One does not have to view the film carefully to
see its wish to resist the Nazi way. But despite its gay shots of British
soldiers singing "We're Going to Hang Out our Washing on the Sieg-
fried Line," it does refuse to pretend that their experience will be
beautiful.

The Communist press saw where Kline's sympathies lay and attacked
the film. Following the Party line, James Dugan suddenly lost all the
eagerness to organize against Hitler that his *Crisis* review had proclaimed. Kline has failed, he says, to match murderers Churchill and
Hitler, and readers are warned away from the film as not useful "to
the real anti-war forces of America." Those who adhered to the Party
line could not comprehend, Kline recalls, that it was against his conscience not to favor the British. He had been in Czechoslovakia and
Poland: he knew the enemy. His disturbance over the Soviet-Nazi
pact—which he did not approve—may have been a component in his
sense of the tragedy of war, but it is a minor component at best, and
it neither undermines his pro-British position nor muddles his humanism.[20]

Still, filmmakers who take the time to stretch beyond the newsreel
should attain a fuller viewpoint than does Kline of a situation's depths—
through careful analysis of cause and effect, through rendering the
human experience of the events, and through a well-developed, personal perspective. *Lights Out in Europe* fails to do any of these things
well, especially in its rendering of human experience, and it remains
reportage that does not probe to the deeper and more universal levels
of *Crisis, The Spanish Earth, Heart of Spain* or, more recently, *Hearts
and Minds, The Sorrow and the Pity*, and *Memory of Justice*.

VI ■ Frontier Films and *Native Land:*
■ Doing the Impossible, 1937-1942

In accompanying Ivens to China and Kline to Europe during 1938-1940, we left Frontier Films as *People of the Cumberland* and *Return to Life* were being released—in the late spring and late summer of 1938. By this point, even though they were about to hire the lively Arnold Perl to scout up new projects, there was no point in asking what next? It had long been decided. From its first days in 1937, Frontier had planned a civil liberties film based on the U.S. Senate's LaFollette Committee findings concerning union busting and the tactics of massive corporate labor spying.[a] The group had planned a four-reel picture based on the four-page script that they had turned over to Michael Gordon and Willard Van Dyke, but by the time they retrieved the script late in 1937, the notion had expanded. On 3 December, Frontier "issued a call for volunteer extras (men) to appear in a huge mass meeting and parade" for *Native Land.* And by the time they went on location in the summer of 1938, Maddow, in collaboration with Hurwitz and Strand, had finished writing a completely organized, feature-length script.[1]

Why *Native Land?*

We have noted that the film was first tentatively entitled *Labor Spy.* The CIO was bearing the brunt of the assault upon progressive or-

[a] They were also influenced by Leo Huberman's book, *The Labor Spy Racket* (New York: Modern Age Books, Inc., 1937).

ganizations, and congressional committee hearings were uncovering the insidiousness of some of its powerful and vicious opposition. The CIO was no idle victim: "At the time we were writing the script and preparing the production," Hurwitz recalls, "the militant trade union movement had made tremendous gains, had fought its way through government and employer repression, and had succeeded in making union organization a right confirmed by law." As with the Spanish Loyalist forces, this was a struggle to which Frontier people felt closely connected. Like the CIO, like the Communist Party with which some of them were affiliated, and like so many other political and cultural groups on the left, they found themselves under attack, targets or potential targets of the red scare and of the right-wing congressional investigating committees that were its official voice.

Not only their politics but the practice of blockbooking prevented the wide distribution of their films, and the "dream" content of the usual Hollywood film had long ago incapacitated the average American for response to the social documentary. Accordingly, Frontier wanted to loudly assert the right of both militant labor and of themselves, under the Bill of Rights, to exist and to be heard. *Native Land*, intended to provide heroic models of courage for the struggle against fascism in America and intended to assert the right to jobs, fair pay, free speech, and free assembly, was also intended as a "spearhead" against the practice of blockbooking. Frontier hoped that the film's impact would be powerful enough to open a new noncommercial distribution base in America to fulfill the perennial dream of American documentary artists on the left.[2]

In still another way the fight of the militant unions—the outsiders—for a place in America touched a deep chord. Many of them sons of Jewish immigrants who had chosen exile from their native lands, they did not yet think of themselves, in the terms Alfred Kazin learned growing up in Brooklyn, as fully "Americans":[b] we have seen how far they were from the class backgrounds, the native, instinctual traditions of a Pare Lorentz or a Willard Van Dyke. As Jews, too, they were vividly aware of the terrifying anti-Semitism in Fascist countries and of the undisguised anti-Semitism of individuals and groups at home who prided themselves on what they thought to be their own unadulterated Americanism.[c] They were outsiders as film artists too, ap-

---

[b] See ibid., p. 175n. This should not be taken to mean that they were not fully and confidently engaged as Americans on the American social, political, and cultural scene.

[c] In 1953, both Robert Gorham Davis and Daniel J. Boorstin attributed the attractiveness of the Communist Party in the late thirties to the "good measures" that the Party supported: "against anti-Semitism, against Fascism, for minority rights" [Davis]. "As a Jew, that had a certain appeal to me, naturally" [Boorstin]. See Eric Bentley, ed.,

parently having failed to make the popular art Americans expected from film, and apparently having failed to strive for the riches that the industry seemed to promise people of their talent. And so *Native Land* was to be about themselves.

A group of shots in its first sequence (which was also the first sequence they edited) supports this theme of self-portrayal: a waving American flag precedes two juxtaposed shots of statues of an immigrant and a frontiersman that in turn are followed by close-ups of the flag, a bust of Lincoln, and the flag again. The narration, written by Maddow and spoken by Paul Robeson, himself so painfully aware of the persecution of his own people in America, echoes the image alignment:

> One nation indivisible, with liberty and justice for all, the immigrant, hungry for bread and for liberty, the brave and the persecuted, the pioneer in the Kentucky forest. We established a bill of rights, and, led by Lincoln, we fought a civil war to extend those rights to the whole people.

The final word commences a slow pan that carries the Statue of Liberty from left frame to right.

Relatively unknown filmmakers, the Frontier people had developed with acute consciousness a style and a form that were appropriate to both their political purposes and their personal impulses in making this film. Highly aware of being an artistic avant garde, of drawing on all the resources of their medium, in *Native Land* they would enhance their dialectical structure by alternating acted, powerfully dramatic stories with straight documentary sequences. Their filmmaking experience, they pronounced early in 1939, assured them "that this full use of film craft will attain the maximum of audience impact."[3]

The impact they hoped for was intended to satisfy goals both conscious and not so conscious. The sheer force of the "tight fistful of emotion" that Hurwitz expected the *Native Land* audience to come away with would not only strengthen the fight against domestic fascism and the struggle for union organization, would not only open up distribution channels for labor films, but it would also call respectful attention to the filmmakers as an individual group of American artists; it would end, they hoped, their relative isolation. Along with the pioneers, the immigrants, and the blacks, along with Paul Robeson— whom they had known from the start they wanted for the narration of *Native Land*[4]—they would finally be accepted with their proud differences: they would be welcomed for their original talent and art,

Thirty Years of Treason: Excerpts from Hearings Before the House Committee on Un-American Activities, 1938-1968 (New York: Viking Press, 1971), pp. 586, 605.

and they would be received and paid notice to for their essentially American, if radical, point of view. At last, they hoped, they would be established in *their* native land on their own terms

Filming in a Goldfish Bowl

At the end of 1937, Frontier told David Platt that 1938 would see the release of their civil liberties film. In October of 1938, Meyers, writing for *TAC*, announced that it would be ready by the end of the year. In December, *TAC* carried an impressive production-still by Elinor Meyer from the film's farm sequence, together with a quotation from Maddow's commentary. The shooting script for another sequence of *Production No. 5* (*Native Land*'s temporary working title) turned up in the January issue of *One Act Play Magazine*. In the spring of 1939, Hurwitz and Strand screened several episodes for Richard Watts, Jr., the film critic for the *New York Herald Tribune*, and told him their plans for the remainder of the film. He came away, he later reported, thinking it destined to be an important work. On 2 June 1939, Hurwitz and Strand showed "the still incomplete and unnamed documentary film" to the participants at the third American Writers' Congress at the New School for Social Research.[5]

The next announcement I have come across is in the February 1940 issue of *Direction*. There the reader found more stills and learned that the shooting was completed and that release could be expected within two months. *Films* echoed this promise in its spring number. Then *Living Films*, published in December 1940, revealed that Maddow was at work on commentary and lyrics: the film would soon be out. Three months later, Leyda reported that this "courageous" film was nearly finished. And evidently the final editing did begin in the last months of 1940. The scoring and dubbing were completed by late autumn of 1941, and the answer print came in on the day after Pearl Harbor, 8 December. Finally, on 11 May 1942, the eighty-three minute *Native Land* was premiered at the World Theatre in New York.[6] The film had taken nearly four and one-half years of the creative lives of Hurwitz, Maddow, Meyers, Berman, and Strand. Hurwitz and Strand had worked on no other films during this period; Meyers and Berman on only some quick minor projects for Frontier. Maddow had done this as well, in addition to a few outside projects.

In 1938, Frontier Films had $7,000 and a feature-length script. Estimating a total cost of $40,000, the group went to work, figuring that money would come in at a rate to keep the cameras cranking. But scout Arnold Perl wasn't coming up with any new projects, perhaps because films were not easy to come by in those days for any independent group, but perhaps also because he may have run into political hostility. Hurwitz and Strand had thought it was red-scare attitudes that had helped to pluck *The City* from their grasp, and Roger Baldwin, although he was sympathetic to Frontier, would not push the ACLU to back *Native Land* because he worried, Hurwitz recalls, that the group was "too left, too labor-conscious."

The result was that between the release of *Return to Life* and the premiere of *Native Land*, only three films had engaged Frontier talent. The first was *The History and Romance of Transportation*, a six-minute short created by Berman, Maddow, and Meyers entirely out of stock shots, using "ingenious cutting and sound," for the Chrysler exhibit at the World's Fair.[d] Work on the second film began late in 1939 when Michael Martini, in from Detroit, appeared at Frontier's office with his edited footage of the UAW's successful 1939 strike against General Motors in Flint and Detroit. Maddow and Berman added a sound track, with Maddow (as Wolff) getting credit for the commentary, which he probably wrote in haste in conjunction with Martini. Earl Robinson took charge of the music. The result, *United Action*, is a very long film, a historically interesting but cinematically dull record of the strike. Still, it is possible that enough money came in from this to pay Maddow's and Berman's salaries for a few weeks. Maddow has no memory of working on the film, and Hurwitz is correct when he states that it should not really be considered a Frontier film.[7]

The third film, *White Flood*, also completed early in 1940, was, according to Maddow, "a made job, in order to be able to pay us a salary to work on it." The footage came principally from William Osgood Field, a member of the board of directors of Frontier who had made a wide variety of scientific and cultural films and who had worked on *Spain, the Fight for Freedom* in 1937. *White Flood* was pieced together from his own Alaskan filming, from Alpine footage shot by Sherman Pratt, and from snowstorm scenes that were shot by Frontier cameras. Berman, with the help of Maddow and Meyers, scripted and edited the film, which was turned over to Hanns Eisler for his Rockefeller Foundation-funded experiments with film music.[8]

White Flood is not in any sense a political film. A study of glaciers, it is startlingly beautiful. The unusual, striking camera angles and

[d] I don't know if this film still exists. The Chrysler Corporation Library in Detroit has carton upon carton of unlabeled film in storage, much of it separate films spliced together. It would be an enormous job to ferret out *The History and Romance of Transportation*, if it is there at all.

movements—as they capture waterfalls, rock texture, waves in a flood, stunningly sculptured ice in water, distant peaks, new dimensions of landscape opening as a boat rounds a lake curve—do not call attention to themselves but reveal the personal vision of Field, a dedicated naturalist. The visual poetry is reinforced by the dissonances in Eisler's fine score. Drums rumble forward as huge slabs of glacier drop into the ocean. Shrill tones of string instruments or the isolated notes of single woodwinds rise against the deeper, more mellow woodwinds to suggest the cold and eerie nature of the deserts of ice. The words, which record the history of the last ice age and the "strange new life" that succeeded, are informative, but this is not their primary purpose: rather they are bent on endowing the imagery with even more poetic dimension. They animate the forces that they evoke—"the snow rose up into a mount of ice that crept out and spread death across the flowery plains, advancing, shrinking back, advancing again"—constructing an aura of power and mystery. Even at its most instructional, the commentary remains poetic:

> Years of snow, millions of tons packed down into a field of silence, the birthplace of the glacier. The grains of snow turn slowly into ice underneath. Layers of snowstorm feed the stream of twisted ice. Hardly melted at noon and frozen at sunset, the newly formed ice bends slowly over the uneven valley floor, and breaks. A great crack opens, a crevice. In this way the glacier splits and grinds over stony obstacles underneath. It is cracked, wrenched, broken into hundred-foot pinnacles. But slowly these frozen streams converge into a river of ice, a river in slow motion, crushing forward a few feet a day.

An uninsistent existential thrust lends further dimension: man lives on "a thin crust over a burning globe," knowing his condition may fatally alter with a few degrees difference in the annual world temperature. An unfortunate final statement tells us that man must match his brain with the changing mountains, something the film had been only implicitly, if at all, concerned with until that point.

White Flood gave Berman, Maddow, and Meyers regular income for a short while, but long before this, the money coffer had emptied out. In mid-summer of 1939, all production work on *Native Land* was forced to a halt while a fund-raising venture, already under way, shifted into high gear. Theodore Strauss reported in May of 1942 that

> during that first six-month layoff they began the first of the several hundred showings of the incomplete film [*Native Land*] in Wash-

ington, New York and Hollywood. Congressmen saw the rushes; Hollywood directors and stars paid $5 per [person] to view the truncated version and in some cases subscribed additional funds, and in New York at innumerable screenings any person who looked as though he had a dollar and a vague interest in films was hustled into the projection room for a gander. A committee of 1,000 women was formed to take contributions from 25¢ up. Jo Davidson presented a sculpture and Reginald Marsh a painting to be sold. Raffles, auctions and benefit parties were held in homes and halls from Greenwich Village to the upper East and West Sides.

Frontier estimated that by 1942 fifteen thousand people had seen some portion of the film and that five to six thousand had contributed to the $60-75,000 it finally cost. "It was," Strand sourly remarked when it was all over, "like making a film in a goldfish bowl." Everyone at Frontier was engaged in taking rushes to show at various little meetings, responding to questions, making the pitch. Well-known artists were also enlisted: at one gathering Lillian Hellman, at another Thomas Mann, rose after the screening to appeal for funds. This continuous process could not always keep pace with costs once production began again. Another hiatus of three to four months occurred in the spring of 1940, followed by further halts, shorter in duration.[9]

The sheer lack of money was the principal cause of delay, but another contributing factor was the growth in the conception and in the scope of *Native Land*. Strand and Hurwitz constantly fed Maddow new material from the outpourings of the LaFollette Committee, and so the film, Strand recalls, "kept getting bigger and bigger and bigger and bigger." A moment of self-awareness on Hurwitz's part also required the creation of new sequences. Hurwitz tells the story:

> At a certain stage I was stuck. I felt there was something crucial missing, and I didn't know what it was . . . and I invited Hudson, who had been a longshoreman. I don't remember his first name now, very big guy, hands about that big. He was a Party representative in relation to trade unions or something. And I said, "Come in and look at this film. Tell me what you think." So then we went down to his house afterwards. I don't know whether I was alone or someone was with me. And he put his finger right on it. . . . He said, "Well, you have a film so far in which people are acted on, and that's true, but you don't have enough action in response from the people." That gave me the clue, and I built

several sequences as a result. Immediately. He was absolutely right. He was talking in political terms, but I interpreted it in terms of dramatic construction.

The final process, from answer print to premiere, was slowed by Paul Robeson's decision to rehearse the commentary for weeks, as if he were preparing for a play. Then there was the suddenly perceived need for an epilogue and the decision to have Marc Blitzstein compose a new song or two for Robeson to render with the Almanac Singers, the folk-singing group formed in 1940 by Woody Guthrie, Lee Hays, Millard Lampell, and Pete Seeger.[10]

Willard Van Dyke believes that another cause for the delay was "a kind of perfectionist attitude on the part of some of those filmmakers." When Theodore Strauss raised that question with Strand, Strand was understandably defensive: "At least as much effort went into financing the film as went into the actual making of it," and the nine-to-one shooting ratio "was decidedly thrifty by any standards of filmmaking." But one can be a perfectionist with a relatively low shooting ratio—in rehearsing actors, setting up shots, editing—and Hurwitz and Strand fit the definition. Hurwitz had a reputation, especially among his antagonists in the early thirties, for taking undue time on his films, and Maddow cites his own curiously strong memory of Hurwitz at the editing table, working, working, working at his takes of the billowing American flag. Strand is almost legendary for the time he devoted to print-character and to the quality of a single still photograph. The shooting ratio, furthermore, was not always low. June Gitlin, then June Prensky, whose husband worked one summer for Frontier Films, recalls:

> I worked for Local 65 at that time, and Paul Strand was looking for a switchboard to shoot a scene. I got permission from the union for him to shoot the scene there, and I almost got fired. Paul was a perfectionist, and I remember that one very important shot in the scene showed a key being depressed or flicking down by itself. He shot that scene many, many times, and of course the entire office was disrupted and in addition the bill for electricity came to the union to pay. It all worked out in the end.[11]

Whatever the amount of time taken and whatever the degree of perfectionism, however, the completed work made it all worthwhile: *Native Land* remains a beautifully made and perennially timely film, as the enthusiastic audience reaction to its rerelease during the Watergate era testifies.

The financial strain was compounded by the fact that, as Hurwitz puts it, *"The City* had been taken out—I'm using a pleasant term for it, instead of what I might have said at the time—of Frontier Films." The popularity of that film (which was made by Henwar Rodakiewicz, Steiner, and Van Dyke) at the 1939 World's Fair may have been a painful goad to Frontier, but the lasting bitterness was caused principally by the loss of vital income. And that loss was tragic, for *Native Land* came too late to save Frontier as an organization. Van Dyke's memory, whatever its personal undertones, is a close approximation of the response the film received in 1942:

> You're in the middle of the war, and the last thing anyone wants to hear about is the May Day Massacre at Bethlehem Steel [a representative sequence in *Native Land*],[e] the last thing that was to be considered or talked about, you know, by any of us. We were all working together now. The greater threat, we thought at least, was Hitler, and we had to destroy him before we began to wash our own dirty linen in public again. And so that film died on the vine, and with it the last remnants of Frontier Films.[12]

Had *Native Land* been finished on schedule, moreover, Frontier might have been able to go on to other films, the tension would surely have been lessened, and Frontier might have achieved the cohesion to continue as a tough-minded, independent, progressive film group after the war. Even a few more months of life might have evoked from the group another film or two and thus a somewhat less buried tradition to which filmmakers of subsequent decades could turn for inspiration.

Despite all this, it is by no means certain that Frontier would have achieved the cohesion that would have enabled it to continue. The strain of *Native Land* told on everyone, and resentments and tensions built, but it is equally as true that *Native Land* simply exacerbated problems that were already present. To understand this, we need to look more closely at both the people and the dynamics of the core group.[f]

At Their Best: The Friendships

Ben Maddow is solid and energetic, and his resolute features grow flexible as he engages with the world, listening, reflecting, working

---

[e] Van Dyke was actually referring to the Memorial Day Massacre at Republic Steel, in 1937.

[f] By "core group" I mean Berman, Hurwitz, Maddow, Meyers, Strand, and to some

out his responses and ideas on the old films, the old experiences, the old relations. Agreeing and disagreeing with the thoughts I tested on him, he colored the past, somewhat more clearly than other interviewees, with his more recent experiences. He and his wife Frieda, who had danced with the Martha Graham Company during the thirties, invited me to dinner in their home perched on a Hollywood hill. After dinner, my recorder before us, Ben and I sat on the couch in a long, two-leveled living room, talking, looking for a while at photographs by Strand and at photographs in Maddow's own recently published *Edward Weston*. After about two hours, Frieda joined us.

Throughout most of the evening, Maddow was strongly critical of the films, of himself at the time, and of other Frontier people. As a result I was caught off guard by the following picture:

MADDOW: My god, we had all our meals together, all of our personal affairs were known to one another, we had no separate lives. And if you ever saw a group of six to eight guys trying to decide where to go to lunch . . .

F. MADDOW: I remember once—I didn't really know him at that time—I was at somebody's house, with two other women, and Marie said, "Some guys are going to come from Frontier Films," and we got all excited. We were going to have a party. . . . Then they all came in together in this bunch and stood together in their coats. I don't even think they took off their overcoats. We didn't get to meet anybody; they just met each other.

MADDOW: (delighted): Just standing there, god knows, there was always something to discuss. That's what I mean, it was precisely like that.

ALEXANDER: In a way this description of the group eating together, moving around together, undercuts many of the other things you have been saying, about the tension.

MADDOW: Oh, the tension was still there.

Both Strand and Hurwitz verified that this episode is representative of the group's closeness, although Strand himself did not take great part in its more social aspects. Inez Garson, then Inez Perl, tells of the long, lively, and serious evening gatherings of Frontier at the Perls' West 33rd Street apartment under the 9th Avenue El in 1938 and 1939: Strand, seldom present, was a bit removed, an elder statesman whom the younger filmmakers looked up to.[13]

---

extent Perl—those who gave most of their time and personal energy to Frontier. Lerner is considered later. I have been unable to gain access to Leyda, who was influentially involved on two films and personally close to at least two of the core members but who was also well out on the fringe of the group, very occupied with other matters.

The friendships were strong. Maddow and Arnold Perl, a former poet, met each other through a City College professor who was in Pen and Hammer.[g] They roomed together in the West 33rd Street apartment, where Maddow became the Perls' boarder after Arnold's marriage. Lionel Berman, also a member of Pen and Hammer, became godfather to the Perl baby, the first Frontier child. Hurwitz, who first introduced Frieda to Ben, recalls thinking of Maddow as his "closest friend," as a brother. Maddow, on the other hand, despite their contemporaneity, thought of Hurwitz as a father: "He'd take me around to things. If he wanted to go to an exhibit, he would take me along and tell me what this was, what that [was] . . . his education was really far superior to mine, which had been mostly technical." According to Maddow, his own closest friend at that time was Sidney Meyers. And at Berman's funeral, Meyers called Berman his "first teacher" and "saving brother."[14]

This kind of closeness informed their working relationships as well. According to both Hurwitz and Strand, in spite of disagreements, they had a "real collaboration," worked "very well together," drew upon each other's abilities and dedication, and were a "motor force" for Frontier Films. And Hurwitz tells of the intimate creative relationship between editor and writer:

> If I would say here's the problem, Ben . . . here is what the image does, this is the central idea, but it needs to have a thrust that begins way back . . . and it should include . . . And I'd give him a whole complex thing, and he would take it away and come back with simply beautiful stuff. Then we would take it and work over the moviola with it, and I'd be absolutely free to enter his words . . . and we'd work it out together and marry it to the picture. It was just marvelous, the kind of true working together that is very rare.

Talking about the first years of committed, spirited work at Frontier, Irving Lerner mused, "How can anybody say anything except good things about those experiences?" For him, it was a profound and inspiring period.[15] Clearly the strength and the similarity of their personal, political, and aesthetic roots tied the films and the filmmakers together on many levels.

Like the Group Theatre and its counterparts in the other arts at the time, Frontier wanted to be a close family.[16] We have seen that some of its members came together out of the alienation of their particular

[g] An academic version of the John Reed Club for left-wing writers.

backgrounds in the cities and out of their relative newcomer status in America. What should be stressed, however, is that they *all* shared a critical perspective on the prevalent film forms that they associated with the values and behavior that had caused the Depression. They came together out of shared convictions, out of joblessness, out of their neglect as unestablished young artists (most of them), out of their belief in collectivism as one feature of the socioeconomic solution, and out of their young and vital conviction about their own talents and the rightness of their ideas. As a family, as a cooperative, they accorded each other high respect and support, they reached out to draw in other artists, and they attempted through their films to speak personally to their audience.[h]

One measure of their closeness at the time is the lasting strength of their friendships and their enmities. It must be clear by now that a painful sidelight to my research has been the stories about bad blood between people. I have been told in confidence about "crooks," "lousy bastards," and "cowards," about one man's preventing another from receiving a job offer, about two men, once the most intimate of friends, who have not spoken to one another for nearly twenty years. Life, of course, is like that, but the fact does not dilute the poignancy. On one occasion, one of my interviewees walked me to a subway entrance at 2:00 A.M., stunned by what had happened during our long talk. For years he had repressed all the love he had felt for his friend and had fixed only on the bitter residue of their broken friendship. But our talk had cracked the psychic cement, and the old warmth had rushed through. Something of the same, though milder and less clear, had happened in my interview with the other friend. And waiting for my train to come through the long tunnel, I was suddenly moved to think how those intense old emotions and affinities had, so many years later during a few odd hours of 1974, flicked out, trying to reach under, over, through the years and the sense of betrayal to become once again a living part of the two people who had felt them.

The Monster

"Things are apt to happen when you are trying to do the impossible," Paul Strand told me at the outset of our interview, as we faced each

---

[h] It is consistent that, like the Group Theatre, Frontier, with its cooperative desire, showed no interest in the Brechtian aesthetics of alienation that, in the interests of political action, shatter the shared emotional experience of the audience. They sought, on the contrary, to engage the audience fully, making it one with them in experience and outlook.

other across the table in the narrow alcove leading from kitchen to garden in his and Hazel Strand's basement apartment in New York City:

> And in certain respects Frontier Films was an impossibility in the America of that time. And I can understand . . . that towards the end of our really phenomenal effort to exist as a group . . . there would be strains and tensions, and I understand very well that they could resent, and thus some of them must have resented very sharply the precedence that was finally given to *Native Land*.[17]

Side by side with the friendships, the mutual admiration, and the shared collective spirit, the reasons for the strains and resentments are clear. Some are directly attributable to *Native Land*; others lie in the nature of the organization, of the individual filmmakers, and even of the Frontier aesthetics.

The delays on *Native Land* caused tremendous strain. Both Maddow and Strand refer to that film as a "monster" that gobbled all the money and devoured everyone's time. They all felt it, probably most of all Hurwitz and Strand, who had the heaviest personal investment in the outcome. For Hurwitz, the continual work, alternating with the maddening suspensions, became "a very intense proposition . . . an immense emotional problem." And Strand remembered:

> Either we had to make that film or we would have the biggest flop that ever came down the pike. With two or three very good films, yes, but not for five years. We *had* to finish it. . . . What if we had failed to finish the film and had been left with a bunch of footage, after working three years and spending, say, fifty thousand dollars. That's what we both faced. . . . I had a name at stake. And I'm a very stubborn man: I never like to start things I don't finish. . . . So we finished it. And it's a world classic, whatever you say about this or that. It has weaknesses. Of course it has weaknesses. Thank God it got made, I say. That is, I thank our tenacity, because it took a terrific amount of tenacity.[18]

It took tenacity, in part because the precedence given to *Native Land* meant a marginal existence. Frontier's income ideal was a subsistence level salary, at first thirty-five dollars per week, then fifty dollars. Yet year after year, weeks and sometimes months would pass without salary. This became, Maddow recalls, a "crucial issue." Sometimes living on a meal a day, at one time depending on the largesse of a couple who were earning very little money themselves, he felt depressed and powerless.

> Frieda remembers that the day after I first went out with her, we were at the same cafeteria at lunch hour. I saw her and she saw me, and I refused to recognize her because I only had a dime in my pocket and had to pay for that soup and roll. . . . Well, this sort of humiliation built up, and I was offered a job by Van Dyke . . . and I seized upon it, of course I did.

Maddow believes himself to have been the worst off, but everyone felt the pinch. Perl's wife had a job, Meyers' wife had a job, people picked up odd dollars, but nobody was living very decently. Strand recalls "all the hardships and all the pain that people suffered to make . . . possible" each one of their productions: "We had hardly any money at all at any time."[19]

How to keep going on empty pockets when all signs indicate that you *are* in fact attempting the impossible? The members watched with dismay as the Group Theatre, with which they felt closely identified, floundered and folded at the end of 1940. And who was going to sponsor films according to the Frontier point of view? Cabaret TAC began to dissolve when it took the Communist Party line on the Soviet-Nazi Pact in late 1939, when it was denounced as a Communist front, and when Actors' Equity ordered its members to withdraw from participation.[i] Little encouragement there. It is indeed a tribute to their conviction and "tenacity" that not only Hurwitz and Strand but also Berman, Maddow, Meyers, and Perl stuck to the finish on *Native Land*.

The problem with money was compounded by something much more serious. For four years, in Maddow's words, *Native Land* "devoured the professional lives and talents of everyone connected with it." Had they gained more film experience in these crucial developmental years, it is possible that the high quality of their later work, both in and out of Hollywood, might have been even higher. For Berman, Meyers,[j] and even Maddow (although he took substantial part

---

[i] This lively East Side theater was formed during the 1937-1938 season. Foremost actors and composers volunteered their services in writing and performing material, and the proceeds went to Loyalist Spain. Berman, Strand, and Edna Ocko were executive board members. See Morgan Y. Himelstein, *Drama Was a Weapon: The Left-Wing Theatre in New York, 1929-1941* (New Brunswick, N.J.: Rutgers University Press, 1963), p. 206.

[j] Meyers also lost time through a serious illness—a virus infection of the cerebellum—beginning in September 1939 and lasting several months. Frontier kept up his salary during this period. Edna Meyers interview.

in the film), the pain of inactivity was increased by the fact that *Native Land* was not their film, no matter how much they joined in on consultations. Hurwitz recalls:

> It came out one day. I don't know who told it to me, either Sidney or Ben. The making of *Native Land* clearly was not a democratic process in which everybody was involved in everything. They had evidently talked among themselves about it. Maybe Lionel [Berman] was in on it. They had concluded, "Well, listen, we don't mind Joris making [his own] film—that's Joris's film—so why do we mind: Leo and Paul have a right to make their [own] film." Although it should have been ironed out by then, that over-simple idea of what collaboration should be still lingered.[20]

And even though Hurwitz and Strand themselves had the satisfaction of making *Native Land*, they were aware that the lengthy delays were stalling their own growth as filmmakers.

Hurwitz's statement seems to indicate an anticollaboration development. I remarked on this, suggesting it natural that the others, as talented artists, would wish to break off and make their own films— that a cooperative like Frontier was inevitably doomed. Hurwitz sharply cut in on me: "Not necessarily!"[21] Other members had been given full control of earlier films, he argued, and this could have continued. *The History and Romance of Transportation* and *White Flood* are minor but valid examples, he believes. Still, the huge Hurwitz/Strand project ate up all available resources, and the others had no films to control.

But forces other than *Native Land* were gathering to dissolve Frontier Films. In order to explore these, let us turn to the separate perspectives of three of the filmmakers.

The Undercurrents Surface

Irving Lerner's departure from Frontier is somewhat instructive. Compared to himself and to Meyers, Maddow pictures Lerner as a very minor figure in Frontier productions but says that as someone "very sensitive to photographic values" his advice was highly valued and that his contribution was substantial. He shared the "written and edited by" credits on *China Strikes Back* and participated in postproduction on *Heart of Spain, People of the Cumberland,* and *Return to Life.* Shortly after this, he eased out of the group.

Lerner's name does not leap forth either in discussion of controversial developments in the decade or in talk of Frontier Films. He was seldom at the center of things. For much of the thirties he spent dull days figuring out duties for Amtorg at the Custom House and as many as five evenings a week in movie houses as a film critic. Unaggressive and not especially verbal, he was a well-liked, probably fairly easygoing person. His decision to concentrate on editing after his work on *The World Today* was both a professional decision and a personal one. Troubled by the divisive rivalries that Ivens and Paul Rotha had discovered in the New York documentary world, feeling he was not "strong enough to engage in that kind of competition," he felt he would "survive longer" if he stuck to his editing. It is conceivable that the bitterness on both sides over *The City* touched this tender spot, made him chary of Frontier, and encouraged him to work for the rest of the decade as a freelance film artist.[k]

I am uncertain about the extent of political differences between Lerner and the rest of the Frontier members, for Lerner was vague on this, and a follow-up letter was never answered. Asked if the Moscow Trials had caused any splits in Frontier, as they had so virulently elsewhere, he replied:

LERNER: Some of those things happened there too. It certainly happened in my case.
ALEXANDER: What happened with you?
LERNER: Well, I just got less and less involved, that's all . . . because of what I was learning, along with what I was forced to do, and getting fed up with things of this kind, and [long pause] I just found it, I found more important things to do than to hold trials like Steiner's to prove he wasn't a Trotskyite. I wouldn't raise an issue, I would just kind of fade away, I felt it wasn't worth fighting for.[22]

My guess is that Lerner did not very substantially alter his basic radical left convictions but that he disliked conflict and desired more freedom in his work.

A closer look at Ben Maddow can lead us more succinctly to the

---

[k] A partial list of Lerner's credits follows. In 1939 he served as cameraman for Flaherty on *The Land*. He also took charge of production for the Educational Film Institute of New York University, which was producing films on contemporary economic topics under a grant from the Alfred P. Sloan Foundation. In this position, he worked on and edited Van Dyke's *Valley Town* (1939-1940), edited Van Dyke's *The Children Must Learn* (1940), and was involved in the production of John Ferno's and Julian Roffman's *And So They Live* (1940). In 1940 he also edited Dial Films' *Day After Day*, and in 1940 and 1941 he directed his own film, *A Place to Live*. In 1941 he edited a film by Mark Marvin and Hans Burger, *Boogie Woogie Stomp*, Van Dyke's *To Hear Your Banjo Play*, and another film by Van Dyke's group, *Here is Tomorrow*. Before entering the Office of War Information in 1942, he edited the second of Julian Bryan's films on South American countries, *Colombia, Crossroads of the Americas.*

causes of the strains. Very close to Frontier, and convinced of the
correctness of its goals, he was not entirely comfortable in the cooperative for a number of reasons. We have seen that he felt his poverty
keenly. His own family was poor, and in the past he had worked more
than the others "with the outside people," as a hospital intern and in
the tenements. Thus, perhaps more than some of the others, he had
an urge to escape all this, to seek recognition and security. Although
this was a subordinate urge, it may nevertheless have caused him some
anguish. Hurwitz recalls:

> Ben used to talk to me about his rich sister and his poor sister.
> And his rich sister would say to him, "Ben, you have all kinds of
> talent. It's worth a lot. You can make it fine, write for the places
> that make money. Don't stick around Frontier Films." And his
> poor sister, who was a social worker, I think, or teacher maybe,
> said, "Ben, stick to what you believe in." And he carried this
> conflict around humorously. Of course he would stay with the
> poor sister's advice and not with the rich sister's advice. [23]

And stay he did, until the completion of *Native Land*.

This does not mean that he devoted himself entirely to the work of
Frontier. In 1939, in an indelicate move, Van Dyke invited Maddow
to join the *Valley Town* crew as a writer, and Maddow, although he
was still a member of Frontier, agreed to do so. This enraged Hurwitz
and Strand, in large part, Hurwitz recalls, because it was the renegade
Van Dyke who was doing the hiring.[1] According to Maddow, Arnold
Perl was

> sent by Leo Hurwitz to see me because I had crossed this horrible
> line, this loyalty. And he demanded that I quit the job. I was a
> member of the cooperative and [they said I] had no right to take
> another job. And I just laughed at him. I said, "Do you want to
> pay my rent? If so, fine. Otherwise I'm going to take it." Well,
> then they had a long negotiation with Van Dyke. And if you look
> at the credits, it says "written by David Wolff [Maddow's pseu-
> donym], courtesy of Frontier Films."

Maddow was to stick with Frontier until *Native Land* was completed
and the organization dissolving. But apparently he found this experience so unpleasant that when he received further offers—to write for
Lerner's *A Place to Live* (1940-1941), for Van Dyke's and Herbert
Kerkow's *Here is Tomorrow* (1941), and for Van Dyke's and William

---

[1] Van Dyke and Strand were not on speaking terms at this time, thanks to *Labor Spy*
and *The City*. Interview with Van Dyke, 12 May 1975.

Watts's *Tall Tales* (1941)—he asked for credits as David Forrest. He took on this new pseudonym either to conceal his independent work from Frontier or because Frontier did not want to be associated with those films.[m] Whatever the reason, the disassociation was important: Lerner took *Documentary Film News* "severely to task" for reporting that Muriel Rukeyser and David Wolff had written the commentary for *A Place to Live*: it was not Wolff, he said, but David Forrest. And in December 1941, it was David Forrest who set sail with Van Dyke for Latin America to make *The Bridge*.[24]

The financial strain that Maddow was experiencing was accompanied by growing artistic tensions that must have been felt, at least to some degree, by the others. In May 1936, Maddow published "On Signing Up," a poem that implied wholehearted commitment to the Communist Party's current political and cultural position:

It is clearly time. Take the express. Joyous,
I among a double thousand subway eyes
twitching at anxious headlines, turn
the red card flaring warm at last in my pocket.

In reviews in August 1936 and April 1937, he scolded other poets for being "too personal," for having too "little social awareness." Yet in these years his own impulses toward expanding the "personal" voice were at uneasy war with his politics. This is evident in both "The Sign" (1937) and "The City" (1940), poems in which monoplanes, symbolizing love and solo flight, appear temptingly in moments of respite. In both poems, the horror of the city and the poet's commitment to social change make the monoplanes unattainable.[25]

The war between his personal voice and his politics is evident in Maddow's film theory as well. In an unusual article, "Film into Poem," which appeared in the November 1936 issue of *New Theatre*, he shows his hand. He makes a case for a "cine-poem," a film form that "would correspond to the scope and concentration of poetry," a film form of "close emotion" and "extreme passionate lucidity" that would present "the complex patterns of our lives with a sharp, concise and shattering emphasis," with "excitement," with symbolism, and with "consistent depth and intensity." Consonant with his argument in his February 1936 article on Potamkin that 1930s American film should be muscular

[m] In response to a written query on this, Maddow did not see, or at least did not care to see, any such dynamic. "David Forrest was simply another of a whole set of pseudonyms. I think it had become a game, like putting on a new pair of shoes. Also, I had just learned the disconcerting news, from my father, that I had made the wrong translation from his name: Medvedev doesn't mean Wolf, but Bear." Letter to author, 2 June 1975.

and impactful, the cine-poem nevertheless tends away from straight-forward documentary, and certainly from proletarian art—a tendency that caused the particular form-content tension in his poetry as well.

The last two paragraphs of the article clearly expose Maddow's attraction to an individualist aesthetic. Self-consciously he contends that the cine-poem does not deviate from the approved confines of left art in America:

> First, yielding as it must, greatest interest to a single filmworker or to a very small group, it might well attract genius that is interested neither in the newsreel nor dramatic forms, but looks for a more individualized and intense expression. The results need not be unpopular, even if restricted to audiences that have a certain minimum of taste and intelligence.

However, it becomes clear that the concept stems from his own particular and highly personal modern poetic sensibility:

> The whole idea of the cine-poem arose out of a search for some method of conveying the abrupt sensations of our own lives. A jazz clarinet whirls and leaps to the incitation of a guttural voice; lovers are parted by a subway door: above the street a woman leans from a window, her face noble and dignified with beauty, her chest and spine distorted with tuberculosis. One sees, hears so much that known forms of art cannot contain. Perhaps in the method of the cine-poem, we have a medium which can encompass modern events, their violent compressions and simultaneities.[26]

At times, Maddow clearly wished to be another sort of poet and film artist then his Frontier role allowed.

Maddow's tension may have been a common one among other Frontier people. At the Perls' apartment, these documentary realists would stay up until four in the morning playing the Dadaist and Surrealist game, *cadavre exquis*, each, with some general hint, drawing a composition on one fold of a sheet of paper and the final participant giving a title to the unfolded work.[n] Why, in the postbusiness and witching hours, this inclination toward surrealism?

Both Hurwitz and Maddow were admirers of the poetry of T. S. Eliot and Hart Crane,[o] and they were sympathetic to the difficult,

---

[n] Inez Garson interview. The drawings were sufficiently political in content that the Perls, wary of the House Un-American Activities Committee, destroyed them sometime during the early fifties.

[o] See Maddow's poem, "Remembering Hart Crane," in *Proletarian Literature in the*

personally eccentric experimental impulses and techniques of modern art. Yet, despite the arguments of James Agee and others, theory on the left made it unusual and difficult to incorporate comparable personal techniques within the confines of social realism. Documentary filmmakers, however, may have been less repressed in this way than other artists of the decade, a fact that was conceivably behind Maddow's excitement when he discovered documentary art with Nykino in 1935. For despite whatever lip service they paid to thirties Soviet film, Frontier practice derived always from the experimental, highly subtle technique of Soviet filmmakers of the twenties. The effort that might have gone into the dynamics of complex and obscure juxtapositions in poetry, painting, or surrealist film was, to some extent, diverted into the advanced and still avant-garde technique of subtle utilization of a clear message.

But they were not making cine-poems, and the conflict between their impulses toward personal creativity and political art could be but partially resolved. And the irresolution must have been compounded by at least a touch of the inner tension that is natural to any artist who works in cooperatives in an individualist society. With this in mind, perhaps it is not insignificant that Berman, Hurwitz, Maddow, and Meyers married dancers and that Strand was married at the time to an actress—people who performed in close relation to others, yet were simultaneously fully able to give themselves to their own individual expressiveness as well. In terms of the *Native Land* experience, the difference in strain experienced by, say, Maddow and Meyers, on the one hand, and Hurwitz and Strand, on the other, is that the latter pair were more fully in touch with their own particular artistic visions as a result of being in control of the film. Consequently they felt less acutely the conflict between personal creativity and the formulation of collective political art.

By late 1939, Maddow began to articulate a second artistic frustration, this one peculiar to himself. Whereas he found the combination of dramatized incidents and explanatory narration in Hollywood's *Confessions of a Nazi Spy* "capable of considerable force . . . straight-line, hard-hitting, expository, wasting time nowhere," the film's characterization failed to be "deepening in a psychological sense." Similarly, the following spring, praising Dovzhenko's *Shors* for its intensity, he argued that the hugely proportioned characters caused "an over-awing of the smaller, more contradictory, more confused and human

United States, ed. Granville Hicks et al. (New York: International Publishers, 1935), pp. 201-202. In 1966, Hurwitz wrote, directed, and produced *In Search of Hart Crane* for National Educational Television.

voices. It is Marlowe rather than Shakespeare." In retrospect, applying these observations to *Native Land* he says that the pattern of structural elements followed in that film "is a way of avoiding looking at life and all of its confusions and contradictions." The personae in *Native Land* have no personality, he argues, only the Strand dignity that he believes severely limits Strand's photographs. And while Maddow could justify his own documentary work in his review of *Shors* by saying that "in documentary film . . . the drama of ideas, not of characters, is being constructed,"[27] it is clear that his own developing interest in in-depth characterization was clearly being frustrated by the Frontier form of documentary. It was a similar frustration that, as a writer, would take him from poetry to fiction.

In addition to the economic and political/artistic tensions, Maddow experienced discomfort with the hierarchical structure. Like Van Dyke, he recalls the division in Nykino between the full-time studio group—Hurwitz, Steiner, and Strand—and the others: "But we were also considered like a lower house, so to speak, and the real decisions and rules were all made by Hurwitz and Strand." Strand had a stubborn personality, while Hurwitz, more readily communicative, *knew* where Frontier was headed:

> They were two fathers, and, even though we were contemporary with Hurwitz and all rather bright people, our decisions were essentially the contributions of promising sons. Now the funny part of it is that when Frontier Films was formed and we were asked to join it, this vision persisted. And it persisted in terms of actual power, because the main offices were held and effectual power exercised by those two, maybe by lack of resistance on our part. We felt we were in a cooperative and therefore had to give our best to it.

They half agreed with and half submitted to "what Leo particularly wanted to do," something which eventually, to the admittedly "distorted" and resentful perspective of the lower house, became "a sort of semi-tyranny." Until sometime in 1938, Maddow asserts, it was Hurwitz's "very fierceness of decision" that had made Frontier an exciting reality and its dynamic films possible. Now the opposition became "furious but subdued," fed by hunger, lack of opportunity, and the feeling of repressed creativity: the fact was that the cooperative was not fully a cooperative.[28]

Yet in spite of all these problems, Maddow, Berman, and Meyers held fast to Frontier until the end. Why? Certainly because of the close and genuine friendships I have described as part of the group's dynamic, for one thing, and because of the joint commitment to common social goals, for another. But for Maddow there was a third reason. Whereas Van Dyke limits his description of the Frontier hierarchy to studio and nonstudio, Maddow talks of fathers and sons. When asked why he did not leave when *Native Land* became such a "monstrous growth," he answered, "I think that I personally, because of my own psychological problems—a broken family, really no father—attached myself to this family." This desire for a harmonious family was, I suspect, so central to Maddow's way of thinking that it remains a key to understanding his behavior to this day. During our interview, he often explained, in relation to one subject or another, how we all live in tribes and how difficult and threatening it is to break out of a tribe, how important, in other words, a family is. Accordingly, while the furor over Maddow's joining the crew of Van Dyke's *Valley Town* may sound "very trivial and funny," we can nevertheless understand how it really was "a tough decision" for Maddow to make.[29]

The unpleasantness of that decision could have been compounded by a political meaning that Maddow may have been imparting to it. When I asked him about the relation of Frontier people to the Communist Party, he talked of their feeling out the general line and trying to go along with it: "It was a question of conforming to the tribe or the village that you lived in, and very sincerely."

ALEXANDER: And the Moscow Trials?

MADDOW: We were all tremendously upset by it, but, you see, it meant, again, you had to leave the family, you had to go and say, "Daddy, you told me a bunch of lies. I'm quitting. I'm leaving the house." Well, it was just impossible for us to do that. I think I did it in an indirect way, taking advantage of the fact that I had to earn a living.

ALEXANDER: With the *Valley Town* decision?

MADDOW: Yes. So I was really leaving the group. . . . I could never believe that these trials were real . . . but I don't remember ever saying to anybody, not even to Sidney, with whom I was closest, "I just don't believe this crap." You just wouldn't say that, you might *believe* it in yourself, but you wouldn't say it. It's like saying, "I just don't believe there's going to be a resurrection" if you were in the church. . . . The more you think about it, the closer it is to a family. Slowly you discover that your father has been stealing money from the local bank. Well, gee, you know, you say, Christ, well Harvey had to do it, you know. You can't go up to the fellow and say, you goddamn crook, I'm leaving.

Economic consideration aside, it is possible that the *Valley Town* move reflected both Maddow's disturbance over the Party line on the Trials and his impulse toward separation from the family. But the family for the most part prevailed, and, along with the others, Maddow continued to "feel out" the general Party line. In the November 1938 *TAC*, he published a poem, "Declamation," decrying the Munich betrayal and essentially urging readiness for war. In September 1940, during the period of the Nazi-Soviet nonaggression pact, *Poetry* carried a Maddow poem that echoed the Party's then-standard pacifist credo. "While We Slept" accused statesmen on both sides of creating war and suggested that Americans concern themselves with fighting poverty at home. [30]

Hurwitz is normally rather guarded about access to his time and is not eager to dwell in a past that is, without contradiction, extremely important to him. Through the services of a lucky boon—a mutual friend—I have spent many hours at his kitchen/projection table discussing the 1930s and interchanging ideas about art, about our needs and efforts to break down inhibitions in our teaching, about his present films, about love and aging. From all of these exchanges, I have obtained a strong feeling for his large core of sensitivity and integrity, an integrity he has not always made it easy for others to accept, for with it goes a fierce independence and perhaps a certain pride that has been interpreted in some quarters as arrogance. Very self-assured, he will fight, with some flexibility, to make his beliefs the major force in his relationships and in his work.

Hurwitz verifies Maddow's memory of his and Strand's power. Having committed his life early to the left film movement, Hurwitz had a great "sureness" about it, a propelling "feeling we could make it out of nothing." He understands Maddow's memory of a father-son relationship, for "I was older, although we were the same age, in the sense that my experience with film was greater, that I had begun earlier, that my drive was central in the whole movement to Frontier Films from Nykino, and that I was a kind of binding aesthetic, ethical passion, with Paul working with me on it, and supporting me."

Hurwitz drew heavily upon Strand, a "very forceful person," and translated him to the others, for Strand, if a father at all, was "a rather remote father." After the second of my first two fairly short interviews with Hurwitz, I found myself making a note of my "sense that LH was tough, dedicated, pushed for his concepts, very sincere, and in the end had more control than other independent filmmakers wanted him to have over their direction," feelings that resulted from the tone of voice in which he talked about the departure of Steiner and Van Dyke from Frontier. Frontier meant "starting something new . . . a collective venture based on the idea that much was wrong with American life which required radical change socially and based on the need for self-criticism." Underneath, "it was a matter of what are you here for? Do you want to work with people willing to struggle to get out the right ideas?"[31] Like the others, he had devoted himself to doing the impossible.[P] But to a greater extent than the others, he thought he knew just what had to be done.

Hurwitz's drive and certainty made for difficult professional moments for the others. Maddow exaggerates in saying that rules were passed down from above, for there was always much discussion, but he is certainly not distorting the result of the Hurwitz-Strand leadership. Hurwitz says he "never meant to convey a sense of dictating anybody's point of view, but I was always quite outspoken about what I felt in a situation." Many of the others felt Strand's "dominance in a way that was intolerable," while Hurwitz could take matters and express them more readily. More flexibly?

> Sometimes not necessarily flexibly. Sometimes I was very sure that there was one solution to the problem, in which case I stated it as forcefully as I could and swung the other people in. They may have felt browbeaten because they couldn't meet the logic of my position, and I suspect they did at certain times. I suspect there were times where they felt my force moved them in directions they weren't quite comfortable with, although they never said so to me. In other words, they moved in agreement with me where we started in disagreement.[32]

Both Hurwitz and Strand were aware of the resentments that were building, and their solution, like that of the others, was, unfortunately, to try to ignore it. The concept of self-criticism seems to have been abandoned in this area, and the stress on cooperation, the shared goals, and the friendships were what made it possible to keep working together. "The whole group," Hurwitz recalls, "had a marvelous relationship to each other, and everybody smothered uncivilized feelings," including the jealousy of his coevals toward his leadership and his closeness, first to Steiner and then to Strand. He himself "knew it was there, but I wanted to be blind to it." Now and then Hurwitz would

---

[P] In talking of Hurwitz's power, we must remember that in this cooperative, individual talents and perspectives were essential; they were relied upon. Had this not been so, the group would have folded long before it did. And other personalities were strong and vibrant—everyone testifies to this being true of Berman, Maddow, Meyers. Berman, in particular, appears to have been an active force in holding Frontier together both politically and financially.

try to learn the sources of the tension, as when Meyers would withdraw during a screening of a *Native Land* fragment that Hurwitz had asked his advice on, and Hurwitz would take a walk with him. But on the whole, he held to the warm surface, like the others,[33] and of course it was more in his interest to do so.

In the spring of 1974, I met by chance someone who had taken part in hiring Hurwitz as chairman and head of the Graduate Institute of Film and Television at New York University, a position he held from 1969 to 1974. An unelaborated remark he made about Hurwitz stayed with me: Hurwitz has never left the thirties. An echo of this came in a letter that fall. The writer felt "considered admiration for the man," thought his mind "a particularly bright and stubborn" one that "has survived all the shocks of history," but believed him to be "still stalled in the Marxism of the 'popular front' of the late thirties, with all the concomitant rhetoric of denunciation and optimism." I will allow that such remarks are true to the extent that they recognize the importance that Hurwitz attaches to the events of the thirties: he has aligned himself with Ivens as someone for whom those early experiences were "the seedwork for everything since." I am not prepared to judge whether in any way this has limited his life and work, just as I am not prepared to judge whether decisions to renounce those early experiences have helped or hurt others. But personally, I am very much drawn to his position. While the interviewers for *Cinéaste* admire his political (Marxist/Maoist) consistency,[34] I am attracted to his effort to remain true to the social and economic recognitions that led him to that particular political faith.

In a talk delivered at Brandeis University in 1972, Hurwitz ruminated for a moment on "why people become radical and stay radical, or on the other hand why their thoughts and feelings disappear from their lives." In so doing, he revealed what underlies his continuing commitment:

> Your life moves along on its own track. Your connections with family and a few others are sufficient. Then out of the pressure of circumstances and ideas, your life becomes more widely connected. You understand you are inextricably threaded into your environment. . . . The self is connected to others known and unknown. Why does the environment create the conditions of rich and poor? Why wars? Why oppression of less developed peoples? Why are the prisons so brutalized and filled with the poor, the blacks, the Puerto Ricans? Why, when the adequate means of living are socially feasible, are so many people deprived?

There seems to be an earthquake fault in social relationships. Then you put your finger on it: as in other historic eras (where it is easier to see) economic and social relationships have been outlived but they are fought for and persisted in by people who have the property, power, and privilege.

Well, now you have "dangerous thoughts" in your head. The FBI, your neighbor, the UnAmerican Activities Committee, your colleagues, the newspaper, radio, TV may label them "red." But the empathy you have discovered, your connection with others, is real, to be denied at the risk of losing much of your humanity. You may find your comrades not exactly as selfless as you thought. You may commit yourself to specific loyalties without adequate information, on the basis of your general push and understanding. But you hold on to what you know.

Now the pressures against nonconformity pile up. Along with success, with a good job, do you break the link of empathy, neutralize your ideas and feelings, because there is privilege to protect or to gain? In my short lifetime, I have seen many who did this, including good friends, when the pressure of blacklists, FBI, committee harassment piled up. For them, the judgment that "I was wrong or misled in my estimate of Stalin or the local political line" became an excuse to erase the feeling of human community, a device to cease the continual search for new answers, as change shifts the facts of living again and again. What is sad in this, as I look back, is the defection from self.

This motif of not betraying one's deepest human values is a key and consistent motif for Hurwitz, and it turns up in his talk about those he admires. "There is some kind of extraordinary truth to himself in the whole thing," Hurwitz told me of Ivens, "and I don't see how he would have done the films he did without that sense of truth."[35]

Native Land

Drawings of pioneers and of steamboats at the wharf are proudly presented at the beginning of *The Plow That Broke the Plains* and *The River*, films dyed in a home-grown faith in America. A mill across a calm pond introduces a nostalgic New England sequence at the start of *The City*, a portrait of town living that the sponsors hoped to emulate in modern terms. *Native Land*, another late-in-the-decade effort "to recreate the vision of the pioneer,"[36] makes very different use of the past. Its ten opening shots hold on waves beating against the Atlantic coast, evoking both the final image of *The Wave* and the first images of *Potemkin*. A 7-minute, 106-shot sequence then calls forth ocean and hills, stately and formidable forests, early bridges, churches, and graves, strong bronze statutes of Revolutionary and Civil War heroes and of the immigrant and pioneer, factories, trains, cities, vast tracts of plowed land, a billowing American flag, the Statue of Liberty. All are associated through repeated, interwoven, and parallel images and through the emotive, powerful voice of Paul Robeson:

> We came in search of freedom, but there were dangers in the deep woods. . . . We were alone, but we took hold. . . . We had to defend our freedom with arms . . . we declared our independence. . . . We fought a seven-year war. . . . We established a bill of rights, and led by Lincoln we fought a civil war to extend those rights to the whole people. . . . Freedom . . . more than a word, it was an axe to clear the continent. . . . Freedom, happiness, not always a fact but always a shining hope . . . fought for . . .

A conscious and militant past is evoked and made current. The prologue has already told us in titles that "*Native Land* is a document of America's struggle for liberty in recent years."

Implicit in this significant first sequence is the underlying challenge of the film. We "built liberty into the beams of our houses," built "the old words, the historic documents" into "bridges and dynamos, concrete cities," built democracy "into the steel girders of America." Yet two dangers are posed: the degeneration of those ideals, documents, and words into clichés that are no longer lived, and a careless belief that the victories are permanent. We must rememember that the Bill of Rights is "more than a dream, more than a document": it is "a way of life." How vitally in fact have we integrated what we so easily mouth? *Native Land* is an effort to destroy the clichés and to challenge the complacent, unexamined life.

The victories are never permanent, and thus the final shot of sequence one is also the first of sequence two. We watch an airplane pass above, then follow a tilt down to catch two strong white horses straining through the frame, behind them a Michigan farmer at his plow. Fred's son calls from the distance, and then the camera, cutting back and forth, gradually brings them together, until Fred sweeps the boy onto one horse's broad back. Here, later in the sequence and in later sequences, editing and internal movement unite people, creating a warmth and joy that are to be broken by brutal intrusion. Fred had spoken up at a farmers' meeting; a car has come to the farm. Tension builds as his son, running to tell him, trips and falls, as Fred grows small carrying a huge stone through the frame while his son tells him the visitors have arrived. Fred walks off with the men; the tension increases: his wife's sharp knife cuts into the potatoes; the plow blade, as his son struggles with it, cuts into the ground. A shot sounds; Fred's wife frantically searches for her husband—a segment beautifully shot and cut—and the sequence ends with Fred dead in her arms by the stream. Here we have evidence of the "tight fistful of emotion" that Hurwitz told an interviewer in 1942 the filmmakers had intended for us.[37]

A pan from the farm couple to rocks in the stream, a dissolve to a rockless stream, a tilt to a town bridge—the serenity achieved introduces a key motif, heard over images of towns and cities:

> Man's farm invaded, his liberty attacked, the right of free speech denied to an American. Happened in Custer, Michigan, September 1934. Never heard of it. People never heard of it. Twenty miles down the river people in the next town going their own way, taking their rights for granted. Unaware of what happened to one man far away. People in an American town, busy with work, children, and what's for supper.

The last image under these words is of a street in Cleveland in the spring of 1936, the camera tracking in on a girl washing windows, happy, innocent, singing her way up the stairs. At the end of the sequence, she stands screaming over the body of a murdered union organizer. A dissolve, and we watch a blind man bypassed in Times Square, we learn that there was "nothing in the newspapers, wasn't on the radio." Another dissolve to the Church of Christ in Fort Smith, Arkansas, July 1936. Black and white sharecroppers are meeting to seek the means to a living wage. Immediately, explosively, the sheriff and his deputies arrive, the men flee and are hunted down in the woods. A black sharecropper shot from ambush lies stretched dead on the dusty road. The body of his white friend, caught by a bullet in the back, sags from a barbed wire fence. Transitional shots end this movement of the film: a darkening landscape, a car moving by farm buildings, a pine cone dropping quietly, a circle spreading outward in a pool, headlights descending a hill. "Few knew," we are told, "and few remembered."

Powerfully acted, directed, and edited, these sequences strike one like so many blows. They are followed by a 7½-minute documentary section about Americans getting up, going to work, performing on their jobs, and then attending rallies and union meetings. But union members have become smug, unalert; the camera holds on one man at a meeting: "This man's name was on file in an office building." Then comes the long dramatized story of Harry Carlisle, a labor spy who successfully infiltrates a union, feels rotten about it, yet is forced to carry through. Then dictaphones and typewriters go to work, producing memos from his list and the lists of others like him, and workers are called off their jobs. Still the dialectic continues: the unions are in the open, and union membership grows by bounds, fighting the blacklist and the secret payroll. But the victory is never final: a dramatized sequence tells the story of Frank Mason, a small Tennessee grocer who aided a town union and was terrorized and warned to leave. The famous Ambridge footage of police firing into a crowd of demonstrating workers follows, as well as footage of violent police action in Brooklyn (shot in the early thirties by Leo Seltzer), San Francisco, and elsewhere.

A two-minute shot holds on a preacher in his pulpit refusing to stay silent despite the urging of rich, influential citizens. But we see that such isolated opponents of repression are in danger: the well-known fatal flogging and tarring and feathering of Joseph Shoemaker, a socialist attempting to capture the Florida Democratic Party in 1935, is reenacted. Again, struggle and victory: trains and planes carry thousands of protest letters to Washington, the LaFollette Committee is founded, the villains scurry for cover, but too late—a vast labor spy ring and conspiratorial network is laid bare. A map occupies the screen for two minutes, its changing images dramatically illustrating Robeson's narration, worth quoting in full for the film's tenor:

> The Senate revealed the spies of a secret war all over the country, planted in every local. Forty-one thousand labor spies, an $80 million payroll. The Senate revealed the existence of private armies, armies of criminals organized for secret war in every state in the union, armed vigilantes, strikebreakers, company police paid by private corporations, private arsenals. The Senate revealed private arsenals of tear gas, shotguns, machine guns for war against Americans. Millions of rounds of ammunition, millions of dollars spent in secret, and a system of nationwide propaganda used to attack progressive legislation. Newspapers, lobbies, the radio, full-page advertisements, spending across the whole country, propaganda, arsenals, private armies, spies. The Senate exposed the secret connection, the interlocking parts of an immense conspiracy. Directed by a handful of fascist-minded corporations,

here was a criminal conspiracy to undermine the Bill of Rights, weaken the strength of Americans, exposed. Exposed to the light of day. The American people had won again. Their enemies could no longer operate in disguise. The newly won rights of the people, collective bargaining, unemployment insurance, were backed by the strength of organization. Democracy was coming back.

Then come cemetery scenes; it is Memorial Day, 1937: we see people enjoying the holiday in the street, the park, and the zoo, and then a siren is heard above the merry-go-round, and we are faced with the startling stills of Chicago's Memorial Day massacre, in which police fired on strikers marching toward the Republic Steel plant in South Chicago, killing ten and wounding over sixty more.q A dissolve from the final shot to a grave and a militant graveside speech by a massacre victim's closest friend, concluding, "We don't forget that, never!" Robeson repeats those words, and over a final montage of images from past and present, once again reminds us of the need for alertness and for struggle against those who suppress America's hard-won freedom. "A Frontier Films Production" is titled over the final shot, of the Statue of Liberty.

Native Land is not simply a call for alertness and for the labor movement's continuation of the great battles of the past. Hurwitz saw the line of growth in recent American history and in *Native Land* as "dialectical—the reforms, defeats and victories are all part of one developing process, towards a radical social transformation."[38] In a popular-front film that aimed at a large American audience, it was inadvisable to picture this militantly, explicitly, yet the film makes it clear that in the growth of the unions, Frontier saw—or wanted to see—the possibility for a new social order. Tactically, they set it in familiar terms. People at work are introduced with images of single workers, then pairs, then groups, and then we go to rallies and union meetings:

Here, in the heat and noise of these shops, a new kind of person was being molded, a new kind of American, no longer alone,r but working with others, working together. . . . They learn to work together, and therefore they had to learn to think together, to move together, to act together. . . . The word brother, the word cooperate, the word union. America took up stronger than ever the idea of community action, tenant needs, public forums, com-

q The Film Division of the National Archives has a print of the newsreel footage, which was never released.
r A refrain from *People of the Cumberland.*

mittees, clubs, the idea of union took hold of the American people. These were the new pioneers, facing a new frontier. They put the Bill of Rights into action.

Just as the old words and documents about freedom should be kept vital, so the "idea of union" should infuse itself into our way of seeing, voting, acting. Echoing the early statement that "more than a dream, more than a document, the Bill of Rights meant a way of life," come the words "more than a weapon for democracy, the unions grew to be the center of people's lives."

The labor spy sequence is at the very heart of the film. Like the other dramatized sequences, it involves the viewer in a suspenseful rendering of the themes of social consciousness, conspiracy, and struggle. It unmasks for the viewer a spy who remains masked in the union, setting his weakness and guilt against the heroic union president, against union loyalty in the face of blandishments by the boss, and against the temptations represented by the "red-headed woman" of a union song. As we observe the spy, Harry Carlisle, in the union president's home, in the union itself, and in the office of the corporation that pays him to spy, the filmmakers stress one of their key motifs: the uncovering of fascistic forces in America. The danger of not knowing must be made clear. Behind Carlisle as he is congratulated for catching a spy (a ploy to consolidate his own position in the union) is the slogan on a poster, "Knowledge is power." To create the new America, the new pioneers must be able to recognize and fight their enemies.

Although the labor spy sequence holds our interest, although it serves a significant function, and although Harry Carlisle is by far the most rounded portrait in the film, it is too long and slow, monopolizing nearly one-fourth of the film. The "tight fistful of emotion" experienced during the opening sequences and sustained throughout the succeeding documentary portions is dissipated here, and the viewer becomes a little impatient. This temporary loss of power diminishes the final effect of the film.

Why did this happen? The sequence was originally assigned to Michael Gordon and Van Dyke. When they were removed from the film for having rendered this and the farm sequence inadequately, perhaps Hurwitz and Strand, wishing to prove that they could do it better, lost their perspective. But the cause may be more elusive than that. Harry Carlisle is tempted by money, sells out, divulges names, is told he will go far in the field of labor subversion, and is a weak and troubled man. Ralph Steiner had taken *The City* away and left the Frontier cooperative, tempted, the others thought, by money and position. They also suspected that he had referred to their Communist Party affinities in contexts that had cost them films. We have seen the furor that arose over Maddow's temporary departure to write for *Valley Town*. The songs in the labor spy sequence stress union loyalty against outside temptation: "Which side are you on,/which side are you on?/ My daddy was a miner,/and I'm a mining son,/and I'll stick with the union/till every battle's won." The one sequence dealing with a union— a cooperative—under attack is the one sequence that is out of perspective and usurps time, and it is possible that it was their anger at Steiner in particular, and their fear of dissolution in general, that made the filmmakers lose control in terms of overall pace and impact.

It is possible, too, given both the economic and the political situation of Frontier Films, that an element of defensiveness, even martyrdom, entered into the making of the film. At least one critic, William Boehnel, was struck by this and condemned *Native Land* as entirely defeatist. Although this is not so, it was *almost* so. At one point, as we have seen, Hurwitz felt a snag and had to turn to the former longshoreman Hudson to learn that the film's characters were too predominantly acted upon, with little action of their own in reply. Accordingly, Hurwitz built the protest sequence that leads into the formation of the LaFollette Committee and probably rebuilt the sequence describing the growth of unionism.[39] But enough of the sense of self-righteous martyrdom—a sense of pride in being victims—remains to give the "defeatist" criticism some merit.

I find myself close to the opinion of Bosley Crowther, who reviewed the film for the *New York Times* on 12 May 1942. "A brilliant achievement," *Native Land* is "one of the most powerful and disturbing documentary films ever made. . . . Every sequence, every incident is composed with an eye to rigid suspense, and the sense of violence and outrage is carried straight through the film." On the other hand, the documentary bridges between episodes show

a certain formality . . . which gives them a routine quality; as a whole, the picture lacks the cohesion of its truly superb episodes. That may also be because the actors—Art Smith as the labor spy, Howard da Silva as a "stool pigeon," Fred Johnson as the farmer, and many more—portray such believable characters that one is inclined toward relaxation when they are off the screen.[40]

Crowther is not contradicting himself. The documentary sections carry and elaborate the dominant themes and retain enough of the overwhelming sense of purpose that the drive does not seriously diminish. But they do lack force, and partly thanks to the power of the dramatic sections. The camerawork is good, and yet one doesn't feel—except for the first sequence, which is more experimental than documentary—an overriding *artistic* impulse in either the footage itself or the editing, despite a coherent development of the images. More significant is the fact that the cutting pace—moderately fast with few held shots—imitates that of the dramatic sequences. Unfortunately, in the documentary sequences, this style adds up to too many shots of the same sort of material, and few if any of the images are retained in the viewer's mind. To have equaled the impact of the dramatic sequences, the editor might have slowed the pace to give the nonfiction sequences their own integrity and impact.

Native Land, like Marcel Ophuls' *The Sorrow and the Pity*, reminds us of something potential in ourselves. Strand defines this quality in a 1950 article in which he associates the Frontier productions with Roberto Rossellini's *Open City*. He argues that artists and their audiences must take sides and that realism should be a dynamic art, devoted to changing the world "in the interests of peace, human progress, and the eradication of human misery and cruelty, and towards the unity of all people." The brutal, ugly violence in *Open City*, he points out, is "not isolated," is not conceived "to entertain the audience, but to revolt them, and more important, to remind them of their own heroism as it was expressed in the resistance leaders who were tortured and killed."[41] Because of the national mood caused by our entry into World War II, so critical a film as *Native Land* could have no success on American screens. Yet because *Native Land*, like *Open City*, evokes in us our ability to combat injustice, it remains, as audience response to its recent rerelease demonstrates, a film for all time.

The Frontier Legacy

Frontier knew, probably well before Pearl Harbor, that they had passed the end of an era. They tried to forestall the all too evident fate of *Native Land*, adding an epilogue spoken by Paul Robeson, an epilogue that in later years was removed from the prints:

> This end is our beginning. Today, as never before, we must stand up for our rights as Americans. Together with the peoples of the world we are fighting the greatest enemy of our liberty—

the Hitler axis. This scourge of mankind must be destroyed. We Americans have had to fight for our liberty in every generation.

"Native Land" shows this struggle in our own times. A great and intense conflict. There were many casualties, many wrongs. Yet American labor and the American nation are stronger for having passed through this fire. Labor is producing for victory. We are becoming an organized people, a united people. No appeasers, fifth columnists or native Fascists can divide us. With the united power of field and factory and arms, we will deliver the blows to crush fascism.

For only absolute victory over Hitler and Japan can safeguard our democratic gains and preserve the independence of America.

Needless to say, the epilogue could not save *Native Land*. Nor was the far left any help. When Hurwitz screened it for Browder and Foster, their reactions were very favorable, but they too were committed to the Communist Party's policy of national unity and quietism for the duration of the war. The Party would not aid with the film's distribution for the same reason that Foster was leaving his recently completed book unpublished.

"Don't worry," he said, "the class struggle will be back." He seemed to have a patience I didn't have. I think it was a mistaken patience. You can't have a period of national unity which forgets history. Not without eroding basic principles. I wasn't able to quote Mao on the question of independence and initiative in the united front, but that's the basic argument I made.[42]

In 1942, it was a fruitless argument.

This chapter examines a significant tension, a tension made up of three components. First, Frontier Films was a closely-knit, fun-loving, and very serious family. Second, and to a great extent undermining the family, come the splits, the strains, the growing disaffections. And then, out of the first and in spite of the second, the films themselves emerge. Here Strand's fierce assertion is lodged in my mind: "You can call us everything under the world, but Frontier made *six good films*, and a couple of great films,[s] and nothing can erase that. Let people make up their own minds about the films, because that's the only thing

[s] The six films to which Strand was referring would include *White Flood*, I suspect, along with *Heart of Spain*, *China Strikes Back*, *People of the Cumberland*, *Return to Life*, and *Native Land*. The latter is one film he had in mind as great; *Heart of Spain*, is probably the other.

that counts. We're not interested in Trotskyites and all that crap."[43]

While I agree with Strand to a certain extent, I cannot look only at the films. Clearly the people and impulses behind them are significant too. In my research and interviews I discovered in many of the film-makers the tendencies that would reduce or eliminate their commitment in later years. I learned of the bitterness and the rancor between them, both then and now, and I even stumbled into the crossfire myself a little. As I could have anticipated, I discovered what Martin Duberman found when looking for a perfect educational community at Black Mountain: a cast of strong, often divided personalities, individualists in individualistic America. All three components of the tension deserve attention, and in concluding this chapter, I wish to put them into a final perspective.

Despite, or maybe because of, their individualism, these filmmakers produced, Strand says, six good films and a couple of great films. *How* good and great? Here is Hurwitz's judgment:

> They were not even in their qualities, but they did pioneer a new film form. They were truly independent, non-conformist. They were bold in subject matter and treatment. They provided a key stimulus to a growing generation of filmmakers on the fringes of the film industry in the growing "documentary" field and in Hollywood. They were responsive to important aspects of the human experience and the underlying forces of the time.[44]

I think Hurwitz is right and that the qualities he names make the Frontier films richer and tougher than *The Plow That Broke the Plains*, *The River*, and *The City*, the three most lauded American documentary films of the thirties.

But we cannot stop with such a statement. One way to evaluate the films fairly is to cite a basic disagreement between Ben Maddow and Paul Strand. On the one hand, Maddow faults the Frontier films for the lack of substance in their portrayal of people, who with certain exceptions, are appreciated only for their dignity, who are "used as illustrations, not persons." He faults the films for focusing too much attention on dialectical theory and states that "they could never make a really great film, because they weren't looking at the human heart of things." On the other hand, Strand's particular aesthetics of dynamic realism runs counter to any complexity of character that would undermine his key goal, which was to remind his audience "of their own heroism."[45]

Both perspectives must be taken seriously. In 1935, Hurwitz and Steiner confessed to "something missing" in their pre-Nykino thought and art—a method of engaging the audience. This they traced to their failure to find documentary equivalents for the Hollywood film's hero, plot, and suspense, and to their own shallow presentation of people. These problems were rather superbly overcome at Frontier, and the force of the films is a tribute to the aesthetic that Strand and the others espoused. Although people are not present in the way Maddow would have them—nor are they any more present in the first two Lorentz films and only somewhat more so in Van Dyke's work—they do have significant dimension.

In *The Plow That Broke the Plains*, people *are* primarily illustrations. The film is about forces that affect their lives, yet their appearances are most often token. However, simply because people are not portrayed in their full complexity does not necessarily mean that they are *merely* illustrations, for in cinema the significance of people can be suggested in several ways: (1) by the time devoted to them as individuals; (2) by camera relation, distance, shot-length, feeling for their setting, their movement, and so on; (3) by postures and expressions the filmmakers either call for or capture spontaneously; (4) by a serious concern over themes deeply related to the behavior, freedom, well-being, and responsibility of the people presented. *The Plow That Broke the Plains* is weak on (1), (2), and (3), and thus (4) is inadequate. The Frontier films are strong in (2), (3), and especially (4). Their forceful advocacy of unexploited lives for their subjects raises those subjects far above the category of mere illustrations.

What I do find missing from Frontier's work, however, is something more difficult to define, perhaps something close to Maddow's "human heart of things," a certain profound quality, a tone, an attitude, a depth of love for humanity. It is a quality we find in the films of Marcel Ophuls, a tragic sense not dissociated from the will to political commitment. Although there is tremendous concern and commitment in the films by the Frontier filmmakers, this larger feeling for the human condition is absent.

Still, a significant part of Frontier's legacy is their serious theoretical goal of combining a profound personal sense of the human condition with political art, a goal in some conflict with their aesthetics of impact and their notion of heroism. Other essential parts of their legacy are their refusal to compromise their art for the sake of funding, their achievement of significant form in support of their vision, their wish to bear witness to contemporary injustice, and the lesson they, like Ivens and other film artists of the thirties, learned of the necessity of both making people central and treating them with respect, a lesson separating them from the makers of such recent exploitative documentaries as *Marjoe* and *Grey Gardens*. This legacy is a resource for present filmmakers confronting issues of integrity in the documentary field and seeking to shun the pitfalls of mere technical virtuosity and of so-called neutral, objective documentation.

And it is true, too, that there are many excellent, powerful films born out of a strong social conscience—some films of Peter Davis and Frederick Wiseman for example—which lack the kind of love, the final mature and wise perspective I am describing. Yet while this may make them less than the greatest art, they are highly important for what they evoke in their audiences. And perhaps it is on that basis that Frontier must finally be judged.

As for the filmmakers themselves, while I defend Strand's aesthetics and Frontier's heroes against Maddow's criticism, I would feel badly if I failed to present *my* people in Maddow's fuller mode. They can be significant figures for me only after I have gone through the mill of their limitations, their difficulties, and their failures. All too aware of our own limitations, of our propensities to compromise and to submit to authority, of our pettiness, cruelty, and anger, we need as models humanly flawed people who are like us in all that, but who have nevertheless often been able to carry through their profound commitments.

Van Dyke, Lorentz, Ivens, and Dick: Variations on the Sponsored Film and *Men and Dust*, 1938-1940

The British Connection

Ralph Steiner and Willard Van Dyke hoped that their departure from Frontier Films to make *The City* would enable them to control their own art, to make money, and to make films politically somewhat to the right of the Frontier product. It was at this point of departure that they came under the influence of the British documentary movement (the most prominent and successful extant movement in documentary film) and thus entered the realm of the sponsored film.

Although in 1933 American readers of the English periodical *Film Art* could read of such British documentary films as Paul Rotha's *Contact*, Basil Wright's *Cargo from Jamaica*, and Arthur Elton's *Aero-Engine*, they were unable to see these films. Travelers to England might take a gander: in 1935 Rotha showed Strand his *Shipyard*, which Strand found "competent and desultory"; Evelyn Gerstein found the same film "meticulous and arid" in her January 1936 article entitled "English Documentary Films." American documentary makers were probably fascinated by her news of the wide distribution that their British counterparts had achieved, yet many surely were put off upon learning that the films were "basically government tracts, intended to applaud the progress of the Crown." Gerstein lauded the English for showing "how far a consistent point of view and determination may go in the battle against the commercialized fantasies and wish-fulfillment exercises of Hollywood and Elstree,"[a] but she had important

---

[a] England's equivalent of Hollywood.

distinctions to make between the English films and the films of Joris Ivens, who was becoming such an important influence on American documentary filmmakers at the beginning of 1936:

> In retrospect, their films are more alert as physical commentary than drama. Their documents merely state and illumine; they explore the medium with highly formalized and studied photography and the avidity of the English for details. They posit a social inquiry and resolve it superficially by concluding that slum clearance has been ended by the Gas Company and the abuses of the coal pits blotted out with electricity for all. The Empire takes care of its own.
>
> Joris Ivens' *Borinage* is a document, too. He made it during the Belgian mine strike, with a camera hidden under his coat. The miners sheltered him in their yards, and the film was shipped out of the city each night for developing. *Borinage* is not handsomely photographed, but in the swift, brief mounting scenes of the strike there is a drama of revolutionary truth.[1]

Although her review aroused the curiosity of many American filmmakers, it was to be some time before their interest could be further explored: Rotha's *Face of Britain* was seen for the first time in the United States at the premiere of *The Plow That Broke the Plains* on 10 May 1936, and Basil Wright's *Song of Ceylon* opened in New York in 1937 during the same week as *The Spanish Earth*, but very little else, if anything, had made it across the Atlantic, and there was almost no contact between American and British documentarists until late in 1937.

On a trip to England in the spring of 1937 to purchase films, husband and wife John Abbott and Iris Barry, respectively director and curator of the new Film Library at the Museum of Modern Art, invited Rotha to lecture in the States. According to Rotha, Barry

> at once grasped that the idea which underlay our work had no counterpart in the U.S., except perhaps for the isolated *The Plow That Broke the Plains*. . . . She saw . . . that my . . . visit might be given an added purpose, that of introducing the whole documentary idea of public service using social purpose for progress, to sections of the American public, especially those who might be concerned to promote a documentary movement among American film-makers and imaginative educationists.

Barry arranged with John Grierson, the renowned English documentary film pioneer, for eleven films to be sent to the Film Library collection, both for Rotha's lectures and for distribution.[b] Rotha himself arrived at the end of September.[2]

Rotha's six-month American visit, supported by a Rockefeller Foundation Fellowship, was a very active one. He made many individual contacts, wrote six articles, lectured widely in addition to the weekly course he taught at the Film Library, and delivered thirteen of the twenty-eight three-hour talks in a film course at Columbia, which was attended by thirty-five students, including his friend Richard Griffith, Arthur Rosenheimer, Jr.—who was later to change his name to Arthur Knight—and aspiring filmmaker Rudy Bretz. Everywhere he attempted to propagate the British "documentary idea."

Rotha explained that the major importance of Grierson's original film unit at the Empire Marketing Board was twofold: through the unit's efforts the government came to realize the value of film for public relations; and big industrial firms and public utility concerns began to see film as "a new form of public education from which prestige could be secured." The task of documentary makers in England was to persuade sponsors "to make films of wider social significance" than they originally had planned and to refrain from using them for direct advertising purposes. In all such films, he explained, the socioeconomic significance of the subject must be emphasized: in his own *Shipyard*, for instance, the story of a ship being built stressed the town's dependency on ship-building commissions. The English documentary makers had always attempted to bring alive daily events, to dignify labor, and to improve communications across classes. Eighteen months ago, they had decided to further humanize their films by portraying people more fully.[3]

Although Rotha tried to be generous, he could not entirely disguise his notion that he had come to show backward Americans the right way to make documentary films.[4] When several interesting film projects were suggested to him, he "stalled production on all these," he reported to Grierson, "until at any rate next spring; there are no units here fit to take on such good projects" (p. 203). He talked extensively with the General Education Board at the Rockefeller Foundation about establishing a film unit that would affiliate itself with the British, but felt at the start that "some executive posts would have to be filled from England . . . as there are just not the people here" (p. 203).

Rotha's attitude was not lost on some of the Americans. Because of

---

[b] The eleven films to be sent were: *Night Mail, Granton Trawler, We Live in Two Worlds, Roadways, Weather Forecast, The Smoke Menace, Children at School, Today We Live, Eastern Valley, Enough to Eat?* and *Housing Problems*. *Song of Ceylon* and *Cover to Cover* were already available.

it, he found no friends at Frontier: Strand was especially disinclined towards him (pp. 182, 211), and his relationship with Lorentz, who found him just plain arrogant, was touchy. Lorentz was to remark sarcastically two years later that "the British have sent over several flights of lecturers to explain to our dumb but patient citizenry the meaning of documentary film." Arthur Rosenheimer, Jr., reviewing the 1939 edition of Rotha's *Documentary Film*, found that Ivens' work was inexcusably slighted, and thought the section on American film "so reserved as to be pallid and flabby, underlined by an implicit distaste for both American aims and efforts."[5] Muriel Rukeyser, who liked Rotha and hoped to do a film on silicosis with him, remembers the tension as based in part on jealousy of both Rotha's work and of the success of British documentary and in part on resentment of his tone toward the Americans. She saw his superior stance as a viable teaching method (letter, p. 211).

The dislike was caused not only by Rotha's tone but by British theory and films in general. His left-wing American listeners found no tough-minded political or economic stand in the "sociological approach" to the shipyard, and Rotha may have told some audiences that his visit was delayed by the necessity of finishing *The Future's in the Air*, "a film extolling the efficiencies of British air routes" (p. 173). Rotha's sort of sponsorship, Rosenheimer argued, "is merely one facet of American documentary production."

> Indeed, the greater part of the advanced workers in the American field have come from socially conscious groups that have seen the value of film in presenting their side. Rotha says, "Production must be placed on a firm economic basis," and consequently cuts down on the social criticism that the Americans insist on. His "propaganda for democracy" is naturally held in check by the undemocratic source of his cheques, which manifests itself in his approach to his material.

Agreeing with this, other critics went even further. Gerstein found the British films unable "to search deeper into the realities that underlie the surface," and Hurwitz thought them pale, passionless, restricted in range, playing it safe with their human and political content. At Frontier they were attempting major art and had better sources: "Unlike the Russians, whom they learned from, the English were not letting their minds and hearts move into the deeper layers of their experience. The Russians were turning over a world—inner and outer."[6]

Actually, Rotha knew some of the limitations of the British documentary, however reticent he might have been to talk about them in America. In a speech to a special Labour Party Conference on Film Propaganda the year before he visited the United States, he had pointed out that with such sponsors as the gas company and the British postal service, "to state wages, hours of work, victimisation and conditions of labour has been beyond [the movement's] power." And he argued forcefully "for the formation of a permanent film body attached to the Labour Movement, spreading working-class propaganda through the country by both making and showing films."[7] He was, he wrote Rukeyser in 1938, a believer in the class struggle who felt that under the capitalist system "no working class can exist in decency" (pp. 209-210). But he was also a practical man who fought to make progressive films under whatever sponsorship was available.

If Gerstein, Rosenheimer, Hurwitz, and Strand found the British documentaries safe and shallow, there were others who welcomed Rotha more warmly. During his stay, he had many long, friendly talks with Steiner and Van Dyke. Although the General Education Board film unit had to wait, Rotha could still report to Grierson that he had managed to help set up one unit in the States. This was American Documentary Films, Inc., directed by Steiner and Van Dyke and associated with Raymond Rich, Inc. The latter—"a non-profit-making body of educationists, university people, etc., who undertake all kinds of public relations work for bodies working 'in the public interest' "— was clearly in support of the documentary idea (p. 207).[c] Steiner and Van Dyke wanted to "make money,"[8] and the British notion of enlightened sponsorship would allow them to do that and make socially responsible films as well. The film they had on hand would make an excellent beginning.

The City

Steiner and Van Dyke weathered the furor over their break with Frontier early in 1938 and set to work on *The City*. This film had its beginnings when the American Institute of Planners foresaw in the 1939 World's Fair a chance to present their ideas on urban planning to a large audience. One of its members, Clarence Stein, incorporated Civic Films, raised $50,000 from the Carnegie Foundation, first offered

[c] ADF's letterhead:
American Documentary Films, Inc.
Producers of Films in the Public Interest
11 West 42 Street, New York.

the film to Pare Lorentz, who turned it down, and then contacted Steiner.[d] The Institute's members presented to him what Steiner remembers as a two-hundred-pound barrage of their highly contradictory books and lectures. He threw up his hands and suggested that "Pare can write down in a couple of pages what it's all about." Lorentz agreed to do this initial sketch, but "nothing came and nothing came, so I went out to his house and lived for three days and stood over him with an axe, and finally I took back the simplest thing," an eleven-page outline, in fact, that was to set most of the format and the tone of the completed film. The outline called for a prologue in New England, followed by five sequences: a steel factory and a steel town; an industrial prairie city; a metropolis; a weekend highway outside the metropolis; and the kind of planned community that the Institute proposed. Consonant with Lorentz's strategy in *The Plow That Broke the Plains* and *The River*, the outline urged a short, pointed final sequence, "explaining . . . as simply and quickly as possible, that, (a) the new city exists; (b) where it exists; (c) how it is planned."[9]

The outline was completed sometime before 28 June, and by July, Van Dyke was on location in New England. He was to shoot the prologue and the final sequence, and Steiner would shoot the Pittsburgh (industrial city/steel town), the highway, and the New York (metropolis) sequences; Van Dyke would work on the New York sequence as well. The Rockefeller Foundation gave Edward Anhalt and Rudolph Bretz grants to serve as associate cameramen, and Roger Barlow was brought out from Los Angeles to work as a cameraman with Van Dyke. Aaron Copland, at a turning point in his career and eager to reach a larger audience, jumped at Steiner's request that he compose the score. Morris Carnovsky of the Group Theatre agreed to narrate.

The filmmakers felt themselves to be in competition with Lorentz,[e] especially with his famous method of lyrical narration. The question here, Van Dyke recalls, was "How do you overcome the problem of that voice from on high?" Since they knew that to imitate Lorentz

[d] See pp. 179-180.

[e] Lorentz probably sensed this, perhaps out of some insecurity of his own as a filmmaker. While working on *The City*, Van Dyke had a potential film commission from the Monsanto Chemical Company, and he requested from Lorentz a print of *The River* in order to demonstrate his camerawork. Lorentz refused, and Van Dyke subsequently borrowed a print from the Museum of Modern Art. Lorentz found out and was so angry that he did not speak to Van Dyke for years. Why did Lorentz refuse? All Van Dyke could suggest to me was that perhaps Lorentz feared that Van Dyke would claim the film as essentially his own. (Van Dyke interview 2, and 15 Jan. [no year] letter from Van Dyke to Lorentz, in Lorentz file at Film Study Center, Museum of Modern Art, New York.)

would be absurd, they agreed that they would not employ his technique of using voices over the music (much to Copland's delight).[10] Instead they decided to work with the relation of music and images, resorting to commentary only where absolutely necessary, a strategy that was to be effectively and beautifully carried out.

Henwar Rodakiewicz, who since *The Wave* had worked on Bing Crosby pictures as an assistant to Hollywood director Frank Tuttle (who directed left-wing films on the side in Los Angeles), was invited to assist in forming the film. Credited with the scenario and as an associate in production, Rodakiewicz actually merits much more acknowledgment. He arrived in late July or early August, found Steiner and Van Dyke uncertain about how to unify their material, and quickly developed a shooting script for the prologue. He helped to direct the New England footage which was still outstanding, and then he wrote the rest of the script, served as director in Pittsburgh for the industrial city sequence, and over the last several months of filming worked constantly with Ted Lawrence and Lawrence's wife[f] in the editing room.

By all available accounts, the collaboration was joyful, inventive, stimulating, and dedicated: Rodakiewicz recalled the "painstaking care and the cutting for months and months, getting things sharper and sharper" out of "a devotion to the thing because we felt we had something to say." And "for most of the film," Van Dyke recently reminded Rodakiewicz, "we felt in accord with . . . the city planners."[11]

The accord, however, was by no means entirely blissful. Steiner and Van Dyke had left Frontier partly because they wanted greater artistic independence and preferred not to make propaganda films. But here they discovered that dependence on sponsors meant considerable pressure to follow another kind of line that was not entirely their own. "The clients," Steiner recalls,

> always wanted to know, "what are you doing, what are you doing," and we didn't want to show them, so we would just take anything and put it together all mixed up . . . so they couldn't see sequence or anything. Sometimes we'd take apart the work print and mix it all up and then put it back again.

Why not show it to them? Because, Steiner explained, the sponsors lacked imagination and wanted a straightforward, informational exposition of their position, not the humorous, witty treatment that the filmmakers were at work on. When *The City* was finally previewed,

---

[f] My interviewees do not remember her name. Ted Lawrence has the credit as editor on the film.

Steiner recalls, "one of the [Carnegie Foundation] men had to be taken home in a taxi cab, two people supporting him, and everyone said, 'you have ruined us, you have thrown $50,000 out the window, you have taken a serious subject and made fun of it.' " Rodakiewicz also remembers the screening and the Carnegie Foundation man who "walked out the door and I don't think he's ever been seen since!"[12]

And they got away with somewhat more than making a witty, inventive film. Van Dyke and Rodakiewicz found Lorentz's purposes compatible with their own. The outline read:

> We should get into the industrial village, and the speculation, and the jerry-built houses, but this is the story of brutal, unheeding industrial development, personified by what Frick, and Carnegie and the boys did in the Monongahela Valley and it is so vivid pictorially I do not think we need to comment on the morals, methods, or urges, that built this valley.

Rodakiewicz agreed that "narrative is unnecessary, for the images are brutally vivid," although he also saw that "a carefully spotted narrative might punctuate and give a larger meaning to the sequence." The words he had in mind would have chilled the Carnegie man, "whether a cold, matter-of-fact account of the development of the Monongahela Valley and the growing demand for steel, or excerpts from the annual reports of the large steel industries (incredible as they would sound spoken against the pictures)." Rodakiewicz himself feared that such words would make the commentary "cynical and one-sided."[13]

Rodakiewicz had originally intended to write the narration and might have used words close to those he had in mind, but he couldn't do it to his satisfaction and turned the job over to Lewis Mumford, who was a member of the sponsoring Institute of City Planners.[g] After some consultation with the filmmakers, Mumford did the writing mainly on his own.[14] He decided to give the Pittsburgh images a commentary, and the words he chose were calculated to stress the human waste while avoiding the tangle with the sponsors that Rodakiewicz's words would have caused. Mumford's narration runs as follows:

[g] According to Howard Gillette, the claim by Paul Rotha and Richard Griffith that *The City* is based on Mumford's *The Culture of Cities* is an error. Yet Mumford did have some influence on the film's conception, perhaps through the Institute of City Planners, on the basis of the reputation of his own writing, and definitely as the result of a luncheon talk with Lorentz (who admired his writing), when Lorentz was thinking of taking on the film himself. But, according to Gillette, Mumford took no active part in the original shaping of the film, the writing of the script, or the shooting. He was not brought in until he was asked to write the commentary. See Howard Gillette, Jr., "Film as Artifact: *The City* (1939)," *American Studies*, Fall 1977, pp. 71-85. Phone conversation with Pare Lorentz, 14 Nov. 1978.

It don't make us any happier to know there's millions like us living here on top of it. There's prisons where a guy sent up for crime can get a better place to live in than we can give our children. Smoke makes prosperity, they tell you here, smoke makes prosperity, no matter if you choke on it. We got to face life in these shacks and alleys, got to let our children take their chances here with rickets, typhoid, t.b., or worse. They draw a blank, the kids. They have no business here; this no man's land, this slag heap wasn't meant for them. There's poison in the air we breathe. There's poison in the river. The fog and smoke below rise up and choke us. Don't tell us this is the best you can do in building cities. Who built this place? What put us here, and how do we get out again? We're asking—just asking. We might as well stay in the mills and call that home; they're just as fit to live in.

The "who" and "what" are rhetorical and lead to no further discussion. By tempering his lines, Mumford denied the sequence some of the impact that Lorentz and Rodakiewicz would have liked to give it.

When they first read Mumford's commentary, which they did not have the right to veto, all of them, according to Steiner, "thought it terrible. Perhaps correct from a city-planning point of view and philosophically, but mushy and sententious in the extreme. I still shudder, after all these years, at some of the unnecessary on-the-nose-ness and gooiness." Rodakiewicz found it "too damn wordy and like a well-kept lawn," lacking accurate "briars and brambles and thorns." He resolved then that he would always do his own narration.[15] Mumford did, however, hold to the filmmakers' policy of spare commentary, and whatever his restraint in the Pittsburgh sequence, his words helped to make that sequence disturbing and powerful, probably more, despite his evasions, than the Carnegie man bargained for, and one of the best treatments of industrial negligence and exploitation in the decade.

Rodakiewicz risked tangling with the Institute in another way. To remedy a tame ending in the outline, he planned that contentious voices would argue the merits of the planners' version of the model city, the "Green City." The carping, abusive, cynical voices of a "slick realtor," a demagogue, and a city tough would be combated by the unruffled voice of the Green City itself—and at one point by the voice of Mayor Fiorello LaGuardia, as an advocate for city planning. By touching the sources of congestion, dehumanization, and oppression, Rodakiewicz intended to anger and motivate the audience—to "create answers," he told the skeptical city planners. Although this effort was not in the more militant, declarative mode of Frontier, Rodakiewicz,

Van Dyke, and their colleagues were clearly antagonistic toward the forces of exploitation.

The Planners' Civic Films Committee predictably vetoed Rodakie-wicz's ending, and the result of this veto and of Mumford's tempered words was that the film lacks the full accusatory bite that the filmmakers had wanted. "When you made that film," interviewer G. Roy Levin asked Van Dyke recently, "was there ever any question of talking about why cities were like that?"

> W.V.D. No, no. The city planners simply insisted there be no so-
> ciological or political or any kind of examination of the reasons
> behind, but simply that this is what exists and this is what it could
> be. Not "how do we get there" or "how did we get here."
>
> G.R.L. Did you have any feelings about wanting to or caring to
> talk about causes?
>
> W.V.D. Yes, but we simply couldn't. [16]

The filmmakers suffered another harmful form of intervention. In strong agreement with Lorentz about the necessity for a compact end-ing, they nevertheless had to buckle to the city planners' insistence, from the start, that the planners' idealized Green City solution be spelled out at length. The result is a long, bland final sequence without much conviction. In the completed film, the prologue is 7 minutes, the industrial city sequence 6½, the metropolis 9 minutes and 50 seconds, the highway 2 minutes and 25 seconds, and the final Green City sequence is 17 minutes and 15 seconds—even in strictly structural terms a disaster for the film. [h]

The point of *The City* is direct. The prologue reminds us of the harmony between nature, man, and work in an environment that has remained small and integrated. The following three sequences show man overpowered in his factories, impoverished in the industrial en-vironment, and dehumanized in the metropolis. The Green City is offered as a solution, a modern, urban version of the New England village.

There are almost as many styles in the film as there are sequences. Beneath the credits, a motionless camera portrays New England sta-bility through images of fields and town; sizeable rocks are in the foreground, and we see images of large, old, solid houses. The first post-credit shot holds on a pond, then tilts slowly up to catch the watermill

[h] For later distribution purposes, Civic Films cut a good chunk from the final sequence and smaller chunks from earlier sequences, and this is the version many libraries now have. The Museum of Modern Art distributes the original, which is the one Van Dyke wants shown, despite his dislike for the final sequence.

beginning to turn, a slow leisurely shot that sets the tone for the sequence. Then follows footage of a farmer and his son riding the horse-drawn wagon to town, the boy and dog running through the graveyard, the town hall and town meeting, the blacksmith's shop where the wagon rim is repaired: it is an intimate, convincing, and economically edited sequence with a minimum of talk, and the talk is calculated to enhance the visual images. The intention is to show simply that "this is the way it was,"[17] with the images carrying the message of open air, sunshine, and relaxed friendliness. It is all light and pleasant and beautifully photographed. Yet it is also a perpetuation of the myth of idyllic small-town America—a little bland, unchallenging, *too* sweetly harmonious. More an idealized memory of someone's childhood than a realistic consideration of life in a small town, it is also a world away, politically and dynamically, from the charged, militant use of New England in the prologue to *Native Land*.

One of *The City*'s purposes is to burrow under American slogans and clichés and to show how people actually live. Into the stark industrial sequence, breaking in on the stunning silence over a man trudging home down a smoking hill of molten waste, comes an excited voice:

> Machines, invention, power, block out the past, forget the quiet city, bring in the steam and steel, the iron men, the giants, open the throttle, all aboard, the promised land, pillars of smoke by day, pillars of fire by night, pillars of progress, machines to make machines, production to expand production. There's wood and wheat and kitchen sinks and calico, already made in tons and carload lots, enough for tens, thousands, *millions*, faster and faster, better and better.

By the last "better," the camera has panned across the river from an industrial site to a grim long shot of its workers' squalid houses. A similar narration, this time over New York skyscrapers, ends on "the people yes . . . the people, maybe."

The humor of the metropolis and the highway sequences also pokes fun at the slogans and clichés of the American way of life. As we watch people trying to cross a street and see the signs, signals, and whizzing cars that repress their movements and send them dashing back to sidewalk safety, as we watch the ingenious gadgets that make fast mass lunches and watch as people pleasurelessly gulp them down, as we hear the clicking taxi meter in the city traffic jam, as we listen to jaunty highway music and watch cars stuck in line—and laugh—we are admitting to what we have become, we are acknowledging our human resemblance to the machine and all the inadvertent, unnatural qualities that plague us and lower our dignity. Our amusement is sympathetic too, for the situations are so familiar. We can laugh because this time it is happening to someone else; we, for the moment, are allowed to know better.

The idealized inhabitants of the planners' Green City are not mechanized individuals, of course, but whole, balanced human beings; accordingly, their sequence employs a different brand of humor. A pitcher who tosses too many gifts to opposing batters is thrown into the lake by his teammates. A boy snitches an extra apple from the refrigerator. He pumps up his bike tire and the air escapes, time after time. Other boys tie knots in the clothing of a swimmer. This is a warm, not satirical, humor—traditional rural and suburban American fun—and we are drawn into the scene, into our own, half-remembered, peaceful growing-up, or into the kind of childhoods that stories and films have told us of and that we wish for our children.

The industrial city sequence (a merging of two Lorentz sequences) is the strongest in the film. Shot in the late, leafless fall, it contains little sky and little sense of fresh air: smoke drifts slowly through shot after shot, stultifying most of the images that appear after the opening mill shots, which themselves are controlled by the intense light from the fires, the smallness of the human figures, and the loud, sharp, jarring music. Individual shots, edited less toward the next shot than for their own composition, underscore the static, depressing character of industrial lives. And the composition is excellent, with Steiner's acute eye having picked out the most telling faces, structures, streets, arrangements of milltown houses, and factory outlines.

The film's crucial weakness is one of placement and tone, a weakness resulting only minimally from the sponsors' restrictions on content. The outline placed the industrial town before the metropolis because its "horrible condition . . . is really a prelude to the city"; it "built the city . . . gave it its wealth," and is the basis of its mores.[18] This makes good sense, but the two sequences that follow the industrial city sequence are insufficiently consonant with it.[i] Although they succeed in

---

[i] Rodakiewicz had wanted them to be consonant. In the metropolis sequence, he planned to capture the "pitiful conditions whether in terms of terrible surroundings for lack of feeling for humanity"; "nasty fights, altercations, cursing, parents, loafers at corners"; a shot where "man walks slowly along street, collapses suddenly on steps near pavement, people walk by giving him wide berth." The highway sequence would then be a relieving interlude, for they would "have been bearing down pretty steadily on miserable aspects of congestion." It is obvious that his was not the prevailing voice in the composition of the metropolis sequence. Information from Rodakiewicz, shooting script for *The City*.

depicting the danger, the congestion, and the inhumanity of the chaos, their function is primarily diversionary. Clever, quickly paced, composed of some of the best cutting and internal movement in 1930s documentary film, these sequences were composed primarily for the entertainment of the working middle-class that they portray. The problem is that the audience is so entertained that it forgets the grim industrial city that it has seen just a few minutes earlier. And although some of the industrial city images are effectively cut into the final "you-take-your-choice" shots of the film, they recover only a portion of the grim power of their prior context. Either the metropolis and the highway sequences should have been tougher, or they should have preceded the industrial city sequence in order to give the film a sense of increased urgency immediately before the Green City sequence.

The City received a great deal of critical attention, not all of it positive. James Arthur, Richard Griffith, and an anonymous reviewer for *Film Survey* found it too amusing.[j] Griffith also noted that the film "is much more concerned over the inconvenience which traffic congestion causes the motorist than with the dirt and disease of the slums." And Arthur thought it "unfortunate that with so vast and profoundly tragic a theme, the makers have failed both in their responsibilities to the subject and to their own talents." Griffith quoted from the ending:

> Chaotic metropolis or summery suburb—"each of them is real, each of them is possible. You can take your choice." *Who* can take it? *The City* proceeds as though everyone could, as though it had only to convince us of the *value* of the future town. But people do not live in slums by choice. They need to be shown not only what they ought to have but how they can get it. And this the film does not mention.[19]

I share these criticisms. Yet *The City* was a huge success at the World's Fair, where it was shown twice daily four days a week for a year and a half.[k] It received full-page spreads in *Life* and *The New*

---

[j] The amusement was important to Steiner. He urged Agriculture Secretary Wallace and others to forego a private screening in Washington for the showing at Greenbelt "because we have noticed that the audience enjoys the film far more when in a large group. The treatment of the film is frequently humorous as well as dramatic, so that it is definitely the kind of thing which gains added effect from a public showing, in which laughter and the emotional reaction are very contagious." Letter to James McCamy, assistant to the secretary, 15 June 1939, National Archives.

[k] Many documentary makers and documentary devotees had eagerly anticipated the 1939 World's Fair. In July 1938, praising *Men Make Steel* as an excellent industrial film spoiled by a come-on from its sponsor, U.S. Steel, Lorentz expressed his hopes that the Fair's business, industrial, and governmental films would make "the factual film exciting enough to give audiences once again a curiosity about movies." The critic for *Film Survey*

York Times Magazine and garnered a rave review from Archer Winsten in the *New York Post*. In spite of my own strong reservations about its social reality, however, there are reasons for the major status that the film has claimed since then. It brought to the American documentary film a spirit and humor that the more epic constructions of Lorentz and the more driving productions of Frontier Films lacked.

---

and Richard Griffith concurred. And a newcomer, producer Mary Losey, regarded the Fair as an opportunity to advertise the best documentary work. Together with Philip McConnell, she brought *The City* to the Fair's Little Theatre. This team also was responsible for setting up the extraordinarily comprehensive documentary program in which *The City* was included: *The Plow That Broke the Plains, The River*, the British films *Enough to Eat?, Housing Problems, Kensal House, The Londoners, Children at School, Night Mail, The Transfer of Power, Monkey into Man*, and *North Sea*, Flaherty's *Man of Aran*, the powerful Belgian film by Henri Storck that so impressed Paul Strand, *Les Maisons de la Misère* (see Lorentz, "Movies," *McCall's*, July 1938, p. 57; and Strand, "*Les Maisons de la Misère*," *Films*, Nov. 1939, pp. 89-90), the *March of Time's* Men of Medicine, Roffman's, Kandel's, and Del Duca's consumers' series called *Getting Your Money's Worth, New Earth, The Spanish Earth, The 400 Million, China Strikes Back, Return to Life*, and programs on medicine, Pan America, farming, and so on. The British Pavilion showed a few other British documentaries, the Soviet classics were running at the Soviet Pavilion, the Chrysler Building carried Frontier Films' little *History and Romance of Transportation*, and Joseph Losey, brother of Mary and director of the Federal Theatre's Living Newspaper productions, had experimented with Helen van Dongen and Hanns Eisler on a puppet film, *Pete Roleum and His Cousins*, which ran in the huge hall of the Petroleum Industry. These films were, from all contemporary accounts, the best of the more than five hundred nonfiction films at the Fair.

The other films, it seems, were not so good. The critic Richard Griffith, also a devotee of the British documentary idea and a firm friend of Rotha, was disappointed over the sponsored productions at the Fair. The corporations had not turned to documentary professionals but to Hollywood technicians and commercial filmmakers, and few had made new films for the occasion. There were exceptions, but all too few (see Griffith, "Films of the Fair," *Films*, Nov. 1939, pp. 63-64). Yet Rosenheimer, by then Arthur Knight and by then a better friend of the British point of view, argues in *The Liveliest Art* (1957)—a book that does not once mention Frontier Films—that the Fair was "the real turning point for documentary in America" (p. 271). This belief, shared by Lerner, Van Dyke, and others, has much truth in it. Thanks to the example of the British films, to Mary Losey, to the revelation of how open and undeveloped the field of the sponsored film was, and to the clear popularity that good documentary films could sustain with a general audience, much of the isolation experienced by New York's documentary filmmakers began to break down. As a result, new collaborations began, and, although they were never to come easily, commissions for sponsored films became more frequent. New film units, such as Film Associates, Inc., Realfilm Productions, Inc., Lee Dick, Inc. (later Dial Films, Inc.), and Documentary Film Associates, entered the field.

New supporting organizations also developed. The Rockefeller-Foundation-funded American Film Center came into being in 1939, "its sole objective . . . to develop the use of films for educational and public purposes" (letter from Donald Slesinger, Director of Film Center, to John Fisher of the Farm Security Administration, 9 Apr. 1941, National Archives). Its bulletin, *Film News*, helped filmmakers keep track of what was going on among them. Also formed in 1939, the Association of Documentary Film Producers, an independent organization that was the result of Mary Losey's ongoing efforts, aimed "to develop the artistic and technical standards of independent, creative documentary films, to promote wider production and distribution of such films, to provide a means of communication and cooperation among independent, creative, doc-

As Griffith pointed out, its camera technique and the quality of human intimacy that it applied to contemporary life opened the documentary form to a wider audience than it had previously attracted. John Grierson, who found both the prologue and the Green City sequence tame and unconvincing, praised the film as "one of the first directive social documentaries done in the United States," commending it for its similarity to British documentary.[20] It gave new life and imparted at least some new direction to American nonfiction film.

But it was not only humor and human intimacy that made *The City* popular at the end of the thirties. Although several critics were bored by the Green City sequence, I suspect that very few members of the general public found it at all dull. Here, after years of depression, dissension, and uncertainty, was a harmonious America, an America that was portrayed as if it could control its own destiny in the uneasy face of growing world fascism and militarism. By drawing on aspects of the American Dream, as Richard Barsam notes, by playing on the agrarian myth, by touching on the same instincts that Barry Goldwater tapped in a very troubled 1964, by taking Americans back to nature, to the farm, to childhood, by reminding them of the old clarity and simplicity, the Institute and American Documentary Films had created an oasis. *The City* was successful not only because, as Van Dyke suggests, "its message was something that nobody could object to"[21] but also because it offered the kind of possibilities that many people needed to believe in.

Van Dyke and *Valley Town*

After *The City*, Steiner and Van Dyke, who had both drawn on their own slim funds to finish the film, found it difficult to find work at the

umentary film workers, and to act as a source of information on such films" (see Lewis Jacobs, "Documentary Film Advances," *Direction*, Feb. 1940, p. 14). The Association's officers from June 1940 to June 1941 included: Joris Ivens, president; Paul Strand and Willard Van Dyke, vice presidents; W. O. Field, Jr., treasurer; and Mary Losey, Field's future wife, secretary. Jay Leyda chaired the education committee, Lee Dick the finance committee, and Joseph Losey the membership committee. Alice Keliher, Lionel Berman, Jack Bradford, Lora Hays, and Leo Seltzer (now making films for the WPA) were members of the board (see *TAC*, July-Aug. 1939, p. 17; and *Documentary Film News*, Aug. 1941, p. 1).

In the years before the war dissolved it, the Association sponsored an important documentary series with the Museum of Modern Art and another with the Institute of Arts and Sciences of Columbia University. It sponsored series of lectures, ran a program of educational evenings, published *Documentary Film News*—which advertised the meetings and told of new films, ongoing productions, and new publications—and published *Living Films*, a late 1940 catalogue of members, which included brief biographies

level they desired. Steiner tells the story of a less than ideal sponsor, the Monsanto Chemical Company:

> We wrote and submitted scripts to various organizations that seemed to want a film made. One huge Midwest chemical company wanted a film about the importance of phosphorus in diet to make good bone structure. Our script detailed shots showing American families living on insufficient diets. When we went out to confer with the top executives, one of them objected, saying that to depict undernourished Americans was unpatriotic. Another executive helpfully offered: "You could show undernourished Mexicans; no one cares about them." We did not make that film.

In the late spring of 1939, Van Dyke, Edward Anhalt, and Lee Dick, with the help of Jules Bucher, Hansel Mead, and Peter Stackpole, made *The Candid Camera*, a one-reel promotional film for Zeiss Cameras, in exchange for equipment and the cost of raw film. That summer Charlie Hunterhill, director of the film division at the New York advertising agency Batten, Barton, Durstine, and Osborn, hired the group to make a film for the New Hampshire Savings Bank Association and another for its Massachusetts counterpart. Steiner, Van Dyke, and Ted Lawrence (as editor) took the job. Based on Hunterhill's scripts, the two films were evidently straightforward and uninspired; they are not listed in the filmographies of Van Dyke's work. Disagreement over control of the unit and some unfortunate technical experience on the Massachusetts film conspired to make this the last Steiner-Van Dyke undertaking.[22] American Documentary Films had worked on its final project, and Van Dyke and Herbert Kerkow formed Documentary Film Productions. Their first sponsor was to be the Alfred P. Sloan Foundation.

Alfred P. Sloan, the president of General Motors, was the highest paid corporate executive in America in 1937, an outspoken advocate of the open shop, and notoriously complicit, at least indirectly, in antilabor espionage.[23] In 1939, the Sloan Foundation, run by Sloan's brother, produced a film directed by Walter Niebuhr, first titled *The Challenge*, then, in a shorter version, *Machine: Master or Slave?* Concerned with technological unemployment from the management point of view, the film posed the question of how management could "co-

---

and a list of each artist's films. Mary Losey actively sought film opportunities for Association members, and one frequently comes across letters between her and the Farm Security Administration about films on farm surpluses and nutrition (see, for example, her letters of 30 June and 26 Dec. 1940 to Jack Fisher at the FSA; National Archives), or reports of her presence at meetings between, for example, the Rockefeller-funded Film Center and the Association on public health films.

ordinate its own long-term self-interest with the needs of the workers and the consumer."[24] It was didactic, rudimentary, and dull, and the Sloan Foundation decided to try the subject again. With the intention that the new film and future films would become part of a series of teaching films on economics, the Foundation created and funded an Educational Film Institute at the New York University Film Library, and put Spencer Pollard, a former Rhodes Scholar and Harvard economist, in charge. Pollard asked John Ferno for two films, one on improvements in rural education in Kentucky, the other on agricultural surpluses and nutritional deficits. From Ivens he commissioned a film on economic frontiers in the West and gave the new film on technological unemployment to Van Dyke's and Kerkow's Documentary Film Productions. Together, Van Dyke and Pollard set to work on the outline and script for the latter film.

The result, *Valley Town*, is the film that Van Dyke likes best of all his productions, the film he feels to be most completely his. He, Roger Barlow, and Bob Churchill went on location in the early fall of 1939 in Lancaster, Pennsylvania, where employment was relatively high, and then on to Newcastle, Pennsylvania, one of the most depressed steel towns in the country: the mill was closed and two-thirds of the town was on relief. Early in the shooting, Van Dyke called on Irving Lerner for the editing. Lerner, who became very involved in the film, suggested composer Marc Blitzstein for the musical score; Blitzstein's popular opera *The Cradle Will Rock* had also focused on steel town unemployment. Ben Maddow, borrowed from Frontier Films once the shooting was completed, did the commentary—at white heat in one weekend. According to Van Dyke, these collaborators intended a film that, whether they thought of him or not, was unlikely to warm the heart of Alfred P. Sloan:

> The truth of the matter . . . is that there was a terrible revolution in steel, terrible as far as the workers were concerned, with high-speed machinery displacing as many as thirty workers, thirty-to-one. . . . For that to happen during a depression only accentuated that depression. And it's equally true that the companies never did a damned thing to help ease the shock. . . . And really that's what the film is about. . . . It tries to present those facts with sufficient emotion so that the audience will be moved by it.[25]

Van Dyke was in the habit of being home by 6:00 P.M. to listen to a favorite soap-opera serial in which Ray Collins of the Mercury Theatre portrayed a small-town druggist who agonized through his problems from Monday to Friday. Still intent on avoiding Lorentz's narrative style, Van Dyke postulated, "Well, *some* mayors are really concerned about their towns: why don't I write it from that point of view and get Ray Collins [to play the mayor]? And that's what I did." He also intended to experiment with an inner monologue for the unemployed worker and his wife, whom he found in Newcastle, but yielded to Blitzstein's refinement: a recitative as the man walked home, still jobless, lifting into song when he entered his house.[26]

Valley Town; a Study of Machines and Men, opens with the upper-story facade of an obsolete factory juxtaposed against a bleak sky, the factory completely black except for light behind the configuration of its jagged mouth, nose, and two eyes. A dissolve casts a dawn light over the facade, but makes it scarcely more assuring. We see other facades, then mound-shaped, decaying red-brick structures, discarded wheels, an unused wood-brick building, and an old brick furnace, the woods grown up around them. The mayor begins speaking on the second shot. Mayor for twenty years, he has watched "it happen, the way things change and change again." A typical Maddow touch follows: as we look at fallen bricks and at a collapsing stone entrance mocked by high weeds, we hear "I'm still the mayor of the town, a live town with living people." Wheels fill the frame, and the narration ceases a moment; then over a shot of two wheels he adds, "But I'm mayor of *this* town, too"—of the decay we see. Silence, and the camera holds for a moment to stress both this second town and the mayor's feeling of personal responsibility for it.

The sense of obsolescence and decay deepens. "I've seen it happen," the mayor continues, "the old mill closed, people moving away." And as he speaks, we see a large, jagged, blackened tombstone dominating the frame, behind it naked autumn trees and more tombstones.

And when the new mill opened, different men. They came a thousand miles, they came across an ocean, new men and new voices, another generation. The people came here to work the machines. Well the machines were changed, and the people were changed. It happened once in every man's lifetime, and sometimes twice. But then he got too old to move.

His words carry over gravestones marking steelworkers born in Scotland, Greece, Austria, Rumania, Germany, and Italy. Three more expensive tombstones follow, and a pan adds two that are even more costly. A dissolve takes us in close to another monument, carved with a stunning, detailed bas-relief of a factoryscape, set above a mill owner's resting place. The camera holds, then pans right to catch the actual factories of the town in the distance. The gravestones introduce the steelworkers in terms of death, and they unmistakably link that death to the work the dead have done and to the mill owner. This opening sequence is a masterful setting of mood and tone. In the sequences that follow, people go to work during good times; when changes are slow, men learn to adjust to new machines; steel mills open; workers flock to town; at Christmas the streets fill with shoppers. Then the Depression strikes, the wheels stop, and those who can afford it move on; stores close down, thousands are unemployed; new, high speed strip mills open, but they employ only one man for every thirty that were previously employed. We hear the thoughts of an unemployed worker and his wife; workmen watch the old mills torn down; they walk up to the old factories with which the film began to discuss and lament their situation, and the mayor draws conclusions in a voice-over.

Valley Town is very compact, its unity reinforced by parallel camera movements and positions. Each image has a striking integrity, and sound and image are dynamically related. The narration is forceful but does not dominate: several sequences, in fact, are without voice, and three of them are striking small symphonic movements of music and image. Following Copland's method in *The City*, Van Dyke joined piano and editing equipment and worked closely with Lerner and Blitzstein, "conceiving sections musically the whole time," especially in the first mill sequence: "It was shot as a ballet, edited as a ballet, and scored as a ballet."[27]

Despite the different musical styles of the sequences, the film is straight social documentary except for the recitative and song, which, by way of Blitzstein, are influenced by German expressionism. Stylistically the recitative and song are an intrusion, and some viewers resent the sequence intensely. I happen to find it very effective. It begins at the close of the highspeed strip mill sequence, when dramatically lighted images and shrill, punctuated celebrative music resolve themselves into three rather solemn chords and a distant shot of the unemployed worker on his way home. It is as if a strong shot of a dreary steelworker dragging past his wife into the house in the industrial city sequence of *The City* had tormented Van Dyke's mind. Here, working with an actual unemployed family, he could convey what it *felt like* to be out of work:[1] where *The City* was relatively shallow, he would assay depth.

---

[1] This was also a realization of his desire to direct nonactors, a desire frustrated on *The River*. For a year now, at Kazan's request, Van Dyke had been directing a boy's theater group at a settlement house on the Lower East Side. They wrote and put on a play about a sit-down strike. Van Dyke Buffalo interview.

In medium shot, then close-up on the man, the camera tracks backward at his pace as he plods toward home. He encounters idle acquaintances and a dog scrounging through a garbage can—images of his environment and equivalents of both his state of mind and his self-image.

What am I goin' home for? What th' devil am I goin' home for? Just to walk in the door, to say "No job again?" That what for? There he is, the old [word inaudible]. He used to have a job. Mrs. Cavonki—and Jack Cavonki way out in Pittsburgh, trying to land a job there. Well, *I'm here, I'm trying to keep the home together here!* Home, nice home. We got to get out of this dump, soon. Pete and Joe—we used to hang around together, workin' at the mill. But now, now I can't stand to look at their faces. They're thinkin' and *I'm thinkin', when is that mill going to open again? When do we work?* There's nothin' wrong with me. I can still work. I'm ok. Walk in the door, tell her the same old thing, tell her that again, see that look in her eyes again. I don't want to go home. What am I goin' home for? What th' devil am I goin' home for?

The interior scene is no happier. His wife tries to hide her disappointment as he comes in jobless once again. They sit at the table, the camera moving to extreme close-up on her intense unhappiness and on his hostile eyes as he looks up and resents the pain he knows is in her. On these shots her hidden thoughts explode into a piercing song:

You add up the pennies,
Finding there's always just not enough.
So far you can eat,
And over your head is some kind of roof.
And then you ask yourself, how long?
What happens after all you saved is gone?
....
Look at both of his hands
From not working so long.
Ohhhh, far away, there's a place
With work and joy and cheer,
Far away, oh far away from here.

The camera swiftly pans to a pail beneath the sink and holds on the water dripping into it, rendering the slow, silent, tense passage of time. The wife and a small daughter go to comfort a baby we hear, but do not see, crying. To the words, "I hear that they tell ya we're livin' in a wonderful age, the age of machines and gadgets and things," the husband leaves to put their new toaster in pawn. Hearing his departure, his wife comes to the door, kicks the rug against the crack, and with tears, thinks in song,

> They say they're tearing down the mills.
> Why if that was so I know then
> One day he'd walk right out of here
> And never come back to us again.

As her anguish continues, the camera explores the cracked wall, the broken window patched with cardboard, the dripping sink. She throws her head back against the door for a moment, then reenters the baby's room. The camera moves to the scrounging dog. Two men race to the scene of the falling mill. This sequence perfectly captures the anger, hostility, tension, despair, and deathlike, impoverished spirit that the opening sequence of the film so eloquently anticipated.

"Who built this place? What put us here?" the makers of *The City* managed to ask. But they were not allowed to answer. Under Pollard, Van Dyke felt more freedom, and as the defeated steelworkers thread the street and mount the hill, the mayor, vowing he will do what he can to help them, indicts and laments: "If only we had known, we might have been prepared. But the company never told us, never gave us notice far enough in advance." Framed against overgrown ruins and rusting machinery, against the earth and a meager fire kindled by one group of the workers, the men try to understand what has happened, and the use of their actual voices is a strong example of the film's humanizing process. Into their dialogue, the mayor now and then interjects his own comments:

> Well, we can't blame the machines. They do what they're told to do. They benefit a great many people in a great many towns. . . . Why should these men be thrown away as if they were obsolete? As if they were broken machines? . . . Yes, these men should have had notice, they should have been given dismissal wages, enough solid cash to tide them over and give them a start in another line, maybe another town. . . . It's the same way with millions of trained men . . . it's not a local problem, not these days. Our town by itself can't feed these men, can't afford to retrain them. It's a bigger thing than one mayor in one town can possibly handle. It's a national problem. I know it. New machinery can do a lot of damage unless the right policies go with it.

Simultaneous with the mayor's final remarks, we see close-ups of the displaced workmen—straight-on, respectful shots giving us time to study their sadness, their frustration, and their dignity. At least unconsciously, Van Dyke must have had in mind here the final bland, hopeful children's faces of *The City*, the faces of the happy, well-cared-for, new generation. There the last, long-held shot consists of a boy's face, his hair blowing in the wind. Here, the parallel and more truthful final shot is the somber, tough face of a man of twenty-five confronting unemployment—his hair also blown by the wind. What will he do? He is more kin to the young worker putting the shot at the end of *People of the Cumberland* than he is to the young working fathers of the Green City.

Valley Town was premiered on 14 May 1940, at the Steel Workers' Organizing Committee[m] Convention in Chicago, where, Van Dyke recalls, it was warmly received, much to the displeasure of Sloan. The July 1940 issue of *Film News* subsequently announced:

> Production of documentary films at the Educational Film Institute of New York University has suddenly been suspended and crews called in from the field. . . . Simultaneously the Institute's three completed productions have been recalled for revision. . . . The reasons given are economic and cultural changes due to war and national preparedness.

Ferno's Kentucky film, *And So They Live*, and a second Kentucky film, *The Children Must Learn*, which Van Dyke had been called in to make, had been previewed in April, and together with *Valley Town*, they were now pulled out of circulation. Ivens and Floyd Crosby had only begun shooting for the economic frontiers project out in Colorado. Ferno, whose film had been in production for six weeks, was on location in Peoria County, Illinois. All were notified that their employment was at an end.[28]

For Ferno, this was the second blow under Sloan/Educational Film Institute sponsorship, and Van Dyke, unfortunately, had played a role in the delivery of the first blow. Pollard had either viewed some Ferno rushes from Kentucky or had simply heard rumors of dissension— townspeople being upset, the crew not working well. Consequently, when *Valley Town* production bogged down, he sent Van Dyke and Churchill to another section of Kentucky to make their own version of Ferno's film. The filmmakers tramped through the woods, helped build a privy, and sat in the schoolroom with their cameras for a week

[m] Later the Steelworkers of America, CIO.

before beginning shooting. They came away with a sensitive film that showed both the poignancy and the dignity of the lives of the mountain people and described the new school curriculum designed to help the children overcome the poor health and farming habits of their ancestors. They finished the film before Ferno returned and edited his own, an equally touching film that portrayed the damaged lives more poignantly and in the end was more pessimistic about the future of the poor farmers and their children than Van Dyke's had been. Van Dyke has regrets:

> I should have called Johnny and said, "Johnny, tell me, . . . what is the problem? Are you in difficulties? Anything I can do to help?" instead of grabbing a camera and running down and making another movie. I was anxious to make the movie, but . . . I had some kind of responsibility to my fellow filmmaker, to talk to him about it.

Ferno felt this lack of trust, this willingness to put sponsor before colleague, and he let Van Dyke know it.[29]

The Sloan Foundation would not commit itself to renewal of its grant to New York University's Educational Film Institute, pleading "changed income expectations due to war." That was the official reason. But *Film News* announced:

> There is a report, however, of dissatisfaction with the critical tenor of films and scripts on hand in view of changed world conditions. War and national defense, it is said, make necessary a more constructive approach to economic material. . . . Epilogues providing "more constructive" solutions to problems presented in the completed films are now being prepared; scripts for contemplated productions are being revised.

It was the critical tenor of *Valley Town* that sent Sloan looking at the Ferno and Ivens scripts, and it was hardly surprising that he did not like what he saw there either: his brother was subsequently discharged as Foundation head. But some of the filmmakers were not quite so easily dismissed. Deprived of their livelihoods without compensation, Ferno, Ivens, and members of their crews initiated actions against New York University and the Sloan Foundation. In December they reached a settlement calling for "the payment of salaries for the unexpired period of employment."[n] But if the Foundation lost on the

---

[n] The Sloan-established Educational Film Institute did try very hard to find a sponsor to finish Ferno's film. The National Archives has letters from Mary Losey to the Farm Security Administration, from E. Ashley Bayne to the Department of Agriculture, and

salary issue, it had its way on the completed films and on future production. *And So They Live* and *The Children Must Learn* were released in December or January, the commentary on the former "revised by Edwin Locke," the latter unrevised. Not until December 1941 did the Sloan Foundation renew its grant to the New York University Film Library to distribute Foundation-sponsored films.[30] No new films were to be sponsored through the Educational Film Institute, and only one new Sloan-backed film, *The Bridge*, was to be produced by the Foreign Policy Foundation. This film went to Ben Maddow and Willard Van Dyke for filming in South America.

Valley Town was revised. Van Dyke, who was laboring under the illusion that he had been given a certain amount of freedom, was, I think, taken by surprise when the film was called in. But he did not fight. It hurt that a sponsor was again weakening one of his films—this time drastically—and it hurt that he found himself acceding: "It hurt, because, among other things, Marc Blitzstein [then also under contract for *Native Land*], whom I liked very much, was absolutely furious at me and felt that I had really sold a piece of work down the river and I was a whore."[31] Frontier Films was angry at him for taking Maddow away, Ferno was angry because of the Kentucky film, and Blitzstein was furious at him for not standing up for his own film—all of this must have given him some pause.

The revision of *Valley Town* was made to sound legitimate. With defense production vastly increased, the government was training skilled workers, and unemployment was shriveling. Over shots of men at work in the defense plants, the new epilogue argues that although the economic situation has improved, the lesson of *Valley Town* remains: always plan for job retraining.

But the revisers did more than add an epilogue. Van Dyke, who participated in the revision, recalls that they found the woman's voice too sharp and bitter, and insisted on a change. Although I do not believe that this change was ever made, for the voices sound much the same on the two sound tracks, a more crucial alteration was imposed: on the original print, it is Ray Collins's voice that is sharpest, sometimes ironic, slightly abrasive, and it is not Ray Collins's voice that appears on the revised print. In the new version, the mayor's voice is much toned down, less accentuated.

The revised film opens with a shot tracking through a room to a window overlooking the town: there is no music, for Blitzstein composed no new music for the new material. This shot is then followed

from Spencer Pollard to the Federal Surplus Commodities Corporation. Bayne also looked into other possibilities, including the Sears Roebuck Agricultural Foundation.

by the panning shots of the town from above that follow the final graveyard shot in the original. The entire opening sequence is gone. Also gone is the wife's final song as she stands against the door. The revisers either felt that the sequence was too long or too moving, or they felt uncomfortable with the suggestion that unemployed fathers might be driven to abandon their families. The epilogue plays havoc with the final sequence of the original, which is now cut up and rearranged, with much material eliminated. The men among the rusted machinery are no longer sensitively portrayed, and all the final close-ups are gone, except for the last—kept, I suspect, for the sake of the film's concluding chords. As the epilogue narration takes over, we lose not only the tough dialogue between the workers but also all of the mayor's words that directly indict the companies.°

The film's carefully crafted structure was destroyed in order to present the viewer with a different perspective. The original film tells of company negligence, of people who do not give a damn for other people, and it implies the need for laws and contracts that enforce fairness. The second is milder: the war has improved matters; let us continue to retrain men after peace returns. In the interests of national harmony, of harmony with management, and of harmony with Alfred P. Sloan, the revisers removed what needed most to be remembered.

The original *Valley Town* is now distributed by the Museum of Modern Art, and the revised Sloan version is in bad condition at the Film Library at New York University. But the original was not at first available, and what if it were not available now? I find myself wondering whether it would be better to have the revised version than none at all. Is it better that Van Dyke went along than to have lost the film altogether? And if so, better for whom? In failing to do battle, was Van Dyke failing to point a way for the documentary filmmakers who wished to make tough, committed films but who could survive only with the help of sponsors? Would not a refusal, with all the litigation and stink it would cause, have been more positive than the availability of a film on the necessity of training skilled labor? My disappointment (a disappointment that I believe Van Dyke shares with me) is not, as Richard Griffith's was, that a potential sponsor dried up because someone made too political and too experimental a film.[32] Rather, it is more akin to Marc Blitzstein's criticism that Van Dyke was unable to stand up for the artistic and political integrity of his work.

In the years immediately following *Valley Town*, Van Dyke was one of the most active members of the documentary community, lecturing,

---

° There are other more minor revisions that are unnecessary to describe here.

teaching, leading discussions, writing, and serving as officer and board member of the Association of Documentary Film Producers. Although major assignments were hard to come by and he was to make no films of the stature of *The City* and *Valley Town*, his group, Documentary Film Productions, still managed a decent number of commissions. There were three more films in 1940. One, first titled *Design for Education*, was eventually simply called *Sarah Lawrence*. Van Dyke and Kerkow made an advertising film for General Mills, *The Year's Work*, that caused "a major sensation in the sponsored film field," breaking "down the operating figures of a big company into what the cold integers and fractions mean in terms of men, women, and work." And he and Bob Churchill made a color film for the Whitehead Brothers Company that combined a geological history of sand deposits, the story of the first American foundries, and a contemporary "survey of quarrying sand and its industrial uses."[33]

Nineteen forty-one brought a contract from the Film Division of Cultural and Commercial Relations with South America for a film entitled *Democracy at Play*, with Van Dyke and Joseph Losey producing and Ferno directing. But the money did not come through, and the film was never made. In July, Documentary Film Productions finished a film on social welfare work for the New Jersey Children's Home Society, *The Children Next Door*, for which I have been unable to find any credits. Geza Karpathi and Ricky Leacock brought folk music footage from the Kentucky mountains, and Lerner thought a film could be made around it; Van Dyke joined in, and the result was *To Hear Your Banjo Play*, with Pete Seeger as narrator and performer. When the original sponsor (a government information agency),[34] buried the film because of Seeger's politics, Tom Brandon rescued it. Interested in more such films, Brandon, Maddow, and Van Dyke went south on Labor Day weekend to make *Tall Tales*, a story in which three folk singers sing to each other around a bunkhouse. The last film by Documentary Film Productions was *Here is Tormorrow*. Produced for the Cooperative League of the USA, this is a three-reel film that explains the advantages of cooperative marketing and production. Maddow wrote the script, Van Dyke shot the opening sequence, and Roger Barlow, Kerkow, and Lerner completed the film as Maddow and Van Dyke departed for South America to make *The Bridge*.[35]

Did the experience on *Valley Town* make it less likely in these films and the films to follow that Van Dyke would "try for something strong again?" I asked him this late in our final interview, and he tried to puzzle out the answer. He had told G. Roy Levin in 1970 that all his films had been sponsored by organizations, that he "never had money enough to make the films that [he] wanted to make." In 1973 he had told James Blue that filmmakers who fell into making bland, not quite honest films for the Office of War Information[p] had hurt themselves as filmmakers for good:

The job was to make strategic films to be sent overseas primarily to our allies to explain what kind of people Americans were. . . . And we made a series of films false to the truth about America, but we felt so strongly that this was the way they had to be made, because . . . well, God, you had to beat Hitler. But they were false. . . . You know, you can't remain a whore for three years and then be a virgin again. You just can't.

And he told his interviewers from *Film Culture* in 1956 that the "atmosphere of fear" of the postwar era had kept sponsors and filmmakers tame. He feels now, he told me, that after the late thirties

the kind of film that I did . . . was to a large extent a kind of journeyman film: good, and every once in a while something would kind of flash in it that looked as if, if that had been sustained, it would have been a work of some quality—some distinction. But mainly you can just sort of see through them down underneath some kind of quality that you wondered wasn't out there in front.[36]

Was *Valley Town* the starting point for his inability to sustain his stronger qualities?

It would be very hard to say, but I suspect that the kind of struggle that emerged out of *Valley Town* and having to revise it and so forth—was somehow traumatic. *The Bridge* didn't turn out to be as interesting and good as I expected and partly at least that was because the war intervened. . . . During the war, I felt as if I were making things that were not true pictures of America, and I felt that continued afterward. I never saw an opportunity again to make a film that had the bite.[q] And at least partially that's my own fault.

What Van Dyke describes happened to nearly everyone: the forties and fifties are not marked by many courageous documentary films. Yet

[p] See Richard Barsam, *Nonfiction Film—A Critical History* (New York: E. P. Dutton & Co., Inc., 1973), p. 219, for agreement with Van Dyke about the content of these very well-made films.

[q] In 1963, the United States Information Agency asked Van Dyke for a film on the situation of black Americans. When he screened the rough cut for USIA, they were pleased to see that he had portrayed the United States as having put all its force on the side of integration, but they were uncomfortable when they saw that he had also depicted black Americans speaking out about persecution and inequities. While Van Dyke was away on another film, USIA requested the film from his office and then buried it in a vault. Van Dyke Buffalo interview.

he is reluctant to lay all the blame on the era, for "there are other people who have just simply gone ahead and done it anyway. And maybe I should have. I didn't." As he talked, he decided that he was "too competitive, too tough-minded for" the *Valley Town* experience "to have had any lasting effect." He was affected more by personal and career decisions, he thought: his first children were born at the turn of the decade, he began to feel family responsibilities, believed that private schools were necessary for his offspring who were growing up in New York City, and a stable reputation and consistent income became more important than taking risks on films for which he couldn't find sponsors.[37] If he can indeed be faulted for making films "without bite,"ᵣ then the fault and its causes are common ones.

One of our most professional and skillful documentarists, Van Dyke has worked with, taught, and influenced numbers of other talented filmmakers. Especially during the sixties and early seventies as Director of the Film Study Center at the Museum of Modern Art, he was a staunch, open-minded supporter of fellow filmmakers (and, from my own experience, of scholars and critics who came to him for help). In his recent interview with Van Dyke, James Blue praised him highly for the encouragement the Museum had given to the new American cinema. Van Dyke replied,

> I especially like the film that bears the stamp of the intention of the filmmaker, the creative stamp of somebody who says, "I made this because I had to make it or because I wanted to make it." And partially that may be because a documentary filmmaker always is constricted somewhat by the subject material and by the political thing that surrounds him and by the needs or demands of the sponsor. He's always, or almost always, working under certain kinds of constrictions. The breath of fresh air comes when a man says, "I'm going to make my movie the way I want to make my movie."[38]

And so he has facilitated in others what he could not always facilitate in his own work, the experience of his own constriction becoming a nurturing force for others.

Lorentz and *The Fight for Life*

Although Pare Lorentz had to worry about congressional opponents to the New Deal's use of the media, and although he had to fight for

---

ᵣ I am taking Van Dyke's word about his films. I have seen few of them. His filmography

adequate funding and struggle with government bureaucracy, he was blessed with the fact that he was working in close ideological harmony with his sponsor, the Roosevelt administration. By spring 1938, he had another project underway.

Late in April 1938, he voyaged to London, where he showed *The River* at the annual screening of work by Grierson's General Post Office Unit; he then put the film into distribution throughout the country. Although *The River* was well received, *World Film News* and some others raised the old and by now familiar criticism: there were no people in it. Probably spurred by such comment and by Shelley Hamilton's observation that "the third part of a natural trilogy would be about the people," and perhaps driven by the impulse behind the sharecropper scene in *The River*, Lorentz was already at work on *Ecce Homo!* His recent attempt at a short novel, which depicted the experience of a North Carolinian he had met a few years before, now became the starting point for a film on technological unemployment that would trace the migrations of four workers through the United States. His staff had provided research before he left for England. Lorentz completed a script outline on the *Queen Mary* in the second week of May and reached New York eager to begin.[39]

The CBS Workshop gave him a chance to try his script as a radio play on 21 May. Thomas Chalmers narrated, and Van Heflin spoke the main part of Worker No. 7790 who reminisces about his past up through the early days of the Depression. Later, he and three other migrant workers tell their stories at a Kansas crossroads gas station. When the same program, slightly revised and retitled *Job to be Done*, was broadcast by the BBC a month or so later, the *World Film News* reviewer saw it as a significant step forward: "It was said of *The River* that it humanised nothing. *Job to be Done* humanises a lot. . . . The personal intimate stories . . . make this one of the best bits of radio of the summer."[40]

The half-hour radio play grew to a two-hour feature film script in which the characters of the other three men were combined into No. 7790 in order to eliminate dialogue. The script ended with a New Deal upbeat: a call for the Grand Coulee dam project in the Columbia River Valley to lead to area development patterned on the TVA. Roosevelt was delighted, urged Lorentz to speed ahead, and gave him key support for the founding of the United States Film Service.[s] When the

---

shows that they are interesting and that they are often socially conscious films, and it is possible that he is being overly modest.

[s] The story of the creation and demise of the U.S. Film Service is an interesting one. Although not germane to my purposes, it is well told by Richard Dyer MacCann in *The People's Films: A Political History of U.S. Government Motion Pictures* (New York:

Film Service was established in August, Lorentz and Floyd Crosby, its director of photography, went on location in industrial plants in the Midwest, at TVA, and on the West Coast. But the filming was at first delayed by insufficient funds and then halted when Lorentz went to another project in the late spring of 1939; although he made efforts to resume production, the film was never completed.[41]

Lorentz's project in 1939 and 1940 was *The Fight for Life*. Roosevelt wanted at least one film to dramatize the need for the general health program he planned to submit to Congress. This intention coincided with the desire of Paul de Kruif, the great public health crusader and author, to carry his ideas to people who were unlikely to read his books. Highly impressed with *The River*, de Kruif offered the film rights to any of his books to the United States Public Health Service free of charge, with but one stipulation: that Lorentz make the picture. He and Lorentz met and agreed that Lorentz would film one of the stories from de Kruif's *The Fight for Life*, the story of the Chicago Maternity Center, which had been founded in 1895 by Doctor Joseph B. De Lee.[42]

Lorentz was drawn to the Maternity Center story for a number of reasons. He had been strongly moved by de Kruif's description of a hemorrhaging mother smiling up at a helpless doctor and saying, "You won't let me die, will you?" and he was appalled by the U.S. statistics on infant and mother mortality, which had scarcely improved in a quarter of a century, at least partly because of the inadequate training of obstetricians. These truths, he later wrote to Robert Snyder, were "the major reason for the film." With their nine thousand deliveries without a death, Dr. De Lee and his successors were an inspiring model. In addition, the location of the Center would enable Lorentz to continue exploring one of the basic themes of *Ecce Homo!*: his months of filming in industrial cities had convinced him that it was extremely important to show the poverty that he found there. Whatever other illness they had, Lorentz recalls, in 1938 75 percent of the Cook County Hospital patients suffered from malnutrition. He would not have made the film had he "not been allowed to broaden it to give some indication of the unemployment and living conditions as prevailed then." His early outrage against private, self-interested, and negligent institutions had not abated,[t] and he was particularly drawn

---

Hastings House, 1973) and by Robert L. Snyder in *Pare Lorentz and the Documentary Film* (Norman: University of Oklahoma Press, 1968).

[t] It was not coincidental that at this time the Film Service was producing *Power and the Land*, a film supporting consumers' cooperatives to bring rural electricity to the farmers in areas where the power utilities had refused to do so. Recall Lorentz's 1928 article on utility companies (see Chapter II).

to De Lee's pioneering work in establishing the Maternity Center separately from the other hospitals of Chicago. Finally, it is possible that as a result of his father's death in 1937 and with Lorentz's own approach to his mid-thirties—he would be thirty-four in December 1939—there had been some stock taking. The young intern in the film, he told Bosley Crowther, "goes through the tortures of doubt—first doubt of himself, his profession, and then doubt of the economic system." Although there was no pat conclusion, he added, the experience carried "certain philosophic overtones."[43]

The Fight for Life was the first time Lorentz worked with professional actors—possibly with an eye to future employment in Hollywood.[u] The three principals were played by Myron McCormick as the young intern and Will Geer and Storrs Haynes as the presiding doctors at the Maternity Center. For six weeks prior to filming, this trio was trained in every detail of the Center, living with the interns, McCormick reported, and learning "their ways and their minds until we behaved and thought as they did,"[44] a strategy that made them, in the opinion of some critics, virtually indistinguishable from the supporting cast of nonactors.[v] Dudley Digges played the old doctor, based on De Lee, and Dorothy Adams and Dorothy Urban played the mother and the old woman in the hemorrhage sequence filmed on set in Hollywood.

After some private viewings, *The Fight for Life* opened at the Belmont Theatre in New York on 6 March 1940 to a two-month run and highly laudatory reviews, including Archer Winsten's prediction that "there will be no better motion picture made in 1940" and Frank Nugent's observation that Lorentz had brought to the film "a journalist's objectivity, a dramatist's passions, a crusader's indignation." All this brought numerous bids for the privilege of distribution, with the government eventually deciding to award the contract to Columbia Pictures.[45]

The prologue has two sequences. In the first, a baby is born in a hospital delivery room, but the mother, despite the presence of three doctors and three nurses, dies of acute heart failure. O'Donnell, the young intern in the second sequence, walks the night in great pain over this death and the state of his profession. He drops into a chair in the office of the head doctor of Chicago City Hospital, who has no easy answers to O'Donnell's despair, laments that medical training is

---

[u] Richard Dyer MacCann says "it seems clear that he was trying to impress the film world" (*The People's Films*, p. 99). In 1938, Lorentz had declined a contract worth $1,500 a week (W. L. White, "Pare Lorentz," *Scribner's*, Jan. 1939, p. 11).

[v] This is one aspect of a very interesting production story that may be found in more detail in Robert Snyder's *Pare Lorentz and the Documentary Film*.

so limited—only four of the fifty in O'Donnell's class will get a hospital residency—and sends the young intern to learn in a place "in the slums where two young doctors are bringing modern science to the poor women of the city." The story proper then unfolds, the double tale of the work of the Maternity Center and of O'Donnell's education. We observe him in the early stages of training, then watch him accompany Dr. Hanson in a successful delivery. A montage of assignment boards indicates a number of such experiences in homes of various ethnic-minority families, and then we witness him and Dr. Ballou at the conclusion of a delivery, we follow his involvement in an emergency case in which a pregnant woman nearly goes blind, and finally we accompany him to his own case: after a successful birth, the mother hemorrhages, and aided by Hanson and Ballou, O'Donnell saves her. The contrast with the prologue is stressed by a repeated pattern of intensive close-ups.

In many ways this film was an important departure for Lorentz. At moments it is difficult to believe that the same filmmaker also made *The Plow That Broke the Plains* and *The River*. No other non-Holly-wood film of the thirties holds the camera so long on the actors, so thoroughly explores the possibilities of the fluid camera, or so sub-stantially develops the dramatic potential of the single shot. The result is striking: *The Fight for Life* is a film that is remarkably trusting of its setting and people, a film that comes close to the way we experience life. This quality is most evident in the two scenes where we wait with the drab women in their slum apartments. They pace the floor, and the prologue's pulsing heartbeat motif sets in, over it a tender, low, soothing, flowing cello melody, a combination that conveys the tension of waiting, the inherent danger in the birth that is to come, and the warmth of the environment created by the doctors, the nurse, and the mother herself. The doctors doze or read and watch the woman from their chairs, while she dominates their and our thoughts, moving in and out of, or back and forth in, the frame in a long-held, unmoving camera shot, or controlling camera movement with her own movement in other lengthy shots. The pain comes, and horns blare and blare again as the doctors act; the heartbeat motif intensifies, other musical instruments enter the sound track, and all reach an intense pitch and pace as the delivery begins. Here we find a suspense and involvement as affective as anything that exists in the cinema of the thirties.

In O'Donnell's prologue night-walk scene, after the hospital death, he steps into the night rain and, in a complex and powerful sequence that one critic thought "alone would mark Pare Lorentz one of the real geniuses of the screen,"[46] the young intern passes through the down-town Chicago streets. He moves by the large show windows filled with fashionable women's clothes, surrounded by rich, lively displays of summer vacation scenes by beaches and of chefs preparing elegant restaurant meals, and finally passes a florist's window, with flowers for all occasions, including a funeral. Against this poignant backdrop, and in a low, stunned, almost bitter tone, the young doctor meditates the mother's death.

Lorentz was very definite about the music he needed for this night-walk sequence. When Louis Gruenberg could not compose it,[w] he turned to Joe Sullivan's jazz band. His original instructions to Gruenberg are worth quoting at length:

> Start a gut-bucket, barrel-house, gin mill, Rampart Street, belly-rub, low-down, double-shuffle, boogie-woogie, jug-band blues—call it what you like it's the old Bessie Smith, one-handed piano player blues—the blues played by the illiterate gulf-coast negroes who had no left hand—who hit the bass with their left thumbs to make sure, and then hit the rest of the chord off-beat; the method, so-called, of Fats Waller.
>
> It is a slow time, with deliberate off-beat; it is a hot, crowded saloon with ten cent gin, wanton, weary, bedeviled men and women . . .
>
> I feel, then, that we start one piano under the intern; that we start another piano as he walks out of the hospital; that the minute he hits the street, we suddenly hit the audience in the face with gin, women, despair, cruelty and life, as crude as it is.
>
> Now, here the words create a symphonic pattern. The words themselves carry the meaning and the tempo;—the film and the music continue, not in monotony, but without variation, until that very savage, unrelieved, 4/4 time creates a frightening city . . .
>
> My man is all-important;—he doesn't know where he is . . .
>
> He is drinking gin and talking to himself. He doesn't know there is an orchestra in the room—he doesn't know there are wanton women around him; he pays no attention to the whores, the savage, primitive emotions; he is worried over his own soul, and the noise merely gives him a background against which to retire.[47]

For it is not simply the death over which the young intern despairs. The death is part of something larger that O'Donnell must come to

---

[w] Lorentz worked for twenty-two weeks with Gruenberg, creating an original score for the film. Gruenberg, who had written the music for both *Stagecoach* and the opera *Emperor Jones*, found that his propensities as a composer made it impossible for him to create the music Lorentz needed for this particular sequence. See Snyder, *Pare Lorentz and Documentary*, p. 110.

grips with, the blues at their deepest: "gin, women, despair, *cruelty and life*, as crude as it is."

Later, after Ballou, O'Donnell, and the nurse have completed the successful delivery, lullaby music takes a slightly muted tone as they descend the stairs, and then a new city music blends in and takes over as they enter an alleyway and pause to watch children playing in the wreckage of a house. They leave the alleyway and see a ragamuffin stop just in time to avoid being run over. "Why," O'Donnell asks grimly, "do we bring them into the world?" And so begins the day-walk sequence that Richard Griffith, who did not like the film, thought "searchingly bitter and tragic" and that Lorentz thought was perhaps the best thing he had ever done.[48]

The film's power derives in part from the restraint with which the slum lives have been handled up to this point. We have seen the exhausted faces and the shabby clothing of the women, we have followed the car that carried the doctors through the ruined streets, and we have entered the deteriorating tenements, but none of this deprivation has been stressed. Now, as the three walk the streets, O'Donnell assertively and movingly develops his question:

> We tell our mothers: Give them plenty of milk to drink. We say: Feed them Cod Liver oil and orange juice and green vegetables. We say: Keep them clean, and dress them warmly to fight off influenza and pneumonia. We teach them: The sun will make them strong against rickets and help fight T.B. But where do we tell them to go for the green vegetables? Where do we tell them to move for the sunshine?

After a few more words, a poignant, swelling music commences, and O'Donnell pauses and points—"There is a house in America"—and the camera pans left across a rubble-filled lot to a distant tenement standing alone. The sequence is stepped up cinematically, as the camera sweeps over rows of dilapidated nightmarish homes, while O'Donnell continues in voice-over: "They brought them into all our great cities from the hills and fields to build their machines and roll their steel. And left them in *these* shacks." Here the battered, patched, broken shacks come stunningly to represent the physical condition of their inhabitants: we see them and learn that "here are bad teeth and tainted blood and infected lungs. Here are damaged kidneys and cracked hearts and twisted legs." Scavengers pick rotted food behind warehouses containing millions of pounds of surplus food, while "there are children in this city who never in their lifetime have eaten a decent meal." With overtones of direct accusation, the final, distant shot in the market area holds while a woman scavenger pushes her dolly slowly from frame right to left, past a fruit and vegetable salesman and beneath a large warehouse sign with the words "Company," "Morgan," "fruit and vegetable," and "Burlington Route."

O'Donnell has learned his profession. But something is still missing: he needs to know *why* he is dedicating himself to such a vocation in a world that seems hopeless. If it is no longer the bedeviled night world, it is nevertheless a world that remains overwhelmingly damaging, defeating, chaotic, and unjust. Again he is answered by an older doctor. They pause at the Maternity Center door, and Ballou responds to all we have seen and heard: "Well, it is a time of sadness and trouble; of worn-out ideas and weary people. But since the beginning of medicine, it has been the business of the doctor and the scientist to heal the sick wherever and however he found them. No matter what doubts you have—if you doubt this purpose, you doubt medicine itself."

Inside, O'Donnell and Ballou must turn around for an emergency call to a "steel shack" south of the city where a woman is losing her sight. As O'Donnell waits in a hospital lab for the results of her blood and urine tests, the lesson deepens. The scene is highly charged, the lighting on the lab technician very dramatic. And here we have the only narration (as opposed to dialogue) in the film, a fact that lends even more force to its incantatory tone, spoken in the voice of the head doctor at City Hospital. This voice relates that the endangered woman has inherited "a legacy freely given; all the knowledge of the legions of unknown men of science." The technician running the routine test is not alone, it continues, "he's working with Dobson and Minkowski, Fehling and Bright, Wolhard and Fahr, Benedict and Van Slyke, working with the unbroken line of men against death."

Lorentz's memorandum to Gruenberg tells us why he has given such tonal emphasis to this sequence, for here in this lab are evoked models of quiet, dedicated workers who are fighting against great odds: "Now she is in the hands of a thousand men who worked unknown to bring the meaning of life to the world. . . . Her blood is the blood of humanity, and the *servants of the people* have her life in their hands."[49] [Italics mine.] The meaning of life—the answer to O'Donnell's existential questions—rests in acting as such a servant, in helping to create patterns of order among the cruel and chaotic life of the sick city, in transcending the self-centeredness of other members of the profession and the corruption of the health-care institutions. O'Donnell is now prepared in every way to face the postpartem hemorrhage.

In all three of his films, Lorentz was fascinated by immense forces and by the professional and technical know-how that he thought could bring them under control. His films themselves—for which he hired the best professionals and over which he exercised his own meticulous care—were meant to be living examples of such professional skill, and he intended them to help control the forces they portrayed.[x] But *The Plow That Broke the Plains* and *The River* had been epic films, ultimately more celebrative in nature, charged with the power of the land, the river, of America's size and industry. Now it was as if he had moved in close to study one small, uncompromising, dedicated group of soil conservationists or engineers. The day-walk sequence is more powerful than anything in the first two films and it is even more effective than the industrial city sequence in *The City* because the voices come from men we can relate to—men whose deep feelings rise from involvement with the people and the slums. In the midst of the malnutrition and tuberculosis, here are *heroes*—Ballou, Hanson, O'Donnell and others like them—quiet, obscure men intensely at work, and choosing to work with poverty both *because of* and *in spite of* overwhelming circumstances. Here are the "philosophic overtones" Lorentz promises. We are in the presence of unassuming and inspiring figures who strive to cure because for them there is simply no other alternative.

For Lorentz there is something sacred about this, and one should not fail to perceive a subtle but significant referent in the film. The first shot following the prologue tilts down from the sky to a street, across which a man dashes to call the Maternity Center. In the distance, in almost exactly center frame, is a church. In the final shot of the film, the three doctors drive down a similar street, and we see another church in the same position. The film ends when their car is directly below the church. If there *is* a design to the universe, then the message seems to be that these doctors are in touch with it.

Ivens and *Power and the Land*

In the sponsored film field there are several alternative paths for politically conscious filmmakers to follow. They may, with effort and luck, find sponsors with whom they are in accord, as Frontier Films did on *People of the Cumberland*, as Lorentz did with the Resettlement Administration and the Farm Security Administration, and as the filmmakers on *The City* and *Valley Town* thought they had done. The

---

[x] In an ungenerous review at the time he began *The Fight for Life*, Lorentz indicted Kline and Ivens for failing to control cinematically the immense topics they had taken on in *Crisis* and *The 400 Million* respectively. See Lorentz, "Movies," *McCall's*, June 1939, pp. 4, 87. Also in Lorentz, *Lorentz on Film: Movies 1927 to 1941* (New York: Hopkinson and Blake, 1975), pp. 164-165.

other paths are more problematic. The filmmakers may insist upon
their own style and values even if they are in direct conflict with those
of their sponsors. But here—aside from the obvious likelihood of losing
the film in a direct clash—they must also consider the ethical issues:
Is it right to accept a project one does not believe in, take a salary,
and betray the sponsor? A third direction is for the filmmakers to
divorce their politics and social values from their work and make films
for sponsors regardless of whether they agree or disagree with the
views they are representing. After a while they stop disagreeing, however, or the strain takes a toll on their technique and soul, as Margaret
Bourke-White discovered when her social views altered in the early
thirties and drove her from a career as an eager, successful advertising
photographer.

Some Hollywood leftists of the thirties and forties are among the
best known examples of the strain of this alternative, although they
had not wished to divorce their work from their politics. Herbert Kline
attended a gathering of politically conscious people in the industry in
1936, and heard Donald Ogden Stewart's poignant confession:

> As I remember it we writers were very, very bitter, we were
> very, very disillusioned, and we were above all determined to tell
> the truth about life. That was twelve years ago. I don't know
> whether or not any of you have seen my two latest contributions
> to the screen. One was a vehicle for Marion Davies entitled "Going
> Hollywood" and the other was Miss Crawford's "No More Ladies."
> That isn't exactly what I meant twelve years ago. It isn't as funny
> as that . . . and I am not really blaming the movies for my downfall.
> Nobody came to me with a revolver and said, "You've got to take
> this big salary and have three automobiles and live in this goddam
> sunshine." It's my fault and I simply want to say a few words about
> my present situation and particularly why I am here tonight.[50]

Few cases are cut and dried, and often these are subtle, difficult,
sometimes excruciating matters. Nor are absolute stands called for in
every case. It is possible, as with *The City*, to start a film one believes
in and to continue for the most part to believe in it even when one
learns that some limits will be imposed upon one's politics and vision.
Joris Ivens' next film is another case in point.

In June 1939, Ivens received a call from Pare Lorentz: Would he
be interested in directing a film for the Rural Electrification Administration of the Department of Agriculture? It was the REA's aim to
interest small farmers, denied power by the private utilities, in forming
a cooperative to buy generators and lines from the government on a

low-interest loan. Before this could be done, however, the farmers had to be made more aware of this possibility and its benefits. Lorentz had drawn up an outline and Charles Walker had developed a script: the idea was to film working days on a farm both before and after electrification. Ivens agreed to take the job. It was an opportunity to know more of America than just New York and Hollywood, and it sounded relaxing after the tensions of Spain and China. He liked Lorentz's courage in wanting to hire the maker of the outspoken *New Earth, Borinage, The Spanish Earth,* and *The 400 Million,* especially since Lorentz ran into "some difficulties" in doing so, although evidently nothing very serious.[51]

The writer Ed Locke joined Ivens in Hollywood, where they put together their own preliminary outline, then set out, with cameraman Arthur Ornitz, to find an average, representative farm without noticeable regional characteristics, one "not too poor and not too rich." In July they lodged in the St. Clairsville, Ohio hotel, about six miles from the farm of Bill and Hazel Parkinson. Three weeks later, when suspicions of "these Hollywood people" had dwindled thanks to Ivens' engaging personality, he was invited to install himself and his equipment at the farm. His rapport with the Parkinsons gave him deep satisfaction and reaffirmed the vital sympathies and values upon which he had based his recent films: "I see how much they taught me. They had a direct feeling about the earth, a feeling about their own land. In the evenings, sitting around the fire I talked about Russia and about the wars in Spain and China where the people had to fight for their own land." As "the whole relationship became closer and closer," they went to dance Saturday nights in the miners' Union hall.[52]

A very large portion of *Power and the Land* was reenactment by nonactors. Fascinated by the problems any director faces in working with nonprofessionals and encouraged by Pudovkin's success in this area, Ivens adopted ploys to capture natural behavior, and the film testifies to his overall success. In accordance with his aesthetics in *The Spanish Earth,* he told the Parkinsons what he wanted done but refused to act it out for them, wanting them to behave and move with their own traits and rhythms. Alert to sensitive spots in family relations, he and his crew avoided intruding on them. They learned not to insult the professional pride of Parkinson by asking him, for instance, for the sake of a close-up, to milk an already milked cow. In addition, they sought to center scenes around activities that the family enjoyed: for instance, two long-held shots toward the end of the film give Parkinson space and time to set up his motor and begin sharpening his tool blades.[53]

Ivens worked well with Ed Locke, but, uncertain of the abilities of the young cameraman, Ornitz, and bothered by bad rushes, he was not able to direct smoothly until Lorentz sent Floyd Crosby to join the crew. A greater problem was the postlocation commentary. Lorentz tried to line up John Steinbeck, failed, decided to write it himself, and finally chose to hire Stephen Vincent Benét. Benét overloaded the film with narration, and although Ivens and Helen van Dongen worked sensitively with him to cut words out, it distressed Benét to have them do so, and eventually they had to restrain themselves. No one was satisfied with this uneasy compromise, and as a result, the film suffered.[54] There is too little vital dynamic between image and word, and examples of the superfluity of language abound: as Hazel Parkinson bears a bucket of water from fire to washtub, for instance, the narrator, William Adams, says "heat the water, carry the water, put it in the tub."

Ivens did not want to use either the music of the region or the experimental harmonies of an Eisler but rather to find more traditional music that would be suited both to the farm and to the kind of town audiences he anticipated. This he got, but with uneven relation to the picture. Douglas Moore's original score has excellent moments, but sometimes it provides a dramatic orchestral tone that is clashingly inappropriate to the setting and to the lives of the Parkinsons. The result is that the film improves at several points if one switches off the volume.

But it was with the sponsorship that Ivens found himself most at odds. The goal of *Power and the Land*, he wrote in 1944, was limited and clear: "It had to be a film for general release to show people in towns and on the farms, the importance of rural electrification, and how it develops the prosperity of the American farmer." His 1968 description, however, asserts another emphasis. The film was a New Deal project and Ivens was for the New Deal:

> It was about how the private companies own the electric power in your country. In many other countries electric power is nationalized, but as you know in the United States electric power is privately owned. So those big companies are not interested to send their big lines to isolated farms or little villages where they don't get many customers, to get profits, you see. So the companies didn't give electric power to them.

This was a reversion to his early hopes. At some point in the planning or shooting, Ivens realized that he "could not include the drama of the conflict between farmers and the private utilities" and settled mainly for the undynamic and therefore difficult before-and-after concept of Lorentz. As the shooting ended, however, Ivens again raised the question with Lorentz, who replied from a firm position that Ivens had to respect:

> One point we must be clear on: while I am perfectly willing to agree that you might make a very exciting documentary film from the material you have, unless that film is specifically enough like the original outline approved by the men who gave me the money and who trust me to see that such a picture is made, I feel it would be an unfortunate thing for both of us.[55]

Lorentz's U.S. Film Service was running into congressional attack and at this point a sortie against private enterprise would be disastrous.[y] Ivens continued to try to edge "le problème essentiel" into the film. In an article written after he left location but before composition of the commentary, he set out his position and his strategy for *Power and the Land*:

> In my opinion, it's necessary to find the social reality, then to find the essential drama of that reality. If this drama cannot be made the chief line of the film, another real drama must be found, or it must be compressed into some portion of it. There must be a place in the film for both love and hate. For example, the real drama of rural electrification in the United States is the conflict with the private utilities, who refuse to put up lines to farmers, but who fight any attempt of cooperating farmers to put up their own. In our film on this subject, we had a task into which this natural drama did not fit as a main line, but it will be there—in a short passionate speech by one angry farmer. If the essential drama is ignored, your film will lack both color and, more tragically, conviction.[56]

But the farmer in the film is *not* angry, only matter of fact, and his "speech" is pronounced not by him but by narrator William Adams, mild and a little bemused: electricity "sure would help me out and the woman too, but the power company says—you can see their lines go cross country, see them in the sky, but they don't bring the power down to the farm, say it costs too much, say a lot of things. . . . Helen's always saying if we had running water—power company won't do it."

---

[y] The two men acted out of respect and mutual admiration and there was no bitterness or ill feeling. See Snyder, *Pare Lorentz and Documentary*, p. 127; and Joris Ivens, "Joris Ivens Interviewed by Gordon Hitchens, November 20, 1968, American Documentaries," *Film Culture*, Spring 1972, p. 204.

It is not much, although it is more than Hurwitz and Strand were able to get by Lorentz in *The Plow That Broke the Plains*.

At least one of Lorentz's motivations in sending Crosby out was to instruct the crew to stick to the outline: for one thing, they had been following little Bip Parkinson around the farm and had staged a barn burning, which was quickly extinguished by the Belmont Electric Cooperative of St. Clairsville. Government officials demanded the elimination of this episode from the film, probably because Ivens had left the cause of the blaze in doubt. Talking in 1968 about the hostilities between the Rural Electrification Administration and private power crews, cooperatives, and companies, he recalled: "And even at certain times—I didn't get it in the film—but then there was sometimes also fire, you know, provocations."[57]

Power and the Land is a curious film to come from a major documentary filmmaker of the thirties, so middle-class in its stolid subjects, so simple and straightforward in style. It is neither dramatically dynamic nor deeply moving, which makes it difficult to describe, but it is nevertheless an engrossing film that reveals a great deal about Ivens himself and the passions that inspired him. Sharing the expressive unexpressiveness of its people, it has a slow cutting rhythm that corresponds to their work and character. And thanks to care and skill in shot and scene composition, it also takes on the drab, homely beauty and the real dignity of its subjects.

Over half of the film portrays a day's work without electrical power. There is no dramatic development: each chore comes as a separate impression, the scene varying from barn to house to milk house to fields as the day progresses. Bip, carrying a cornflower across the land, touches the day with some lyricism, while a note from the dairy accompanying the return of some sour milk—inadequate farm-cooling facilities—gives a slightly dramatic rendering of the film's motif. Three sequences serve as transition: a group of farmers join together to harvest one of their number's corn; at lunch they consider the need for power and resolve on a meeting with the government people; a meeting in town takes place, concluding with a changing map that tallies the impressive growth of rural cooperatives between 1935 and early 1940. Poles and lines go up, and one set of lines leads to the Parkinson farm, where in the final eight to nine minutes we share the family's pleasure in the new lights, stove, radio, running water, refrigerator, washing machine, and power tools. The milk to feed the pigs will no longer be sour, and the day's work is done—this time *before* dinner.

The photography is excellent. It is difficult to forget the images of the horses in the fog, cornstalks and corn-flowers in almost abstract composition against the sky, the rolling hills alone or as a backdrop for farm work, light, shapes, and textures on the lantern table as kerosene streams through the old funnel into a lantern base, the farmer with his lips pursed close-up at the meeting in town, the milk container cooling in the trough by the pouring faucet water, Bill Parkinson's disappointment as he walks around the dairy truck. Ivens' sensitivity to people and environment is evident in the camera position; subjects and objects are presented with a certain subtle restraint. Significant paraphernalia such as lanterns and buckets are omnipresent but never overstressed, simply there in the foreground or the background of many shots; in close-up they belong to an action that takes precedence in the frame.

Except for Bip, the six Parkinsons are very reserved, and Ivens makes no effort to probe, to open up their personalities. He places them in their context, so that we see *how* they live. Yet he also takes close-ups of Bill and Hazel Parkinson especially, holding on their slight but telling expressions. Four such shots capture the difference between the two days. On the first, at the end of dinner, Bill rests his arms in weary silence for a moment before rising; Hazel's brief, tired, and affectionate smile as he touches her shoulder on his way back to work registers their plight more accurately than words. At the film's end, she turns from the oven to look at Bill with a fine glow, and he smiles, speaks a quick word, then starts out of the frame before the final fade.

Two anomalous sequences that lend separate dimension bring us close to Ivens' personal concerns. In the first of these, Parkinson moves toward the camera, cutting corn. A tilt composes cornstalk tops and cornflowers against the sky. In the distance, Bip runs toward the cornfield: "A kid is about the best crop there is." Parkinson cutting. Bip looking up. Two cornflowers. Parkinson cuts the cornflower stalk. Bip pulls it from his father, dodging, feinting, laughing, then dashes off as his father playfully reaches his corn-cutting knife out for him. Parkinson cutting. Bip walks to light flute music, his flower held high, beyond the stalks. Parkinson cutting to the sound of a somber horn. The horn holds, then the flute takes over, while flower moves above tall grass, Bip invisible below. The flute as Bip comes over a rise, small in the frame, and a large barren tree and a tall lightning-struck branch stuck in the ground stand starkly, disturbingly, over him. When he is almost out of frame, the horn returns and continues while we hold on the trees and move to a close-up of Parkinson, wiping his brow and looking at what becomes a close-up of an unpicked ear of corn.

The relationship between Bip and his father fascinated Ivens. He captured it in quiet glances between the two and in another mock combat when Parkinson flicks water and then a towel at Bip's teasing head poked out of the shower curtains. In the sour-milk sequence, two lyrical shots bring Bip running to the truck; the sequence ends with Parkinson, dignified but discouraged, slowly walking around the truck. Bip is more fluid and expressive than the adults—the film needs him. He is also the young life that will grow to see a better American farm. But beyond this, the very exceptional symbolism of flute versus horn, flower versus stalk, and barren tree suggest that through him something else is being, perhaps unconsciously, explored.

Ivens was very close to the Parkinsons, but he may have felt himself in uneasy opposition to their lack of resilience, both for cinematic and personal reasons. The anomalous sequence celebrates Bip's liveliness and lyricism against the more stony, drab existence of the hardworking father. The barren tree, then, is a threat, a sign of Bip's future, the future he instinctively resists in his playful combativeness with his parent. The generational coherence is one of vital interchange, as Ivens captures Bip's admiration and love for his father and touches us with the way he activates in Parkinson moments of playfulness and even mild joy. The generational conflict is strongly implied.

Ivens had two brothers, one older and one younger, and an industrious father who had established a firm (Capi) that sold photographic supplies. By Dutch tradition, the oldest brother has the choice of careers—William became a doctor—while the second son must follow in his father's footsteps. We have seen how Ivens dutifully went through the proper technical and business training and became assistant director of Capi. During the same period, however, he also became a filmmaker and a leftist—he had found the cornflower among the stalks of the photographic business—and as a result, he and Helen van Dongen, who also worked for his father, were discharged from their jobs.[58] It is no accident that thereafter Ivens would devote his art to the causes of people who needed freedom from the inequities of free enterprise and by extension from the tyrannies of fascism. In *Power and the Land*, he was once again making such a film. But because he was under a sponsor's restraint, he could not express himself creatively according to his impulses. Before Lorentz cracked down, however, the Ivens crew had picked up the unplanned footage of Bip, who then stood, however accessible this is to an audience, for resistance to the predictable and restrained life of the farm and to the scheme of the film. A great deal of Ivens himself is expressed in that one short sequence. And it was important enough to him that he allowed only one brief sentence by Benét to intrude in it.

The second unusual sequence is the one in which area farmers join to cut one farmer's corn. The pace is quicker than it is elsewhere, the angles unusually sharp, the sunlight strong, human movement relatively swift, the music mellow in tone but forcefully accented, and it is accompanied by a Benét verse chorus spoken at a loud, aggressive pitch, the words acute and biting:

> You and me and the neighbors too,
> We get together and cut the corn.
> The knife goes through and the knife cuts through
> When we get together and cut the corn.
> It's the same job that we used to do:
> We built the forty-eight states that way
> With the sunny day and the stormy day
> And the neighbors working to build them too.
> The knives are cutting the load piled high,
> The sun beats down from the August sky;
> We built our freedom and strength this way.
> From Mississippi to Ioway.
> From Oregon to the docks of Maine,
> We're building it still, together.
> When we get together we're hard to stop:
> We can raise the crop and harvest the crop,
> We can get the power and get the light,
> We can get the things that we want today,
> The neighbors working the selfsame way,
> Working together to cut the corn.

Immediately after "today," a close-up catches Parkinson's knife, glinting in the sun, landing in a gatepost. Two more farmers follow and slam their blades into the same post as they break for dinner. In this sequence, as his father works cooperatively with the others, Bip enters the cornfield, not to wrestle away a precious cornflower but to bring his father a bottle of water, thereby symbolically endorsing collective work and struggle as the correct direction for the future. It is not in the direct references to the power companies but rather through this sequence that Ivens unleashes his creative resources to suggest his sympathies and his solutions to "le problème essentiel" in the rural areas.

The sequence has no other reason for being, and its construction is purposefully out of key[z]: "As in music," Ivens wrote that winter, "there

---

[z] According to Richard Griffith, this sequence caused considerable dispute at the time about its appropriateness to the film. See Griffith, "Power and the Land," NBR, Dec. 1940, p. 16; and Archer Winsten, "Power and the Land is Added at the Rialto," N.Y. Post, 11 Dec. 1940, p. 19.

is often a need for dissonance in saying (or yelling) what you want your audience to hear."[59] It is no accident that the biting, aggressive voice that speaks the chorus echoes the quality of the shouted narration of the angry poem that marks *New Earth's* final sequence where the images expose the damage done by capitalism to the men who made the new land. To be sure, the audience and perhaps Ivens too are protected from the implications of this sequence by elements within the sequence and by what follows. It is American tradition, not rebellion, that the verse dramatically summons up, and the ensuing sequence is very slow. The farmers sit around the pump, and Adams tells how it is done: "Now they talk it over, the country way, the slow, cautious decision of the people."

Despite these sequences, and despite the film's beauty and dignity, *Power and the Land* lacks the color and the strong political testimony of Ivens' previous work. Left on his own, he would have shaped a different film, clearly. In June of 1940, while the final touches were being applied to *Power and the Land*, Ivens, at work on a new film, thought he had considerable license. He wanted to call this film *New Frontier*, as it was to be "about a frontier you can only cross if you change . . . your social situation."

> You can have these technical new steps but if you want to really be the master of your technique, you cannot go on with the economic structure you have now, your capitalist structure. I think you have to take as your inevitable goal a new structure that will have socialist tendencies. That is your last frontier, and your new frontier, for a wonderful United States, you know.[60]

It does not sound like a film RKO Radio Pictures would pick up for distribution, as they did *Power and the Land*, nor one that the farmers and townspeople of St. Clairsville would enthusiastically receive, but it might have been an important and influential film. In any case, as we have seen, *Valley Town* sent the Sloan Foundation nosing into the script for *New Frontier*, and as a result, the film was never made.

Sheldon Dick and *Men and Dust*

One obvious funding alternative for leftist filmmakers has been neglected: one could be independently wealthy. I want to introduce a new filmmaker at this late stage primarily because he made a priceless, unknown little experimental documentary film that is among the best of the decade. Upon his father's death, Sheldon Dick, the fourth son of A. B. Dick, refused one-fourth of the family mimeograph business, evidently because of his distress about the way the money had been gained. He sold his share to his brothers for a guaranteed annuity,[aa] he married Lee Burgess, an actress and the founder of the Truro Tryout Theater in Provincetown, Massachusetts, and he wrote poetry and worked as a still photographer—eventually under Roy Stryker at the Farm Security Administration. In 1939, at age thirty-three, at a time when Stryker was insisting on positive subjects, Dick found himself in the Tri-State Mining Area of Kansas, Missouri, and Oklahoma, stunned by the living and working conditions and by the silicosis death toll. He bought a movie camera and began his first film.[61]

In the meantime, Lee, who had worked for Frontier and American Documentary Films and assisted with *Candid Camera*, directed her first film, the debut of Lee Dick, Inc. This was *School*, a two-reeler sponsored by the Association for Progressive Education and the American Film Center. Lee Dick, Inc. now also produced *Men and Dust*, the film Sheldon brought back from the mining communities. This two-reeler premiered on 22 April 1940 in Joplin, Missouri, and then opened at the New York Theatre on 6 June. Lee Dick directed the commentary, Jules Bucher, assisted by Edward Anhalt, edited the film, Fred Stewart composed the music, and Will Geer, Storrs Haynes, Robert Porterfield, and Eric Walz narrated. Its critical success—it was endorsed by trade unions and health organizations and lauded by Eleanor Roosevelt—led to the company's reincorporation as Dial Films, Inc. and to the making of *Day After Day*, a film about visiting nurses made for the Henry Street Nursing Service. Eventually, Dial was to negotiate with a major company for the production of documentary shorts.[62]

Men and Dust begins as we hear:

This is our land, a great land for a great people. This is our land. We are this nation. This is our country, the richest country in the world. A fertile earth and forests, power, and great industry. We live here.

Firmly stated and set over the humming of a slow regional tune and functional images—farm buildings amidst trees and rising hills, wheat fields at harvest time, combine blades, sturdy forest trees, water streaming over a dam, industrial smokestacks, and farm buildings again—these opening words, in a brief sequence of about thirty-two seconds, establish conventional pride in America. A sharp, very nasal

[aa] This information was obtained from Willard Van Dyke, whose recollections may not be strictly accurate. Dick also had a sister, and I have been unable to find information about how she participated in the financial arrangements.

singing voice enters at the end of the fade that follows, and it continues for fifteen seconds over a single shot of vast distant hills of quarried material, barren gray against a barren gray sky, with a telephone wire skimming the middle ground:

> There are mean things happ'nin in this land,
> There are mean things happ'nin in this land,
> There are mean things happ'nin,
> There are mean things happ'nin,
> Mean things happ'nin in this land.

The shock is on every cinematic level: the nasal voice versus the richer, deeper, first voice, the song versus the words, the held shot versus the series of shots, the barren versus the fertile images, the mean things occurring in America versus the conventional view of its basic goodness.

On first glance this technique may seem a bit facile, until one learns that it is the beginning of a consistent aesthetic tactic, and one that is almost unique for American documentary of the 1930s. Whereas other filmmakers sought to pull the viewer emotionally into the world of the film, *Men and Dust* works in a more Brechtian mode: sequences are constantly interrupted by others that upset their tone, mood, style, and message, as Dick strives to challenge our assumptions and to keep us alert to the disturbing facts. Unlike the films by Ivens, Van Dyke, and Frontier, there is scarcely a shot without voice-over. But it is neither the news narration of the Kline films nor the steady poetic mode of the two Lorentz films; instead, the words shift constantly in their relation to the images—ironic, supportive, angry, sad—and usually contrast with words that precede and follow. Over three shots of barren chadpiles[bb]—two that include a strolling couple, distant and low in the frame—we hear a ballad from another time and place: "I wandered today to the hill, Maggie/To watch the scene below,/The trees and the old rusty mill . . . ," and as we wait for "Maggie" to recur, suddenly, in an abrasive jolt, a tristate radio voice blasts in, and we are in the back seat of a car going by the rotting miners' shacks and hearing, along with flares of music: "This is station WMB thwee. In the Joplin, when the gong rings, at the crossroads of America, the richest country in the world, this is the less taxes, the more jobs. What helps business helps you."

Aside from its unique narration, *Men and Dust* sharply challenges the other standard qualities of the industrial information film. As a

[bb] These are mining waste hills containing siliceous dust.

simple map appears on the screen, a deep voice tells us that "the plains of Kansas, the hills of Missouri, and the Oklahoma dustbowl make the tristate mines." A piece of lead and a piece of zinc appear on the map: these mines provide 10 percent of all American lead and 38 percent of all American zinc. Conventional industrial information follows in conventional form over a series of illustrative shots: the lead is for pewter, the zinc for brass, lead for type, solder, cables, zinc for paint (a man paints a lovely white suburban house), for batteries, for galvanizing. The final example, "lead for toys," is illustrated by a little windup train on a circular track, with toy figures in the center. As the train comes around the bend to front screen, the engine derails, a slightly disturbing note amidst all the product talk, a dissonance followed by two trains, the second filling the frame at a powerful upward diagonal from lower back left to upper front of the frame, with the narrator reciting "twenty million dollar business every year."

A fade leads to more information: we see shots of shafts, buildings, trains, mines, men at work. A fast pace now, images very brief, the earlier bitter nasal voice, in accented verse prose, speeding up, shouting at the very end. Underneath, a chorus humming strong slow beats that quicken into fast train sounds and conclude in a chord. Industrial sounds are mixed in. Narration:

> Scores of mine shafts as far as you can see,
> Big mines, little mines, independent operators,
> Oversized companies with miles of leased railroads,
> Interstate commerce and rich raw products,
> Independent mills being driven to the backwash,
> Trainloads of zinc for the central mill at Carden,
> Lead ore, going to the smelter works at Joplin,
> Lead ore, going to the smelter at Galena,
> Smelter in Galena is the biggest in the district,
> The biggest in the district, the biggest in the district.
> Tons of zinc are coming out hourly,
> Tons of tailings building up mountains,
> Clouds of dust to cover up the little towns,
> Cave-ins over at Baxter Springs,
> Danger of lead poison, danger from dust.
> Men drop down the shaft, down the shaft, *down* the shaft.
> Lead for pipes and bullets and gases.
> Zinc for medicines and batteries and paint.
> Thousands of tons of rock ore daily:
> A million dollar business, a million dollar business,
> Million dollars, million dollars, million, million, million!

The images begin to differ. Simultaneous with the line about lead, a hand pulls the string on a long military field cannon; with the line about zinc, white paint is *flung* against a brick wall, and a paint-brush begins to spread it fast. In the final shot, a train speeds up to and over the camera, then, in a dissolve, runs over a woman in a very faded flower print dress blinking at the camera in medium close-up from the door of her shack.

The absurdly limited viewpoint of the medical film that merely provides objective information on a disease and ignores the social causes of the disease is also savagely brought home. We learn, with the visual aid of chart, pointer, and chest x-ray, that

> breathing silica dust causes silicosis, which is scar tissue in the lungs. Silicosis can be prevented by general ventilation and local suction exhaust of this type, but silicosis never can be cured. It invites tuberculosis, and when death comes, TB will be the cause of it. You can fight TB which is based on silicosis.

Cut to a medium shot of a shack with broken-off screen door. A tougher, darker voice snaps: "You can fight for your life in a two-room shack"— cut to a very dusky interior shot, a man in medium-close shot bending and coughing—"with dust and silica blowing in the window." Chadpile shots follow, then blowing dust, blowing over "the towns and the street, the streets and the houses, the houses and the people, the schools and the children." Under these conditions, the film asks, what chance do people have of fighting "TB which is based on silicosis"?

Implicit in such a question is the answer that people must fight the conditions, and Dick could point to some efforts worth supporting. While he was on location for the film, the mining companies became unfriendly after he attended a local CIO meeting.[63] But there was no worried sponsor to insist that unions be soft-pedaled in the film, and *Men and Dust* firmly backs the rhetoric and the plan for action of the International Union of Mine, Mill, and Smelter Workers: "We know these conditions. Let us fight for health. There is death in the mines for our friends and our enemies. There is no distinction between our lungs. . . . Let's all get together." An official explains the union's four-point program: a Federal Workman's Compensation Law; Federal legislation prescribing minimum standards for working conditions; a cheap housing development away from the chadpiles; and a regional tuberculosis sanitarium. But even here Dick is suspicious of statements without action and of action that comes too late. A dissolve takes us from the union speaker to ill-kept tombstones, and the nasal voice intrudes: "Silicosis, tuberculosis, malnutrition, general diseases. In

the meantime they sicken. In the meantime they die." A second graveyard shot tilts up to trees and hills and dissolves to the first of a set
of eleven still photographs, powerful in their stasis in a moving film,
powerful photographs of the dying, of the old and very young, with
their thin, drawn faces, some a little frightened, all dazed and deadly
serious, wasted bodies in chairs and beds. Their names are called over
a loud slow ticking sound accompanying the wipes that carry us from
one of them to the other. In three cases, the transition is also accompanied by a foghorn sound that is followed by a gong—over the first
still, of Charlie, over the last, of Dewey, and over the little girl, Alice,
holding her dog. Dewey's photograph lunges up at the camera to end
the sequence as the camera returns to the graveyard.^{cc}

Men and Dust is driven by its refusal to allow us to escape the truth
of these lives. As the men flee the impending blast they have rigged
in the mine, a voice calls out to them, "All right Howard, give 'er to
her," then, "C'mon boys, on the lam! Get away from that wall, get
away from that rock. Get away from that rock, get away from that
dust!" And, over the blast, again, "Get away from that dust!" Then
over swirling dust by a bit of lighted wall, "Get away from that dust!"
Then, as headlamps approach through the dust, the sharp piercing
voice grows tight and bitter and shifts to the position of commentator:
"And *come back for more.*" A fade makes us think that the experience
is over, but we are not spared what remains: over a distant chadpile,
the same insistent voice calls again: "Get away from that dust!" The
sound of wind and a moonlike local landscape: "Get away from that
school! Get away, you kids! Get away from that dust, get away from
that dust!" Finally, in a new, dramatic shift of tone, the frame filled
only with dust, a quiet, low tense voice wierdly chants

Dust in the ground, dust in the mills,
Dust in the towns and on the window sills.

It is this constant, mind-jogging and emotion-jogging change of stance,
and this constant refusal of evasion, that make *Men and Dust* so af-
fecting and powerful a film.

What difference did such a film make? Did its viewers find, as did
the brief and fairly positive *New Masses* review, that the film was

---

^{cc} The film would have been better ended here. Unfortunately there follows a rather
sentimental, upbeat sequence of four shots: men at the union meeting, a low angle of
a woman hanging clothes against a background of trees, a smiling workman, a boy
running to his grandfather and being lifted up. A sharp strident voice calls out over the
first shot "Give us health, give us work, give us life," and individual voices call out in
the same demanding tone over the next three shots "Give us health!/Give us work!/Give
us life!" as choral humming lifts to a high pitch.

"slightly arty," or simply "interesting"? Was it shown in a few places and then not seen again? Did people plagued by the Depression they wanted to believe was finally over refuse to connect it to themselves? The film and the commitment behind it, it turns out, was not even sustaining to Dick himself: ten years later, this "socially prominent son of the late A.B. Dick of Chicago," this "literary agent and . . . polo player . . . who retired several years ago," committed a double suicide with his third wife in the living room of his home in the fashionable Greens Farm section of Westport, Connecticut, with three young children and three servants asleep upstairs.[64] So why write about *Men and Dust*?

One reason is that its proceeds fed a good and eventually triumphant cause. It dramatically informed its audience about concrete legislation that needed their support; a speaker accompanying the film could organize a lobbying effort, asking audience members to join support organizations, donate money, write letters, and sign petitions. And here, if only for a moment in his life, someone saw something that so angered him that he chose and was able to transform his rage into a provocative, original statement that engages anyone who sees it. If Van Dyke's compromise over *Valley Town* is a useful negative example, it is also important that we find positive resource in such small and evanescent but vibrant and committed efforts as was Dick's.

The Films on the Left

This question about *Men and Dust* is one that has been sometimes implicit, sometimes explicit throughout this book: Why should we revive the films made by the Workers Film and Photo League, by Kline, by Van Dyke, by Lorentz, by Nykino and Frontier Films, and by Ivens? What value and relevance do they have today?

Let me take the Frontier filmmakers first, for on a much more continuous basis their lives and films reflect the impulse behind Dick's film. Unlike most of us, they were hurt enough by what was deeply wrong in the world to turn their art toward its rectification. Whatever the strains and divisions, they worked together and struggled for original form because they believed that they had something that needed to be said and because they had a vision of how things could change. When they saw the United States become self-celebratory and consolidated in reaction to world events, they kept their eyes on the injustices that had not disappeared simply because people had decided to close their eyes to them. Whatever the ultimate depth of their art, it is significant and useful that they refused, whatever their own weaknesses and whatever the temptations, to compromise in any way the straightforward, impactful statements they wanted to make; they worked in their chosen profession, using their talents, their incomes, and their lives to serve a cause they believed in. And in presenting us with Dr. Bethune, with Mao Tse-tung and Chu Teh, with Myles Horton, and with the protagonists of *Native Land*, they provided us with inspiring examples of people who have devoted their own lives to the struggle for social equality. They and their films thus become personal resources for us in our own lives.

Fight For Life and *Native Land* are films of special significance. Although they could be used, like *Men and Dust*, to raise funds and trigger discussion and action, their most significant value lies in the attitudes they evoke. Both films, dissimilar as they are, ask what other films on the left during this period usually failed to ask: they want to know just what terms you and I will tolerate in life, with what consciousness, what level of authenticity, and what sense of responsibility we will consent to live. For answers and for inspiring examples, Lorentz went to the pioneers in public health[dd] and Frontier Films to the pioneers in the labor movement. In the people they portray, the two films underline the necessity of *ongoing* courage and strength to fight both the cruelty of everyday misery and deprivation and the forces of a depression, of fascism, and of the inner despair and indifference that dehumanize and incapacitate us. For most viewers, *Fight for Life* is more practically inspiring than *Native Land* because its heroes are not martyrs out on the political frontier but people who have chosen quietly to dedicate their skills and so their lives to those most in need of them. But both films achieve what Paul Strand thought the Italian neorealist films and the Frontier films accomplished: they rouse in us our own latent heroism.

Power and the Land has another value. As I mentioned previously, left on his own, Ivens would have shaped a different film. Yet just how militant it would have been is difficult to say, for Ivens had lived for several months with the film's audience (it was in fact premiered in St. Clairsville, on 31 August 1940, with Ivens present), and he had done some thinking. "You eventually bring your finished film," he wrote that winter,

[dd] Lorentz actually thought in such terms. On 17 April 1940, fighting for the survival of the U.S. Film Service, Lorentz told a congressional subcommittee, "I feel this—that we have pioneered, we have learned how to do this work within the government" (see Snyder, *Pare Lorentz and Documentary*, p. 158). Recall his 1931 *Scribner's* discussion of the importance of the pioneering tradition to his generation (see Chapter II).

to the collaborator who has exerted a constant moral pressure upon every function of its making from the start—the *audience*. . . . I believe that the documentary film-maker has a greater responsibility to his audience than the creator of any other kind of films . . . we are constantly touching unfamiliar concepts, social and political themes that the moral propagandists in Hollywood rarely touch, and to influence people's opinions on these closer, but more unusual subjects is a considerable task.

In these terms, *Power and the Land* was a greater success than Ivens' previous films, and a greater success than most films of the decade. It rocked no boats, its premiere earned high plaudits, RKO Radio Pictures took it on for distribution to four thousand theaters, and it garnered many nontheatrical screenings as well. It was both clear and practical, and accordingly, it was in demand. Richard MacCann is accurate in calling it "a leading example of what a government documentary might properly be. It is a straightforward report on social change as it affects one family when it takes advantage of services provided by Congressional and administrative decision."[65]

This kind of practical success recalls two much less skillful and rather flat English films, *Housing Problems* and *Enough to Eat?* Although cinematically unadventurous, the latter and possibly the former became sources of legislative action against the ills they describe. What kind of propaganda films are best, then? Those that work cautiously in consonance with the general outlook of government and population to highlight facts and figures and practical steps and benefits? In one sense, the answer is obvious: *Power and the Land* would bring more immediate positive results for the farmer than would any militant agitational film on the rural electrical power situation.

But the answer is not so simple. There are diverse audiences and different, sometimes long-range political goals. The warning films by Kline, Ivens, and Frontier Films, intended to alert Americans to a threatening world situation, were meant also in large part to open the pocketbooks of the already convinced. *The Plow That Broke the Plains* and *The River*, less immediately "practical" than *Power and the Land*, were meant to create a climate of opinion generally favorable to New Deal policies. But a militant rural power film by the Workers Film and Photo League might lend vital emotional support to those who were already at work for radical change. And by this measure, all of the films considered in this book, whether they can be characterized today as either liberal or left-wing, made their contributions to improvement in the lives of the deprived and disenfranchised in their own country and to the combat of fascism and imperialism abroad. Their goals were sometimes complementary and sometimes even conflicting, but all are part of a viable leftist film tradition, a usable past.

Perhaps the most important lesson for the left lies in Ivens' hardwon approach to filmmaking and to change. It had its beginning in his own strongly empathetic, generous personality, and it was reinforced when Soviet audiences questioned him about the *people* in his films. It was further strengthened by his experience as a filmworker expressing the spirit and the purpose of an industrial project in the Soviet Union (*Song of Heroes*); and it was deepened still more by his years of identification with the Dutch workers as they carried out the land reclamation project he recorded in *New Earth*. From all of these experiences and from his experiences with people in the Borinage, Spain, and China, Ivens himself became sensitized to the difficulties involved in reaching people with social and political themes that are probably still unfamiliar to them.

A person who is aware of these problems knows that viable social change can only rise from the particular conditions and perceptions, past and present, of an exploited people themselves. He or she realizes that the role of artist and educator is to help people define their situations in their own images and language and to facilitate their discovery of workable methods for improving their conditions. Such methods must often be reformist at the outset, and only later, when the audience has been exposed to new possibilities, can they become class-conscious and revolutionary. This awareness means an ability to listen and to see, an ability to communicate authentically, an avoidance of the attempt to impose theories and actions instead of understanding that they must occur organically through the process of realization and struggle. It means a subordination of ego. Artist and educator must enter this process sincerely, or it will not work. That Ivens was sensitive to these things is implicit in his behavior on the Parkinsons' farm, in his accurate rendering of the character, the lives, and the needs of the farmers in *Power and the Land*, and in the film's success in stimulating the formation of rural cooperatives. And although his approach did not bear full fruit in that film, for Ivens was not permitted to express very definitely the more socially conscious farmers' perception of the greed and the easy indifference of the power companies, it is an approach that Ivens would stay with and develop further in later films, including his most recent work in Vietnam and China.[ee]

[ee] *The Sky and Earth* (1965), the *17th Parallel* (1968), and *How Yukong Moved the Mountains* (1975).

This approach implies the kind of community—shared work and purpose, solidarity, love for justice, and love and concern for one another—and openness to new situations that artists and nonartists in the 1930s and in the 1960s at their best were able to achieve. It is a kind of community that too few activists from either decade have managed to sustain because of youthful passion and inexperience, because of cooptation and personal ambition, and because of the sheer lack of a strong, continuous tradition that could teach it by example. Yet it *is* now actively sustained and effective in significant places, and resources for it can be found in the attitudes and in the art not only of a Joris Ivens but in the efforts and the experience, however short-lived, of Frontier Films and in the enduring films that they and some of their contemporaries have left to us. And the lesson they pass on to us is that radical change can occur only with this kind of true community as its basis.

Notes

I

1. Stern, "A Working-Class Cinema for America?" *The Left*, Spring 1931, p. 69.

2. Ibid., pp. 70-71. Jacobs was with the American Prolet-Kino and it is possible that Platt was also. Platt, however, was "in no way involved with the beginnings of the Workers Film and Photo League" and did not join the group until 1933. Letter to author, 30 July 1975.

3. Letter from Brody to author, 25 July 1976.

4. DW, 7 July 1930, p. 4.

5. NM, July 1930, p. 20.

6. Events: DW, 27 Sept. 1930, p. 5 (*Potemkin*); DW, 9 Oct. 1930, p. 2 (Potamkin talk); DW, 5 Nov. 1930, p. 2 (*Fighting Workers*). DW, 29 Nov. 1930, p. 5, has a description of *Harbor Drift*, and DW, 6 Dec. 1930, p. 5, has a negative review signed by Myra Page, who found it a melodramatic film.

7. The first mention of the WF&PL is in DW, 10 Dec. 1930, p. 2 (which also includes the housewarming announcement); DW, 4 Dec. 1930, p. 2, announces a meeting of the Workers Camera League. The addresses are from the DW announcements. EC 1, no. 3 (1931): 37. Potamkin was listed as the New York editor on the first two numbers.

8. Potamkin, "A Movie Call to Action!" WT, July 1931, p. 5.

9. Albany Hunger March, May Day, and dark room: NM, June 1931, p. 22. According to Tom Brandon, several League members owned DeVry cameras, and one or two owned Bell and Howell Eyemoes at this point or later. Sidney Howard later donated proceeds from a satirical article on Hollywood for an Eyemo. See "Pioneers: An Interview with Tom Brandon," by Fred Sweet, Eugene Rosow, and Alan Francovich, *Film Quarterly* 26 (1973): 14.

10. *Arsenal* showing with Platt talk; DW, 10 Jan. 1931, p. 6. Separate *Arsenal* showing: DW, 20 Mar. 1931, p. 2. *China Express* showing and Potamkin lecture: DW, 4 Feb. 1931, p. 2. *Potemkin* showing and symposium on American films: DW, 14 Feb. 1931, p. 2. *Two Days* showing: DW, 12 Mar. 1931, p. 2. *Weavers* showing: DW, 28 Mar. 1931, p. 2.

11. All of the information in these two paragraphs is from Potamkin, "A Movie Call to Action!" pp. 5-6. On classes at the League, see also NM, July 1931, p. 21. The League advertised for proletarian photos in both *New Masses* and the *Daily Worker*: "It is to be understood that worker-photographers intending to exhibit with the American section are to concentrate on the photo of class-struggle and proletarian life. No bourgeois portraiture, nudes, landscapes, still lifes, will be exhibited" (NM, June 1931, p. 22). See also NM, July 1931, p. 21.

12. Russell Campbell, "Introduction" to "Radical Cinema in the 30's," *Jump Cut* 14 (1977): 23.

13. Films for distribution: WT, Jan. 1932, pp. 22-23, 25. Staff, cities, and *Winter, 1931*: NM, Dec. 1931, p. 27.

14. Most of this information is from Sweet, Rosow, and Francovich, "Pioneers: An Interview with Tom Brandon," and from the Balog and Brody interview.

15. Brody interview and letter to author from Brody, 25 July 1976.

16. Material is from: Hurwitz interviews 2 and 3; Leo Hurwitz, "One Man's Voyage: Ideas and Films in the 1930's," *Cinema Journal*, Fall 1975, pp. 1-15; and Michael and Jill Klein, "*Native Land*: An Interview with Leo Hurwitz," *Cinéaste* 6, no. 3 (1974): 3-7.

17. Material is from my own Lerner interview and from an interview of Lerner by George Bluestone, Eugene Anthony, and Fred Carlisle (n.d., transcript furnished by Lerner). Information concerning the shooting at the WIR camp is from the Brody interview. The quotation concerning the educating of children is from DW, 10 June 1931, p. 3.

18. Letter from David Platt to author, 30 July 1975.

19. Material is from the Steiner interview and the Steiner Buffalo interview. See also Ralph Steiner, *A Point of View* (Middletown, Conn.: Wesleyan University Press, 1978). I learned of Steiner's presence at the May Day demonstration from the Lerner interview.

20. Jacobs interview. Jacobs himself paid for the first two issues of *Experimental Cinema*. For his argument that grappling with social issues would affect film form, see Jacobs, "Eisenstein," EC 1, no. 3 (1931): 4.

21. Material is from the Seltzer interview, from biographical material furnished by Seltzer, and from *Living Films*, a 1940 publication of the Association of Documentary Film Producers.

22. The first quotation is from Klein, "*Native Land*: An Interview with Leo Hurwitz," p. 3; the second is from Hurwitz, "One Man's Voyage," p. 9.

23. Edna Meyers interview. The article that she did for *New Masses* appeared in the 12 June 1934 issue on pages 27-28.

24. Hurwitz and Steiner, "A New Approach to Film Making," NT, Sept. 1935, p. 22.

25. Brody, "The Hunger March Film," DW, 29 Dec. 1932, p. 4.

26. Hurwitz, "One Man's Voyage," p. 3.

27. Hurwitz interview 1.

28. *The Left*, Spring 1931, pp. 73-75. The article is signed N. Kaufman; I have not been able to discover who he was.

29. Lerner, "Harry Alan Potamkin," EC 1, no. 5 (1934): 53. For background and development, see also Dudley Andrew, "Harry Alan Potamkin," *Film Comment*, Mar. 1974, pp. 55-57, and Lewis Jacobs, "Introduction," in Harry Alan Potamkin, *The Compound Cinema: The Film Writings of Harry Alan Potamkin* (New York: Teachers College Press, 1977).

30. Lerner, "Harry Alan Potamkin," p. 53. Lerner quoting Hamilton. This tribute is accompanied by Brody's still of the death mask by Adolph Wolf.

Seltzer remembers going with Brody and others to give blood: Seltzer interview. See *Close Up*, Sept. 1932, pp. 206-207, for a description of the lecture series given by Potamkin.

31. *Hound and Horn*, Apr.-June 1933, p. 485. In a report submitted to the New York League upon completion of *Hunger 1932*, Hurwitz argued that it was the task of the revolutionary film to document the masses' daily struggle and "to dramatize these events so that their ideological and political meaning is conveyed, and the effect is persuasive. We must think of our films as having the same capacity as union organizers." Hurwitz, "Survey of Workers Films: A Report to the National Film Conference," NT, Oct. 1934, p. 27.

32. These points are gleaned from a number of separate statements in Potamkin's writing.

33. NM, June 1930, p. 15, and Dec. 1932, p. 21.

34. Potamkin, "Film Problems of Soviet Russia," EC 1, no. 1 (1930): 4.

35. Potamkin, "Populism and Dialectics," EC 1, no. 2 (1930): 16-17.

36. NM, June 1930, p. 14, and Aug. 1930, p. 13. Hurwitz, film can be "a very important political weapon, more effective at this time than carloads of bullets and machine guns" (NT, Oct. 1934, p. 27).

37. Stern, "A Working-Class Cinema for America?" p. 69; EC 1, no. 3 (1931): 30. Potamkin: "What Will Mr. Peet Do About It?" NM, Nov. 1930, p. 23, and Oct. 1930, p. 16.

38. Steiner interview. Van Dyke interview 1.

39. Potamkin, "What Is the Program of the Workers Cultural Federation?" DW, 18 July 1931, p. 4.

40. Hurwitz interview 2, and Lerner and Seltzer interviews. Jacobs knew Potamkin, and he was one of those who volunteered his blood (Jacobs interview).

41. WT, Jan. 1932, p. 22.

42. Hurwitz, "One Man's Voyage," p. 30. According to Lerner, an effective antidote to dangerous Hollywood film "is the showing of films made by the Film and Photo League and other workers' films. Only two years ago the League had the honor of presenting Esther Shub's Soviet compilation *Cannons or Tractors*[?] to 8,000 workers in New York alone. Another such compilation could be made of Film and Photo League newsreels. And neither would need any commentator. Its effectiveness would depend upon the proper selection of shots and their truthful and precise juxtaposition" (Lerner, "A Dry Martini with Cyanide," NM, 19 June 1934, p. 30).

43. Solomon P. Rosenthal, "Change of Socio-Economic Attitudes Under Radical Motion Picture Propaganda," vol. 25, no. 166, Archives of Psychology, Columbia University (New York, Apr. 1934).

44. *Close Up*, Sept. 1932, p. 213. The effectiveness of such juxtaposition was also being tested in 1931 by Sender Garlin, coeditor of the *Labor Defender*, in an ambitious tour of the United States. His talk on "The Soviet 5-Year Plan and the Hoover Plan" was backed with the latest pictures of Soviet factories, collective farms, and other institutions and personalities, and with pictures of "breadlines, lynching, class-war prisoners, mass terror—*and how*

the workers are fighting back!" More than capacity audiences turned out for this talk in Baltimore, Worcester, Mass., and elsewhere. See Garlin, "USSR— 1917-1931," *Labor Defender*, Nov. 1931, pp. 205, 225.

45. Sweet, Rosow, and Francovich, "Pioneers: An Interview with Tom Brandon," p. 19.

46. Brody, who was one of the cameramen, reported on the failure to make a sufficient record: Brody, "The Hunger March Film," p. 4. The rest of the information in this paragraph comes from Hurwitz interview 2.

47. Brandon lecture at the Museum of Modern Art in New York, 6 June 1973. Seltzer on the Supreme Court incident and the zoom lens: Seltzer interview. Scottsboro: Jacobs interview; Louis Berg, "All Quiet in Morgan County," NM, May 1933, p. 3; Hurwitz interview 2. Brody on Seltzer and on Gastonia: Brody interview. For the arrest of Martin Harris, a New York League cameraman, for filming a strike in New Jersey, see NM, 19 June 1934, p. 24, and NT, July-Aug. 1934, p. 19.

48. Seltzer interview. Modesto, California incident: DW, 16 Apr. 1934, p. 5. Balog: DW, 11 June 1934, p. 5, and 21 June 1934, p. 5; NT, July-Aug. 1934, p. 19.

49. First sentence in this paragraph: Hurwitz interview 2. *Hunger 1932*: Hurwitz, "Survey of Workers Films," p. 27. Last two sentences: Hurwitz interview 1 and Brody interview.

50. Information for these three paragraphs comes from Sweet, Rosow, and Francovich, "Pioneers: an Interview with Tom Brandon," and from Brandon, Brody, and Seltzer interviews. The Vorkapich and Vidor information is from DW, 20 June, 27 July, and 17 Aug. 1934. Brody on costume ball: DW, 25 Apr. 1934, p. 5. Proceeds to CP: DW, 17 May 1934, p. 5.

51. Tom Brandon owns the Mooney film. I was not present when he showed it publicly in New York in 1974, and I have been unable to see it subsequently. My information is from documents and reviews at the National Archives. Material on Seltzer and Howard is from Sweet, Rosow, and Francovich, "Pioneers: An Interview with Tom Brandon," p. 19, and from the Seltzer interview. Other information is from "Filmography," compiled by Russell Campbell and William Alexander, *Jump Cut* 14 (1977): 33.

52. On the *agitki*, see Jay Leyda, *Kino* (New York: Macmillan, Inc., 1960), pp. 132-139. Potamkin, WT, Apr. 1932, p. 19.

53. Variety of angles: Seltzer interview. Editing: Seltzer, "A Total and Realistic Experience" (interview with Russell Campbell), *Jump Cut* 14 (1977): 27.

54. Tom Brandon in conversation: 3 Dec. 1973.

55. Hand viewer and editing: Seltzer interview. Hurwitz and Steiner, "New Approach," pp. 22-23; and Hurwitz, "The Revolutionary Film—Next Step," NT, May 1934, p. 14.

56. Information about *Harbor Scenes* is from the Jacobs interview. The Hurwitz quote is from "The Revolutionary Film," p. 14.

57. *Winter, 1931*: Brandon interview. For information on the children of the Depression film, see Sweet, Rosow, and Francovich, "Pioneers: An In-

terview with Tom Brandon," p. 20. This film got as far as the shooting script, which Lester Balog did for Nancy Naumburg: Balog interview. Crucible of events: Hurwitz, "The Revolutionary Film," p. 15.

58. Hurwitz, "Survey of Workers Films," p. 28, and John Gessner, "Movies About Us," NT, June 1935, p. 20.

59. NM, Dec. 1931, p. 27.

60. WT, Feb. 1932, pp. 29-31. That Ballam had the hunger march film and possibly *Cannons or Tractors?* is evident from DW announcements of his appearances in various parts of the country.

61. For his distribution campaign policy, see Sweet, Rosow, and Francovich, "Pioneers: An Interview with Tom Brandon," p. 22. Audience estimate: Michael Gold, "Change the World!" DW, 2 Oct. 1934, p. 5. Film circuits: NT, Dec. 1934, p. 25; DW, 27 Oct. 1934, p. 5, and 5 Nov. 1934, p. 7 (Michael Gold, "Change the World!").

62. Seltzer, "A Total and Realistic Experience," p. 26. For more information on the still section of the League, see Anne Tucker, "Photographic Crossroads: The Photo League," special supplement to *afterimage*, Apr. 1978, and Ms. Tucker's book of the same title, to be published by Alfred A. Knopf, Inc., New York.

63. DW, 18 Apr. 1934, p. 5.

64. Organization of symposium and delegation: DW, 14 Sept. 1934, p. 5. Position paper: DW, 17 Dec. 1934, p. 5. Brandon on the League's interpretation of censorship: "Who Are the Forces Behind the 'Legion of Decency' Drive?" DW, 21 Aug. 1934, p. 5. League in court: DW, 28 Jan. 1934, p. 5. Protest on Chicago: DW, 21 Mar. 1934, p. 7.

65. May Day leafleting: DW, 11 June 1934, p. 5. Thaelmann film: DW, 28 June 1934, p. 5; 10 Sept. 1934, p. 5; 13 Sept. 1934, p. 3; 14 Sept. 1934, p. 3; 15 Sept. 1934, pp. 2, 7; 20 Sept. 1934, p. 5; NM, 2 Oct. 1934, p. 46. Blander: DW, 25 July 1934, p. 5; 1 Aug. 1934, p. 5; 14 Sept. 1934, p. 5.

66. Shortened run of *Thunder Over Mexico*: DW, 12 Feb. 1934, p. 5. As an additional part of the strategy against these two films, Brandon and Brody teamed up for reviews of both *Thunder Over Mexico* and *S. A. Mann-Brand*: "A Mexican Trailer," NM, Sept. 1933, p. 28, and "Epic of an Era," NM, 26 June 1934, pp. 29-30. Prevention of English version: NM, 26 June 1934, p. 29. Information on *S. A. Mann-Brand* campaign: Hurwitz, NT, "Hisses, Boos and Boycotts," July-Aug. 1934, pp. 10-11. Loss of business at Yorkville Theatre: Brody, DW, 20 July 1934, p. 5. Picketing of *No Greater Glory*: Brandon, "What's Doing in the Film and Photo League Branches," DW, 14 Sept. 1934, p. 5. Cancellation of *Man of Courage*: Platt, DW, 9 Mar. 1935, p. 7.

67. Maria Baker, "Film Conference," NT, Sept.-Oct. 1933, p. 24.

68. WT, July-Aug. 1933, p. 9. In this half-page "Call," the word "creative" appears twice, signalling an admission that things had been allowed to lapse.

69. On the formation of the Hollywood group: NT, Feb. 1934, p. 23. On the First National Film Conference: NT, Nov. 1930, p. 30. See also "Film-Photo League Issues Call for National Film Conference in September," DW, 29 Aug. 1934, p. 5.

70. FF, 15 Feb. 1935, pp. 19-20, and 7 Jan. 1935, p. 12. Facts on Tischler: Brody interview.

71. On the formation of the Chicago plan and the Film Production Committee: DW, 31 Dec. 1934, p. 5. It is probable that *Criminal Syndicalist Law on Trial* is about the "racket conspiracy case" in Chicago. The trial began on 22 January 1934. Alderman Oscar Nelson and others were accused of a criminal conspiracy to control the laundry, cleaning and dyeing, carbonated beverage, and linen supply businesses in Chicago.

72. *Cannon Fodder* was about imperialist war and was composed of newsreel footage of American, English, Japanese, and other world armies. *Living Wage or Death* concerned a strike; it was criticized for oversimplifying the "business of getting workers out on strike" and for boring the viewer by listing all of the strikers' demands. Criticism of L.A. films: FF, 7 Jan. 1935, pp. 12-13.

73. N.Y. League revision: DW, 10 Dec. 1934, p. 5.

74. Brandon report: FF, 15 Mar. 1935, p. 9. FF focus on Hollywood: DW, 23 Mar. 1935, p. 7. Gessner: "Movies About Us," p. 20.

75. Potamkin, "Movies and Revolution," NM, Dec. 1932, p. 21.

76. Potamkin, "Film Problems of Soviet Russia," pp. 3-4; Potamkin, "Pudovkin and the Revolutionary Film," *Hound and Horn*, Apr.-June 1933, p. 482. Kurella (the article is signed this way, and I have no other information on the writer): EC 1, no. 3 (1931): 12.

77. Seaver, "Literature at the Crossroads," NM, Apr. 1932, p. 12, and Rahv, "The Literary Class War," NM, Aug. 1932, p. 7.

78. DW, 10 June 1931, p. 1.

79. Brody interview.

80. Brody, DW, 18 Jan. 1934, p. 5. League film reviewers did not hesitate to criticize inadequate Soviet films (although they may have hesitated to call any of them complete failures), but they never questioned the glowing picture of the Soviet Union conveyed by those films. For a particularly accepting review, see Julian Roffman on *Soviet Russia Today*, DW, 6 Mar. 1935, p. 5.

81. Jacobs interview.

82. Steiner interview, and Steiner, *Point of View*, p. 9. Quotations are from the former. In the latter, Steiner changes the second location to "Park Avenue near Harlem underneath the New York Central Railroad elevated tracks."

83. Seltzer and Brody interviews.

84. Maria Baker, "Film Conference," NT, Sept.-Oct. 1933, p. 24.

85. Potamkin, "Movies and Revolution," p. 21.

86. NT, Sept.-Oct. 1933, p. 3.

87. Potamkin, "Notes on the Film: A Proposal for a School of the Motion Picture," *Hound and Horn*, Oct.-Dec. 1933, pp. 140-143.

88. Tom Brandon's article: "Workers Study the Film," NT, Jan. 1934, pp. 14-15. List of instructors: EC 1, no. 5 (1934): 54. Jacobs says he was not an instructor: Jacobs interview. Seltzer does not remember doing any teaching; if he did, he says, it did not turn out to be much: Seltzer interview.

89. Brandon interview. Brandon quoting Meyers: Sweet, Rosow, and Francovich, "Pioneers: An Interview with Tom Brandon," p. 15.

90. Klein, "*Native Land*: An Interview with Leo Hurwitz," p. 4. Balog and Brody interview.

91. Brody, "The Revolutionary Film: Problem of Form," NT, Feb. 1934, pp. 21-22. Platt, "*The Unknown Soldier Speaks* Reveals the Power of Newsreels," DW, 26 July 1934, p. 5. Platt was executive secretary in January (DW, 9 Jan. 1934, p. 5). I am assuming he still held this position in July.

92. Hurwitz, "The Revolutionary Film," p. 15.

93. Steiner interview; and Hurwitz and Steiner, "New Approach," p. 23. See *Film Art*, no. 5 (Winter 1934), for a description of one of the exercises they used.

94. Hurwitz, "The Revolutionary Film," p. 15; Steiner (in collaboration with Hurwitz), "Revolutionary Movie Production," NT, Sept. 1934, p. 23. Hurwitz collaborated with Steiner on the September *New Theatre* article (Steiner interview and Hurwitz interview 2). Hurwitz says that he was eager to find a place in the League to develop artistically as a filmmaker (interview 2). Brandon feels that Hurwitz and Steiner formed this new unit before the time was right for it (Brandon interview). Lerner recalled that, like Brody and Platt, the other faction wanted to use film to create and aid political action, "but we felt that the more skilled and artistic we were, the better job the films would do" (Lerner interview).

95. NT, Oct. 1934, pp. 27-28.

96. Freeman, "Ivory Towers—White and Red," NM, 11 Sept. 1934, pp. 20-24. Michael Gold, "Change the World!" DW, 5 Nov. 1934, p. 7.

97. *Sweet Land*: Hurwitz interview 2. *Battle in the Barnyard* was not completed, for reasons I have been unable to determine. The 28 February 1935 issue of the *Daily Worker* (p. 5) says that the Workers Animated Film, part of the cultural department of the WIR, is filming its *first* animated film, *Rugged Racketeering*.

98. *Café Universal*: Steiner interview, and Steiner, *Point of View*. Stills of this film may be found in *Theatre Arts Monthly*, Nov. 1933, pp. 831-834. On the completion of *Pie in the Sky*: Ray Ludlow, "*Pie in the Sky*," NT, May 1935, p. 19.

99. Lerner, "A Revolutionary Film," NM, 25 Sept. 1934, p. 30. Such pseudonymous horn blowing was common in Party publications, and this example must have delighted the three protagonists.

100. Steiner (in collaboration with Hurwitz), "Revolutionary Movie Production," p. 23. Quite possibly he is poking at Brandon, Platt, and others here. He goes on to say that the leadership should concentrate the major part of its time, energy, thought, and money on the few highly talented and committed filmmakers. Hurwitz interview 2.

101. NT, Nov. 1930, p. 30.

102. NT, Nov. 1934, p. 27; Seltzer, "Technically Speaking," FF, 7 Jan. 1935, p. 9.

103. Kern reviews: "Three Workers Films," FF, 7 Jan. 1935, pp. 10-11, and "World of the Movies: Development of a White-Collar Worker," DW, 27 Dec. 1934, p. 5. Naumburg working independently: Brody interview.

Lerner review: *"On the Waterfront,"* NM, 4 Dec. 1934, pp. 28-29. As far as I have been able to determine, the film remains lost.

104. Platt, "A Reply to Michael Gold," DW, 16 Nov. 1934, p. 5.

105. Campbell, "Introduction," p. 25.

106. Brody interview. Letter from David Platt, 30 July 1975. Seltzer interview, biographical information furnished by Seltzer, and film credits listed in *Living Films*, a 1940 publication of the Association of Documentary Film Producers.

107. Magazine film: Sweet, Rosow, and Francovich, "Pioneers: An Interview with Tom Brandon," p. 17. Dates and other films from pages of *New Masses* and *New Republic*. NM, 12 May 1936, p. 29, has an advertisement describing the content of *The Birth of New China*, a feature-length film edited by Roffman. For information about *Getting Your Money's Worth*, see also *Living Films*. Lerner's praise of *Getting Your Money's Worth*: NM, 21 Sept. 1937, p. 29. Tom Brandon owns at least one reel of this series; I have been unable to determine whether the other films still exist. Between 1935 and 1938, Roffman also worked for *The March of Time*, helping to produce some of its most prominent numbers: "Men of Medicine," "The Father Devine Story," "The Huey Long Story," and "The Disinherited." Before returning to Canada to join the National Film Board in 1940, he codirected a film in Kentucky, *And So They Live*, for the Sloan Foundation and he directed *A Report to the People* for President Roosevelt.

108. On the proceedings of the Nykino group: NT, Dec. 1934, p. 25; Mar. 1935, p. 13; and Feb. 1935, p. 30. Hurwitz interview 2. Steiner says that *Harbor Scenes* and *Granite* were completed and that they were lost during his temporary move to Hollywood years later (*Point of View*, p. 13).

109. Ludlow, *"Pie in the Sky,"* p. 19. Steiner interview.

110. *Left Front*, May-June 1934, p. 15.

II

1. Seaver, NM, June 1933, p. 13.

2. Daniel Aaron, *Writers on the Left* (New York: Harcourt, Brace & World, 1961), p. 396.

3. Strand interview, "Power of a Fine Picture Brings Social Changes: Paul Strand, of Frontier Films, Explains Success of 'The Wave'," *N.Y. World Telegram*, 4 Mar. 1939, p. 11.

4. Information here and in the succeeding paragraphs is from Calvin Tomkins' excellent profile on Strand in *The New Yorker*, 16 Sept. 1974, pp. 44-94, and from Nancy Newhall, *Photographs, 1915-1945: Paul Strand* (New York: The Museum of Modern Art, 1945). Quotations, unless otherwise noted, are from Tomkins.

5. See Carlos Chávez, "Mexico," *Films*, Summer of 1940, pp. 20-21, for some detail on the background for this series and for its very limited execution.

6. Frank Brandenburg, *The Making of Modern Mexico* (Englewood Cliffs,

N.J.: Prentice-Hall, Inc., 1964); Howard F. Cline, *Mexico: Revolution to Evolution, 1940-1960* (New York: Oxford University Press, 1962).

7. Everything in this and the preceding paragraph is from the Strand interview.

8. "Reflection of their own lives": Strand interview. Platt, DW, 18 May 1937, p. 7. Strand's statement to the Secretariat quoted by Sidney Meyers, "*Redes*," NT, Nov. 1936, p. 22. After a year of futile correspondence with the Mexican archival bureaucracy, I gave up on trying to locate a copy of this statement in which, Strand told me, he cited Flaherty as an example.

9. Strand interview. Statement to Secretariat.

10. Information on Rodakiewicz: Rodakiewicz Buffalo interview and Rodakiewicz interview.

11. "Virgin effort" and following information and quotations: letter to author from Fred Zinnemann, 18 Apr. 1975. According to Strand, he and Rodakiewicz witnessed the fishing scene very carefully before shooting and broke it down into its elements for the editing. Some preediting was done on the film before the editor arrived on the scene. Strand interview. Rodakiewicz's return: Rodakiewicz interviews.

12. Payment of villagers: Zinnemann letter, 18 Apr. 1975. Production problems: Garrison Film Distributors' publicity brochure. Revolutionary content: Strand, "Power of a Fine Picture," p. 11; Rodakiewicz interview. Rushes: Zinnemann letter and Rodakiewicz interview. Sewing machine: Zinnemann letter. Voltage: letter to author from Gunther von Fritsch, 18 Aug. 1976.

13. Water close-ups: Rodakiewicz interview. Direction: letter from Fred Zinnemann to author, 4 June 1975. Editing: von Fritsch, letter to author, 18 Aug. 1976. Musical score: Garrison Film Distributors' publicity brochure. Request for further time and funds: von Fritsch letter. Uncertain fate of film: Strand interview.

14. Quoted in Garrison Film Distributors' publicity brochure.

15. Rodakiewicz interview.

16. Van Doren, "Films; on Horror's Head," N, 8 May 1937, p. 545. Hamilton, "*The Wave (Redes)*," NBR, May 1937, pp. 12-13. Nugent, "The Screen," *N.Y. Times*, 21 Apr. 1937, p. 18. Van Dyke, "The Interpretive Camera in Documentary Films," *Hollywood Quarterly*, July 1946, pp. 405-406.

17. Meyers, "*Redes*," p. 22. Strength and nobility: Tazelaar, "On the Screen: *The Wave—Filmarte*," *N.Y. Herald Tribune*, 21 Apr. 1937, p. 18. Physical beauty and refusal to falsify: Herbert Weinstock, clipping in Museum of Modern Art file on *The Wave*.

18. Welcome to group: Strand interview. Trip to Soviet Union: Harold Clurman, *The Fervent Years* (New York: Hill and Wang, 1957), p. 150, and Tomkins, profile on Strand, pp. 68, 70. Eisenstein: Tomkins, p. 72.

19. Highest impact: quoted by Tomkins, profile on Stand p. 70. Strand interview.

20. Lerner interview. Steiner Buffalo interview.

21. Hurwitz's first meeting with Strand: "One Man's Voyage: Ideas and Films in the 1930's," *Cinema Journal*, Fall 1975, p. 6; and Lola Ridge, "Paul

Strand," *Creative Art*, Oct. 1931, pp. 313-316. Strand's reappearance: Hurwitz interview 3.

22. Information on Berman is from: Brandon interview; Maddow interview; letter to author from Berman's widow, the late Louise Berman, 23 Sept. 1975; letter to author from Berman's sister, Hortense Socholitzky, 18 Aug. 1976; and "Lionel Berman," a booklet printed privately after his death. The first and second quotations are from Hortense Socholitzky's letter, the third from the booklet, and the rest from accounts given by Berman's stepson, Thomas R. Branston (also from the booklet).

23. Meyers on Berman: "Lionel Berman" (booklet). Quotation by Meyers' sister, plus information on Clinton orchestra and Cincinnati Symphony: Jay Leyda, "Vision is my dwelling place," *Film Culture*, no. 58-59-60 (1974), pp. 2-36 (quotation is from p. 4). Other information from Edna Meyers interview.

24. Maddow interview. Maddow's interest in film before this point is signalled by his assisting Gertrude Armstrong with an article, "Wall Street Hollywood," NM, 14 Aug. 1934, pp. 29-30 (Maddow believes he revised Armstrong's text: letter to author, 18 Aug. 1976).

25. Maddow interview and letters from Maddow to author, 24 Dec. 1974 and 2 June 1975.

26. Maddow, "Red Decision," *Symposium*, Oct. 1932, pp. 443-453.

27. Maddow, "On Signing Up," *Poetry*, May 1936, p. 71. Substitute family: Maddow interview.

28. Maddow, "Images of Poverty": *Partisan Review*, Oct.-Nov. 1935, pp. 9-10. On rereading the poems: letter to author, 24 Dec. 1974. Depression intellectuals: Maddow interview.

29. Lerner, "The Screen: *The March of Time*," NM, 9 July 1935, p. 30.

30. Leo Hurwitz and Ralph Steiner, "A New Approach to Film Making," NT, Sept. 1935, pp. 22-23.

31. As early as 30 Jan. 1934, Hurwitz had argued that Victor Trivas's antiwar film, *Hell on Earth*, "gives no hint of the underlying causes of war" and "lacks the basic dialectic of dramatic conflict, which dulls the story and renders the final effect inadequate" ("*Hell on Earth* at the Acme is Vital Anti-War Film" DW, p. 5). Although the *Daily Worker* published the review, it did not much approve of it, and had David Platt write a second, much more laudatory one for the 5 Feb. 1934 issue (p. 5).

32. Eisenstein, "The New Soviet Cinema, Entering the Fourth Period," NT, Jan. 1935, pp. 9, 21.

33. Jay Leyda, *Kino: A History of the Russian and Soviet Film* (New York: Macmillan, Inc., 1960), Chapters XII-XIV. "Artistic dictatorship" is his phrase (see p. 299).

34. See: Eisenstein, "The New Soviet Cinema"; Marie Seton, "A New Generation," NT, Jan. 1935, pp. 16, 21; Friederick Wolf, "Dramatizing Our Times," NT, Feb. 1935, p. 24; Lerner, "More About *Chapayev*," NM, 12 Feb. 1935, pp. 29-30; Lerner, "The Soviet Film," NM, 5 Mar. 1935, pp. 29-30; G. W. Pabst, "A Letter to F. Ermler on *Peasants*," NT, Oct. 1935, p. 5. See also the following articles on *Chapayev*: William Troy, "Films: Blood and

Glory," N, 30 Jan. 1935, p. 140, and Otis Ferguson, "Not in Mournful Numbers," NR, 6 Feb. 1935, pp. 360-361.

35. Criticism of left theater: Kline, NT, Sept. 1934, p. 3; Dec. 1934, pp. 22-23; Feb. 1935, p. 3; Mar. 1935, pp. 22-23. Progress of left theater: Blake, "From Agitprop to Realism," NT, Jan. 1935, p. 28. On the deepening of the left theater's artistic work: NT, June 1935, pp. 3-4. Substantial shift: Lawson, "The Crisis in the Theater," NM, 15 Dec. 1936, pp. 35-36.

36. First call: NM, 22 Jan. 1935, p. 20; second call: NM, 1 Oct. 1935, p. 33. Revolutionary films: Hurwitz's letter to NM, 12 Mar. 1935, p. 21; Hurwitz and Steiner, "A New Approach to Film Making," pp. 22-23. Progressive films: Lerner, "The Plow That Broke the Plains," NT, July 1936, p. 19.

37. Cowley, "What the Revolutionary Movement Can Do for a Writer," *American Writers' Congress*, ed. Henry Hart (New York: International Publishers, 1935), pp. 60-61. For further discussion of the effect of the Roosevelt administration, see Richard H. Pells, *Radical Visions and American Dreams: Culture and Social Thought in the Depression Years* (New York: Harper & Row, Inc., 1973), pp. 86-94 (quotation is from p. 93).

38. Leyda, *Kino*, pp. 323-324.

39. William Stott, *Documentary Expression and Thirties America* (New York: Oxford University Press, 1973), pp. 238-257.

40. Richard Dyer MacCann, *The People's Films: A Political History of U.S. Government Motion Pictures* (New York: Hastings House Publishers, Inc., 1973), p. 62.

41. Lorentz, "A Young Man Goes to Work," *Scribner's*, Feb. 1931, pp. 205-208.

42. Lorentz, "Public Service," *Plain Talk*, Aug. 1928, pp. 235-238. Pare Lorentz and Morris Ernst, *Censored: The Private Life of the Movies* (New York: J. Cape and H. Smith, 1930), p. 153.

43. Brody, "Movie Notes," *Labor Defender*, Jan. 1931, p. 17. Arch Mercey, "The Teaching of Social Studies Through Documentary Films," p. 5 (abstract of remarks made 5 Aug. 1938 at the Institute on Visual Instruction in Higher Education).

44. Lorentz, *Vanity Fair*, Jan. 1934, p. 46.

45. On the machinery of business overpowering the country: Lorentz, "Young Man," p. 208. Promised outline for New Deal Film: letter from LeCron to Lorentz, 28 Feb. 1935, National Archives. On the RA's innovative public relations programs: Mercey, "The Teaching of Social Studies," pp. 3-4. Other information here and in what follows comes from MacCann, *The People's Films*, Chap. 4; Robert L. Snyder, *Pare Lorentz and the Documentary Film* (Norman, Oklahoma: University of Oklahoma Press, 1968), Chap. 2; J. P. McEvoy, "Young Man with a Camera," *Scribner's Commentator*, July 1940, pp. 43-44; W. L. White, "Pare Lorentz," *Scribner's*, Jan. 1939, pp. 7-11, 42; and Lorentz, "Dorothea Lange: Camera with a Purpose," *U.S. Camera Annual* 1 (1941): 94-95.

46. Snyder, *Pare Lorentz and Documentary*, p. 26.

47. Concert: Steiner interview and Steiner, *A Point of View* (Middletown,

Conn.: Wesleyan University Press, 1978), pp. 12-13. Praise of *Pie in the Sky: Town and Country*, 15 Apr. 1935, p. 32. Lerner, "*The Plow That Broke the Plains*," pp. 18-19.

48. Lorentz's lack of sympathy for radical school critics: *Vanity Fair*, Dec. 1932, p. 46, and Oct. 1933, p. 39. *Pie in the Sky: Town and Country*, 15 Apr. 1933, p. 32. Lorentz's praise of Steiner and Strand: Willard Van Dyke, "Letters from 'The River'," *Film Comment*, Mar.-Apr. 1965, pp. 46-47.

49. MacCann, *The People's Films*, p. 56; McEvoy, "Young Man with a Camera," p. 36; Steiner interview.

50. Lerner, "*The Plow That Broke the Plains*," pp. 18-19. Outline approval: Lerner, and Hurwitz interview 2. Strand account: Tomkins, profile on Strand, p. 72. Hurwitz account: Hurwitz interview 2.

51. Strand quote: Tomkins, profile on Strand, p. 72. Hurwitz quote: Hurwitz interview 2. Top hat scene: Tomkins, profile on Strand, p. 72; also Hurwitz interview 2. Telegram: Hurwitz interview 2.

52. Steiner account, including target practice: Steiner interview. Hurwitz account: Hurwitz interview 2. Forceful letters: Hurwitz interview 3. Strand's letter from Hardin, Montana, 9 Oct. 1935: Stieglitz correspondence, Yale University Library (not to be quoted elsewhere without permission from Georgia O'Keeffe, Hazel Strand, and the Yale University Library). Dart game: Hurwitz interview 3. Hurwitz and Strand differ in their accounts of Steiner's detachment; Strand remembers it more clearly than Hurwitz.

53. Nykino ideas: Hurwitz, "One Man's Voyage," pp. 12-13 (ideas they had been germinating, dramatic structuring, and interactive needs); and Michael and Jill Klein, "*Native Land*: An Interview with Leo Hurwitz," *Cinéaste* 6, no. 3 (1974): 5 (plot to identify with, empathy, and opposition). Livestock: Lerner, "*The Plow That Broke the Plains*," p. 19.

54. No clash of wills: Tomkins, profile on Strand, p. 74. Lorentz's anger: Steiner and Strand interviews. White, "Pare Lorentz," p. 9. According to Hurwitz, White interviewed him, Steiner, and Strand, as well as Lorentz, for this piece. Lorentz's ultimatum: Van Dyke, "Letters from 'The River'," pp. 45-46. Van Dyke says Denver, not Dalhart, but he must have it wrong.

55. Desire not to disrupt entire project: Lerner, "*The Plow That Broke the Plains*," p. 18. Rest: Steiner and Strand interviews and Hurwitz interview 3.

56. Account of credits: Van Dyke, "Letters from 'The River'," p. 46. Their surprise: Tomkins, profile on Strand, p. 74; Strand interview and Hurwitz interview 3.

57. Lorentz, "Dorothea Lange," p. 96. For corroboration, see *Hard Times*, ed. Studs Terkel (New York: Pantheon Books, 1970), pp. 261-262.

58. A. Roger Paxton, "Fiddling While the Great Plains Burn: The Neros of the New Deal," NM, 21 July 1936, pp. 8-9; Edwin Rolfe, "The 'God of Floods'," NM, 9 Feb. 1937, p. 5.

59. Use of lenses: MacCann, *The People's Films*, p. 63. Lorentz, *McCall's*, July 1936, p. 15.

60. Lerner, "*The Plow That Broke the Plains*," p. 18. Strand's words as

reported by Lorentz to Van Dyke: "Letters from 'The River'," p. 46. MacCann, *The People's Films*, p. 65.

61. Mrs. Duke: Snyder, *Pare Lorentz and Documentary*, p. 49. Lorentz, "Agriculture: Mother Nature Lays Down a Withering Calamitous New Deal, Reducing More Crops Than AAA Decreed," *Newsweek*, 9 June 1934, p. 3. Lorentz, *McCalls'*, July 1936, pp. 15, 84.

62. Van Dyke, "Letters from 'The River'," p. 46. Lorentz, "Dorothea Lange," pp. 94-95, 98.

63. Paul Rotha, *Documentary Diary: An Informal History of the British Documentary Film, 1928-1939* (London: Secker & Warburg, 1973), p. 202.

64. Hamilton, "*The Plow That Broke the Plains*," NBR, June 1936, p. 10.

65. Ferguson, "They, the People," NR, 5 Aug. 1936, pp. 381-382.

66. Hurwitz, "One Man's Voyage," pp. 11, 13.

67. Steiner income: Steiner, *Point of View*, p. 19. Maddow interview.

68. Steiner's inability to work: Van Dyke, "Letters from 'The River'," p. 46. On mentioning Steiner to Strand: MacCann, *The People's Films*, p. 64. Hurwitz's and Strand's gloomy outlook: Steiner interview.

69. Decisions in Nykino made by Hurwitz and Strand: Maddow interview. Hurwitz on relation with Strand: Hurwitz interview 3. Steiner's sense of betrayal: Steiner interview. He is referring specifically to later events, but what he describes was happening in 1935.

70. Steiner Buffalo interview. Steiner continues to hold Strand's art in high esteem: see Steiner, *Point of View*, p. 11.

71. Maddow interview and Hurwitz interview 3.

III

1. Background information on Ivens is from Joris Ivens, *The Camera and I* (New York: International Publishers, 1969), p. 18. Subsequent references are to this edition and will be cited by page number in the text.

2. Information on Ivens' lectures and film showings in New York is from the following sources: Hans Wegner, *Joris Ivens, Dokumentarist der Wahrheit* (Berlin: Henschelverlag, 1965); Helen van Dongen, "Joris Ivens in America," *Film Art*, Autumn 1936, p. 15; handout from Museum of Modern Art Film Study Center file on Ivens; NM, 21 Apr. 1936, p. 29; NR, 22 Apr. 1936, p. 324; N, 27 May 1936, p. 688; James Shelley Hamilton, "Joris Ivens," NBR, May 1936, pp. 9-10; Irving Lerner, NM, 31 Mar. 1936, p. 29; and author's interviews with Hurwitz, Lerner, Maddow, and Strand.

3. Ivens, *The Camera and I*, p. 87. His description of work on this film is from pp. 81-93. For more material on the making of *Borinage*, see Ivens, "Making Documentary Films to Meet Today's Needs," *American Cinematographer*, July 1942, p. 299.

4. Criticism of Soviet audiences; search for alternatives to hero and plot: Lerner, NM, 31 Mar. 1936, p. 29. Argument against "objectivity": Ivens,

"Making Documentary Films," p. 299; Ivens, "Note on the Documentary Film," *Direction*, Apr. 1940, p. 15. Importance of editing: Ivens, "Making Documentary Films," p. 332; van Dongen interview. Beauty of physical labor: Maddow interview.

5. Lerner, NM, 31 Mar. 1936. Strand interview. Hamilton, "Joris Ivens," p. 11. Ferguson, "Guest Artist," NR, 15 Apr. 1936, p. 278.

6. Lerner, NM, 31 Mar. 1936. Personal attributes: much testimony to this, but especially in the Helen van Dongen interview. Beauty under surfaces of life: Hamilton, "Joris Ivens," p. 9. Hurwitz interview 1. Leyda and Meyers, "Joris Ivens: Artist in Documentary," *The Magazine of Art*, July 1938, p. 393. In Jay Leyda, "Vision is my dwelling place," *Film Culture*, no. 58-59-60 (1974), pp. 9-10, Leyda identifies this statement as Meyers'.

7. Lerner interview. Hurwitz interview 1. As spur to Nykino effort: Hurwitz, "One Man's Voyage: Ideas and Films in the 1930's," *Cinema Journal*, Fall 1975, p. 13. Strand interview. Van Dyke interview 1.

8. Hurwitz interview 1. Meyers reports Strand's opinion in "*Redes*," NT, Nov. 1936, p. 22. Both Strand and Lerner felt the photography was not up to Dovzhenko's earlier work: Lerner, "Dovjenko's *Frontier*," NT, Jan. 1936, p. 24. Maddow, "Film into Poem," NT, Nov. 1936, pp. 23, 36. Meyers, "The Screen: *Frontier*," NM, 7 Jan. 1936, p. 30.

9. Wegner, *Joris Ivens*, p. 61. "Der grosste Teil der Anwesenden erkannte das Neue an diesen Filmen, nicht nur wegen ihrer filmischen Gestaltung und ihrer unmittelbaren Frische, sondern auch wegen ihrer direkten Stellung-nahme" [the greater part of those present recognized what was new in these films, not only because of their filmic form and their immediate freshness, but also because of their direct point of view]. Ivens' stay in Hollywood: Leyda and Meyers, "Joris Ivens," p. 164.

10. Ivens, "Note on Hollywood," NT, Oct. 1936, pp. 8-10, 28.

11. Lerner and Meyers, "Are Newsreels News?" NT, Apr. 1937, p. 45. See also William Alexander's "*The March of Time* and *The World Today*," *American Quarterly*, Summer 1977, pp. 182-193.

12. Lerner, "The Screen, *The March of Time*," NM, 9 July 1935, p. 30.

13. Willard Van Dyke, in G. Roy Levin, *Documentary Explorations: Fifteen Interviews with Filmmakers* (Garden City, N.Y.: Doubleday & Company, Inc., 1971), p. 184; editorial, NT, Sept. 1936, p. 3; David Platt, "Newsreel With Punch in *The World Today*," DW, 6 May 1937, p. 7.

14. Lerner, "Sights and Sounds," NM, 11 May 1937, p. 29. According to Hurwitz, "the general attitude was that we had no trouble doing better than *The March of Time*, so we didn't take it as a model" (Hurwitz interview 3).

15. First two quotations: Ben Belitt, "The Camera Reconnoiters," N, 20 Nov. 1937, pp. 557-558, from his interview with Paul Strand: they refer to past and present purposes of the cooperative. More complete background: Hurwitz interview 3. Lerner, NM, 18 Aug. 1936, p. 29. Hurwitz and Steiner, "A New Approach to Film Making," NT, Sept. 1935, pp. 22-23.

16. A third was planned, but no one I have talked with has been able to remember the subject.

17. Lerner, "Sights and Sounds," p. 29. Hurwitz interview 2. Other credits from interviews with Hurwitz, Lerner, Maddow, and Edna Meyers.

18. Sunnysiders: Lerner, "Sights and Sounds," p. 29; and David Platt, "Films 1937-38," *Direction*, Jan. 1938, p. 28. *March of Time* staff: Lerner, "Sights and Sounds," p. 29. Hurwitz interview 3.

19. Information in this paragraph from Van Dyke Buffalo interview and from Kent Harber, "Photography and Film through the Eyes of Willard Van Dyke," *The Daily Californian* 10, no. 3 (1978): 3.

20. Van Dyke Buffalo interview and Van Dyke interview 2. Lerner interview.

21. First three quotations: "Thirty Years of Social Inquiry: an Interview with Willard Van Dyke by Harrison Engle," *Film Comment*, Spring 1965, p. 25. Last quotation: Van Dyke Buffalo interview.

22. Ella Winter: Van Dyke interviews 1 and 2. Van Dyke, "The Photographs of Dorothea Lange—a Critical Analysis," *Camera Craft*, Oct. 1934, pp. 461-467.

23. Van Dyke, "Thirty Years of Social Inquiry," p. 25. Van Dyke interview 2.

24. Collier: Van Dyke Buffalo interview. Departure: Buffalo interview and Van Dyke interview 2.

25. Van Dyke Buffalo interview and *Harper's Bazaar* (see, for example, Dec. 1935, pp. 134, 136, 140-143, 146-149).

26. Lorentz negotiations: Van Dyke interview 3. Station wagon: Van Dyke Buffalo interview. Van Dyke has said many times since that this opportunity "was one of the most important things that ever happened to me" (Van Dyke, "Thirty Years of Social Inquiry," pp. 25-26). Earn Respect: Van Dyke Buffalo interview. Final touches: Van Dyke in Levin, *Documentary Explorations*, p. 185.

27. Van Dyke, "Letters from 'The River'," *Film Comment*, Spring 1965, pp. 38-56. The descriptions and quotations in the rest of this section are taken from this source unless otherwise noted.

28. See Van Dyke's own, different analysis of the graveyards in "Thirty Years of Social Inquiry," p. 27.

29. Father: Van Dyke Buffalo interview. Malaria and feelings about New York: Van Dyke in Levin, *Documentary Explorations*, pp. 186-187. In his interview with Kent Harber, Van Dyke gives a great deal of importance to his feeling for the "positive American spirit" (Harber, "Photography and Film," p. 12).

30. Information in this and the following paragraph is from Richard Dyer MacCann, *The People's Films: A Political History of U.S. Government Motion Pictures* (New York: Hastings House, 1973), pp. 71-77; Robert L. Snyder, *Pare Lorentz and the Documentary Film* (Norman, Oklahoma: University of Oklahoma Press, 1968), Chap. 3; and W. L. White, "Pare Lorentz," *Scribner's*, Jan. 1939, pp. 7-11, 42.

31. Letter from Lorentz to Donald C. Blaisdell, 7 June 1937; copy in the National Archives.

32. Hamilton, *"The River,"* NBR, Nov. 1937, p. 12. Awards: Snyder, *Pare Lorentz and Documentary,* pp. 69-74.

33. Quotations from Lorentz *"The River"* (narration for), *Film Comment,* Spring 1965, pp. 57-60. When I have been able to notice the difference, I have revised where words are different in the actual film.

34. Rotha's suggestion: Rotha, *Documentary Diary: An Informal History of the British Documentary Film, 1928-1939* (London: Secker & Warburg, 1973), p. 202. Rotha was privately scornful of the film, and in his *Documentary Film: The Use of the Film Medium to Interpret Creatively and in Social Terms the Life of the People as it Exists in Reality,* 3rd ed. (London: Faber and Faber, 1952), while arguing its importance in popularizing documentary film in America, stated that it had the same faults as *The Plow That Broke the Plains*: "lack of human beings, 'difficult' music, and again a tacked-on end with the propaganda message" (p. 200). In her review, *"The River* Damned," which appeared in the July 1938 edition of *World Film News,* Muriel Rukeyser also criticized the omission of people (p. 121). Praise of Film: Hamilton, *"The River,"* p. 11.

IV

1. Van Dyke Buffalo interview. Los Angeles: Rodakiewicz interview. Sklar letter to author, 4 July 1975. NT, Mar. 1937, p. 50.

2. The brochure is in the Frontier Films file at the Film Study Center of the Museum of Modern Art in New York.

3. Hurwitz, "One Man's Voyage: Ideas and Films in the 1930's," *Cinema Journal,* Fall 1975, p. 14.

4. Playwrights and key contacts: NT, Mar. 1937, p. 50. Frontier's predispositions: Frontier Films brochure. Farm film and civil rights film: *N.Y. Times,* 25 Apr. 1937, X, p. 4. Poughkeepsie: Van Dyke letter to author, 31 July 1975. Watts and John Doe film: Ben Belitt, "The Camera Reconnoiters," N, 20 Nov. 1937, pp. 557-558. John E. Devine, *Films as an Aid in Training Public Employees* (New York? 1937).

5. Van Dyke interview 1. Hurwitz interview 2. Steiner interview and Steiner Buffalo interview.

6. Belitt, "The Camera Reconnoiters," pp. 557-558.

7. Willard Van Dyke, "Letters from 'The River'," *Film Comment,* Mar.-Apr. 1965, p. 54. Hurwitz: Michael and Jill Klein, "*Native Land*: An Interview with Leo Hurwitz," *Cinéaste* 6, no. 3 (1974): 3-7.

8. Frank A. Warren III, *Liberals and Communism* (Bloomington: Indiana University Press, 1966), p. 133.

9. Archibald MacLeish, "Spain and American Writers," in *The Writer in a Changing World,* ed. Henry Hart (New York: Equinox Cooperative Press, 1937), pp. 57-58. Ivens, *The Camera and I* (New York: International Publishers, 1969), p. 103.

10. "Joris Ivens Interviewed by Gordon Hitchens, November 20, 1968,

American Documentaries," *Film Culture*, Spring 1972, p. 191. Hans Wegner, *Joris Ivens, Dokumentarist der Wahrheit* (Berlin: Henschelverlag, 1965), pp. 61-62. A. Zalzman, *Joris Ivens* (Paris: Editions seghers, 1963), p. 59. Van Dongen Buffalo interview. The National Archives has a print of the twenty-minute version of Warner Brothers' *Black Legion*.

11. Ivens, *The Camera and I*, pp. 103-104. Van Dongen Buffalo interview.

12. All information here and in the previous two paragraphs is from Ivens, *The Camera and I*, pp. 104-128.

13. Choice of Welles: Ivens, *The Camera and I*, p. 128, and van Dongen Buffalo interview. Preview dates: John McManus, "Down to Earth in Spain," *N.Y. Times*, 25 July 1937, X, p. 4. Ivens on the narration: Zalzman, *Joris Ivens*, p. 62. Hellman et al. on the narration: Ivens, *The Camera and I*, p. 129, and van Dongen Buffalo interview. Ivens' agreement: van Dongen Buffalo interview. Quote: Ivens, *The Camera and I*, p. 129.

14. Archibald MacLeish, "The Cinema of Joris Ivens," NM, 24 Aug. 1937, p. 18.

15. Quotations are from Ivens, *The Camera and I*, pp. 125-127.

16. John McManus, "The Screen; *The Spanish Earth*, at the 55th St. Playhouse, is a Plea for Democracy—*Gangway* at the Roxy," *N.Y. Times*, 21 Aug. 1937, p. 7. Reply: Zalzman, *Joris Ivens*, pp. 123-127. Call for objectivity: Ivens, *The Camera and I*, p. 137. "Ivens Interviewed by Hitchens," p. 211.

17. Winsten quoted in Ivens, *The Camera and I*, p. 133.

18. Maddow interview and Hurwitz interview 3.

19. Roosevelt's reaction: Ivens, *The Camera and I*, p. 131. March's guests' contributions: McManus, "Down to Earth," p. 4. Amount raised and chasses: Ivens, *The Camera and I*, p. 132. MacLeish speech: MacLeish, "Spain and American Writers," p. 66. Efforts to get major theater distribution: Ivens, *The Camera and I*, p. 132. Distribution: "Ivens Interviewed by Hitchens," p. 194; and Belitt, "The Camera Reconnoiters," pp. 557-558. Ivens was especially pleased by *Time's* praise of the film as "a sort of portfolio of portraits of the human soul in the presence of disaster and distress" and by James Dugan's pointing out that in creating an emotional relationship between spectator and film the filmmaker had accomplished what he had previously believed documentary incapable of achieving. See Ivens, *The Camera and I*, p. 135.

20. Information in these paragraphs from: Kline interview; Kline, "Films Without Make-Believe," *The Magazine of Art*, Feb. 1942, pp. 58-59 (youthful traveling and reading, reaction against "misery and poverty," picked up by labor theaters, Broadway producer); NT, Mar. 1934, p. 22 (announcement of dramatic reading of Kline's play), June 1935, p. 26 (27 May lecture announced), and June 1936, p. 17 (*New Theatre* tour to Soviet Union announced); NM, 5 Feb. 1935, p. 7 (picketing of Ohrbach), 20 Apr. 1937, p. 19 (anticensorship speech in Boston), 12 Mar. 1935, p. 27 (critical symposium on *Panic* announced), and 12 Nov. 1935, p. 2 (symposium on *Squaring the Circle* announced); and N, 22 Jan. 1936, p. 104 (changes in *Squaring the Circle*).

21. Kline, "A Festival of People's Art," NT, Nov. 1936, pp. 9-10.

22. Kline resigns editorship of *New Theatre*: NT, Mar. 1937, p. 2. Joins

Loyalist cause: Kline interview and NM, 30 Mar. 1937, p. 2. With Karpathi: Kline, "Films Without Make-Believe," p. 59. NM articles: 13 Apr. 1937, pp. 7-8; 20 Apr. 1937, p. 19; 20 July 1937, p. 2. Other articles can be found in *Theatre Workshop*, Apr.-July 1937, p. 2, and *N.Y. Times*, 18 Apr. 1937, X, p. 2. The English poet Stephen Spender worked with Kline at EAQ.

23. Information in these paragraphs from: Kline, "Films Without Make-Believe," pp. 58-60 (Karpathi at Kline's door, subject of film, crude thread of a story, Bethune and Karpathi agreeing, learning to operate Eyemo, writing by the great foreign correspondents); Kline interview (Ivens advising Kline to direct the film); and an unidentified clipping dated 13 Sept. 1937 in the *Heart of Spain* file at the Film Study Center of the Museum of Modern Art, New York (living with blood unit, Karpathi wounded).

24. Kline on Hurwitz and return with Bethune: Kline interview. Revision of scenario by Strand and Hurwitz: Kline, "Films Without Make-Believe," p. 56. Hurwitz the night before: Hurwitz interview 1. Strand on images and footage: Strand interview. Maddow at moviola: Maddow interview. Leyda and North: Tom Brandon, in program for "A Missing Chapter in the History of U.S. Documentary Films," at the Museum of Modern Art, New York, 15 May 1974. Scraping the barrel: Strand interview. Lerner on sound: Lerner interview.

25. Elizabeth Noble, *"Heart of Spain,"* NM, 5 Oct. 1937, p. 18.

26. Ibid.

27. Hurwitz interviews 1 and 2.

28. Disagreement with Potamkin: Maddow, "Harry Alan Potamkin," NT, Feb. 1936, p. 33. Criticism of Hayes: Maddow, "Hopes for Poetry," NM, 4 Aug. 1936, p. 28. Meyers applauds films in various reviews for *TAC*. Praise of *Shors*: Maddow, *Films*, Spring 1940, p. 56. See also William Alexander, "Frontier Films, 1936-1941: The Aesthetics of Impact," *Cinema Journal*, Fall 1975, pp. 16-28.

29. Premiere and opening: NM, 14 Sept. 1937, p. 29, and 2 Nov. 1937, p. 27. Brandon: Fred Sweet, Eugene Rosow, and Alan Francovich, "Pioneers: An Interview with Tom Brandon," *Film Quarterly* 26 (1973): 23. Ambulance tour: NR, 22 Sept. 1937, p. 190, and clipping dated 8 Dec. 1937, from an Albany newspaper in *Heart of Spain* file at the Film Study Center, Museum of Modern Art, New York.

30. Kline departure and arrangements: Kline interview and Hurwitz interview 3. Sensational film: Lerner interview.

31. Inappropriateness of film for newsreel and enthusiasm of filmmakers: Lerner interview. Jay Leyda, "Vision is my dwelling place," *Film Culture*, no. 58-59-60 (1974), p. 8. Theater distribution: Sweet, Rosow, and Francovich, "Pioneers: An Interview with Tom Brandon," p. 23.

32. "The poem in *China Strikes Back* was entirely my own. It was my idea of how the translation of a Chinese poem should sound, although I think I had never read any such translations except the rather curious ones produced by Ezra Pound." Letter from Ben Maddow, 24 Dec. 1974.

33. Van Dyke interview 2. Letters to author from Vera Caspary, 22 June

1975, and George Sklar, 4 July 1975; also DW, 30 Dec. 1937, p. 7. Strand interview.

34. Information is from Irene Thomas's (executive secretary of the committee) letter of 16 Mar. 1937 to *New Masses* (p. 18) and from a four-page appeal inserted between pp. 350-351 of the 27 Mar. 1937 issue of *The Nation*. Clyde as sponsor: conversation with Hurwitz, 18 Nov. 1974.

35. Dobbs and Lynch: N, 27 Mar. 1937, pp. 350-351. Vigilantes: *Direction*, Apr. 1938, p. 29. Steiner Buffalo interview, with some minimal editing for better readability.

36. Strand interview.

37. Lorentz, *The Roosevelt Year: A Photographic Record* (New York: Funk & Wagnalls, Inc., 1934), pp. 50-51.

38. Van Dyke interview 2.

39. Van Dyke interviews 1 and 2; Hurwitz interview 2; Strand interview.

40. Steiner interview.

41. Stein contacts Steiner: Van Dyke Buffalo interview. Steiner screening the films and resignation from Frontier: Buffalo interview. Berman to Devine: Devine, *Films as an Aid in Training Public Employees*, p. 56. Resignation date: Van Dyke interviews 1 and 2. Conference with Stein: I was asked not to divulge the source of this information; Berman was one of the two members.

42. Lawsuit: Steiner interview and Van Dyke interview 2. Steiner's version of the resulting trouble: combination of Steiner interview and Steiner Buffalo interview.

43. Steiner interview. Strand's world view: Van Dyke in Richard Dyer MacCann, *The People's Films: A Political History of U.S. Government Motion Pictures* (New York: Hastings House, 1973), p. 64.

44. On salary: Hurwitz, "One Man's Voyage," p. 14. In retrospect: Steiner interview; G. Roy Levin interview with Van Dyke, *Documentary Explorations: Fifteen Interviews with Filmmakers* (Garden City, N.Y.: Doubleday & Company, Inc., 1971), p. 185. Lerner and Maddow interviews. According to Steiner, at least one purpose in the founding of American Documentary Films, Inc. was to make money (Steiner Buffalo interview).

45. Hurwitz interviews 2 and 3.

46. Van Dyke Buffalo interview and Van Dyke interview 2. Steiner Buffalo interview and Steiner interview. Strand interview.

47. Van Dyke interview 2. Hurwitz quotation: first paragraph, interview 3; second paragraph, Klein, "*Native Land*: An Interview with Leo Hurwitz," pp. 3-4.

48. Eric Bentley, *Thirty Years of Treason: Excerpts from Hearings Before the House Committee on Un-American Activities, 1938-1968* (New York: Viking Press, 1971), p. 260.

49. Conversation with Hurwitz, 12 May 1975.

50. Steiner Buffalo interview.

51. Hawes's film: Steiner Buffalo interview. Hollywood: Steiner interview. Commercial photography: Steiner Buffalo interview.

V

1. Details on production: Kline interview and letter to author from Kline, 19 Apr. 1975. The Medical Bureau and the North American Committee to Aid Spanish Democracy aided in the production. See NR, 20 July 1938, p. 316. Premiere: *TAC*, Aug. 1938, p. 6.

2. Conversation with Hurwitz, 18 Nov. 1974. Strand interview. Lewis Jacobs, "Two Pictures of the Month," *Direction*, Sept.-Oct. 1938, p. 23.

3. Background information: Ivens cited in *N.Y. Herald Tribune*, 5 Mar. 1939. Fund raising: A. Zalzman, *Joris Ivens* (Paris: Editions seghers, 1963), p. 63, and "Joris Ivens Interviewed by Gordon Hitchens, November 20, 1968, American Documentaries," *Film Culture*, Spring 1972, p. 193. To Paris and back: Ivens, *The Camera and I* (New York: International Publishers, 1969), p. 142, and Zalzman, *Joris Ivens*, p. 63. Friends: Sidney Meyers, "Film: To the Editor," *TAC*, Oct. 1938, p. 12. At this time Strand was comparing himself unfavorably to the Dutchman (Ivens) who took his camera to the very battlefields where the great issues were fought: letter to author from David Prensky, 17 Aug. 1976.

4. Information in this paragraph from: *N.Y. Herald Tribune*, 5 Mar. 1939 (cutting to 6,000 feet); Ivens, "We Document a Nation at War," *TAC*, Feb. 1939, p. 19 (Nichols not able to go to China); Ivens, *The Camera and I*, pp. 179-180 (lower costs in New York and no pay); Ivens, "Ivens Interviewed by Hitchens," pp. 193-194 (medical aid); van Dongen Buffalo interview (New York and Hollywood editing and no pay).

5. Ivens, *The Camera and I*, pp. 165-166; p. 167.

6. Information in these paragraphs from: Ivens, *The Camera and I*, pp. 141 (purposes frustrated), 145 (officers from among the people), 149 (Madame Sun Yat-sen), 150 (Chinese art, etc.), 160 (General Tu), 176-178 (true and staged demonstrations); Robert Grelier, *Joris Ivens* (Paris: Les éditeurs Français réunis, 1965), p. 84 (inability to reach former red army and duplication of shots in 16mm).

7. Ivens, *The Camera and I*, pp. 169-170, 174. Despair and Nichols: Zalzman, *Joris Ivens*, p. 67, and Grelier, *Joris Ivens*, p. 84. Eisler: Maddow interview.

8. Ivens, *The Camera and I*, pp. 182, 169.

9. Premiere: Kline interview. Backing: Hans Burger, "Filming a European Crisis," NBR, Mar. 1940, p. 7, and Arthur L. Mayer, "A Plea for Unpopular Films," NBR, May 1940, p. 6. Czechoslovakia: *TAC*, Nov. 1938, p. 21. World War II and various reasons: Kline interview. Mayer is the person who put Stein in touch with Steiner; he may have been unfriendly toward Frontier Films, but I have no information confirming this. Kline told me that some of his filmmaking friends were surprised at how good the Czech film was; he also mentioned the people I name as those who were encouraging. See Herbert Kline, "Films Without Make-Believe," *The Magazine of Art*, Feb. 1942, pp. 58-63.

10. Great correspondent: Kline, "Films Without Make-Believe," p. 58. Description of film: Kline interview.

11. The scripts: Kline interview. Two crews: "Script Trouble," is unidentified clipping in *Crisis* file in Film Study Center at the Museum of Modern Art. Probably contemporary with the opening of the film.

12. Information from: "Script Trouble" (see note 12) (permits to film Czech army, film hidden in basement, and not able to tell about smuggling film out); Kline, "Films Without Make-Believe," p. 62 (pretending to be pro-Nazi, etc., troop of SA men doing Kline's bidding); Burger, "Filming a European Crisis," pp. 8-9 (events as they broke and lies of Nazi guides); James Dugan, "Film on Czechoslovakia," NM, 21 Mar. 1939, p. 28 (leaving Sudeten after Munich); and Kline interview (antagonists murdered, editing in Bata Shoe Film Dept., getting collaborators out of Czechoslovakia).

13. Credits: Kline interview, and *Variety*, 15 Mar. 1939, p. 16. *Living Films* (a 1940 publication of the Association of Documentary Film Producers), p. 17. Ten best: NBR, May 1940, pp. 6-7.

14. Travelogue: *Variety*, 15 Mar. 1939, p. 16, and Kate Cameron, "Crisis, a Film Record of Czech's Travail," clipping erroneously identified in handwriting as the *N.Y. Daily News*, 12 Mar. 1939, in *Crisis* file in Film Study Center at the Museum of Modern Art.

15. Hamilton, "*Crisis*," NBR, Mar. 1939, p. 22. Dugan, "Film on Czechoslovakia," p. 30. Meyers, "Movies," TAC, Apr. 1939, pp. 15, 22. Previous summer: Jay Leyda and Sidney Meyers, "Joris Ivens: Artist in Documentary," *The Magazine of Art*, July 1938, p. 393 (the words cited are Meyers'). Maltz, and Meyers' reply: TAC, May 1939, pp. 24, 27.

16. Information in these paragraphs from: Kline interview (Rosa Harvan and Peter Mayer, cameramen killed and cameras lost); Kline, "Films Without Make-Believe," p. 61 (strafing); *Time*, 22 Apr. 1940, p. 90 (knew his next destination, strafing, filming locations); and "Censors Place Eager Cameras on Skimpy Diet," *N.Y. Herald Tribune*, 21 Apr. 1940 (uninteresting material and censorship in France). A *New Republic* article, dated 22 Apr. 1940, agrees that Kline scooped "a lot of watchful cameras."

17. Newsreels: *N.Y. Herald Tribune*, 21 Apr. 1940, VI, p. 3; NR, 22 Apr. 1940, p. 536. Franz Hoellering, "Films," N, 20 Apr. 1940, p. 521.

18. Information in this paragraph from: *Direction*, May 1940, p. 18 (remaining in Warsaw with others gone); Julien Bryan, "War Is, Was, and Always Will Be, Hell," *U.S. Camera Magazine*, Feb.-Mar. 1940, pp. 88-92 (trip through Rumania from Switzerland, long account of his experience, escape); and *Thirty-Five Years After* (travel from Switzerland, masquerade as Swede), a film made in tribute to Bryan in 1974 (finished in 1975) when he returned to Poland just before his death. It includes *Siege*.

19. Hoellering, "Films," p. 521.

20. James Dugan, "Murder, Ltd.; Herbert Kline's War Film and a Remake from Hollywood," NM, 16 Apr. 1940, pp. 30-31. Kline interview.

VI

1. Four-reeler: Strand interview. Extras: DW, 7 Dec. 1937, p. 7. Feature-length script: Irene Thirer, "Paul Strand and Leo Hurwitz Offer Data on *Native Land*," *N.Y. Post*, 9 May 1942, p. 13.

2. Militant trade union movement and spearhead: Michael and Jill Klein, "*Native Land*; An Interview with Leo Hurwitz," *Cinéaste* 6, no. 3 (1974): 5. In *One Act Play Magazine*, the Frontier members wrote hopefully and optimistically about a growing audience for progressive films (see the Jan. 1939 issue, p. 665).

3. *One Act Play Magazine*, p. 666.

4. "Fistful of emotion": Theodore Strauss, "Homesteading Our *Native Land*," *N.Y. Times*, 3 May 1942, X, p. 3. Robeson: Thirer, "Strand and Hurwitz Offer Data on *Native Land*," p. 13.

5. David Platt, "Films 1937-38," *Direction*, Jan. 1938, p. 28. Meyers, "Film: To the editor," *TAC*, Oct. 1938, p. 12. Meyer still: "Program for American Audiences," *TAC*, Dec. 1938, p. 3. Richard Watts, "Documentary Film," *N.Y. Herald Tribune*, 16 May 1942, p. 15. Writer's Congress: Strauss, "Homesteading Our *Native Land*," p. 3.

6. *Direction*, Feb. 1940, p. 15. *Films*, Spring 1940, p. 95. Association of Documentary Film Producers, *Living Films: A Catalog of Documentary Films and Their Makers* (New York, 1940), pp. 14, 26. Leyda, "Courage in Films," *Direction*, Apr.-May 1941, p. 27. Editing (which went on while the filming was in process): Strauss, "Homesteading Our *Native Land*," p. 3; and *Documentary Film News*, Apr. 1942, p. 7. Answer print: Klein, "*Native Land*: An Interview with Leo Hurwitz," p. 6.

7. $7,000 and $40,000: Strauss, "Homesteading Our *Native Land*," p. 3. Baldwin: Hurwitz interview 2. Although Baldwin's name appears on the Frontier letterhead in 1941 as a member of the advisory board, he may have been less friendly in 1938 when Frontier was trying to raise funds and showed him the script. "Ingenious cutting": James Arthur, "Films at the Fair," *TAC*, July-Aug. 1939, p. 30. Maddow interview. Hurwitz interview 1.

8. Maddow interview. Information on the film: Association of Documentary Film Producers, *Living Films*, pp. 10, 55. Meyers and others give Berman major credit for the film: "Lionel Berman," booklet printed privately after his death.

9. Strauss quote: Strauss, "Homesteading Our *Native Land*," p. 3. *Times* says $60,000; Strand said $75,000. Goldfish bowl: Strauss, "Homesteading Our *Native Land*," p. 3. Rushes: Hurwitz interview 3. Hellman and Mann: Strand interview. Hiatus and halts: Strauss, "Homesteading Our *Native Land*," p. 3. Strand recalls that no money came from unions: contributors were mostly well-to-do liberals concerned with civil rights.

10. Strand interview. Hurwitz interview 3. Robeson: *Documentary Film News*, Apr. 1942, p. 7. Blitzstein: Thirer, "Strand and Hur•itz Offer Data on *Native Land*," p. 13.

11. Van Dyke Buffalo interview. Strauss, "Homesteading Our *Native Land*," p. 3. Maddow interview. Letter from June Gitlin to author, 6 June 1975.

12. Hurwitz interview 3. Van Dyke Buffalo interview.

13. Maddow interview. Strand interview and Hurwitz interview 3. Inez Garson interview.

14. Inez Garson interview; Hurwitz interview 3; Maddow interview; "Lionel Berman" (booklet).

15. Strand interview and Hurwitz interview 3. Lerner interview.

16. See Richard H. Pells, *Radical Visions and American Dreams: Culture and Social Thought in the Depression Years* (New York: Harper & Row, Inc., 1973), pp. 257-258.

17. Strand interview.

18. Maddow and Strand interviews. Hurwitz interview 3.

19. Salary: Hurwitz, "One Man's Voyage: Ideas and Films in the 1930's," *Cinema Journal*, Fall 1975, p. 14; Hurwitz interview 3. Maddow interview. Strand interview. Edna Ocko Meyers remembers that she and Sidney got by all right, that they didn't feel uncomfortable: Edna Meyers interview.

20. Maddow, letter to author, 13 Oct. 1974. Hurwitz interview 3.

21. Hurwitz interview 3.

22. Maddow and Lerner interviews.

23. Hurwitz interview 3.

24. Hurwitz interview 3. Maddow interview. *Documentary Film News*, Aug. 1941, p. 6; Sept. 1941, p. 6; Nov.-Dec. 1941, p. 5.

25. Maddow, "On Signing Up," *Poetry*, May 1936, p. 71. Reviews: NM, 4 Aug. 1936, p. 28; 27 Apr. 1937, p. 23. Maddow, "The Sign," NM, 4 May 1937, p. 20. Maddow, "The City," *Poetry*, Jan. 1940, pp. 169-175.

26. Maddow, "Film into Poem," NT, Nov. 1936, pp. 23, 36.

27. *Confessions*: Maddow, "Fact into Film, *Confessions of a Nazi Spy*," *Films*, Nov. 1939, p. 83. *Shors*: Maddow, "Film Intensity: *Shors*," *Films*, Spring 1940, p. 56. *Native Land* avoids looking at life and limitations in Strand photography: Maddow interview. The drama of ideas in documentary film: Maddow, "Film Intensity; *Shors*," p. 57. For the same notion, see Maddow's speech, "The Writer's Function in Documentary Film," *Proceedings of the Writers' Congress, Los Angeles, 1943* (Berkeley: University of California Press, 1944), pp. 100-101.

28. Maddow interview.

29. Maddow interview.

30. Maddow interview. Maddow, "Declamation," *TAC*, Nov. 1938, p. 13. Maddow, "While We Slept," *Poetry*, Sept. 1940, pp. 316-317.

31. Hurwitz interview 3. Hurwitz interview 2.

32. Hurwitz interview 3.

33. Strand interview. Hurwitz interview 3 and conversation with author, 12 May 1975.

34. Hurwitz interview 1. Klein, *Native Land*: An Interview with Leo Hurwitz," p. 5.

35. Hurwitz, "One Man's Voyage," pp. 8-9. Hurwitz interview 3.

36. The quotation, previously cited in Chapter III, is from Van Dyke, "Letters from 'The River'," *Film Comment*, Mar.-Apr. 1965, p. 54.

37. "Fistful of emotion": Strauss, "Homesteading Our *Native Land*," p. 3.

38. Klein, "*Native Land*: An Interview with Leo Hurwitz," p. 7.

39. William Boehnel, "World Theatre Shows *Native Land*," *N.Y. World-Telegram*, 12 May 1942, p. 10. Hurwitz interview 3.

40. Bosley Crowther, " 'Native Land,' Impassioned and Dramatic Documentary on American Civil Liberties, Presented at the World," *N.Y. Times*, 12 May 1942, p. 16.

41. Strand, "Realism: A Personal View," *Sight and Sound*, Jan. 1950, p. 26.

42. Epilogue quoted by David Platt in clipping at the Film Study Center, Museum of Modern Art—from a review of the film, probably in DW. Klein, "*Native Land*: An Interview with Leo Hurwitz," p. 6.

43. Strand interview.

44. Hurwitz, "One Man's Voyage," p. 14.

45. Maddow Interview. Strand, "Realism: a Personal View," p. 26.

VII

1. Strand interview. Evelyn Gerstein, "English Documentary Films," NT, Jan. 1936, pp. 7, 36.

2. Paul Rotha, *Documentary Diary: An Informal History of the British Documentary Film, 1928-1939* (London: Secker & Warburg, 1973), pp. 171-173. Subsequent references are to this edition and will be cited by page number in the text. In 1937, two other filmmakers of the British documentary movement, Tom Baird and Edgar Anstey, made brief appearances.

3. Paul Rotha, "The Documentary Method in British Films," Lecture delivered in the motion picture course at New York University and later published in NBR, Nov. 1937, pp. 3-9. For Rotha's purposes in the United States, see also Rotha, *Documentary Diary*, p. 201.

4. He was encouraged by some Americans: John Marshall told him "I hope that some of your documentary knowledge and experience will brush off on some of our people here. They have a lot to learn" (Rotha, *Documentary Diary*, p. 176).

5. Rotha's effect on Strand: Strand himself expressed his lack of enthusiasm in my interview with him. Lorentz, "Movies," *McCall's*, July 1940, p. 4; also in Lorentz, *Lorentz on Film: Movies 1927 to 1941* (New York: Hopkinson and Blake, 1975), p. 190. Arthur Rosenheimer, Review of Paul Rotha's *Documentary Film*, *Films*, Nov. 1939, p. 109. See the third edition of Paul Rotha's *Documentary Film: The Use of the Film Medium to Interpret Creatively and in Social Terms the Life of the People as it Exists in Reality* (London: Faber and Faber, 1952), pp. 213-214, where Sinclair Road further slights Ivens and plugs the sponsored film.

6. Rosenheimer, Review of Rotha's *Documentary Film*, pp. 108-109. Gerstein, "English Documentary," p. 36. Hurwitz, "One Man's Voyage: Ideas and Films in the 1930's," *Cinema Journal*, Fall 1975, pp. 11-12.

7. Paul Rotha, "Films and the Labour Movement," address at Edinburgh, 3 Oct. 1936. Document at Museum of Modern Art Library.

8. Make money: Steiner Buffalo interview.

9. Steiner Buffalo interview. Telephone conversation with Lorentz, 14 Nov. 1978. Outline for *The City*: copy in possession of author. Lorentz has doubts that the outline is the one by him: letter to author, 1 Dec. 1978.

10. Completed before 28 June: date on outline. Information in these two paragraphs is from Rodakiewicz interview, Rodakiewicz Buffalo interview, Van Dyke interview 2, Van Dyke Buffalo interview, and G. Roy Levin, *Documentary Explorations: Fifteen Interviews with Filmmakers* (Garden City, N.Y.: Doubleday & Company, Inc., 1971), p. 188 (how to overcome that voice from on high?).

11. Rodakiewicz Buffalo interview (Van Dyke was interviewer) and Rodakiewicz interview.

12. Steiner Buffalo interview. Rodakiewicz interview.

13. Outline for *The City* (see note 9). Rodakiewicz, "Treatment of Sound in 'The City'," in *The Movies as Medium*, ed. Lewis Jacobs (New York: Farrar, Strauss & Giroux, 1970), p. 282; and shooting script for *The City*, copy in possession of author.

14. Rodakiewicz interview.

15. Steiner, undated letter to Howard Gillette, July 1975. Rodakiewicz interview.

16. Rodakiewicz, shooting script for *The City* and note written on the script in 1975. Veto: note written on the script. Levin, *Documentary Explorations*, p. 189.

17. Outline for *The City* (see note 9).

18. Ibid.

19. James Arthur, "Films at the Fair," *TAC*, July-Aug. 1939, p. 33. Richard Griffith, "Films at the Fair," *Films*, Nov. 1939, pp. 63-64. Anonymous reviewer: *Film Survey*, June 1939, p. 1.

20. Archer Winsten, "*The City* opens Saturday at the World's Fair," *N.Y. Post*, 23 May 1939, p. 15. Griffith, "Films at the Fair," pp. 63-64. John Grierson, *Grierson on Documentary*, ed. Forsyth Hardy (New York: Praeger, 1971), pp. 218-220.

21. Richard Barsam, *Nonfiction Film—A Critical History* (New York: E. P. Dutton & Company, Inc., 1973), p. 115. Van Dyke Buffalo interview.

22. Own funds: Steiner Buffalo interview. Monsanto: Steiner, *A Point of View* (Middletown, Conn.: Wesleyan University Press, 1978), p. 15. *Candid Camera*: Van Dyke interview 2. Disagreement: Van Dyke interview 2. There is some discrepancy between sources concerning the Hunterhill films: Steiner refers only to the Massachusetts film (Buffalo interview), and the *Film News* issue of Nov. 1940 reports only that Kerkow directed and Bob Churchill photographed the New Hampshire version (p. 7).

23. See Sidney Fine, *The Automobile Under the Blue Eagle* (Ann Arbor: University of Michigan Press, 1963), pp. 152-155.

24. From a circular by the Educational Film Institute, New York University.

25. "Truth of the matter" quotation: Van Dyke Buffalo interview; Van Dyke interview; Lerner interview; and Willard Van Dyke, "Thirty Years of Social Inquiry; an Interview with Willard Van Dyke by Harrison Engle," *Film Comment*, Spring 1965, p. 27 (on Blitzstein, plus some other production details).

26. Druggist and Mayor: Van Dyke Buffalo interview. Inner monologue and Blitzstein refinement: Van Dyke, "Thirty Years," p. 27.

27. Van Dyke, "Thirty Years," p. 27.

28. *Film News*, July 1940, p. 1, and June 1940, p. 5. Foundation orders to cease production: Spencer Pollard to Philip Maguire, vice president, Federal Surplus Commodities Corporation, Dept. of Agriculture, 1 July 1940, National Archives. Pollard was trying to persuade Maguire to take over sponsorship of Ferno's Film.

29. Van Dyke interview 1 and Van Dyke Buffalo interview.

30. Report: *Film News*, July 1940, p. 2. *Valley Town* responsible for look at Ferno and Ivens scripts and Sloan's brother's dismissal: Van Dyke interview 2. Actions: *Film News*, Dec. 1940, p. 5. Renewed grant: *Film News*, Jan. 1942, p. 3.

31. Van Dyke interview 2.

32. Griffith, in Rotha's *Documentary Film*, pp. 316-317. It should be noted that Griffith has his chronology backward on this film and on *Machine: Master or Slave?*

33. *Year's Work: Documentary Film News*, Dec. 1940, pp. 2, 4. Sand film: ibid., p. 3. Documentary Film Productions was trying to sell the British "documentary idea": Van Dyke interview 2.

34. Van Dyke says this was "the head of the State Dep't agency that preceded the U.S.I.A." (letter to author, 17 Nov. 1978). This is possibly the Foreign Information Service, established at this time by William J. Donovan, Roosevelt's new Coordinator of Information. See John W. Henderson, *The United States Information Agency* (New York: Praeger, 1969), p. 30.

35. *Democracy at Play: Documentary Film News*, Aug. 1941, p. 2, and Van Dyke interview 2. *Children Next Door: Documentary Film News*, Aug. 1941, p. 5. *To Hear Your Banjo Play*: Van Dyke interview 2. Brandon interest and Labor Day trip on *Tall Tales*: Van Dyke interview 2. *Here is Tomorrow: Documentary Film News*, Nov.-Dec. 1941, p. 6, and Van Dyke interview 2.

36. Levin, *Documentary Explorations*, p. 185. James Blue: Van Dyke Buffalo interview. *Film Culture* interviewers, Jonas Mekas and Edouard Laurot: "The American Documentary—Limitations and Possibilities," *Film Culture* 2, no. 3 (1956): 8.

37. Van Dyke interview 2.

38. Van Dyke Buffalo interview: I have trimmed the prose a little.

39. Screening of *The River*: Robert L. Snyder, *Pare Lorentz and the Documentary Film* (Norman: University of Oklahoma Press, 1968), pp. 71-72; Rotha, *Documentary Diary*, p. 218. No people: David Thompson, "Old Man

River," *World Film News*, July 1938, p. 119. Hamilton, *"The River,"* NBR, Nov. 1937, p. 11. Short novel: Snyder, *Pare Lorentz and Documentary*, p. 96; Richard Dyer MacCann, *The People's Films: A Political History of U.S. Government Motion Pictures* (New York: Hastings House, 1973), p. 96. *Queen Mary*: Snyder, *Pare Lorentz and Documentary*, pp. 72-73.

40. Text of radio play (BBC version) is in *World Film News*, Sept. 1938, pp. 216-217, 219. Review: ibid., p. 219.

41. Information from Snyder, *Pare Lorentz and Documentary*, pp. 81, 83-84, 99, 100-102, and from MacCann, *The People's Films*, p. 96.

42. Information from Snyder, *Pare Lorentz and Documentary*, pp. 102-103, MacCann, *The People's Films*, p. 96, and Sigrid Arne, "Young Man with a Movie Camera Finds a Great Story to Tell," AP Feature Service piece no. 27A, 13 Feb. 1940, no page numbers.

43. Hemorrhaging: Arne, "Young Man." Snyder, *Pare Lorentz and Documentary*, p. 104. See also *N.Y. Times*, 17 Mar. 1940, X, p. 4. Extremely important to show poverty; Cook County Hospital: "Lorentz on Film," Program 2, National Educational Television, 1961. Need to broaden scope of film: Snyder, *Pare Lorentz and Documentary*, p. 104, and Bosley Crowther, "Lorentz Experiments," *N.Y. Times*, 10 Mar. 1940, X, p. 5.

44. McCormick quoted in "Trio of Actors All but Earns Trio of M.D.'s," *N.Y. Herald Tribune* 17 Mar. 1940, pp. 3-4.

45. Archer Winsten, *"The Fight for Life* at Belmont Theatre," *N.Y. Post*, 7 Mar. 1940, p. 11. Frank Nugent, "Grim Reality Note," *N.Y. Times*, 10 Mar. 1940, X, p. 5.

46. Winsten, *"The Fight for Life* at Belmont Theatre," p. 11. See also *TAC*, 15 Mar. 1940, p. 9.

47. Work with Gruenberg: Crowther, "Lorentz Experiments," p. 5; Lorentz, "Pare Lorentz's Music Instructions for *The Fight for Life*," in *Twenty Best Film Plays*, ed. John Gassner and Dudley Nichols (New York: Crown Publishers, 1943), pp. 1,083-1,084.

48. Richard Griffith, *"The Fight for Life,"* NBR, Mar. 1940, p. 13. Because he was uncomfortable with "fictionizations of fact" and thought them an improper direction for documentary films to take, Griffith condemned the film. Later, in Rotha's third edition of *Documentary Film*, Griffith had opened his horizons a bit, finding that *Fight for Life* was a viable documentary in the mainline tradition of that genre, and stating that it was "impossible not to recognize this film as a masterpiece."

49. The words, based on De Kruif's speech to the 1938 class of the University of Chicago Medical School (see Snyder, *Pare Lorentz and Documentary*, p. 108), are spoken over the heartbeat motif and the low single notes of an oboe. Gruenberg: Lorentz, "Music Instructions," in Gassner and Nichols, *Twenty Best Film Plays*, p. 1,086.

50. Margaret Bourke-White, "Photographing This World," N, 19 Feb. 1936, p. 217. Kline, "Hollywood Fights Back," N, 13 May 1936, pp. 612-613.

51. Call from Lorentz: A. Zalzman, *Joris Ivens* (Paris: Editions seghers, 1963), p. 67. Outline and script: Snyder, *Pare Lorentz and Documentary*, p.

123. Reasons for taking job: Ivens, *The Camera and I* (New York: International Publishers, 1969), p. 187. Difficulties: "Joris Ivens Interviewed by Gordon Hitchens, November 20, 1968, American Documentaries," *Film Culture*, Spring 1972, p. 204.

52. Outline and farm: Ivens, *The Camera and I*, pp. 197-198, 187. Ivens and Parkinsons: ibid., pp. 189, 193-194, 205; Zalzman, *Joris Ivens*, p. 68; "Ivens Interviewed by Hitchens," p. 196; van Dongen Buffalo interview.

53. Ivens, "Collaboration in Documentary," *Films*, Spring 1940, pp. 35-38; and Ivens, *The Camera and I*, pp. 193-194.

54. Ornitz/Crosby: Snyder, *Pare Lorentz and Documentary*, pp. 125-126. Steinbeck/Benét: ibid., p. 127; Ivens, *The Camera and I*, pp. 195-196; van Dongen Buffalo interview.

55. Clear goal: Ivens, *The Camera and I*, p. 187. Early hopes: "Ivens Interviewed by Hitchens," p. 196. Could not include drama: Ivens, *The Camera and I*, p. 190. Lorentz to Ivens: Snyder, *Pare Lorentz and Documentary*, p. 127.

56. Problème essentiel: Zalzman, *Pare Lorentz*, p. 69. Strategy: Ivens, "Collaboration," p. 32.

57. Crosby: Snyder, *Pare Lorentz and Documentary*, pp. 125-126. Government officials: Zalzman, *Pare Lorentz*, p. 69. Hostilities: "Ivens Interviewed by Hitchens," p. 203.

58. Dutch tradition and brother: van Dongen Buffalo interview. (The younger brother became a lawyer: Ivens, *The Camera and I*, p. 14.) Discharged from jobs: van Dongen Buffalo interview.

59. Ivens, "Collaboration," pp. 41-42.

60. "Ivens Interviewed by Hitchens," pp. 212-213. This was Ivens in retrospect, but the Institute announced that his projected film was to be on both economic and social frontiers (see *Film News*, Apr. 1940, p. 2).

61. Information on Dick: Van Dyke interview 2. In mining area: NM, 26 Mar. 1940, p. 28. See also *Film News*, 31 Jan. 1940, p. 3.

62. *School*: Association of Documentary Film Producers, *Living Films: A Catalog of Documentary Films and Their Makers* (New York, 1940), p. 50. Other information from ibid. and *Film News*, Apr. 1940, p. 6, and June 1940, p. 5. It was also voted one of three short films of distinctive merit for April 1940 by the Film Review Board of *Good Housekeeping* (see April 1940 issue, p. 93).

63. *Film News*, 31 Jan. 1940, p. 3.

64. NM, 26 Mar. 1940, p. 28. *N.Y. Times*, 13 May 1950, p. 34.

65. Winter article: Ivens, "Collaboration," pp. 41-42. Distribution: Zalzman, *Pare Lorentz*, p. 69. MacCann, *The People's Films*, p. 103.

Bibliography

I have not listed all of the articles and newspaper columns consulted in the course of my research but only those actually cited in the text. I do not list here citations of newspaper advertisements or of brief notices in anonymously written columns; those are, however, documented in the footnotes. In a few cases I have listed works not cited—for example, poems by Ben Maddow that I came across—in the knowledge that they are hard to find and in the belief that the reader might wish to locate them.

Books

Aaron, Daniel. *Writers on the Left.* New York: Harcourt, Brace & World, 1961.

Association of Documentary Film Producers. *Living Films: A Catalog of Documentary Films and Their Makers.* New York: Association of Documentary Film Producers, 1940.

Barnouw, Erik. *Documentary: A History of the Non-Fiction Film.* New York: Oxford University Press, 1974.

Barsam, Richard. *Nonfiction Film—a Critical History.* New York: E. P. Dutton & Company, Inc., 1973.

Beattie, Eleanor. *A Handbook of Canadian Film.* Toronto: P. Martin Associates, 1973.

Bentley, Eric. *Thirty Years of Treason: Excerpts from Hearings Before the House Committee on Un-American Activities, 1938-1968.* New York: Viking Press, 1971.

Brandenburg, Frank. *The Making of Modern Mexico.* Englewood Cliffs, N.J.: Prentice-Hall, Inc., 1964.

Campbell, Russell. "Radical Cinema in the United States, 1930-1947: The Work of the Film and Photo League, Nykino, and Frontier Films." Ph.D. dissertation, Northwestern University, 1978.

Cline, Howard F. *Mexico: Revolution to Evolution, 1940-1960.* New York: Oxford University Press, 1962.

Clurman, Harold. *The Fervent Years.* New York: Hill and Wang, 1957.

Devine, John E. *Films as an Aid in Training Public Employees: A Report to the Committee on Public Administration of the Social Science Research Council.* New York? 1937.

Fine, Sidney. *The Automobile Under the Blue Eagle.* Ann Arbor: University of Michigan Press, 1963.

Gassner, John, and Dudley Nichols, eds. *Twenty Best Film Plays*. New York: Crown Publishers, 1943.

Grelier, Robert. *Joris Ivens*. Paris: Les éditeurs Français réunis, 1965.

Grierson, John. *Grierson on Documentary*. Edited and compiled by Forsyth Hardy. 2d ed. rev. New York: Praeger, 1971.

Hart, Henry, ed. *The Writer in a Changing World*. New York: Equinox Cooperative Press, 1937.

Henderson, John W. *The United States Information Agency*. New York: Praeger, 1969.

Himelstein, Morgan Y. *Drama Was a Weapon: The Left-Wing Theatre in New York, 1929-1941*. New Brunswick: Rutgers University Press, 1963.

Huberman, Leo. *The Labor Spy Racket*. New York: Modern Age Books, Inc., 1937.

Ivens, Joris. *The Camera and I*. New York: International Publishers, 1969.

Jacobs, Lewis, ed. *The Documentary Tradition, from Nanook to Woodstock*. New York: Hopkinson and Blake, 1971.

————: *The Movies as Medium*. New York: Farrar, Strauss & Giroux, 1970.

————. *The Rise of the American Film: A Critical History*. New York: Harcourt, Brace & Company, 1939.

Kazin, Alfred. *Starting Out in the Thirties*. Boston: Little, Brown and Company, 1962.

Knight, Arthur. *The Liveliest Art: A Panoramic History of the Movies*. New York: New American Library, 1957.

Levin, G. Roy. *Documentary Explorations: Fifteen Interviews with Filmmakers*. Garden City, N.Y.: Doubleday & Company, Inc., 1971.

Leyda, Jay. *Kino: A History of the Russian and Soviet Film*. New York: Macmillan, Inc., 1960.

Lorentz, Pare. *Lorentz on Film: Movies 1927 to 1941*. New York: Hopkinson and Blake, 1975.

————. *The Roosevelt Year: A Photographic Record*. New York: Funk & Wagnalls, Inc., 1934.

————, and Morris Ernst. *Censored: The Private Life of the Movies*. New York: J. Cape and H. Smith, 1930.

MacCann, Richard Dyer. *The People's Films; A Political History of U.S. Government Motion Pictures*. New York: Hastings House, 1973.

Miller, Lina D., ed. *Directory of Social Agencies*. New York: Charity Organization Society of the City of New York, 1930-1931.

Newhall, Nancy. *Photographs, 1915-1945: Paul Strand*. New York: Museum of Modern Art, 1945.

Pells, Richard H. *Radical Visions and American Dreams: Culture and Social Thought in the Depression Years*. New York: Harper & Row, Inc., 1973.

Petric, Vladimir. "Soviet Revolutionary Films in America, 1926-1935." 2 vols. Ph.D. dissertation, New York University, 1973.

Potamkin, Harry Alan. *The Compound Cinema: The Film Writings of Harry Alan Potamkin*. Edited with an introduction by Lewis Jacobs. New York: Teachers College Press, 1977.

Rotha, Paul. *Documentary Diary: An Informal History of the British Documentary Film, 1928-1939*. London: Secker & Warburg, 1973.

————. *Documentary Film: The Use of the Film Medium to Interpret Creatively and in Social Terms the Life of the People as it Exists in Reality*. 3d. ed., rev. and enl. London: Faber and Faber, 1952.

Snyder, Robert L. *Pare Lorentz and the Documentary Film*. Norman: University of Oklahoma Press, 1968.

Steiner, Ralph. *A Point of View*. Middletown, Conn.: Wesleyan University Press, 1978.

Stott, William. *Documentary Expression and Thirties America*. New York: Oxford University Press, 1973.

Sworakowski, Witold S. *The Communist International and Its Front Organizations: A Research Guide and Checklist of Holdings in American and European Libraries*. Stanford: Hoover Institution on War, Revolution, and Peace, 1965.

Terkel, Studs. *Hard Times: An Oral History of the Great Depression*. New York: Pantheon Books, Inc., 1970.

Tucker, Anne. *Photographic Crossroads: The Photo League*. New York: Alfred A. Knopf, Inc., forthcoming.

Warren, Frank A. III. *Liberals and Communism*. Bloomington: Indiana University Press, 1966.

Wegner, Hans. *Joris Ivens, Dokumentarist der Wahrheit*. Berlin: Henschelverlag, 1965.

Williams, Jay. *Stage Left*. New York: Charles Scribner's Sons, 1974.

Zalzman, A. *Joris Ivens*. Paris: Editions seghers, 1963.

Zuker, Joel. "Ralph Steiner: Filmmaker and Still Photographer." Ph.D. dissertation, New York University, 1976.

Articles

Agee, James. "Art for What's Sake." *New Masses*, 15 Dec. 1936, pp. 48, 50.

Alexander, William. "Frontier Films, 1936-1941: The Aesthetics of Impact." *Cinema Journal*, Fall 1975, pp. 16-28.

————. "Frontier Films: Trying the Impossible." In *Prospects: An Annual of American Cultural Studies*, ed. Jack Salzman. 4 vols. New York: Burt Franklin & Company, Inc., 1979, vol. 4.

————. "*The March of Time* and *The World Today*." *American Quarterly*, Summer 1977, pp. 182-193.

Andrew, Dudley. "Harry Alan Potamkin." *Film Comment*, Mar. 1974, pp. 55-57.

Armstrong, Gertrude, and Ben Maddow. "Wall Street Hollywood." *New Masses*, 14 Aug. 1934, pp. 29-30.

Arne, Sigrid. "Young Man With A Movie Camera Finds a Great Story to Tell." AP Feature Service piece no. 27A, 13 Feb. 1940. In *Fight for Life* file at the Film Study Center, Museum of Modern Art, New York.

Arthur, James. "Films at the Fair." *TAC*, July-Aug. 1939, pp. 29-30, 33.

Baker, Maria. "Film Conference." *New Theatre*, Sept.-Oct. 1933, pp. 24-25.

Belitt, Ben. "The Camera Reconnoiters." *Nation*, 20 Nov. 1937, pp. 557-558. Also in Lewis Jacob's *The Documentary Tradition*, pp. 141-145.

Berg, Louis. "All Quiet in Morgan County." *New Masses*, May 1933, pp. 3-5.

Blake, Ben. "From Agitprop to Realism." *New Theatre*, Jan. 1935, p. 28.

Boehnel, William. "World Theatre Shows *Native Land*." *New York World-Telegram*, 12 May 1942, p. 10. In *Native Land* file at Film Study Center, Museum of Modern Art, New York.

Bourke-White, Margaret. "Photographing This World." *Nation*, 19 Feb. 1936, pp. 217-218.

Brandon, Tom. Film Program. Pacific Film Archive, 13 May 1973.

———. "A Missing Chapter in the History of U.S. Documentary Films." Program at Museum of Modern Art, New York. 15 May, 1974.

———. "Pioneers: An Interview with Tom Brandon." By Fred Sweet, Eugene Rosow, and Allan Francovich. *Film Quarterly* 26 (1973): 12-24.

———. "What's Doing in the Film and Photo League Branches." *Daily Worker*, 14 Sept. 1934, p. 5.

———. "Who Are the Forces Behind the 'Legion of Decency' Drive?" *Daily Worker*, 17 Aug. 1934, p. 5; 18 Aug. 1934, p. 7; 20 Aug. 1934, p. 5; and 21 Aug. 1934, p. 5.

———. "Workers Study the Film." *New Theatre*, Jan. 1934, pp. 14-15.

———, and Sam Brody. "Epic of an Era." *New Masses*, 26 June 1934, pp. 29-30.

———, and Sam Brody. "A Mexican Trailer." *New Masses*, Sept. 1933, p. 28.

Brody, Sam, translator and commentator. "Dziga Vertov on Film Technique." *Film Front*, 28 Jan. 1935, pp. 7-9.

———, translator and commentator. "Dziga Vertov on Kino-Eye: Excerpts from a lecture given in Paris in 1929." *Film Front*, 7 Jan. 1935, pp. 6-8.

———. (as "Lens"). "Flashes and Close-ups." *Daily Worker*, 18 Jan. 1934, p. 5.

———. (as "Lens"). "Flashes and Close-ups." *Daily Worker*, 20 July 1934, p. 5.

———. "The Hunger March Film." *Daily Worker*, 29 Dec. 1932, p. 4.

———. "Movie Notes." *Labor Defender*, Jan. 1931, p. 17.

———. "The Movies as a Weapon Against the Working Class." *Daily Worker*, 20 May 1930, p. 4.

———. "The Revolutionary Film: Problem of Form." *New Theatre*, Feb. 1934, pp. 21-22.

Bryan, Julien. "War Is, Was, and Always Will Be, Hell." *U.S. Camera Magazine*, Feb.-Mar. 1940, pp. 88-92. Also in Lewis Jacobs's, *The Documentary Tradition*, pp. 167-174.

Burger, Hans. "Filming a European Crisis." *National Board of Review Magazine*, Mar. 1940, pp. 7-9.

Cameron, Kate. *"Crisis*, a Film Record of Czechs' Travail." *New York Daily News*, clipping erroneously identified in handwriting as *New York Daily News*, 12 Mar. 1939, in *Crisis* file in Film Study Center, Museum of Modern Art, New York.

Campbell, Russell. "Introduction" to "Radical Cinema in the 30's." *Jump Cut* 14 (1977): 23-25.

———, and William Alexander. "Filmography." *Jump Cut* 14 (1977): 33.

Chávez, Carlos. "Mexico." In section on "Films by American Governments." *Films*, Summer 1940, pp. 20-21.

The City. Review. *Film Survey*, June 1939, p. 1.

Cowley, Malcolm. "What the Revolutionary Movement Can Do for a Writer." In *American Writers' Congress*, ed. Henry Hart. New York: International Publishers, 1935.

Crowther, Bosley. "Lorentz Experiments." *New York Times*, 10 Mar. 1940, X, p. 5.

———. " 'Native Land,' Impassioned and Dramatic Documentary on American Civil Liberties, Presented at the World." *New York Times*, 12 May 1942, p. 16.

Dugan, James. "Film on Czechoslovakia." *New Masses*, 21 Mar. 1939, pp. 28-30.

———. "Murder, Ltd.: Herbert Kline's War Film and a Remake from Hollywood." *New Masses*, 16 Apr. 1940, pp. 30-31.

———. "Zinc Miners in the Movies." *New Masses*, 26 Mar. 1940, p. 28.

Educational Film Institute, New York University. "Two Film Studies of Machines, Jobs, and Men." Circular located in *Valley Town* file, Film Study Center, Museum of Modern Art, New York.

Eisenstein, Sergei. "The New Soviet Cinema, Entering the Fourth Period." *New Theatre*, Jan. 1935, pp. 9, 21.

Ferguson, Otis. "Guest Artist." *New Republic*, 15 Apr. 1936, p. 278.

———. "Not in Mournful Numbers." *New Republic*, 6 Feb. 1935, pp. 360-361.

———. "They, the People." *New Republic*, 5 Aug. 1936, pp. 381-382.

———. "Where Was Moses . . ." *New Republic*, 22 Apr. 1940, p. 536.

Freeman, Joseph. "Ivory Towers—White and Red." *New Masses*, 11 Sept. 1934, pp. 20-24.

Friberg, Carl [C.O.N.]. "The Film is a Weapon." *Left Front*, May-June 1934, p. 15.

Frontier Films. "Film Sequence, Frontier Films' Production No. 5 (Temporary Working Title)." *One Act Play Magazine*, Jan. 1939, pp. 664-667.

———. Frontier Films brochure. Frontier Films file, Film Study Center, Museum of Modern Art, New York.

Garlin, Sender. "USSR—1917-1931." *Labor Defender*, Nov. 1931, pp. 205, 225.

Garrison Film Distributors. Publicity brochure for *The Wave*. In *Wave* file at Film Study Center, Museum of Modern Art, New York.

Gerstein, Evelyn. "English Documentary Films." *New Theatre*, Jan. 1936, pp. 7, 36. Also in Lewis Jacob's *The Documentary Tradition*, pp. 112-115.

Gessner, John. "Movies About Us." *New Theatre*, June 1935, p. 20. Also in Lewis Jacobs's *The Documentary Tradition*, pp. 94-96.

Gillette, Howard, Jr. "Film as Artifact: *The City* (1939)." *American Studies*, Fall 1977, pp. 71-85.

Gold, Michael. "Change the World!" *Daily Worker*, 2 Oct. 1934, p. 5.

———. "Change the World!" *Daily Worker*, 5 Nov. 1934, p. 7.

Griffith, Richard. *"The Fight for Life." National Board of Review Magazine*, Mar. 1940, pp. 11-13.

———. "Films at the Fair." *Films*, Nov. 1939, pp. 63-64.

———. *"Power and the Land." National Board of Review Magazine*, Dec. 1940, pp. 14-16.

Harber, Kent. "Photography and Film through the Eyes of Willard Van Dyke." *The Daily Californian* 10, no. 3 (1978): 3-12.

Hamilton, James Shelley. *"Crisis." National Board of Review Magazine*, Mar. 1939, pp. 21-22.

———. *"Joris Ivens." National Board of Review Magazine*, May 1936, pp. 9-11.

———. *"Lights Out in Europe." National Board of Review Magazine*, Apr. 1940, pp. 12-13.

———. *"The Plow That Broke the Plains." National Board of Review Magazine*, June 1936, pp. 9-10.

———. *"The River." National Board of Review Magazine*, Nov. 1937, pp. 11-12.

———. *"The Wave (Redes)." National Board of Review Magazine*, May 1937, pp. 12-13.

Hoellering, Franz. "Films." *Nation*, 20 Apr. 1940, p. 521.

Hogenkamp, Bert. "Workers' Film in Europe." *Jump Cut* 19 (1978): 36-37.

Hurwitz, Leo. *"Hell on Earth* at the Acme is Vital Anti-War Film." *Daily Worker*, 30 Jan. 1934, p. 5.

———. "Hisses, Boos and Boycotts." *New Theatre*, July-Aug. 1934, pp. 10-11.

———. Letter to the editor. *New Masses*, 12 Mar. 1935, p. 21.

———. *"Native Land*: An Interview with Leo Hurwitz." By Michael and Jill Klein. *Cinéaste* 6, no. 3 (1974): 3-7.

———. "One Man's Voyage: Ideas and Films in the 1930's." *Cinema Journal*, Fall 1975, pp. 1-15.

———. "The Revolutionary Film—Next Step." *New Theatre*, May 1934, pp. 14-15.

———. "Survey of Workers Films: A Report to the National Film Conference." *New Theatre*, Oct. 1934, pp. 27-28.

———. "Vanderbilt is Star in Phoney Anti-Nazi Film." *Daily Worker*, 7 May 1934, p. 5.

———, and Ralph Steiner. "A New Approach to Film Making." *New Theatre*, Sept. 1935, pp. 22-23.

Ivens, Joris. "Collaboration in Documentary." *Films*, Spring 1940, pp. 30-42.
――――. "Joris Ivens Interviewed by Gordon Hitchens, November 20, 1968, American Documentaries." *Film Culture*, Spring 1972, pp. 190-223.
――――. "Making Documentary Films to Meet Today's Needs." *American Cinematographer*, July 1942, pp. 298-299, 332-333.
――――. "Note on Hollywood." *New Theatre*, Oct. 1936, pp. 8-10, 28.
――――. "Note on the Documentary Film." *Direction*, Apr. 1940, p. 15.
――――. "We Document a Nation at War." *TAC*, Feb. 1939, pp. 18-19, 29.
Jacobs, Lewis. "Documentary Film Advances." *Direction*, Feb. 1940, p. 14.
――――. "Eisenstein." *Experimental Cinema* 1, no. 3 (1931): 4.
――――. "Two Pictures of the Month." *Direction*, Sept.-Oct. 1938, p. 23.
Job to be Done. Comment. *World Film News*, Sept. 1938, p. 219.
Kaufman, N. "Evolution of the Soviet Cinema." *The Left*, Spring 1931, pp. 73-78.
Kern, Ed (as "Ed Kennedy"). "Three Workers Films." *Film Front*, 7 Jan. 1935, pp. 10-11.
―――― (as "Ed Kennedy"). "World of the Movies: Development of a White-Collar Worker." *Daily Worker*, 27 Dec. 1934, p. 5.
Klein, Michael. "*Native Land*: Praised Then Forgotten." *Velvet Light Trap*, Winter 1975, pp. 12-15.
――――, and Jill Klein. See Hurwitz, Leo.
Kline, Herbert. "Behind Loyalist Lines." *New York Times*, 18 Apr. 1937, X, p. 2.
――――. "Conversations in the Trenches." *New Masses*, 20 July 1937, pp. 5-6.
――――. Editorial. *New Theatre*, Sept. 1934, p. 3.
――――. Editorial. *New Theatre*, Feb. 1935, p. 3.
――――. "A Festival of People's Art." *New Theatre*, Nov. 1936, pp. 9-10.
――――. "Films Without Make-Believe." *The Magazine of Art*, Feb. 1942, pp. 58-63. Also in Lewis Jacobs's *The Documentary Tradition*, pp. 148-157.
――――. "Hollywood Fights Back." *Nation*, 13 May 1936, pp. 612-613.
――――. "Killed in Action." *New Masses*, 20 Apr. 1937, p. 19.
――――. Letter to the editor. *Theatre Workshop*, Apr.-July 1937, p. 2.
――――. "The New Plays." *New Theatre*, Mar. 1935, pp. 22-23.
――――. "Script Trouble." Unidentified clipping in *Crisis* file in Film Study Center, Museum of Modern Art, New York.
――――. "The Voice of Spain." *New Masses*, 13 Apr. 1937, pp. 7-8.
――――. "Writing for Workers Theatre." *New Theatre*, Dec. 1934, pp. 22-23.
Kurella. "The Five-Year-Plan and the Cultural Revolution." *Experimental Cinema* 1, no. 3 (1931): 12.
Lawson, John Howard. "The Crisis in the Theatre." *New Masses*, Dec. 1936, pp. 35-36.
Lerner, Irving. Correction sent to *Documentary Film News*, Sept. 1941, p. 6.
―――― (as "Peter Ellis"). "Dovjenko's *Frontier*." *New Theatre*, Jan. 1936, pp. 24, 42.

Lerner, Irving. "A Dry Martini with Cyanide." *New Masses,* 19 June 1934, pp. 29-30.

———. "Harry Alan Potamkin." *Experimental Cinema* 1, no. 5 (1934): 53.

——— (as "Peter Ellis"). "More About *Chapayev.*" *New Masses,* 12 Feb. 1935, pp. 29-30.

——— (as "Peter Ellis"). "On the Waterfront." *New Masses,* 4 Dec. 1934, pp. 28-29.

——— (as "Peter Ellis"). "The Plow That Broke the Plains." *New Theatre,* July 1936, pp. 18-19.

——— (as "Peter Ellis"). "A Revolutionary Film." *New Masses,* 25 Sept. 1934, p. 30.

——— (as "Peter Ellis"). "The Screen." *New Masses,* 31 Mar. 1936, pp. 29-30.

——— (as "Peter Ellis"). "The Screen." *New Masses,* 9 Feb. 1937, pp. 28-30.

——— (as "Peter Ellis"). "The Screen." *New Masses,* 21 Sept. 1937, p. 29.

——— (as "Peter Ellis"). "The Screen: *The March of Time.*" *New Masses,* 9 July 1935, pp. 29-30.

——— (as "Peter Ellis"). "The Screen: *The March of Time* and the Share-croppers." *New Masses,* 18 Aug. 1936, p. 29.

——— (as "Peter Ellis"). "Sights and Sounds." *New Masses,* 11 May 1937, p. 29.

——— (as "Peter Ellis"). "The Soviet Film." *New Masses,* 5 Mar. 1935, pp. 29-30.

——— (as "Peter Ellis"). "Three Songs About Lenin." *New Masses,* 20 Nov. 1934, p. 30.

——— (as "Peter Ellis"), and Sidney Meyers (as "Robert Stebbins"). "Are Newsreels News?" *New Theatre,* Apr. 1937, pp. 12-15, 44-45.

———, and Ralph Steiner. "Technical Advice to Movie Makers." *New Theatre,* Nov. 1934, p. 27.

Leyda, Jay. "Courage in Films." *Direction,* Apr.-May 1941, p. 27.

———. "Three Songs About Lenin: Film News from the Soviet Union." *New Theatre,* Nov. 1934, p. 10.

———. "Vision is my dwelling place." *Film Culture,* no. 58-59-60 (1974), pp. 2-36.

———, and Sidney Meyers (as "Robert Stebbins"). "Joris Ivens: Artist in Documentary." *The Magazine of Art,* July 1938, pp. 392-399, 436, 438. Also in Lewis Jacobs's *The Documentary Tradition,* pp. 158-166.

"Lionel Berman." Booklet written by several persons and printed privately after Berman's death in 1968.

London, Kurt. "Film Music of the Quarter." *Films,* Spring 1940, pp. 46-47.

[Lorentz, Pare.] "Agriculture: Mother Nature Lays Down a Withering, Calamitous New Deal, Reducing More Crops Than AAA Decreed." *Newsweek,* 9 June 1934, pp. 3-4.

[———?] *The City.* Outline. In possession of William Alexander.

———. "Dorothea Lange: Camera with a Purpose." *U.S. Camera Annual* 1 (1941): 94-98.

——. *Fight for Life* (text). In *Twenty Best Film Plays*, ed. John Gassner and Dudley Nichols (New York: Crown Publishers, 1943), pp. 1,088-1,112.

——. *Job to be Done* (text). In *World Film News*, Sept. 1938, pp. 216-217, 219.

——. "Lorentz on Film." Program 2, National Educational Television, 1961.

——. "Movies." *McCall's*, July 1936, pp. 15, 84. Also in *Lorentz on Film*, pp. 135-136.

——. "Movies." *McCall's*, Feb. 1937, pp. 14-15, 93. Also in *Lorentz on Film*, pp. 136-138.

——. "Movies." *McCall's*, Sept. 1937, p. 12.

——. "Movies." *McCall's*, July 1938, pp. 4, 57. Also in *Lorentz on Film*, pp. 154-157.

——. "Movies." *McCall's*, June 1939, pp. 4, 87. Also in *Lorentz on Film*, pp. 164-165.

——. "Movies." *McCall's*, July 1940, pp. 4, 99. Also in *Lorentz on Film*, pp. 190-194.

——. "Pare Lorentz's Music Instructions for *The Fight for Life*." In *Twenty Best Film Plays*, ed. John Gassner and Dudley Nichols (New York: Crown Publishers, 1943), pp. 1,082-1,087.

——. "Public Service." *Plain Talk*, Aug. 1928, pp. 235-238.

——. "Reunion." *Story*, Sept. 1934, pp. 19-23.

——. "*The River*," narration for. *Film Comment*, Spring 1965, pp. 57-60.

——. "The Screen." *Vanity Fair*, Dec. 1932, pp. 46-47, 64.

——. "The Screen." *Vanity Fair*, Oct 1933, pp. 39-40, 63-64. Also in *Lorentz on Film*, pp. 118-120.

——. "The Screen." *Vanity Fair*, Jan. 1934, pp. 45-46, 60.

——. On War Films: Note on Communist Films. *Town and Country*, 15 Apr. 1935, pp. 31-32.

——. "A Young Man Goes to Work," *Scribner's*, Feb. 1931, pp. 205-208.

Ludlow, Ray. "Pie in the Sky." *New Theatre*, May 1935, pp. 19-20.

McEvoy, J. P. "Young Man with a Camera." *Scribner's Commentator*, July 1940, pp. 43-48.

MacLeish, Archibald. "The Cinema of Joris Ivens." *New Masses*, 24 Aug. 1937, p. 18.

——. "Spain and American Writers." In *The Writer in a Changing World*, ed. Henry Hart (New York: Equinox Cooperative Press, 1937), pp. 56-62.

McManus, John. "Down to Earth in Spain." *New York Times*, 25 July 1937, X, p. 4.

——. "The Screen; *The Spanish Earth*, at the 55th St. Playhouse, is a Plea for Democracy—*Gangway* at the Roxy." *New York Times*, 21 August 1937, p. 7.

Maddow, Ben (as "David Wolff"). "Acts of God." *Partisan Review*, Apr.-May 1935, pp. 69-71.

——. "August 22, 1927-1933." *New Masses*, Aug. 1933, p. 11.

Maddow, Ben (as "David Wolff"). "The City." *Poetry*, Jan. 1940, pp. 169-175.

———. "The Communist Party of Germany." *Dynamo*, Summer 1934, pp. 1-6.

——— (as "David Wolff"). "Comrade and Master." *Dynamo*, May-June 1935, pp. 29-32.

——— (as "David Wolff"). "Declamation." *TAC*, Nov. 1938, p. 13.

——— (as "David Wolff"). "Fact into Film: *Confessions of a Nazi Spy*." *Films*, Nov. 1939, pp. 81-85.

——— (as "David Wolff"). "Film Intensity: *Shors*." *Films*, Spring 1940, pp. 55-61.

——— (as "David Wolff"). "Film into Poem." *New Theatre*, Nov. 1936, pp. 23, 36.

——— (as "David Wolff"). "The Front in Darkness." In *Proletarian Literature in the United States*, ed. Granville Hicks et al. (New York: International Publishers, 1935), pp. 200-201.

——— (as "David Wolff"). "Green in the Halls." *Dynamo*, May-June 1935, pp. 16-18.

——— (as "David Wolff"). "Harry Alan Potamkin." *New Theatre*, Feb. 1936, pp. 28, 33.

——— (as "David Wolff"). "Hopes for Poetry." *New Masses*, 4 Aug. 1936, p. 28.

——— (as "David Wolff"). "Images of Poverty." *Partisan Review*, Oct.-Nov. 1935, pp. 9-10.

———. "Obsequy." *Poetry*, May 1931, p. 79.

——— (as "David Wolff"). "On Signing Up." *Poetry*, May 1936, p. 71.

———. "Red Decision." *Symposium*, Oct. 1932, pp. 443-453.

——— (as "David Wolff"). "Remembering Hart Crane." In *Proletarian Literature in the United States*, ed. Granville Hicks et al. (New York: International Publishers, 1935), pp. 201-202.

——— (as "David Wolff"). "The Sign." *New Masses*, 4 May 1937, p. 20.

——— (as "David Wolff"). "A Summer Night." In *New Masses: An Anthology of the Rebel Thirties*, ed. Joseph North (New York: International Publishers, 1969), pp. 61-62.

——— (as "David Wolff"). "The Trumpeter." *New Masses*, 25 Feb. 1936, p. 14.

———. (as "David Wolff"). "Two Poets." *New Masses*, 27 Apr. 1937, p. 23.

——— (as "David Wolff"). "While We Slept." *Poetry*, Sept. 1940, pp. 316-317.

———. "The Writer's Function in Documentary Film." *Proceedings of the Writers' Congress, Los Angeles, 1943* (Berkeley: University of California Press, 1944), pp. 98-103.

———, and Gertrude Armstrong. "Wall Street Hollywood." *New Masses*, 14 Aug. 1934, pp. 29-30.

Maltz, Albert. Letter to the editor on *Crisis*. *TAC*, May 1939, p. 24.

Mayer, Arthur L. "A Plea for Unpopular Films." *National Board of Review Magazine*, May 1940, pp. 4-8.

Mekas, Jonas, and Edouard Laurot. "The American Documentary—Limitations and Possibilities." *Film Culture* 2, no. 3 (1956): 8.

Mercey, Arch. "The Teaching of Social Studies Through Documentary Films." Abstract of remarks made 5 Aug. 1938 at the Institute on Visual Instruction in Higher Education. Copy at the National Archives.

Meyers, Sidney (as "Robert Stebbins"). "Film: To the Editor." *TAC*, Oct. 1938, p. 12.

———— (as "Robert Stebbins"). Letter to the editor, replying to Albert Maltz's criticism of his review of *Crisis*. *TAC*, May 1939, pp. 24, 27.

———— (as "Robert Stebbins"). "Movies." *TAC*, Apr. 1939, pp. 14-15, 22.

———— (as "Robert Stebbins"). "One Man's Contribution." *TAC*, Nov. 1938, p. 6.

———— (as "Robert Stebbins"). "Paul Strand's Photography Reaches Heights in *The Wave*." *Daily Worker*, 4 May 1937, p. 7.

———— (as "Robert Stebbins"). "*Redes*." *New Theatre*, Nov. 1936, pp. 20-22.

———— (as "Robert Stebbins"). "The Screen: *Frontier*." *New Masses*, 7 Jan. 1936, pp. 29-30.

"News Clips of the Week." *New York Times*, 25 Apr. 1937, X, p. 4. (About Frontier Films.)

Nichols, Bill. "The American Photo League." *Screen*, Winter 1972/1973, pp. 108-115.

Noble, Elizabeth. "*Heart of Spain*." *New Masses*, 5 Oct. 1937, p. 18.

Nugent, Frank. "Grim Reality Note." *New York Times*, 10 Mar. 1940, X, p. 5.

————. "The Screen." *New York Times*, 21 Apr. 1937, p. 18.

————. "The Screen: *Spain in Flames*, Depicting the Spanish Revolution, Opens at the Cameo—*Holy Terror* at the Palace." *New York Times*, 30 Jan. 1937, p. 21.

Pabst, Georg Wilhelm. "A letter to F. Ermler on *Peasants*." *New Theatre*, Oct. 1935, p. 5.

Paxton, A. Roger. "Fiddling While the Great Plains Burn: The Neros of the New Deal." *New Masses*, 21 July 1936, pp. 8-9.

Platt, David. "Films 1937-38." *Direction*, Jan. 1938, pp. 22, 28.

————. "Flashes and Close-ups." *Daily Worker*, 9 Mar. 1935, p. 7.

————. "*Hell on Earth* at Acme is Fine Anti-War Film." *Daily Worker*, 5 Feb. 1934, p. 5.

————. "The Movie Front: National Film Conference." *New Theatre*, Nov. 1934, p. 30.

————. "*Native Land* is Powerful Expose of America's 'Little Hitlers'." *Daily Worker*, 12 May 1942, p. 7.

————. "A Reply to Michael Gold." *Daily Worker*, 16 Nov. 1934, p. 5.

————. "*The Unknown Soldier Speaks* Reveals the Power of Newsreels." *Daily Worker*, 26 July 1934, p. 5.

————. "Photographer Must See, Think—Strand: Creator of *The Wave* urges Film Photographers to Create Images and Remember Social Aspects of Subject to be Screened." *Daily Worker*, 18 May 1937, p. 7.

Platt, David. "Newsreel with Punch in *The World Today*; Labor Productions Presents a 'March of Time' With a Labor Slant that Defends the Sunnysiders and Takes the Hide Off The Black Legion." *Daily Worker*, 6 May 1937, p. 7.

Porter, Katherine Anne. "On *The Wave*" (letter). *New Masses*, 18 May 1937, p. 22.

Potamkin, Harry Alan. "Film Problems of Soviet Russia." *Experimental Cinema* 1, no. 1 (1930): 3-4. Also in Potamkin, *The Compound Cinema*, pp. 310-312.

———. "Hollywood or Lenin Hills." *New Theatre*, Apr. 1934, pp. 9-10.

———. "Lands, Films & Critics." *Close Up*, Sept. 1932, pp. 206-207.

———. "A Movie Call to Action!" *Workers Theatre*, July 1931, p. 5. Also in Potamkin, *The Compound Cinema*, pp. 583-586.

———. "Movies." *New Masses*, Oct. 1930, p. 16. Also in Potamkin, *The Compound Cinema*, pp. 474-475.

———. "Movies and Revolution." *New Masses*, Dec. 1932, p. 21. Also in Potamkin, *The Compound Cinema*, pp. 511-514.

———. "Notes on the Film: A Proposal for a School of the Motion Picture." *Hound and Horn*, Oct.-Dec. 1933, pp. 140-143. Also in Potamkin, *The Compound Cinema*, pp. 587-592.

———. "Populism and Dialectics." *Experimental Cinema* 1, no. 2 (1930) 16-17. Also in Potamkin, *The Compound Cinema*, pp. 176-178.

———. "Pudovkin and the Revolutionary Film." *Hound and Horn*, Apr.-June 1933, pp. 480-493. Also in Potamkin, *The Compound Cinema*, pp. 422-434.

———. "What Is the Program of the Workers Cultural Federation?" *Daily Worker*, 18 July 1931, p. 4.

———. "What Will Mr. Peet Do About it?" *New Masses*, Nov. 1930, p. 23.

———. "Workers Films." *Daily Worker*, 31 May 1930, p. 3.

Rahv, Philip. "The Literary Class War." *New Masses*, Aug. 1932, pp. 7-10.

Ridge, Lola. "Paul Strand." *Creative Art*, Oct. 1931, pp. 313-316.

Rodakiewicz, Henwar. *The City*. Shooting script. Copy in possession of William Alexander.

———. "Treatment of Sound in 'The City'." In *The Movies as Medium*, ed. Lewis Jacobs (New York: Farrar, Strauss & Giroux, 1970), pp. 278-288.

Roffman, Julian. "Soviet News Film Living Refutation of Hearst's Lies." *Daily Worker*, 6 Mar. 1935, p. 5.

Rolfe, Edwin. "The 'God of Floods'." *New Masses*, 9 Feb. 1937, pp. 3-6.

Rosenheimer, Arthur (later Arthur Knight). Review of Paul Rotha's *Documentary Film*. *Films*, Nov. 1939, pp. 106-109.

Rosenthal, Solomon P. "Change of Socio-Economic Attitudes Under Radical Motion Picture Propaganda." Vol. 25, no. 166, Archives of Psychology, Columbia University (New York: April, 1934).

Rotha, Paul. "The Documentary Method in British Films." *National Board of Review Magazine*, Nov. 1937, pp. 3-9. Originally delivered as a lecture at a New York University motion picture course.

————. "Films and the Labour Movement." Address at Edinburgh, 3 Oct. 1936. Document at Museum of Modern Art Library.

Rukeyser, Muriel. "*The River* Damned." *World Film News*, July 1938, p. 121.

Seaver, Edwin. "Literature at the Crossroads." *New Masses*, Apr. 1932, pp. 12-13.

————. "The Authors and Politics." *New Masses*, June 1933, p. 13.

Seltzer, Leo. "Technically Speaking." *Film Front*, 7 Jan. 1935, p. 9.

————. "A Total and Realistic Experience." Interview with Russell Campbell, *Jump Cut* 14 (1977): 25-27.

Steiner, Ralph. "*Café Universal*: Scenes from a Film About War, by Ralph Steiner, with Actors from the Group Theatre." *Theatre Arts Monthly*, Nov. 1933, pp. 831-834.

———— [with the collaboration of Leo Hurwitz]. "Revolutionary Movie Production." *New Theatre*, Sept. 1934, pp. 22-23.

————. "Why Don't More Photographers Take Pictures That Make People Laugh?" *PM Daily*, 1 Sept. 1940, pp. 48-49.

————, and Leo Hurwitz. "A New Approach to Film Making." *New Theatre*, Sept. 1935, pp. 22-23.

————, and Irving Lerner. "Technical Advice to Movie Makers." *New Theatre*, Nov. 1934, p. 27.

Stern, Seymour. "A Working-Class Cinema for America?" *The Left*, Spring 1931, pp. 69-73.

Strand, Paul. "Power of a Fine Picture Brings Social Changes: Paul Strand, of Frontier Films, Explains Success of 'The Wave'." Interview. *New York World Telegram*, 4 Mar. 1939, pp. 89-90.

————. "*Les Maisons de la Misère*." *Films*, Nov. 1939, pp. 89-90.

————. "Letter to *Art Front*." Feb. 1937, p. 18.

————. "Realism: A Personal View." *Sight and Sound*, Jan 1950, pp. 23-26.

Strauss, Theodore. "Homesteading Our *Native Land*." *New York Times*, 3 May 1942, X, p. 3.

Sweet, Fred, et al. See Brandon, Tom.

Tazelaar, Marguerite. "On the Screen: *The Wave*—Filmarte." *New York Herald Tribune*, 21 Apr. 1937, p. 18.

Thirer, Irene. "Paul Strand and Leo Hurwitz Offer Data on *Native Land*." *New York Post*, 9 May 1942, p. 13.

Thomas, Irene. "Southern Labor Colleges." Letter to the editor. *New Masses*, 16 Mar. 1937, p. 18.

Thompson, David. "Old Man River." *World Film News*, July 1938, pp. 118-119.

Tomkins, Calvin. "Profiles (Paul Strand)." *The New Yorker*, 16 Sept. 1974, pp. 44-94.

"Trio of Actors All but Earns Trio of M.D.'s." *New York Herald Tribune*, 17 Mar. 1940, pp. 3-4.

Troy, William. "Films: Blood and Glory." *Nation*, 30 Jan. 1935, pp. 139-140.

Tucker, Anne. "Photographic Crossroads: The Photo League." Special Supplement to *afterimage*, Apr. 1978.

Van Dongen, Helen. "Joris Ivens in America." *Film Art*, Autumn 1936, pp. 15-16.

Van Doren, Mark. "Films: On Horror's Head." *Nation*, 8 May 1937, p. 545.

Van Dyke, Willard. "The American Documentary—Limitations and Possibilities: An Interview with Willard Van Dyke by Jonas Mekas and Edouard Laurot." *Film Culture* 2, no. 3 (1956): 6-9.

———. "The Interpretive Camera in Documentary Films." *Hollywood Quarterly*, July 1946, pp. 405-408.

———. Interview. By G. Roy Levin. In *Documentary Explorations: Fifteen Interviews with Filmmakers* (Garden City, N.Y.: Doubleday, Inc. 1971), pp. 175-193.

———. Letter to Pare Lorentz. In Lorentz file at Film Study Center, Museum of Modern Art, New York.

———. "Letters from 'The River'." *Film Comment*, Mar.-Apr. 1965, pp. 38-56.

———. "The Photographs of Dorothea Lange—a Critical Analysis." *Camera Craft*, Oct. 1934, pp. 461-467.

———. "Thirty Years of Social Inquiry: An Interview with Willard Van Dyke by Harrison Engle." *Film Comment*, Spring 1965, pp. 24-37.

Watts, Richard. "Documentary Film." *New York Herald Tribune*, 16 May 1942, p. 15.

Weinberg, Herman. "Cinema America." *Film Art*, Winter 1934, pp. 28-31.

Weinstock, Herbert. *The Wave*. Unidentified clipping in Film Study Center *Wave* file, Museum of Modern Art, New York.

White, W. L. "Pare Lorentz." *Scribner's*, Jan. 1939, pp. 7-11, 42.

Winsten, Archer. "*The City* Opens Saturday at the World's Fair." *New York Post*, 23 May 1939, p. 15.

———. "*The Fight for Life* at Belmont Theatre." *New York Post*, 7 Mar. 1940, p. 11.

———. "*Power and the Land* is Added at Rialto." *New York Post*, 11 Dec. 1940, p. 19.

Wolf, Friederick. "Dramatizing Our Times." *New Theatre*, Feb. 1935, p. 24.

"The Workers Film & Photo League of the W.I.R." *Workers Theatre*, Jan. 1932, pp. 22-23.

Index

Library of Congress Cataloging in Publication Data

Alexander, William, 1938-
    Film on the left.

    Bibliography: p.
    Includes index.
    1. Moving-pictures, Documentary—United States—
History and criticism.   I.   Title.
PN1995.9.D6A38   791.43′53   80-8534
ISBN 0-691-04678-6
ISBN 0-691-10111-6 (lim. print. ed.)

William Alexander is Associate Professor of English at the University of Michigan.